WALLED LAKE CITY LIBRARY
WALLED LAKE, MICHIGAN

6/2010

DEMCO

PARADISE
BENEATH
HER FEET

PARADISE
BENEATH
HER FEET

HOW WOMEN
ARE TRANSFORMING
THE MIDDLE EAST

Isobel Coleman

A Council on Foreign Relations Book

RANDOM HOUSE

NEW YORK

The Council on Foreign Relations (CFR) is an independent, nonpartisan membership organization, think tank, and publisher dedicated to being a resource for its members, government officials, business executives, journalists, educators and students, civic and religious leaders, and other interested citizens in order to help them better understand the world and the foreign policy choices facing the United States and other countries. Founded in 1921, CFR carries out its mission by maintaining a diverse membership, with special programs to promote interest and develop expertise in the next generation of foreign policy leaders; convening meetings at its headquarters in New York and in Washington, D.C., and other cities where senior government officials, members of Congress, global leaders, and prominent thinkers come together with CFR members to discuss and debate major international issues; supporting a studies program that fosters independent research, enabling CFR scholars to produce articles, reports, and books and hold roundtables that analyze foreign policy issues and make concrete policy recommendations; publishing *Foreign Affairs*, the preeminent journal on international affairs and U.S. foreign policy; sponsoring independent task forces that produce reports with both findings and policy prescriptions on the most important foreign policy topics; and providing up-to-date information and analysis about world events and American foreign policy on its website, www.cfr.org.

The Council on Foreign Relations takes no institutional position on policy issues and has no affiliation with the U.S. government. All statements of fact and expressions of opinion contained in its publications are the sole responsibility of the author or authors.

Copyright © 2010 by Isobel Coleman

All rights reserved.

Published in the United States by Random House, an imprint of The Random House Publishing Group, a division of Random House, Inc., New York.

RANDOM HOUSE and colophon are registered trademarks of Random House, Inc.

Grateful acknowledgment is made to Mary Anne Weaver for permission to reprint an excerpt from "Gandhi's Daughters: India's Poorest Embark on an Epic Social Experiment" by Mary Anne Weaver (*The New Yorker*, January 10, 2000), copyright © 2000 by Mary Anne Weaver. Reprinted by permission of the author.

Library of Congress Cataloging-in-Publication Data
Coleman, Isobel.
Paradise beneath her feet : how women are transforming the Middle East / Isobel Coleman.
p. cm.
Includes bibliographical references and index.
ISBN 978-1-4000-6695-7
eBook ISBN 978-0-679-60369-6
1. Women's rights—Middle East. 2. Women's rights—Religious aspects—Islam. 3. Muslim women—Social conditions—Middle East. I. Title.
HQ1236.5.M65C65 2010
305.48'6970956—dc22   2009037967

Printed in the United States of America on acid-free paper

www.atrandom.com

2 4 6 8 9 7 5 3 1

First Edition

3 9082 11443 0419

For Cullen, Struan, Julian,
Josephine, and Adrienne

Jahmah said to the Holy Prophet, "O Messenger of Allah, I desire to go on a military expedition and I have come to consult you." He asked him if he had a mother, and when he replied that he had, he said, "Stay with her because Paradise lies beneath her feet."

—AN-NASAI, Muslim scholar (ca. 829–915)

A mother is a school. Empower her, and you empower a great nation.

—HAFEZ IBRAHIM, Egyptian poet (1872–1932)

CONTENTS

INTRODUCTION

Education is like sun and water. Without it,
you can't grow anything. But if girls are educated,
they can change our whole society.
—Afghan mullah, 2004

T he village is nothing more than a few mud houses clinging to a
rocky hillside. A beaten footpath forces its way between stone
walls, past broken orchards of stunted fruit trees and across the dry
creek bed that gouges its way down the slope and across the valley. We
are in Hazarajat, the central highlands of Afghanistan. The snow-
capped peaks of the Hindu Kush mountain range loom over the plains.
There are no roads. After a twelve-hour overland trek from Kabul, our
old Toyota Land Cruiser strains the last half mile to the village. The
car's wheels bump and spin excruciatingly over watermelon-sized rocks
and the hard-packed dirt of the arid winter fields.

My traveling companion, Dr. Shukria Hassan, is a quiet, unassum-
ing woman in her mid-forties whose gray-streaked hair and ruddy face
creased from the sun make her look old beyond her years. She is a local
daughter, well-known in these parts for her community health work
with the Hazara, an ethnic minority treated as poor cousins in Afghan
society. She serves as the health director for Future Generations
Afghanistan, a local nonprofit organization that helps bring healthcare and educational improvements to remote villages like this.

I had heard that Future Generations was working with local religious leaders to provide literacy classes for girls, and I wanted to learn
more. Afghan society was still reeling from the Taliban's severe Islamic
fundamentalism that had fiercely suppressed women in the name of
religious purity, even prohibiting girls from attending school. But here

were Afghan mullahs, heads of their local religious communities, consciously using the mosque itself as a classroom for girls. Not only were they defying Taliban extremism against girls' education, they were also invoking Islam as justification for their actions.

Knowing my interest in girls' education in the Middle East, part of my research for the Council on Foreign Relations, the New York–based foreign policy organization where I work, Dr. Hassan offered to show me this mosque-based school in Hazarajat. I knew that if international efforts to get girls in school in Afghanistan had any hope of success, they would have to avoid the cultural backlash that had doomed previous initiatives. They would have to work with local groups, they would need the support of local leaders, like this Hazara mullah, and, most important, they would have to find ways to work with the pervasive and powerful force of Islam, not against it. Indeed, having Islam on the side of change might be the only way to move forward with sensitive cultural shifts like girls' schooling, or more broadly, women's empowerment, in conservative Islamic societies like Afghanistan.

When our Land Cruiser can go no farther, we get out and hike the path down the hill to the village mosque where the classes for girls are held. Spring is near, and the last patches of snow on the hillside are melting in the weak sun. The mosque is indistinguishable from the other houses except for a flag of green, the color of Islam, flying above its straw-and-mud-thatched rooftop. The mullah, waiting in the doorway, shoos the chickens away and beckons us inside. We give each other a traditional greeting, right hand pressed over our hearts with a nod of acknowledgment. Most conservative Muslim men refuse to touch a woman who is not a close family member so I have learned to avoid the awkwardness that usually ensues when I extend my hand to shake.

The mosque consists of one large room, lit by harsh light from the bare bulb dangling from the ceiling. It is slightly dank, with strong body odors mixing with the unmistakable smell of wet wool. A gas heater in the corner struggles to warm the room while adding a distinct propane smell to the mix. Money sent home from village refugees working in other countries paid for the mosque's windows and the thick red carpets covering the stone floor. On one side of the room is a poster of the Islamic holy city of Mecca. On the other side hangs a picture of a brooding Ayatollah Khomeini, the leader of Iran's Islamic Revolution. The mosque, built and maintained by local families, is about twenty years old. These classes offer the first opportunity for women to use the mosque regularly. Usually they only enter this building for funerals or other specific occasions.

The room is packed with women of all ages, from infants in arms to wizened grandmothers. Most are between the ages of nine and sixteen and all are attending the equivalent of first grade. These students are too old to start in the national school system; about a quarter of them are married, and their mothers-in-law are taking care of their children while they attend these classes. They want to learn to read and write so they can help their children with schoolwork and better solve the family's problems at home. The youngest students—five of them are only six years old—are attending the mosque school since the only state school in the area is more than an hour away by foot, too far for them to walk.

The mullah stands and immediately quiets everyone. This is clearly a special occasion, an improvised town hall meeting in honor of our visit. Flanked by two elderly village leaders, he begins with a short prayer and then politely thanks Dr. Hassan's organization for helping to support girls' education in the village. He also thanks me for making the long journey from Kabul.

Looking around the room, the mullah speaks with the confidence of a convert to a cause. "Education is like sun and water," he says in a strong voice. "Without it, you can't grow anything. But if girls are educated, they can change our whole society." The force and faith behind these simple words could mean a whole world of progress, not just for the girls in this room but for the millions of girls around the globe who are deemed unworthy of an education.

The teacher, Fatima, stands by the mullah's side, beaming with pride. She wears a long dress over baggy pants, her hair carefully covered by a large white cotton scarf. She carefully unfolds a piece of paper and reads, a bit nervously, from a letter written by the students. "Education is better than sitting in a corner of the house . . . The Prophet Muhammad (Peace be upon Him), says that women must be educated . . ." The women and girls sitting on the floor nod in agreement. Fatima has been teaching for eight months, her first experience working outside her home. She is one of the few literate women in the area, having completed high school in the 1960s—Afghanistan's "golden years." The 1960s were a relatively peaceful time for the country, a period of even some small progress with the building of a few roads and schools under the benign leadership of Afghanistan's last, long-serving king, Zahir Shah.

After Fatima finishes her presentation, I ask the students what they want to be when they grow up. Their dreams come tumbling out. Gulafzar, a ten-year-old with rosy cheeks and huge dark eyes, says she wants to be a doctor; Nahid, a seventeen-year-old mother with a tired face, insists she wants to be a teacher even as she cradles her baby in her arms. Around the room, their young voices ring out: "Teacher . . . doctor . . . doctor . . . pilot . . . teacher . . ." Their enthusiasm is infectious and their dreams speak to the larger thirst for education among Afghan girls.

The closest secondary school, however, is in Ghazni, a six-hour drive from this village under the best of conditions. Since there are no female dorms at the school, it is impossible for girls to attend unless their families relocate to live nearby. I know the odds are low that any of them will be able to continue their education much beyond the equivalent of a few years of primary school. But these girls are arguably among the lucky ones in rural Afghanistan. With strong community support for their education, they at least have a chance to learn to read and write. Despite the fact that polls show that nearly 90 percent of the Afghan population approves of girls' education, nonetheless, among the 10 percent who oppose it, there are extremists who are willing to use violence to impose their conservative views. In vast regions of the country, especially in the south and east where the conservative Pashtun tribes are predominant and the Taliban has its strongest foothold, few, if any, girls attend school. Even the most determined have been driven away by resurgent Taliban intimidation, including fatal attacks on girls' schools.

The Taliban, an extreme fundamentalist movement, came to power after the years of bitter civil war that engulfed Afghanistan in the wake of the Soviet occupation. In late 1979, Soviet forces invaded the country to prop up Afghanistan's puppet communist government. Then, for nearly a decade, Soviet advisers pushed various modernization plans on the country while fighting a brutal guerrilla war against the Afghan mujahideen, the resistance fighters who battled in the name of holy war, or jihad.

An important aspect of the Soviets' effort to remake Afghanistan focused on women's advancement. The Soviets reasoned that if they forced rural Afghan families to send their girls to school, development would follow. Indeed, female education is highly correlated with improved family health, reduced fertility, and greater national prosperity. However, the Soviets' heavy-handed educational policies, with coed classrooms and men teaching girls, even in the countryside, were seen as subverting the country's social codes and religious laws. Protecting Afghan girls from the godless ways of the Soviets became a powerful rallying cry for the mujahideen. Hundreds of thousands of Afghan families fled the country, many of them telling aid workers in camps in Pakistan that they would rather be refugees and remain true to their Islamic faith than submit their girls to the atheism of Soviet-run schools.

The Soviets failed to tame Afghanistan and on February 15, 1989, the last Soviet tanks retreated. Their withdrawal, however, did not bring the Afghans their longed-for peace. Instead, fighting broke out among the mujahideen fighters themselves, and the country was plunged into a civil war that lasted until 1996. The commanders of various mujahideen groups ruthlessly leveled Kabul as they battled each other for control of the capital city. Whatever "modernizing" the Soviets achieved during their nearly decade-long occupation was soon obliterated.

Out of this chaos, the Taliban emerged from southern Afghanistan. Many Afghans, tired of years of war, initially embraced the brutal peace imposed on the country by this conservative movement. Over time, though, the Taliban's cruelty and extreme interpretations of Islamic law began to take a toll on the Afghan people. Their harsh constraints on women, which they justified in the name of Islam, were particularly onerous. Women were beaten for not wearing the all-encompassing burqa, for appearing in the streets without a male guardian, even for laughing out loud in public. In front of crowds chanting "*Allahu Akbar*" (God is great), the Taliban stoned to death women accused of adultery. Although the toppling of the Taliban in 2001 heralded some improvements for women, educational opportunities remained slim. Even today, schools for rural girls, like this mosque-based effort in Hazarajat, are still the exception.

Later, after the class, Dr. Hassan and I sit on the floor and drink tea with the mullah. The village children press their faces against the window, watching us curiously. Most of the people in the village, including the mullah, have never met a foreigner, let alone an American. They assume that I must work for the government and that I have the power to bring their village the development they desperately need—not just a school, but clean water, electricity, and medicine. I try to explain that I am just a writer, but the mullah presses me with a list of the villagers' needs. He shakes his head sadly when the subject of the Taliban arises. "Islam is the religion of education, for both boys and girls," he explains with a defensiveness now familiar to me from similar conversations with other Afghans. "The Taliban are ignorant people who don't understand the basics of Islam. The Prophet says that women must be educated." The mullah seems proud that he's playing even a small part in reversing the Taliban's educational suicide.

"There's no other place for the women to gather, and it's important for our future that they learn to read . . ." The mullah sighs, and exasperation creeps into his tone. "But the mosque is getting too crowded. It's fine for the short term, but once a school is built, the women should study there." He looks wistfully out the window, at the desolate countryside with no roads, no electricity, and no irrigation for the barren fields. He shrugs his shoulders as if to acknowledge that it might be many years before a school is built in the village. In the meantime, it's the mosque or nothing. "Please, America," he says, looking directly at me, "don't leave us."

In 2002, Leslie Gelb, then the president of the Council on Foreign Relations where I was a senior fellow working on the Middle East, asked me to develop a program on women and foreign policy. I hesitated, protesting that I knew very little about gender issues. In fact, a program focused on women's issues struck me as, well, decidedly out of the mainstream. I had studiously avoided taking any women's studies courses in college and graduate school. "Women's rights" for me conjured up images of cranky, privileged women trying to get into all-male golf clubs. I had grown up in a "post-feminist" America, attended good schools, and achieved professional success with the support of important male mentors along the way. Gender issues had never been on my radar screen. Gelb, however, is persistent, and at his urging I read widely. Very quickly, I was intrigued and humbled.

It did not take long for me to understand that women's struggle for justice in much of the world is about the most basic human rights. It is also central to many of the most pressing foreign policy concerns: alleviating poverty, promoting economic development, improving global health, building civil society, strengthening weak and failing states, assisting democratization, tempering extremism. I soon came to appreciate that gender is one of the most critical lenses through which to examine a whole host of foreign policy priorities, and I accepted Gelb's challenge.

From the beginning, the most pressing question for me was how can women's rights progress in those places, like Afghanistan, where deeply entrenched religious and cultural traditions argue against it? Indeed, across the Islamic world, women's rights are one of the most contentious political and ideological issues. Attitudes toward women have helped to define and set apart the broader worldviews of conservative and progressive Muslims. Conservatives link women's piety to the purity and Islamic authenticity of their societies. They use religious justifications to enforce that piety through a limited public role for women, gender segregation, and harsh punishments for any perceived transgressions. Assertions of women's rights are often portrayed as anti-Islamic. For decades, powerful Islamists have successfully smeared women's groups as being slavish followers of an illegitimate, neo-colonialist Western agenda.

In this toxic environment, it is clear that women's empowerment, like many things, cannot be imposed on a country or a culture from the outside. Men and women within these conservative communities must first find their own reasons and their own justifications to allow women a fuller role in society. Increasingly, they are finding those reasons within Islam itself. This book is about how those efforts are coming together, slowly, in an emerging global movement of "Islamic feminism" (or Muslim feminism, as it is also called) and how that movement is transforming the broader Middle East.*

Islamic feminism is the promotion of women's rights through Islamic discourse. Just as conservatives have used Islam as a barrier to women's empowerment, Islamic feminists are turning that argument on its head and using Islam to promote gender equality. They argue that Islam, at its core, was intended to be progressive for women and that its teachings support equal opportunities for men and women alike. By firmly grounding their arguments within Islamic discourse, Muslim feminists offer a culturally acceptable and sustainable way to expand opportunities for women. This approach also allows them to press for their rights without feeling that they have to compromise their religious identity. Their efforts hold out the promise of a more stable and prosperous Middle East. Their ideas are part of a broader reform movement within Islam, one of the great ideological struggles of the twenty-first century.

The mullah I met in Hazarajat is an unwitting Islamic feminist in his use of Quranic arguments to support girls' education, but no doubt he would cringe at the term "feminism" in any form, and he would go to great lengths to distance himself from the Western cultural baggage it carries. So too would many of the activists I would term Islamic feminists. They see themselves simply as Muslims pursuing rights for women within Islam. But asked whether they believe that the spirit of the Quran is one of gender equality, and whether Islamic discourse can and should be used to promote women's empowerment, their answers will be a resounding yes.

Islamic feminism incorporates the ideas of numerous Muslim (and

*Some make distinctions between the terms Islamic feminism and Muslim feminism, noting that Islamic feminism can and does include non-Muslims in the dialogue. Indeed, several non-Muslims have made important contributions to Islamic feminism, including Elizabeth Warnock Fernea, whose 1998 book, *In Search of Islamic Feminism*, was one of the first to explore the emerging movement, and also the scholar Margot Badran, who has been writing and speaking about Islamic feminism for many years.

non-Muslim) intellectuals and activists. Some of its leading proponents
are men—distinguished scholars who contend that Islam was radically
egalitarian for its time and remains so in many of its texts. Islamic feminists claim that Islamic law evolved in ways inimical to women not due
to any inevitability or intention in its core beliefs, but because of selec-
tive interpretation by patriarchal leaders. They argue that the worst
practices toward women, like those of the Taliban, in fact represent a
subversion of Islamic teaching, its corruption by tribal customs and traditions. Seeking to revive the equality that the religion originally
bestowed on women, they advocate rereading the Quran, putting the
texts in historical context, and disentangling them from patriarchal and
tribal practices and other local traditions.

The great potential of Islamic feminism is its grassroots appeal. Secular feminism—both in the Middle East and in the West—has always
been the province of urban elites and intellectuals, and that has long
been its greatest weakness. Social change takes time to make its way
from city salons and urban newspapers to the countryside, especially in
places with few roads and little public education. Because it strives to
work within the values of Islam, not against them, Islamic feminism has
the potential to be embraced by local leaders, perhaps most importantly by religious leaders, like the Hazara mullah, who can lend their
authority to the difficult changes at hand.

Islamic feminism can and should be viewed as part of a much larger
struggle taking place today within Islam itself. Khaled Abou El Fadl,
one of the world's leading Islamic scholars, describes these times
as a transformative moment for Islam, a competition between two
opposing worldviews—"moderate" versus "puritanical" Islam.[1] (Other
scholars use terms such as "liberal" or "progressive" Islam versus "conservative" or "extremist" Islam to explain this same divide.) As Abou El
Fadl explains, while all Muslims agree on a core set of beliefs and practices (such as a belief in monotheism, accepting Muhammad as God's
messenger on earth, praying five times a day), there are several related
areas of profound disagreement. These include differences in understanding and applying Islamic law (sharia), different approaches to
modernity, different perspectives on the legitimacy of holy war (jihad)

and terrorism, and, of course, different views on the role of women in society.

In every country across the Islamic world, the role of women is contested. Attitudes toward women represent a stark fault line between those promoting economic reform, human rights, and democratization on the one hand and those who adhere to austere, fundamentalist notions of society on the other. The diametrically opposed attitudes between the mullah who is willing to bring girls into his mosque to educate them and the Taliban who burn down girls' schools merely for existing is but one extreme example of how these disagreements play out in various Islamic societies around the world today.

The outcome of this struggle matters enormously. While the more dramatic subjects of jihad and terrorism dominate headlines, it is instead attitudes toward women's rights that will, over the long run, have a far more profound role in shaping the economic and social development of these countries and their interactions with the West.

While women's empowerment can be framed as a moral issue, it is— perhaps most critically—also a vital economic issue. Put simply, economies cannot prosper without the full participation of half the population. Investing in girls' education and creating economic opportunities for women have been proven to have tremendous positive benefits for the broader development of a country. They are powerful levers for raising per capita incomes, and the advantages are transmitted directly to the next generation. Study after study shows that women use their income to invest more in the family than do men. Indeed, as many within the international development community now recognize, women's empowerment is the low-hanging fruit of poverty reduction.

Women's active participation in the public sphere is also critical to the broader development of civil society. It should come as no surprise that countries that suppress women are far more likely to have authoritarian regimes and are more prone to extremism.

In our post-9/11 world, talk of a "clash of civilizations" between the West and the Islamic world is widespread. At the heart of this talk is the presumption that Muslim-majority countries and Western liberal democracies do not share the same values, yet there is a surprising convergence between these groups on one subject in particular: Overwhelming majorities (85 percent or more) in both Western and Muslim-majority countries concur that democracy is the best form of government and the one they desire for their country.[2] Although women's political participation does not necessarily lead to democracy, democracy certainly cannot happen without it.

The big differences in attitudes between the West and Muslim-majority countries arise around social issues. Respondents in Muslim countries are less tolerant of homosexuality, abortion, and divorce. But the biggest gaps involve attitudes toward women, especially in the perspectives of younger generations. While youth in Western societies presume equality between the sexes, younger generations in Muslim countries have, in many cases, grown up in an environment more overtly religious than that of their parents' generation and have remained deeply traditional in their views on gender roles. As these younger generations assume positions of power in their respective countries, it will become even more difficult to find common ground on these issues. As some have noted, what we really have on our hands is a "sexual clash of civilizations," an expanding cultural chasm between Muslim-majority countries and the West over gender.[3]

Undoubtedly, the rise of political Islam, or "Islamism" as it has also been called, has contributed to prevailing conservative views on women in the Middle East. Political Islam began its steady rise in the wake of Egypt's ignominious defeat in the 1967 Arab-Israeli War, when cultural pride could no longer sustain the political hopes of millions of Arabs across the Middle East. As the luster of Arab nationalism began to fade, a wave of Islamism swept over the region, filling an ideological vacuum. The 1979 Islamic Revolution in Iran, the jihadi fight against the Soviets in Afghanistan, the ceaseless Arab-Israeli struggle—all have served to invigorate and sustain political Islam across the broader Muslim world. In recent years, the U.S.-led war on terror, the invasions of Afghanistan and Iraq, and the successes of Hizbullah and Hamas against Israel have infused new energy into Islamist movements. Throughout the region, the Muslim Brotherhood's slogan, "Islam is the solution," continues to resonate with a broad cross section of society that believes that a renewed dedication to Islam is the best way to address their problems.

Islamist movements depict women's freedoms as sowing the seeds of cultural corruption. For many Islamists, women's empowerment—social, economic, or political—represents nothing more than a slippery slope toward Western decadence and godless secularism, toward widespread adultery and prostitution and the end of family life. On these grounds, some religious and tribal leaders resist girls' education, and powerful Islamist pressure groups have successfully protected unequal laws in the name of upholding sharia, particularly in the realm of family law. Linking feminism with the "heresy" of the West is good politics, and helps turn patriarchy into patriotism. This is what makes Muslim feminism a potentially powerful force for women's rights, since it undercuts the argument that feminism is an illegitimate Western influence.

Women's empowerment in the Middle East has also suffered due to its long association with colonialism and secularism. During the tumultuous decades of decolonization in the region, as Western empires retreated, a number of military leaders came to power whose attempts to modernize their societies included forcibly diminishing the role of the religious establishment and overturning centuries of cultural traditions. The best known of these was Mustafa Kemal Atatürk, the heavy-handed founder of modern Turkey. His success as a leader and a modernizer inspired imitators in other countries who tried to follow in his secular footsteps.

Inevitably, these reformers focused on women since women's lack of education and rights were such a glaring difference with the West. They believed, accurately as it turned out, that improving women's status through better access to education and public life would benefit their country as a whole. While some of these leaders made real investments and reformed laws to benefit women, others made superficial changes, emulating the West to appear "modern." Their shortcut to modernization often began with the cultural touchstone of women's dress, as they struggled, and mostly stumbled, with the symbolic lifting of the veil. For opponents of these cultural changes, feminism became synonymous with a rejection of local culture in favor of that of the West. It became a class issue, with urban elites embracing social change as much as rural traditionalists resisted it. And it also became a political issue, pitting strong-armed rulers with deep ties to former colonial powers against entrenched religious authorities whose status and power were threatened by secularism.

Tied to the fortunes of the region's authoritarian rulers, secular feminism rose and fell as they did. And over the last several decades, from Algiers to Baghdad to Tehran, many of those secular leaders have fallen, undone by rampant corruption, brutality, and ultimately, their failure to deliver on the promises of modernization.

Today, secular governments across the region are constantly fighting a rearguard action against Islamism. Even in Turkey, elections in 2007 delivered political control to the Islamic Justice and Development Party (AKP), causing many to fear the end of Atatürk's legacy of secularism. The Turkish military threatened to intervene, as it has in the past, to keep the flame of secularism alive, and it continues to keep watch in the wings. In other secular countries, like Tunisia, it takes the mechanisms of a none-too-subtle police state to maintain a secular system.

It is fair to say that secularism as a political force is on life support across the Middle East. While secular opposition groups exist in every country, they are mostly comprised of urban intellectuals and lack a grassroots following. They struggle to compete against better-organized, better-financed, and more widely supported Islamist movements and their networks of mosque-based social services.

Given the cultural, religious, social, and political sensitivities to women's empowerment, as well as the negative connotations of secular feminism and the ascendance of political Islam in the region, Islamic feminism may very well be the most promising way to promote gender justice today across the broader Middle East. Popular or not, women's empowerment remains a crucial aspect of development in these countries. It is a goal in which the broader global community clearly has a vested interest.

While Islamic feminism explicitly works within Islam, and can therefore seem less threatening than secular feminism, it nonetheless questions aspects of traditional Islamic orthodoxy. Many Muslim feminists are strong proponents of *ijtihad*, the process of arriving at new interpretations of Islamic law through critical reasoning, rather than blindly following the views of past scholars. (Literally, *ijtihad* can be translated as "self-exertion.") In the early centuries of Islam, the process of *ijtihad* helped shape Islamic law. Whenever the Quran and Sunnah (the traditions and sayings of the Prophet Muhammad) did not explicitly address an issue (say, a new discovery or phenomenon), or when jurists could not reach a clear consensus on an issue, a qualified legal scholar could use independent reasoning to come up with a solution that he believed was consistent with the Prophet's intent. This legal ruling, expressed as a fatwa, could then be accepted or rejected by the followers of the scholar as they wished.

Ijtihad was a vibrant legal process until the end of the tenth century by which point many doctrines were settled by jurists representing the various schools of law. Around this time, influential orthodox Sunni *ulama* began to argue against the process of independent reasoning, claiming that it could distort Islam. Some of these Sunni scholars instead advocated for a more literal reading of religious texts. Reformers resisted, warning that a rigid interpretation of sharia, the existing body of Islamic laws, could be profoundly unhelpful in answering contemporary questions. But over the centuries, the literalists gained ground, leading to what some have referred to as a "closing of the gates of *ijtihad*" among more orthodox Sunni schools.[4]

At the heart of Islamic feminism is an attempt to push those gates of reasoning wide open. Across the Muslim world, Islamic feminists are now combing through centuries of Islamic jurisprudence to highlight the more progressive aspects of their religion. They are seeking—and finding—accommodation between a modern role for women and the Islamic values that more than a billion people in the world follow.

Despite significant restrictions on women across much of the Muslim world, the last several decades have seen rising levels of female literacy and, due to globalization, greater exposure to international media in almost every country. Islamic feminists are taking advantage of these changes to shift the terms of religious debate. Networks across countries are forming to help even illiterate peasant women marshal the religious justifications they need to push back on centuries of tribal customs and traditions that have been sustained in the name of Islam.

For all its practical and strategic advantages, Islamic feminism is not without its challenges. For starters, it is unpalatable to diehard secularists, both in the West and in the Middle East. After my visit to the mosque-based school in Afghanistan, I gave a talk in New York about the possibilities of working with religious leaders in some of the most conservative regions of the world to promote girls' education. When the discussion turned to the use of the mosque itself as a classroom for girls, a woman in the audience interrupted. This was exactly the wrong approach, she insisted. "We should be working to dislodge religion, not further entrench it." Clearly, she has never been to the central highlands of Afghanistan, I thought to myself, and might not appreciate the political and cultural realities of the region. Those who have tried to dislodge religion in such places have a long history of failure. Outright opposition to religion is simply counterproductive in many Muslim-majority countries today (as it is in many Western countries). If the advancement of women's rights in the Middle East depends on the removal of Islam, Muslim women will be waiting a long time indeed.

At a conference in Morocco sometime later, I discussed the concept of Islamic feminism with a history professor from Tunis University who is also an adviser to the minister of higher education in Tunisia. He smiled knowingly, and leaned back in his chair as he adjusted the cuffs on his pinstriped suit. "Ah, they have gotten to you," he said. "The Islamists want women to play on their field, where they can tie them up in religious arguments forever. No, no. Secularism is the only way forward for women." If we take a long-term perspective, over many decades, the Tunisian professor might ultimately be right. But outside of Tunisia and Turkey today, where does secularism have a chance in the near term in the Middle East?

Later in our conversation, the professor admitted that despite Tunisia's ban on women wearing the headscarf in public offices and schools, over 80 percent of the female students and faculty at the university defiantly still wear one in class. "We cannot enforce the ban on hijab," he bemoaned. "We would have to shut down the university if we tried." Measured by the ubiquitous hijab, Islamism is alive and well in Tunisia, despite, or indeed perhaps because of, the country's enforced secularism. Many Muslim women have embraced this aspect of their religion almost as an assertion of their rights in and of itself. Across the region, the headscarf is as much a symbol of resistance to authoritarian secularism as it is a sign of piety.

Although Islamic feminists themselves see Islam as having room to accommodate and empower them, their efforts are denigrated by Islam bashers, many of whom dismiss Islam as an inherently misogynist religion and who refuse to allow that it can be a force for women's empowerment. Some of the women you will read about in the pages of this book—Muslim women who are leading the charge to promote progressive interpretations of Islam—have been accused of whitewashing their religion.

Critics contend that by emphasizing the parts of the Quran that are progressive for women, and minimizing those sections that are harder to reconcile with gender equality, Islamic feminists are simply glossing over the fundamental issues. Yet, one can argue, is this not the same process of interpretation and contextualizing that has occurred over the centuries in every major religion in the world?

Indeed, many Islamic feminists see their efforts as a critical driver of a larger reform initiative within Islam. As Muslim women themselves engage more deeply with Islamic texts and jurisprudence, through casual study groups, as scholars and activists, or even by pushing for formal training to become religious leaders themselves, they are forcing debate over Islamic interpretation and the intent behind some of the most widely held tenets of the religion.

The different ways Islam can be interpreted was driven home for me on a trip to the region some years ago. In Saudi Arabia, a Western-educated Saudi friend tried to explain away his country's restrictions on women. He told me earnestly that the only reason women in Saudi Arabia cannot drive, vote, or travel without a male guardian is because Muslim women are so revered. "These restrictions are only to protect women," he good-naturedly insisted. To prove his point, he quoted a well-known hadith, or saying, of Muhammad: "Paradise lies beneath the feet of mothers." Later on the same trip, when I was discussing these issues with a group of Saudi women, one of them spoke up enthusiastically. "You know," she announced, stabbing her finger in the air, "we deserve all these rights and more, because Muhammad said that 'Paradise lies beneath a mother's feet!'"

Finally, some Islamic feminists will undoubtedly disappoint Western observers with their anti-Western, anti-globalization, and anti-Zionist views. Some do not condemn armed struggle as terrorism. Some of the more conservative women condone certain deeply entrenched social practices, like polygamy, that others believe to be repressive. While their conservative dress, their religious discourse, their support for Islamist causes, and their working-class roots may sustain the status quo in some ways, these are precisely the factors that provide some Islamic feminists with the credibility and influence they need within their communities to be effective agents of change.

Some of the women profiled in the following pages are deeply devout. Others are not. Some wear the headscarf for reasons of piety, others do so only for tactical reasons. They adhere to social conventions in an effort to enhance their credibility. A few eschew the headscarf completely—their understanding of Islam does not require it. But all of them are using Islamic discourse in one way or another to promote women's access to education, to jobs, and to the public sphere, access that is already transforming Muslim societies.

The book is organized in two sections, the first providing some historical background on the contested status of women in the Middle East and the rise of Islamic feminism, and the second looking at specific ways that women's empowerment is playing out in five countries in the greater Middle East. Chapter 1 in the first section explains why we should care about the status of women in the Middle East. It examines the extensive evidence that investing in women creates a virtuous cycle—smaller, healthier families raising better-educated, more productive children in stronger civil societies. Specifically, it explores the three legs of the stool on which women's empowerment stands: access to income, education, and political voice.

Chapter 2 in the first section then examines the rise of Islamic feminism, from its roots in the late nineteenth century with the attempts of various Muslim scholars, confronted with the economic and technological challenge of the West, to "modernize" Islam, to the more recent, groundbreaking work of contemporary men and women scholars who are reading the Quran in a more progressive way. It shows how the rise of political Islam, and the failures of secular authoritarianism, have in many ways necessitated Islamic feminism. It looks at the success of activists in forming transnational networks and using global communications and media to spread the ideas of Islamic feminism, as average Muslim women themselves enjoy rising levels of education and the ability to read the sacred texts for themselves.

The second part of the book focuses on how Muslim women are transforming their societies in five deeply conservative countries in the greater Middle East region—Iran, Pakistan, Afghanistan, Saudi Arabia, and Iraq. This strategic crescent contains more than 330 million people, nearly 50 percent of the world's known oil reserves, an unstable nuclear power (Pakistan), and one aspiring to nuclear capabilities (Iran); one of the world's richest states (Saudi Arabia) and one of the poorest (Afghanistan); Sunni-majority countries (Saudi Arabia, Afghanistan, and Pakistan), and the spiritual and political centers of resurgent Shiism (Iran and Iraq). It is also the setting for two active wars. The stability of our world as we know it will likely be determined in this volatile part of the globe. The future of women's rights within each will be central to determining the future of these societies.

While every country has its unique circumstances, these five illustrate the major trends occurring across the broader region: women's demands for greater educational and economic opportunities; their efforts to gain a political voice; the shift in influence from secular elites to mass-based Islamist movements and the class issues this entails; women's quest for legal rights, particularly in the sensitive area of family law; and the influence of new media, especially satellite television, on shaping the public's perceptions of the role of women in society. The differences across these countries are clearly significant, but the commonalities of women's struggles run deep.

Many of the women I describe here are courageous, determined, and inspirational. In these pages you will meet unsung heroes like Nasreen Parveen, a once-destitute Pakistani slum dweller who, through pluck and entrepreneurship, is creating a better life for her children. Champions like Dr. Sakena Yacoobi struggle under medieval conditions to deliver healthcare to women in Afghanistan. Dr. Haifa Jamal al-Lail, the dean of one of the leading women's universities in Saudi Arabia, quietly but persistently resists some of the most conservative forces within the kingdom to push for greater educational opportunities for young women.

At the same time that these women are making their insistent progress, however, girls' schools are being burned down, women leaders are being imprisoned or assassinated, and progressive laws are being overturned. There is no mistaking that women and women's issues are very much on the front lines of a war that is taking place between advocates of modernity, tolerance, and plurality and those who use violence to enforce rigid orthodoxy and reject modernity.

Ultimately, this is a hopeful book. Cultural change can and does happen, albeit often slowly. Islamic feminism is a growing force that is easing that process of cultural change for millions of Muslim men and women by fighting for progress while respecting religious faith. The process will not be linear: The history of women's empowerment around the world and through the ages has been that of two steps forward, one back, and sometimes even two or three steps back. But history is on the side of the Afghan mullah who knows that "if girls are educated, they can change our whole society."

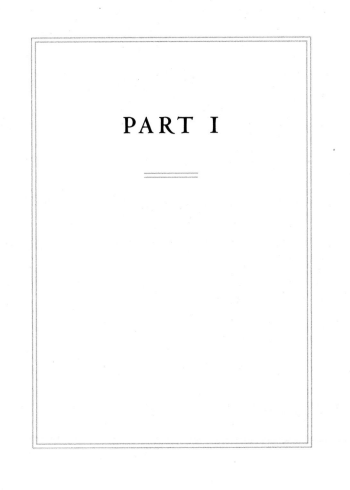

PART I

CHAPTER 1

WHY WOMEN MATTER
The Payoff from Women's Rights

A mother is a school. Empower her and
you empower a great nation.
—HAFEZ IBRAHIM, Egyptian poet (1872–1932)

Across the dusty Mogadishu courtyard, the Somali women shouted instructions to each other as they cooked, adding their voices to the already considerable din—dogs barking, babies crying, the occasional staccato of distant machine-gun fire. The temperature hovered around a hundred degrees, and although a tattered tarp provided some meager cover from the searing sun, it also trapped the scalding heat from the kitchen fires. Orange flames licked the bottom of the giant makeshift pots provided by the Red Cross—fifty-gallon drums cut in half, with handles welded onto the sides for maneuvering. The women used long poles, like broomsticks, to stir the mush inside, a bland but nutritious concoction of rice, beans, and oil. Sweat poured down their faces. The smell of perspiration, food, and woodsmoke was pungent.

Outside the burned-out building, a guard stood by the doorway. The drooping flags of the Red Cross and the Red Crescent stirred occasionally in the faint breeze off the Indian Ocean. By late afternoon, a line of people began to form, and soon it was hundreds deep—mothers with babies on their backs, gaunt-faced children waiting listlessly by their parents' sides, a few young men chewing *khat* leaves, a natural stimulant that suppresses hunger but also makes them high. When the guard blew his whistle, the line moved slowly forward, flip-flops shuffling in the dust. The poorest were barefoot. The guard made the young men leave their Kalashnikovs at the door.

Inside the courtyard, the volunteer "kitchen mamas" worked efficiently, slopping the mush into whatever containers people carried—a cup, a plate, a ripped carton. Dipping in with their hands, the Somalis ate quickly. The bold colors of the women's *direhs*—their long, billowing traditional dresses—brightened the otherwise dismal surroundings. Remarkably, they somehow managed to keep their petticoats out of the dust.

It was the summer of 1991, and Somalia was embroiled in a full-blown civil war, a war that tragically continues today. Hundreds of thousands of refugees fled the fighting, and as drought compounded the already tenuous situation, famine ran rampant. Relief groups struggled to provide aid, but thousands of people were dying by the day. Red Cross efforts to feed the hungry were largely thwarted by widespread looting. Convoy trucks were routinely attacked and robbed by rival clans who used the food to feed their own militias, or to barter for weapons, while the women and children starved. By some estimates, a quarter of Somali children under the age of five perished during the famine. As Geoffrey Loane, the director of Red Cross efforts in Somalia at that time, recalls, "This was not the finest hour for Somali men."[1]

Somali women, however, rose to the challenge. Loane, a soft-spoken Irishman, smiles remembering how the women of Mogadishu came to him with a plan to get food to the starving people. "They proposed a solution, a practical solution totally in keeping with their local culture. Rather than transporting big shipments of food to large feeding centers, which only encouraged the looting, the women suggested we help them set up communal kitchens in neighborhoods across the city. The Red Cross would supply them with firewood and water, and run a constant stream of small loads of food to them via donkeys. They would immediately cook the food and serve it to the hungry, averting starvation and eliminating the food's cash value. We thought it was worth a try. Before we knew it, the women had totally taken charge. They set up more than three hundred of these communal kitchens, run by kitchen committees comprised of twenty to thirty women. Each of these kitchens was dishing out between one and two thousand meals, twice a day. They became the lifeline of Mogadishu."

The kitchens took shape in the rubble of destroyed buildings—what was left of the whitewashed villas that once graced Mogadishu's palm-tree-lined streets. Even the city's elegant mosques, a tribute to its historic past as a great trading port, had not escaped the ransacking. Once the Red Cross was on board, the women negotiated with the warlords to appropriate space for their communal kitchens. Some of these kitchens even had links with local schools, where meals provided an incentive for both students and teachers to continue attending classes even during the brutal chaos of the war.

Andrew Natsios, the United States' special coordinator for Somalia relief efforts at the time, remembers going into Mogadishu at the height of the fighting and, to his amazement, stumbling upon a functioning school in the middle of the civil war. There were at least ten classrooms full of grammar-school children. How is that possible, he wondered? Though he had been told that all the schools in Mogadishu had been shut down due to the fighting, in truth some thirty thousand kids were still attending classes. The formal education system had collapsed along with the government, but the women had devised a way to keep the schools functioning. The kitchen mamas were using some of the food aid to pay the teachers in a makeshift food-for-work program. Natsios recognized the effectiveness of this grassroots effort, and the United States started giving small grants not only to the Red Cross, but to several women-led local organizations that were focused on keeping the schools running. The results were spectacularly successful for many months until the warlords caught wind of the transactions and began robbing the women's groups to finance their militias.[2]

"These women were incredibly determined and courageous," remembers Loane, the Red Cross director. One in particular stands out in his memory: Dhabo Issa, a tall Somali woman with a commanding presence and fiery temper. The Red Cross hired her to manage the complicated logistics for the kitchen program in the southern part of the city. Loane's eyes sparkle recalling Dhabo Issa's grit: "She was a pearl of pearls." But when I ask him what became of her, his smile fades. As the famine receded and the kitchens were closed, the women lost what little power they had garnered. After the "Black Hawk Down" fiasco, when U.S. troops were fatally dragged through the streets of Mogadishu, international support for the peacekeeping effort disappeared. "The last I heard," sighs Loane, "Dhabo Issa had become a refugee in London, working as an office assistant. I felt like saying to her boss, 'Man, don't you know who you have photocopying for you? This woman deserves a Nobel Prize for her kitchen work.'"

On the Front Lines of Development

The efforts of the Somali women to keep their children in school, despite the violence, chaos, and famine, are inspirational but by no means unusual, as anyone who has worked in a disaster area or a war zone knows. Although women are often the victims of violence and oppression, by dint of their child-rearing responsibilities they are also the backbone of society—the ones responsible for keeping families intact, feeding and educating the children, and raising the next generation.

Poor women's suffering has long been a surefire way to pull on the heartstrings of rich donors, but in recent years there has been a newfound appreciation for the role that these women play in breaking the cycle of poverty and stabilizing fragile societies. Development experts now widely recognize women's role as critical to economic progress, healthy civil society, and good governance, especially in developing countries. Providing women with more and better opportunities to fulfill their social, economic, and political roles is now deemed so essential for reducing poverty and improving governance that women's empowerment has become a development objective in its own right. The key levers for change, from the ground up, are clearly female education and women's access to income. Top down, women's leadership—at the local and the national level—is also important.

In 2000, all the world's countries and top development institutions agreed to an action plan to eliminate extreme poverty, disease, and hunger by 2015. The resulting UN Millennium Development Goals (MDGs) include the promotion of gender equality and the improvement of maternal health as two of its eight targets—not simply as a nod to social justice, but in recognition that women's empowerment is a driver of poverty alleviation. (Progress on the gender equality/women's empowerment MDG is measured by increases in girls' access to schooling, improvements in women's access to wage-paying jobs, and increases in the share of women within national parliaments.) Across the MDGs, women's empowerment is considered so essential that it underpins all of the other goals.

Unfortunately, too little progress has been made on all the MDGs, and on the ones that focus on women in particular. In fact, of all the MDGs, the least progress has been made on the goal of improving maternal health. More than half a million women die each year and several million more are severely disabled from childbirth. These grim maternal health statistics give an all too clear picture of the low status of women in parts of the world.

The good news is that with concerted government efforts, women have made progress in many countries: Gender gaps in infant mortality rates, calorie consumption, school enrollment, literacy levels, access to healthcare, and political participation have narrowed steadily in many developing countries in recent decades, particularly in East Asia and Latin America. Those changes have benefited societies at large, improving living standards, increasing social entrepreneurship, and attracting foreign direct investment.

Yet significant gender disparities continue to exist, and in some cases to grow, in three regions of the world: South Asia, the Middle East, and sub-Saharan Africa. Although the conservative, patriarchal constraints on women living in these areas are increasingly recognized by the international community as a drag on development, empowering women is nonetheless still considered a subversive proposition by many who live in these regions.

In some societies, women's rights are at the forefront of a protracted battle between religious extremists and those with more moderate, progressive views. In the name of Islam, numerous women leaders have been assassinated; hundreds of girls' schools have been destroyed in Pakistan and Afghanistan; across South Asia, the Middle East, and even in Muslim communities in Europe and North America, thousands of young women—mothers, wives, sisters, daughters—have been murdered by close male relatives for supposed "honor crimes"; in Somalia in 2008, in front of a crowd of a thousand people, a thirteen-year-old girl was stoned to death for adultery after her family told local authorities that she had been raped; in Iraq, Afghanistan, and Pakistan,

Islamic vigilantes throw acid on women's faces for not fully covering themselves. In Palestine, Sunni extremists belonging to shadowy groups such as the "Swords of Islamic Righteousness" threaten to slit the throats of female broadcasters "from vein to vein" if they do not wear strict Islamic dress.[3] All these acts of violence are justified by their perpetrators as upholding sharia, as conforming to the will and rule of God. Yet moderate Muslims condemn this violence as perverted extremism that flies in the face of Islamic values.

The debate over women's rights within Islam is not a new one. For centuries, Islamic scholars, thinkers, and activists have been pondering this question of women's rights, and reaching very different answers. In today's increasingly global world, however, the stakes are higher than ever—for everyone. Societies that invest in and empower women are on a virtuous cycle. They become richer, more stable, better governed, and less prone to fanaticism. Countries that limit women's educational and employment opportunities and their political voice get stuck in a downward spiral. They are poorer, more fragile, have higher levels of corruption, and are more prone to extremism.

Womenomics

There is a familiar self-help aphorism, "If you give a man a fish, he will eat for a day, but if you teach him to fish, he will eat for a lifetime." A veteran development expert once quipped to me: If you teach a man to fish, he will eat for a lifetime, but if you give a woman title to the fish pond, she will clean it up, preserve it for the next generation, stock it with new fish, and create a fish farm to employ the village.[4]

When I repeated this saying to the Nobel Prize winner Muhammad Yunus, founder of Grameen Bank and one of the architects of the global microfinance movement, he smiled knowingly. Grameen now focuses almost exclusively on women borrowers, although in its early days, Grameen's goal was to have a 50/50 split between male and female borrowers. And then something happened:

> We started noticing something new. Money that went to the
> family through the woman brought so much more benefit to the

family than the same amount of money going to the family through the man. It was very clear. Women took very good care of it. And being a poor woman, she had an amazing skill, the skill to manage a scarce resource . . . And she brought this excellent skill of managing a scarce resource to the little money we gave her. She got the largest, biggest mileage you can ever think. And if mother is earning money, children become the first beneficiary of it and everybody else gradually benefits from it. She is the last person to benefit. So we saw those things and we kept talking about it and we changed our policy. We said: Forget about 50/50. Who says 50/50? Let's concentrate on women. And that's when we came to this. And gradually we moved from 70 to 80 percent, 90 percent and stayed like that.[5]

When Yunus launched Grameen in the early 1970s, the microcredit concept—providing loans to very poor people with little or no collateral—was simply revolutionary. Grameen's mission of making loans to the poorest of the poor in Bangladesh, most of whom had virtually no formal education, little previous business experience, and certainly no collateral, broke all the rules of banking. Moreover, to focus on rural Muslim women, who, bound by their traditions, had rarely left their homes nor spoken to a man outside their family, pushed the limits of common sense. How could they know how to put the loans to good use to be able to pay them back? At the time Grameen started, 85 percent of Bangladeshi women were illiterate; many abided by *purdah*—a range of practices that seclude women as a way of ensuring modesty. In its most conservative form, *purdah* restrictions prevent women from being seen by any man outside her immediate family.

Yunus persevered in his commitment to lending to women, but not without arousing the hostility of the establishment. Early on, he received a threatening letter from the central bank demanding to know why such a high percentage of Grameen's borrowers were women—this was simply too radical a departure from convention. After debating how to reply, he sent back a letter demanding an explanation for why all the other banks had such a high percentage of male clients. Not surprisingly, his letter went unanswered.[6] (The bankers' reluctance to give women any financial control was certainly not unique to Bangladesh. When Grameen started in 1977, less than a decade had passed since a married woman in Texas had gained the right to secure a loan, own property, or start a business without her husband's written approval.[7])

Over the past thirty years, Grameen has achieved remarkable results—millions of clients (97 percent of them women) have started a myriad of businesses, improved the lives of their families, and repaid their loans. Grameen's model has been replicated around the world. Today, the business of microcredit has become virtually synonymous with small loans for women. Women comprise 85 percent of the world's 115 million microcredit borrowers, with many microfinance institutions devoted exclusively to serving women. They focus on women for a variety of reasons, including that women make up the majority of the poorest citizens of the world and are therefore obvious targets for poverty alleviation programs; and women frequently have limited access to jobs that pay a salary, so they are forced to find opportunities in the informal sector of the economy. Women also have very high repayment rates, no doubt because with such limited options, their access to microcredit is a financial lifeline that they protect at all costs.

But the driver for many microfinance organizations' focus on women is related to what Yunus discovered in the early days of Grameen: the social benefits of giving control of money to women rather than to men. Numerous studies show that increases in household income benefit a family more if the mother, rather than the father, controls the cash. Increases in female income, for example, improve child survival rates twenty times more than increases in male income, and children's height-weight measures improve about eight times more. Likewise, female borrowing has a greater positive impact on school enrollment, child nutrition, and healthcare than male borrowing.

Put simply, women tend to invest more in their families than men do. And this has been proven true around the world. Several decades ago, public officials in the United Kingdom began to notice that child welfare benefits were not being spent as intended and that a fair portion of the money was frittered away on alcohol and tobacco. In the late

1970s, the family allowance benefit was transferred away from fathers and instead given directly to mothers. Pretty soon, a significant shift in household expenditures occurred. For example, household spending on tobacco noticeably declined, while spending on children's clothing increased.[8] Similar results have been documented in countries as diverse as South Africa[9] and Mexico.[10] The bottom line is that health, nutrition, and educational outcomes for children improve more when benefits are managed by women than by men.

Economic Empowerment in the Heart of the Muslim World

When Roshaneh Zafar set out to build a microfinance institution in her native country of Pakistan, she knew from the outset that she wanted to focus on women. "I had every advantage as a child," she says in her clipped English accent, her long dark hair falling softly on her shoulders. "I was raised in a family that practiced gender equality, and I got the best education. Just like a privileged child in any country, I felt an obligation to give back."[11]

Roshaneh was raised in an intellectual family in Lahore, the capital of Pakistan's Punjab. The city combines remarkable Muslim architecture from the days of the great Mughal Empire in the seventeenth century with an overlay of imposing redbrick Victorian buildings built by the British raj in the nineteenth century. Lahore is the civic heart of Pakistan, the focal point of the country's vibrant nonprofit sector, and home to many prominent women activists.

Sensing that financial independence would position her to help other women, Roshaneh wanted to be a businesswoman from an early age. "I was inspired by my maternal grandmother," she says. Her grandmother was Malika Pukhraj, a famous singer of semiclassical South Asian music. When she was only eight, Malika started singing in the court of Maharaja Hari Singh, the last maharaja of the princely state of Jammu and Kashmir. She was revered in Pakistan and India until her death in 2004 at the age of ninety-three. "She was a remarkable woman," recalls Roshaneh, "a real diva who earned her own living through music. She always insisted to me that women should be independent and that financial independence was most important," she recalls.

After private schooling in Pakistan, Roshaneh Zafar went off to study business at the prestigious Wharton School at the University of Pennsylvania. By the time she graduated with her degree, she realized she was more interested in trying to tackle the structural drivers of poverty than in the business world itself. She began to believe that financial markets simply were not able to address the needs of the majority of people living in her part of the world. So she shifted course.

Roshaneh got a master's degree in International and Development Economics from Yale and then, in 1990, joined the World Bank, where she spent four years researching the impact of social investment on women. As she traveled across South Asia and talked to hundreds of women about how they could actively participate in economic development, she heard a similar refrain. Women would say, "You think we don't want a better future for our families? You think we don't want to provide a better life for our children? Give us money and we will make better choices."[12]

A chance meeting with Muhammad Yunus at a conference in 1993 launched Roshaneh on the path of microfinance. Yunus sent her a plane ticket to Dhaka to study the Grameen Bank model. By 1996, Roshaneh had founded the Kashf Foundation in her hometown of Lahore.

Kashf, which means "revelation" in Arabic, began as a research program focused on understanding how best to provide microfinance to poor women. But Roshaneh Zafar soon took the plunge into lending herself. Naturally, she got her first start-up funds from her grandmother, who seeded the organization with 150,000 rupees (a little less than $4,000 at the time).

Women's empowerment has always been at the heart of Kashf's mission. From the outset, 100 percent of its borrowers have been women, and women have always comprised at least half of its staff. "People told me when I started Kashf, 'You're crazy! This is Pakistan. You will never get women to borrow from you and you won't get women to work for you.' But within three months we had debunked both of those myths," recalls Roshaneh. One of Kashf's first borrowers was the wife of the local mullah—a person with significant influence in the community but set in traditional ways, an unlikely supporter of Kashf's innovative business. "This was transformational, for me, for my mind-set. I realized then that what is important to poor people is access to credit." Kashf quickly evolved into the fastest-growing microfinance institution in Pakistan, almost doubling in size each year.

Like most microfinance organizations, Kashf charges a high interest rate—around 36 percent. This high rate is necessary to cover the costs of making lots of relatively inefficient small loans to many people and collecting the interest payments regularly. But when viewed against the alternative for most Kashf clients—loan sharks who charge upward of 300 percent a year—Kashf's rate seems like a bargain. And with a 98 percent repayment rate, Kashf was the first microfinance institution in Pakistan to become financially sustainable.

When I first met Roshaneh in the fall of 2003, Kashf had already expanded to 65,000 clients, making it one of the larger microfinance organizations in the world. But Roshaneh has still bigger ambitions for her organization. As she explains, with three-quarters of Pakistan's population of 180 million people surviving on the equivalent of two dollars a day, there are millions and millions of households that could benefit from access to microfinance. And Roshaneh is determined to provide it through Kashf. Her organization is gunning to reach 750,000 clients by 2010.

With the direct, self-assured, and efficient style of the business-woman she was groomed to be, Roshaneh ticks through the positive impact Kashf has on the lives of its clients. Borrowers report a 30 percent rise in income after just one year. Nearly a third of Kashf clients have made it over the poverty line, whereas those in a control group show almost no change in poverty levels. Kashf clients spend more on nutrition, healthcare, and education for their children.

Roshaneh is even more enthusiastic about how Kashf improves the confidence of its female clients. Initially, Kashf had implemented a Grameen-like social contract for its borrowers, with a heavy emphasis on improving the status of women. Grameen makes each of its clients promise to abide by a set of "Sixteen Decisions" (including promising not to pay dowry, educating their children, planting trees, eating vegetables, and arranging for clean drinking water), which they recite at the start of their group meetings. In the beginning, Kashf had a similar set of principles but Roshaneh was never comfortable with the rote approach. "We always believed that a social program has to be interactive and participatory to be effective."

Instead, Kashf began to implement community-specific programs to get men and women to talk about gender issues, discussing everything from installing streetlights for safety to encouraging reproductive health and family planning. It also launched a very successful interactive theater, which works with local theater groups to develop plays with social messages. One such play features a father who is selling his thirteen-year-old daughter to an older man. The audience is required to come up with an ending for the play, determining in this case whether the father should go through with the sale or not. "The plays are a highly effective way to empower both boys and girls in the communities we serve," explains Roshaneh. As Kashf expands into more conservative rural areas of Pakistan, with more conservative mores, the plays serve as conversation starters that help pave the way for social change.

Speaking like a Muslim feminist, Roshaneh Zafar insists that Pakistan's Islamic conservatism is not an impediment to Kashf's growth. Rather, it is Pakistan's patriarchal culture that limits women's participation in activities outside the home. "Islam encourages women to be active in business. Just think of Khadijah." Khadijah was the Prophet Muhammad's first wife. She was a wealthy, older businesswoman who hired Muhammad to drive her caravans. Impressed with his integrity and acumen, Khadijah proposed marriage and he readily accepted. Khadijah is revered not only as the first convert to Islam, but also for her important financial contributions to the early growth of the religion. She is an inspiration to millions of entrepreneurial Muslim women around the world today.

To meet the needs of its clients, Kashf is always developing new products. Aware that many of its customers have no choice but to save their money in pots buried in the backyard or under their mattresses, Kashf has introduced savings accounts and launched a bank so it can take deposits. It has also introduced insurance products (life insurance is mandatory for borrowers so if anything happens to them their family is not saddled with debt) and is piloting a home improvement loan.

Kashf's "emergency loan"—a 4,000-rupee (about $50 U.S. dollars), no-questions-asked loan—is already very popular. Some women use the emergency loan to cover school fees, to deal with a health issue, or simply to take advantage of a business opportunity. To keep costs down, Kashf is constantly looking for helpful new technologies. It is currently experimenting with cashless banking via mobile telephones, an innovation already popular in the Philippines.

Like the Islamic feminist movement itself, Kashf is sensitive to the need to work within, rather than against, the world it is trying to reform. Recognizing the reality of Pakistan's patriarchal society, Kashf allows male relatives to control loans, but studies confirm that even with men directing the loans, women borrowers feel that their stature in the family has improved. Nearly 90 percent of Kashf borrowers report greater self-confidence stemming from more autonomy. More than half say that their spouses respect them more, allow them to make more decisions, and give them more say over household expenditures.[13] Similarly, studies of women in microfinance programs in other countries have observed reduced domestic violence against women borrowers, suggesting this is a consequence of women being regarded as more valuable economic members of the family once they start generating income via their microcredit loans.

A broad set of research demonstrates that across many countries, microfinance indeed empowers women, as defined by improvements in the woman's ability to influence or make decisions that affect her life. These include major family decisions, as well as decisions regarding family planning, her children's lives, household expenditures, and her microfinance-supported business.

Roshaneh Zafar also notes that Kashf clients become more aware politically, and more engaged in civic matters. When she asked her clients before an election if they were voting simply as directed by their husband or father, they rejected this notion. "The women insisted: 'We make our own choices. We vote for candidates who will build schools and better roads, provide electricity and clean water.' When women are involved in political decision making, they will often address social-service issues with more consistency than men," Roshaneh says.

"They Don't Laugh at Me Anymore"

On the outskirts of Lahore where Kashf is based, congested city streets give way to narrow dirt roads clogged with foot traffic and the jumble of small shops and homes. Every inch of space is filled with activity—vendors hawking fresh-squeezed sugarcane juice from pushcarts, men sharpening knives on the side of the road, women selling eggs from cardboard boxes and live chickens in mesh bags. Donkey carts laden with freshly threshed grass weave through the street chaos. Open sewers run along the side of the muddy streets and piles of garbage clog the lanes. Kashf opened its first branch office in these slums in 1998. Although it is beginning to expand into more rural areas, nearly a third of Kashf's clients are still in the slums around Lahore where the organization first started.

In March 2008, I visited Kashf's original branch office accompanied by the organization's energetic, thirty-something-year-old CEO at the time, Sadaffe Abid, who joined Kashf as its seventh employee and helped it achieve its tremendous growth. In the branch office, I meet a few of Kashf's clients and chat with them about their businesses. Some of the women are new to Kashf, just starting out with their first loan. Others have been clients for years. Several of the women have used their loans to start local pushcart businesses. One sells fruits, another sells vegetables. Hina, for example, sells fresh milk and has recently added a sideline of ice cream. "When I started out, I didn't have enough money to change my clothes," she tells me through a translator. "I would wear the same clothes for three or four days. But now I can change my clothes." On this day, she wears a spotless pale yellow *shalwar kameez* with sequins and a matching *dupatta* covering her head. A not-so-small diamond stud glistens in her nose.

Another woman has worked up to a larger loan, which she used to buy several motorized rickshaws. Her husband drives one, her son the other, and together they make enough to cover the installment payments on the rickshaws, interest on the loan, and a small profit. As each woman tells her story, many of them express to God how grateful they are for the Kashf opportunity. A few of them mention Khadijah, the Prophet Muhammad's first wife, as their role model. I think to myself that these illiterate Pakistani women are the foot soldiers of Islamic feminism.

One woman in the group, Nasreen Parveen, stands out. She makes a beeline to me when I enter the room and begins telling me her inspirational life story. She explains that she was married to an auto mechanic who owned a small shop with his brother in the village of Lidher, not far from Kashf's first branch office on the outskirts of Lahore. Nasreen looked after their two small children and the family scraped by on her husband's earnings. But when her husband died, Nasreen lost everything. Her brother-in-law refused to provide her with her husband's share of the shop, and as a lowly woman, she had no recourse. She was penniless, relying on handouts from family members.

One day in 1998, a Kashf loan officer came knocking on her door. At first, she was scared of the concept of taking a loan. "The Kashf person came asking all sorts of questions—what work do you do? How many children do you have? I didn't know why they wanted this information. It took me a long time to agree to the loan," she explains sheepishly. Now, it is hard to imagine this indomitable woman being reluctant.

With 4,000 rupees, Nasreen bought some sweets, which she sold from over her bed. She repaid her first loan, and took out another, adding more items to her burgeoning store, which she moved from her bed to a wooden stool in the street. Today, Nasreen's store occupies the whole first floor of her little house. Five years ago, when she moved the shop back inside, she bought a large freezer that she stocks with ice cream, cold drinks, and ice. Now her shelves are filled with dry goods, bottled drinks, snacks, and cleaning products. Taking my hand, she insists that we visit her shop.

On the way to her home, through muddy streets clogged with bicycles, motor scooters, and carts pulled by oxen, Nasreen points out her deceased husband's repair store that her brother-in-law kept. "I'm now better off than all of them!" she says with vindication. "My relatives all invite me places now. Before, they didn't invite me any-where. When you have no money, you don't get invited places."

Her home is down a side alley, wide enough for only one car to squeeze through at a time. Across the road there is a vacant lot piled high with garbage; on either side of her house are crumbling buildings. But her brick home is neat and tidy, her front door painted a bright, welcoming green. I sense she is a bit of a local celebrity. As she walks down the road, the sun glinting off her golden *shalwar kameez*, she looks almost regal. Men and women pile out into the street calling her name. "Nasreen!" "Nasreen!"

"They used to laugh at me, make fun of me behind my back, and say, what are these women doing getting together? But they don't laugh anymore," Nasreen says, shaking her head knowingly and waving back to her customers. As she speaks, she keeps flipping open her new cell phone, waving it around and slipping it back into the folds of her dress, clearly proud of her new gadget.

Her little store is dark and cool, and chock-full of goods: folded cloths and cotton dress materials on the shelves, soaps for washing and cleaning, plastic containers filled with spices and individual snacks. Over the makeshift counter, bags of sweets hang from a string. With her increased income, Nasreen says she and her children are eating better food and making regular visits to the doctor. Both of her chil-dren are in school—seventh and eighth grade—already beyond the level when most kids in Pakistan drop out.

Nasreen introduces me to her thirteen-year-old son Adil, who helps in the store after school. Adil is a handsome boy, almost as tall as his mother, with soft features and an easy smile. He examines us for a moment with his dark, serious eyes, and then, with a gravity beyond his years, demonstrates the workings of the store. Nasreen tells me that she has just taken out a 4,000-rupee emergency loan from Kashf, which she gave to Adil to buy kites for the upcoming kite festival. "He has almost sold them all and has already made a three-thousand-rupee profit!" she says with great satisfaction. Adil breaks into a smile and gives Nasreen a thumbs-up.

Education, Education, Education

If good things happen when women have access to income, access to education is an equally strong elixir. In recent years, a veritable cottage industry has emerged to extol the benefits of educating women. When he was the chief economist at the World Bank in the early 1990s, Lawrence Summers promoted girls' education through research that showed that investing in girls' education "yields a higher rate of return than any other investment available in the developing world."[14]

Oprah Winfrey agreed. Ever the savvy investor, she opened a $40 million Leadership Academy for Girls in Johannesburg in 2007, proclaiming, "When you educate a girl, you begin to change the face of a nation."

Oprah has a slew of strong statistics on her side. If the goal is slowing population growth, improving children's health and nutrition, reducing infant mortality, increasing the likelihood of the next generation attending school, combating the spread of HIV/AIDS, and even improving agricultural productivity, girls' education is indeed a powerful lever. While the benefits of educating boys are numerous, mounting evidence shows that the social returns to educating girls are even greater.[15]

Due to the central role women play in the domestic sphere, increasing a mother's schooling has a larger positive impact on the next generation than does adding to a father's schooling by the same number of years. Educating mothers drives lower child mortality, promotes better birth outcomes (such as higher birth weights), and leads to better child nutrition. One study that examined child nutrition across sixty-three countries found that female education was more important in reducing malnutrition than was improved healthcare or food availability.[16] Educating girls enables them to earn a higher income, make smarter family decisions, and better access available services. Female education also guarantees earlier and longer schooling for their children. In parts of rural India, husbands now require lower dowries for women with even a few years of education, partly because they know their literate wives will provide better educational opportunities for their own children.[17]

Girls' education also lowers birth rates, which by extension helps developing countries improve per capita income. Better-educated women have fewer children than less-educated women because they tend to marry later and have fewer years of childbearing. They are also better able to make informed, confident decisions about spacing their children. Increasing the average education level of a woman by three years has been linked to a reduction of individual birth rates by one child.[18]

Results from India show that keeping girls in school is a more effective way to reduce unrestrained population growth than aggressive family planning initiatives.[19] The state of Kerala has the highest female literacy rate in India, at around 90 percent, and women there average fewer than two children, a fertility rate slightly below replacement level. In contrast, less than half of women in the state of Rajasthan are literate, and they have more than four children on average, despite numerous family planning programs.[20] The strong correlation between female literacy and fertility shows up around the world. Among the Arab states, Tunisia has the highest level of female literacy and the lowest fertility rate.[21] In contrast, Yemen has the lowest level of female literacy and the highest fertility rate.

Female education can also boost agricultural productivity. Economists at the International Food Policy Research Institute, an organization that aims to reduce world hunger and malnutrition through its research, have been studying why female farmers in developing countries often experience lower yields than male farmers and have concluded that female farmers produce less primarily because of lower educational levels.[22] Women's lower literacy levels make them less able to utilize basic seed and farming techniques.

Similarly, World Bank reports indicate that in areas where women have very little schooling, providing them with at least a year of primary education is a better way to raise farm yields than increasing access to land or fertilizer.[23] With just a bit of education, they can make much more of the farm assets they have. All else being equal, better-educated female farmers are also more likely to grow cash crops in addition to subsistence crops, keep livestock, and plant modern varieties of seeds.[24]

These findings are important because farming in many parts of the developing world is increasingly becoming women's work. Over the past several decades, men have left the countryside to seek employment in cities, leaving the farms largely to women. Indeed, in some countries, women produce upward of 80 percent of the food for both household consumption and for sale.[25] Today, women constitute more than half the farm labor across Africa, the Middle East, and parts of South Asia.[26] But in these same regions, women have less access to education than men, and agricultural productivity has suffered as a result. As land becomes increasingly scarce and fertilizers yield diminishing returns, the next green revolution in many poorer and ecologically fragile regions of the world may well depend on increases in girls' education.

Keeping girls in school also helps protect them from HIV infection. The feminization of the AIDS epidemic across the African continent has forced frank discussions about the link between the low status of girls and the spread of the disease.[27] Girls attending secondary school have much lower levels of sexual activity than their peers who have dropped out of school. Likewise, they are much more likely to understand the causes of HIV/AIDS and to take precautions to prevent its transmission. In fact, education, especially for girls, is such a driver of safer behavior and reduced infection rates that it has been described as a "social vaccine" and hailed by various experts as the single most effective weapon against HIV/AIDS.[28]

Of all the benefits of promoting girls' education, perhaps the most important is that it improves a country's long-term economic growth rate, which is what ultimately lifts a population out of poverty.[29] Higher levels of female education allow more women to be productive, which in turn raises household incomes and reduces family poverty. With an educated female workforce, developing countries are better able to attract foreign direct investment. Export-oriented textile businesses, light manufacturing, and service centers depend on female labor— perhaps because women are better suited to the less-physical work, perhaps because female employees are more docile. Although many in the West look upon these factories as "sweatshops," the fact is that millions of women have lifted their families out of poverty by working in these export-oriented businesses.

It is no coincidence, then, that in the last half century the regions of the world that have most successfully closed gender gaps in education have also achieved significant economic growth: East and Southeast Asia and Latin America. Conversely, regions with lagging economic growth—South Asia, the Middle East, and sub-Saharan Africa—are those that have lagged in their investments in girls' education. Today, illiteracy among adult females is highest in South Asia (55 percent), the Arab states (51 percent), and sub-Saharan Africa (45 percent). Had these three regions closed their gender gaps in education at the same rate that East Asia did from 1960 to 1992, the additional growth in per capita income would have lowered poverty levels significantly.[30]

It is true that many countries across the broader Middle East are now catching up with the rest of the world on girls' education. Most states have now achieved full enrollment of girls at the primary level, and many are closing the gaps between boys and girls at higher levels. In some countries, like Iran and Jordan, women significantly outnumber men at the college level. Even so, there are some notable laggards on girls' education in the Middle East. Among the Arab states, Yemen, Iraq, and Morocco are burdened with the largest gender gaps in education, and with barely a majority of girls in school in Pakistan, and only a third of Afghan girls in school, the next generations in these countries are, it seems, condemned to lives of continuing poverty.

Shaking Up the Political Status Quo

Rasalpura is a dusty village of a few hundred adobe houses in Rajasthan, one of India's poorest and most conservative regions. For as long as anyone could remember, an upper-caste landowner named Charan Singh had led Rasalpura's local council, the *panchayat*. In 1993, however, a lower-caste, illiterate woman named Chaggibai Bhil took over from Charan Singh under an innovative government program to get more women into politics, causing a local uproar.

The program was the result of a constitutional amendment known as the Panchayat Act, which gave more power to *panchayats*, including all-important control over local expenditures. Then, as part of a grand social experiment, the amendment also reserved a third of council seats, and a third of council leadership positions (*sarpanch*), for women—many of whom would be Dalits, or "untouchables," the lowest caste, who are destined by birth to work disposing of human waste and dead animals.

Although the caste system in India was officially banned after Independence in 1947, and several times since then for good measure, this social structure nonetheless remains a pervasive force in rural life. About 20 percent of India's population is still identified as part of the untouchable caste. Despite several decades of affirmative-action policies, still today, Dalits are often segregated at village functions, their children are not allowed to sit next to higher-caste children in school, they are prohibited from using common goods such as the village pond and well, and they are not allowed to ride bicycles in the village. They are also frequently subjugated as bonded labor, an illegal but accepted practice.[31] Remarkably, the Panchayat Act mandated that on a random, rotating basis, a third of the *panchayats* must now be headed by women, including Dalit women. The village of Rasalpura was about to become a political guinea pig.

Forced to hand over power, Charan Singh and his supporters picked Chaggibai Bhil as their stand-in, in the belief that this husbandless, uneducated woman would be easy to manipulate. When Mary Anne Weaver, the veteran *New Yorker* journalist, visited with Chaggibai a few years after her election, it was clear that things had not played out as the men expected:

> "At the first village assembly after my election," Chaggibai said, "Charan Singh conducted the meeting, and he refused to allow me to speak. I had canvassed all the women and all the Dalits from my villages to attend, and more than four hundred people came. Charan Singh was furious. When he was *sarpanch*, all the meetings were held in secret, mostly at his home." The crowd was so large that it spilled out of the *panchayat* building and into the village square and its tiny lanes; some people even perched in the trees. When Charan Singh realized how many women had shown up, his anger turned to rage. "He began shouting," Chaggibai went

on. "He said, 'Why are women required? Go back to your villages at once!' And all the women left."

Chaggibai and her growing army of women and Dalits began to mobilize. The women went from door to door, some under the protection of husbands or sons; some were in *purdah*, others were not. Since the point of *panchayats* is to give villagers control over local development schemes, planning, and spending, Chaggibai was determined to find out precisely what the villagers of Rasulpura considered their greatest needs. The villagers, from all castes, responded, largely enthusiastically.

"Look at what I inherited." Chaggibai pulled a sheaf of papers from her briefcase and waved them in the air. "Unfinished projects. Pending projects. Chaos. Anarchy."

She then proudly enumerated some of her own accomplishments: she had covered a number of village drains (which had posed acute health hazards, she said) and repaired a school building and some roads; she had completed the *panchayat* building—so that meetings could now be held in open session—and a small irrigation project. She also refused to sanction the embezzlement of village funds.

"She did away with all the unnecessary frills of the *panchayat*," Sister Carol said.

"She even stopped tea-drinking," another woman chimed in.

"Tea!" Chaggibai flailed her arms, and her voice began to rise. "Charan Singh and his friends each drank, on average, five cups of tea every time they met—that means sixty-five, sixty-five cups of tea, with four spoons of sugar each." She quickly calculated. "Do you have any idea how much that costs? It costs the equivalent of ten books for children in school."[32]

Weaver's reporting vividly illustrates the kind of shake-up that the architects of the *panchayat* revolution hoped for when they reserved seats for women. Of course, not every village has a female leader as strong-willed as Chaggibai Bhil. When the Panchayat Act was first passed, there was widespread concern that female *sarpanch* would be mere stand-ins for husbands or fathers who were not able to hold the position themselves. It was also widely assumed that if there were any active women, they would likely hail from the better-educated upper castes.

In reality, though, women were proxies for men in only about a third of the women-led *panchayats*. In two-thirds of the reserved councils, they were clearly in control. And contrary to conventional wisdom, the women from the lower castes, who were used to working in the fields with few inhibitions, were far more active and forceful on the *panchayats*, despite their poverty and illiteracy, than upper-caste women.

For years, Esther Duflo, an economist at MIT and cofounder of MIT's Poverty Action Lab, has been studying the *panchayat* revolution. Her results are revealing. Her audit of the villages shows that male and female *panchayat* heads do make different investment decisions, and that across India, female *panchayat* leaders actually deliver more and often better quality public goods and services than male leaders while taking significantly fewer bribes.[33] Ironically, however, despite the better service and lower corruption levels of the female *sarpanch*, surveys reveal that villagers—both men and women—are less satisfied in the performance of women leaders in providing all services. This attests to the deep biases that persist in traditional India, and elsewhere, against women in leadership roles.

Intriguing research from other countries echoes Duflo's finding that the women *panchayat* leaders demonstrate lower levels of corruption than men. Several studies show that, as the proportion of parliamentary seats held by women rises, corruption declines, even after controlling for other factors shown to affect corruption such as income, education, openness to trade, and the extent of ethnic divisions.[34] Extensive research over several decades shows that women are less tolerant of dishonest or illegal behavior than men. And studies from the business world show that women managers are less likely than men to pay bribes to government officials, even after controlling for other factors like the size of the business and the education level of the manager.

The World Bank has been particularly interested in this research. Combating corruption has been one of its highest priorities over the past decade, since corruption is a clear drag on economic and social development. Might increasing female participation in government be a way to improve governance? While it is still hard to conclude that women are intrinsically more honest than men (they might simply be more risk averse, or, by dint of being newer to government or the business world, approach their public obligations with less cynicism), it is obvious that when women are excluded from the public sphere, if nothing else it is a symptom of deeper, structural issues.

Several years ago, Steven Fish, a political scientist at the University of California at Berkeley, waded into the controversial question of why Muslim-majority countries are democratic "underachievers." Fish examined a number of possible explanations. Are Muslim-majority countries less democratic because, on average, those states are poorer than non-Muslim countries? Is it because they are more prone to violence? Is it because they are less secular than non-Muslim societies? Do they have lower levels of interpersonal trust? Did they not "benefit" from a British colonial heritage, and/or did they "suffer" from a communist heritage? Is it because they are ethnically diverse? Are they burdened by the curse of oil? With careful analysis, Fish debunked each of these explanations and then moved on to the status of women in these societies.[35] By measuring a number of factors, including relative literacy rates, sex ratios (markedly fewer women in the population is usually a sign of inferior nutrition and healthcare for girls and the prevalence of female infanticide or sex-selective abortion), and the percentage of women in government, his analysis showed that while the status of women and girls is certainly not the only factor explaining the link between Islam and authoritarianism, it accounts for a large part of it. He concluded that societies that marginalize women generally count both fewer antiauthoritarian voices in politics and more men who join fanatical religious and political factions—two factors that stifle democracy.[36]

The "civilizing" effect of women on society is a theme that runs through world history, but it is getting new scrutiny in the post-9/11 world. Like corruption, religious extremism seems to thrive in environments where women are excluded from the public sphere—just look at the Taliban in Afghanistan, the worst-case manifestation of this Islamic "Lord of the Flies" scenario. Somalia threatens to head in the same direction as al-Shabab, an extremist Islamic group, gains control of the country.

Bangladesh, once the eastern arm of Pakistan, offers an interesting counterexample. Thirty years of slow, steady empowerment of women through the grassroots efforts of organizations like Grameen and BRAC (Bangladesh Rural Advancement Committee), Bangladesh's other remarkable organization devoted to poverty alleviation, has provided an important bulwark against rising fundamentalism and extremism evident elsewhere in the region.

Although the research on the positive impact of women in government is intriguing, it is all too easy, of course, to think of awful women leaders and ones who simply vote along party lines with the men. Reformist leaders throughout the broader Middle East, however, see real benefit in increasing the number of women in government. Progressives in Morocco, Jordan, Egypt, Iraq, Afghanistan, and Pakistan have successfully pushed for legislation to reserve seats for women, both explicitly and implicitly as a way to counter extremism.

A Long Struggle Through History

The expansion of women's rights in much of the world was one of the seismic shifts of the twentieth century. The new constitutions that emerged from the wreckage of wars, revolutions, and decolonization almost always included a de rigueur extension of political rights to women. Women's suffrage shifted from inconceivable to requisite in a matter of decades, making it all too easy to forget the long struggle through history that preceded this progress. Nowhere has the advancement of women's rights been easy, in great part because it collides with the twin powers of culture and religion.

In America, it took nearly seventy-five years from the launch of an official suffrage movement in 1848 until women finally achieved a constitutional right to vote in 1920. During that time, conservative Christians sustained a consistent rhetoric that giving women rights was against the teachings of the Bible and would undermine the family. Even today, women in the U.S. continue to struggle with issues of unequal pay, discrimination, and violence.

In China and India, government policy has long promoted women, but patriarchy dies hard. The continuing desire for male babies in both countries, which together account for 40 percent of the world's population, is still so strong that widespread sex-selective abortions are leading to markedly fewer female births than male births.[37] The result-ing "marriage squeeze" in coming decades will be an unprecedented phenomenon, leaving 15 percent or more of the boys born today in China and India unable to find wives.[38] This gender-skewing of the population may very well give rise to a generation of restless young men, prone to crime and other aggressive behaviors.[39]

In sub-Saharan Africa, even in the last decades of the twentieth cen-tury, the status of girls in society was rarely discussed as international aid agencies struggled with the intractable issues of African poverty. Women's rights were long considered too controversial for mainstream foreign policy, but over the past twenty years, this has begun to change. As research has advanced, girls' relative disadvantages in healthcare, nutrition, and education have come to be understood as important drivers of the region's poverty, not just consequences of it, and there-fore worthy of action.

Clearly, the status of women remains an unresolved issue in many parts of the world, but in no place are tensions greater than within Muslim societies today. Not only are the issues infused with the usual burdens of culture and tradition, but they are also deeply intertwined with questions of Islamic identity itself.

In many Muslim societies, attitudes toward women—what they can wear, what rights they have within the family, and their access to the public sphere—have become litmus tests of Islamic piety. Islamist groups have long resisted liberalizing trends for women. As political Islam has surged in recent decades, Islamists have demonstrated their power, and their commitment to Islam, by blocking further changes, imposing social constraints, and introducing new restrictions on women. (Many secular governments have largely acquiesced in this process in an attempt to curry favor with Islamist groups and burnish their own Islamic credentials.)

The Arab world, the twenty-two countries stretching from Morocco across North Africa to the Arabian Peninsula, is home to the world's nearly 350 million Arab people. Although Arabs comprise only about 20 percent of the world's Muslim population, the Arab states play an outsized role in the Islamic world.[40] Arabia was the birthplace of Islam and Arabic is the language of the Quran. Islamic scholarship is rooted in the Arab world. The great centers of Islamic learning are mostly Arab. Today, the significant oil resources of the Arab Gulf countries ensure their continued cultural, social, and religious influence in the broader Islamic world.

In 2002, the United Nations Development Programme (UNDP) issued its first Human Development Report for the Arab states. The report, written by Arab scholars in Arabic, put the issue starkly: Despite significant gains, the Arab world has lagged behind other developing regions. Its income growth per capita has been dismally low over the past twenty years. The authors blamed the region's weak performance on three factors: lack of freedom, lack of knowledge, and lack of women's empowerment.[41]

To the extent that any UN document could be a "bestseller," the Arab Human Development Report was a blockbuster. The report was groundbreaking for its level of self-criticism, and some of the more discouraging statistics were repeated frequently in the global media: Out of seven world regions, the Arab world has the lowest freedom score, including measures of political process, civil liberties, political rights, and independence of the media; less than 2 percent of the region's population uses the Internet; since the ninth century, the cumulative total of books translated into Arabic (about ten thousand) is what Spain translates in one year.

Perhaps the most widely reported findings of the report related to the status of women. While giving credit for the significant strides Arab women have made in education in recent decades, the report noted that only women in sub-Saharan Africa score lower in terms of their participation in economic, professional, and political activities. Arab maternal mortality is double that of Latin America and the Caribbean, and four times that of East Asia; two-thirds of the Arab world's 65 million illiterate adults are women.

Published less than a year after 9/11, the first Arab Human Development Report was widely read, quoted, and applauded in the West for its direct and open treatment of a range of sensitive issues by Arab "insiders." Not surprisingly, it generated a range of defensive responses in the Arab world where many critics derided the report for airing the region's dirty laundry. While the report garnered far less, and mostly negative, attention in the Arab world than it did in the West, it did spark some debate about the range of needed reforms, especially around the role of women in society.

In the fourth Arab Human Development Report, issued in 2005, which focused specifically on women's empowerment, the authors acknowledged up front that in the polarized environment of today's Middle East, an Arab intellectual who espouses "Western" ideas of gender equality faces outright dismissal.[42] But in the body of the report, the authors went to great lengths to show that women's empowerment is not some foreign concept imposed on the Arab states by outsiders; nor is it in any way contradictory to the tenets of the Islamic faith. Rather, the outmoded attitudes toward women prevalent across the region are rooted in custom and tradition, not required by religion itself.

The authors emphatically reiterated that an increase in the status of women is in fact a prerequisite for an Arab Renaissance. They repeatedly called for more enlightened interpretations of Islamic jurisprudence through the process of *ijtihad*, or independent reasoning, to support women's advancement. While not using these exact words, they were in fact advocating for Islamic feminism.

The Arab states of course differ greatly from each other in many economic, social, and political ways, and also from other Muslim-majority countries. It would be wrong to generalize about the status of women, since each country has its own unique cultural and political circumstances. But the Arab Human Development Reports capture a fact that is true across all Muslim-majority countries: The role of women in society is deeply contested on Islamic grounds. Moreover, Islam is being used to perpetuate repressive cultural practices that are not unique to the Arab world. The authors of the reports, and other reformers across the broader Middle East, recognize that women matter. They understand that the great challenge is to find ways to empower women without pitting women's rights against deeply held religious values. Whereas conservative Islamic interpretations have been a big part of the problem, more progressive interpretations of Islam can be part of the solution.

In revolutionary fashion, Islamic feminism is trying to alter the terms of what has long been a no-win debate. By showing that women's empowerment is consistent with Islamic values—indeed, they insist that Muhammad was way before his time in extending numerous rights to women—Muslim feminists are trying to harness the power of religion for change, rather than working against it.

CHAPTER 2

GENDER JIHAD

The Rise of Islamic Feminism

*Why is it that we can find some Muslim men saying that
women in Muslim states cannot be granted full enjoyment of
human rights? What grounds do they have for such a claim?
None—they are simply betting on our ignorance of the past,
for their argument can never convince anyone with an
elementary understanding of Islam's history.*

—Fatima Mernissi, Moroccan sociologist
and Islamic feminist

Allahu Akbar. The imam's voice is confident as she begins the prayer. Facing the *qibla* that points the direction to Mecca, she allows each verse to fill the conference room—now a makeshift prayer room—before moving on to the next. *Bismillah ar-Rahman ar-Rahim.*

Outside, the sun hangs low in the Spanish sky. The autumn days are noticeably short. Behind the imam, a small congregation of about thirty men and women stands shoulder to shoulder. *Al Hamdulillahi Rabbil Aalamin.* They move a bit awkwardly at first, self-conscious, acutely aware of the unusual circumstances of this event. However, as the verses continue, the room finally eases into a comfortable and familiar rhythm. *Allahu Akbar.*

The congregation bows, straightens, and prostrates in unison. In this room, everyone is equal. *Subhana Rabbiyal Aala.* Covered in a simple veil and with prayer beads in her hand, the imam gently puts her forehead to her prayer rug and rises up again. The others respectfully follow. *Allahu Akbar.* God is great.

Despite the usual repetition of the phrases familiar to Muslims around the world, this is no ordinary Friday prayer. Men and women are praying together, side by side; it is a bold act—not quite unprecedented, but close to it, in Islamic tradition. Many mainstream Muslim leaders, scholars, and lay people have harshly condemned such a practice, claiming that Islam does not allow men and women to pray together.

Far more shocking, however, is that a woman is leading the prayer. The imam is Dr. Amina Wadud, an American academic who converted to Islam in the 1970s and has taught Islamic studies for several decades. Dr. Wadud is no amateur. She speaks Arabic, has studied at al-Azhar University in Cairo, the leading center of Sunni Islamic scholarship in the world, and has painstakingly researched the simple but revolutionary act she is now performing. By her understanding of Islam, it is a woman's right to lead prayer. Indeed, like many Muslim feminists, she believes that Islam is all about gender equality—it simply has not been practiced that way over the centuries.

This unique prayer session is taking place in Barcelona at the historic International Congress on Islamic Feminism. Hosted by the Catalan Islamic Board, a group of mostly Spanish converts to Islam, the conference has brought together some of the leaders of the growing Islamic feminist movement. As a concept, Islamic feminism has been ridiculed in the West—dismissed as nothing more than an oxymoron—and condemned and demonized by conservative Muslims. But ignoring critics on all sides, hundreds have gathered in Barcelona to discuss the challenges facing Muslim women today. Several of the talks focus on how Islamic texts have been misinterpreted and misunderstood to justify a whole range of misogynistic and sometimes violent cultural practices.

This is not Wadud's first experience leading a mixed congregation. In fact, she made headlines in 2005 when she very publicly led Friday prayers in New York City in front of about a hundred men and women. Media from all over the world covered that event as protesters marched resolutely outside, carrying signs reading "Mixed-Gender Prayers Today, Hellfire Tomorrow" and "May Allah's Curse Be Upon Amina Wadud."

The hostility surrounding that event, including fatwas—legal opinions from Islamic scholars—denouncing her actions, was hardly unexpected. Indeed, Wadud led the New York prayer service as a bold act of defiance.[1] The controversy served its purpose, stirring debate among Muslims around the world about the validity of women leading prayers. One Muslim blogger, who disagreed with the notion of women leading prayer, nevertheless acknowledged that the debate was refreshing "because age-old traditions are being questioned, and this is healthy for the Muslim community . . . and because I learned something new: there are some Muslim scholars who agree with women leading the prayer. I never knew that before, and I am happy to learn something new about my faith."[2]

Wadud is not the most likely of Islamic feminists. Born Mary Teasley, she grew up in a religious Methodist family in Maryland. Her father was a minister at the local church, where he was known fondly as "The Rev."[3] A motivated, ambitious, and intelligent student, Wadud was the first in her family to go to college, attending the prestigious University of Pennsylvania. Attracted by Islam's message of justice and racial equality, she converted, and took a Muslim name, choosing Amina after Muhammad's mother.

Not long after converting, Amina Wadud began to wonder whether the Islamic justice she admired was somehow limited to Muslim men. In too many instances, she noticed, Muslim women were often mistreated or made to feel inferior. Unwilling to accept this glaring contradiction in her new faith, she began a lifelong study of the Quran to understand what exactly the true message of Islam was as it relates to women. Soon enough, her meticulous research convinced her that much of what has been used to justify the mistreatment of women under Islam is actually misinterpretation of the Quran. This reaffirmed her faith, and also helped convince her to fight to reclaim these rights.

Wadud went on to get a Ph.D. at the University of Michigan, and continued her graduate studies in Egypt for several years, becoming fluent in Arabic and delving ever deeper into the Quran. In 1992, she published *Quran and Woman: Rereading the Sacred Text from a Woman's Perspective*. The book catapulted her into the pantheon of Islamic feminists. Like other Muslim feminists, Wadud argues that all the rights women need are there within Islam—it is just a matter of stripping away non-Islamic customs and patriarchy and understanding the true essence of the religion.

Muslim feminists fundamentally respect their religion, but today they are playing an important role in questioning who has the right to interpret that religion. Some, like Wadud, are demanding more of a say inside the mosque. Others are working with local nongovernmental organizations (NGOs) to promote women's rights within Islamic societies. Activists are spreading Islamic feminist thinking across borders. Satellite television shows are forcing discussion about conventional interpretations of religion, subtly bringing Islamic feminism into people's living rooms. Leaders of Muslim thought in the West are pushing the boundaries of the debate.

In one of the boldest changes, Muslim women are beginning to pry open the doors of Islamic religious authority itself. They are forging the way for women to become a part of the *ulama*, the Islamic community of religious scholars. They are training as jurists to be able to issue fatwas on the all-important sharia. Women are moving up the ranks at Cairo's al-Azhar. They are studying jurisprudence in Qom, Iran's religious center. In Morocco, they are training as *murshidat*, female religious leaders able to do everything that a male imam does except lead the prayers in the mosque. In the tiny but influential Wahhabi state of Qatar, a woman is even the head of the College of Sharia at Qatar University.

Amina Wadud has dubbed women's struggle to achieve the equality promised them in the Quran a "gender jihad."[4] Today, there are millions of Muslim men and women around the world waging their own gender jihad. Some are very public and intentional in their efforts; others toil silently, often unaware of the role they are playing in a larger reform movement. But all of them position women's rights not as a Western or secular imposition, but as a genuine Islamic value.

While the intellectual roots of Islamic feminism reach back to the nineteenth century, the current movement is very much a product of the social and political dynamics of recent times. Its growing strength lies in its appeal across social classes and political and ideological lines. It is driven not only by devout Muslims seeking to reconcile their faith with a modern role for women, but also by secularists who believe that in their increasingly religious societies, fighting theology with theology is a tactical necessity. Overall, it is a struggle particularly important to Muslim youth, who constitute 60 percent of the population of the Middle East. This generation is growing up in an environment that is more overtly religious than that of their parents, where secularism is on the defensive and Islamic identity is a hot-button political issue. For many young people, however, the issue is not between secularism and Islamism. Religion has won. The fundamental question they must answer is what form of Islam will govern their lives. At its heart, Muslim feminism is the search for that elusive middle ground between the demands of religion and the needs of modernity.

Launching a Movement

The Moroccan writer Fatima Mernissi is, in many ways, the godmother of Islamic feminism. One of the first women in her family to learn to read and write, Mernissi went on to become a renowned scholar, activist, and clarion voice for women's rights within Islam. Her writings on Islamic feminism have inspired several generations of likeminded reformists across the Muslim world.

Born into a harem in the ancient city of Fez in 1940, Mernissi was raised in a society where old traditions and modernity rubbed up against each other like tectonic plates. She grew up surrounded by grandmothers, aunts, sisters, and female cousins, all of them sequestered behind the walls of the family compound in Fez. Ahmed the doorkeeper sat in a chair by the entrance and physically prevented any of them from leaving. In her memoir, *Dreams of Trespass: Tales of a Harem Girlhood*, she describes her childhood as a time of chaos.[5] While French soldiers occupied the country and were noisily camped down the street from the family home in the old medina, for Mernissi, the greater turmoil stemmed from the women's yearning to leave the confines of the harem.

All the adult women in the compound were illiterate, including Mernissi's mother. Although forbidden to do so, the women would secretly listen to the radio and entertain each other by telling stories and playacting feminist heroines, usually ones imported from Egypt. Mernissi's mother was determined that her own daughters would have a different life than she did, and she told young Fatima again and again that it was her obligation to transform the world. Despite the restrictions of the harem, her mother insisted that male superiority was "nonsense." "Allah made us all equal," she frequently reminded her daughter.[6]

Mernissi attended Islamic classes with her cousins. The children sat cross-legged on the ground and memorized passages from the Quran, while the formidable teacher kept them in line by whipping them with her riding crop. Mernissi's life was irrevocably changed when the leading religious authorities in Fez supported a girl's right to attend school. At her mother's urging, Mernissi's father agreed that the girls in the family could enroll in the new nationalist primary school, modeled on the French system, where they would learn math, foreign languages, and geography. They would also play sports and be taught by male teachers.

The harem way of life Mernissi describes in *Dreams of Trespass* rapidly disappeared in the wake of Morocco's independence from France in 1956. Liberated by her education, Mernissi took full advantage of the new opportunities presented to elite women in Morocco's modernizing society. She got a master's degree in politics from Muhammad V University in Rabat, studied political science at the Sorbonne, and received a doctorate from Brandeis University in Massachusetts. She then returned to Morocco to teach at the university in Rabat. Living up to her mother's expectations, she also became an outspoken activist and intellectual.

By the early 1970s, when Mernissi returned to Morocco, the lives of middle- and upper-class urban women had been transformed by their access to education and to the workplace. But across much of the countryside, the low status of women had barely changed. Female literacy in many rural areas was still in the single digits. Although Morocco's 1962 constitution granted men and women equal political and civil rights, women's de facto rights continued to be dictated largely by custom and tradition. Moreover, the *mudawana*, Morocco's sharia-based code of laws governing personal status and the family, contradicted—and more often than not trumped—the constitution.

Under the *mudawana*, polygamy was legal and women were considered minors; they were disadvantaged in divorce, custody, and inheritance. Beginning in the early 1970s, reformers made various attempts to change the *mudawana*, but these were stymied by religious conservatives and the rising political influence of Islamists. Opponents successfully depicted reform efforts as being a rejection both of Islam and of Morocco's rich legal tradition in favor of foreign laws. In 1979, some token changes were made, but at this point there were few substantive reforms.

It was in this context that Mernissi began publishing her thoughts on women and Islam. In 1973, she published *Beyond the Veil: Male-Female Dynamics in Modern Muslim Society*, a book version of her doctoral dissertation. It is mostly a critique of patriarchy in Morocco, but also begins to develop the argument that a big gap exists between theory and practice for women's rights in Islam. Then, in 1987, she published in French her seminal work, *Le Harem Politique*, which was translated into English some years later with the catchier title *The Veil and the Male Elite: A Feminist Interpretation of Women's Rights in Islam*.

Mernissi began *The Veil and the Male Elite* with an anecdote. When she asked her local grocer, a barometer of public opinion in Morocco, if a woman can be a leader of Muslims, he responded in horror, "No!" A schoolteacher standing nearby brought the discussion to a conclusive end by lobbing in a well-known hadith, or saying, of the Prophet: "Those who entrust their affairs to a woman will never know prosperity." Silenced and furious, Mernissi left the store determined. "I suddenly felt the urgent need to inform myself about this hadith and to search out the texts where it is mentioned, to understand better its extraordinary power over the ordinary citizens of a modern state." Working with various religious scholars, she immersed herself in Islamic history and jurisprudence to trace the evolution of this particular hadith and others that are regularly used like sledgehammers against women. Her results were, to say the least, controversial.

In Islam, there are several sources of authority. The highest level of authority is the Quran itself, which Muslims believe is literally the word of God transmitted through His Prophet on Earth, Muhammad. The Prophet's Companions, those early Muslims who had direct contact with the Prophet, memorized verses of the Quran and passed that oral tradition on to others. Like the Christian Bible, the Quran was not fully compiled until some years after the death of Muhammad.[7] However, few Muslims question the authenticity of the Quran itself.

The next source of authority is the hadith, the narrations of Muhammad. Over the ages, Islamic jurists have looked to the hadith as an essential source of clarification for the Quran. Understanding Muhammad's way of life and knowing what Muhammad said, did, and approved (or disapproved) of in others provide critical insight in determining how Muslims should try to live their lives today.

The hadith, however, were not systematically collected or written down until well over a century after the life of Muhammad. When the scholars of the time finally got around to this monumental task, they were faced with the problem that many hadith flatly contradicted each other, and some were at variance with the Quran. Moreover, many hadith were of suspicious origins. Soon, a whole industry developed to determine a hadith's *isnad*, or chain of transmission—who first witnessed the action or heard the comment, and who then passed it on to whom—to establish the validity of each hadith. Those hadith with the strongest *isnad*—say, ones with multiple, reliable transmitters that could be traced back directly to the time of Muhammad—naturally have the greatest authority. (Some of the weaker hadith first appeared several centuries after the life of Muhammad, miraculously retrieved from the dustbin of history.) By the ninth century, various scholars had evaluated the *isnad* of thousands of hadith, and included those they viewed as authentic in their collections. Since then, this stamp of approval has remained largely unchanged.

In *The Veil and the Male Elite*, Mernissi delved into the history of the hadith quoted by the schoolteacher in the grocery store. She noted that this hadith was included in the collection of Imam al-Bukhari, the meticulous and highly regarded ninth-century hadith scholar, giving it great authenticity. However, she had no trouble unearthing good reasons to challenge its validity. She showed that it was only remembered a full quarter century after the death of Muhammad, and the person who claimed to have heard Muhammad uttering those words had been accused of lying in other instances, making him unreliable. Mernissi went on to say that while this "misogynistic" hadith is exemplary of the problem, it is not unique.[8] There are many questionable hadith that have been used systematically to suppress women's rights in Islam.

The Veil and the Male Elite was banned in Morocco. Islamic scholars and Islamists around the world accused Mernissi of shoddy, if not inventive, scholarship and denounced her. But by then it did not matter—she had launched a movement. By the time of the book's publication, numerous women across the Muslim world were completing doctorates, often at European or American universities, and embarking on academic careers. While some were staunchly secular and admitted to being inspired by the gender-equality ideals of Western feminism, many were also practicing Muslims and several were people of deep faith. Inevitably, they began to examine the reality of their lives versus the scriptures they upheld. Like Mernissi, they started to return to primary sources and question the interpretations that have held sway for centuries. Scholars such as Asma Barlas from Pakistan, Leila Ahmed from Egypt, and Ziba Mir-Hosseini from Iran embarked on similar processes of contextualizing the Quran, arguing forcefully that human rights and women's rights were a true part of the Muslim tradition.

A central tenet of Islamic feminism is that Muslim women should not have to choose between their faith and their rights. There are ample rights for women within Islam, if only the patriarchal practices and interpretations can be stripped away from Muhammad's revolutionary message of equality. In the preface to the English edition of *The Veil and the Male Elite*, Mernissi made her point clear: "Why is it that we can find some Muslim men saying that women in Muslim states cannot be granted full enjoyment of human rights? What grounds do they have for such a claim? None—they are simply betting on our ignorance of the past, for their argument can never convince anyone with an elementary understanding of Islam's history. Any man who believes that a Muslim woman who fights for her dignity and right to citizenship excludes herself unnecessarily from the *umma* and is a brainwashed victim of Western propaganda is a man who misunderstands his own religious heritage, his own cultural identity."[9]

For the thought-leaders of the Islamic feminist movement, the quest for middle ground is often a deeply personal one. Although few

can claim like Mernissi to have been born into a harem, many prominent Islamic feminists come from traditional, conservative backgrounds and yet have been educated and trained professionally in a
more liberal, secular environment—often in the West. Muslim feminism is their path to reconcile their two worlds while also playing an
important role in a broader Islamic reform movement.

By the 1990s, female Muslim scholars and activists were carefully
staking out positions that allowed them to retain their Islamic identity
while questioning the patriarchy of their religion. Some identified
themselves as Islamic feminists, while others—like Mernissi herself—
have never been comfortable with that label because of the strong negative connotations of the word "feminism" within their societies.
However, the phrase took hold and became useful in describing the
efforts of these scholars to bridge the chasm between feminism and the
demands of Islam. Their ideas and scholarship are groundbreaking, but
they are certainly not unprecedented. In many ways, they are picking
up where a group of male reformers left off a century ago in making the
case that Islam can and should accommodate women's rights.

Early Islamic Feminists

The intellectual foundations of Islamic feminism were laid in the late
nineteenth century when various Muslim scholars attempted to "modernize" Islam as a means of confronting the challenges of Western
colonialism. Faced with Western economic, military, and technological
superiority, Muslim intellectuals from Delhi to Cairo entered a period
of profound reflection. They emerged convinced that Islam's core
belief system was well suited to the demands of the modern world, but
that Islamic law had strayed greatly from the progressive and dynamic
nature of early Islam. Having evolved in rigid and reactionary ways,
Islamic law was now a clear barrier to the advancement of Muslim societies. For these Islamic modernists, the future of the Muslim community depended on reform, and a central component of their reform
agenda focused on women.

In India, the intellectual grandfather of the modernist movement
was Sir Syed Ahmed Khan (1817–1898), one of the most influential

Muslim thinkers of his time. A man of considerable girth, his many formal portraits invariably show him seated, hands clasped, his flowing white beard cascading over his large barrel chest, and an array of medals pinned to his jacket. Born into a noble family in Delhi, Sir Syed was working as an administrator for the British East India Company when the Indian Rebellion of 1857 occurred. When the dust settled on the violence, in which Indian soldiers mutinied against their colonial masters, Sir Syed had lost several relatives, including his mother.

In the aftermath of the fighting, Sir Syed wrote his famous work, *The Causes of the Indian Mutiny*, an attempt to explain the real reasons for the rebellion to a British audience and alleviate the perception that the revolt was simply Islamic treachery against British rule. It captures, at times painfully, Sir Syed's efforts to bridge two worlds. Despite the horrors of the rebellion and the harsh way in which it was put down by the British, he remained a deeply loyal colonial subject, clearly in awe of British power and technological sophistication. Yet he grieved for his Muslim compatriots and the relative decline of Muslim society, and ached for an Islamic Renaissance that would revitalize the Muslim community.

Sir Syed, like many other reformist scholars, believed that Islam itself was not the problem—the issue was the way it had been interpreted over the ages. He devoted his life to promoting modern education in India, which he hoped would encourage his compatriots to challenge the moldy doctrines preached by the *ulama*. He was passionate about the need for India's Muslims to acquire scientific training and English language skills to compete against the West and maintain their influence within the British raj. His greatest educational legacy was undoubtedly the Muhammadan Anglo-Oriental College at Aligarh, which he founded in 1875, and which later became the Aligarh Muslim University. Modeled explicitly after the universities at Oxford and Cambridge, the purpose of the college was to train young Muslim minds in rationalist and scientific thinking.

Women's rights were an important element of Sir Syed's modernist project. He was personally inspired by the influence of strong female role models in his own life—especially his mother and a female tutor who taught him to read the Quran. He also felt compelled to dwell on this subject because Christian missionaries often pointed to the mistreatment of women in their unrelenting criticisms of Islam. The missionaries focused on the widespread restrictions on girls' education, the prevalence of child marriage, and gender segregation (*purdah*), which they noted was strongest in those parts of India where the influence of Islam was greatest.[10]

In response, Sir Syed favorably compared the current Islamic laws of the 1870s with English laws for women. "England greatly favors the freedom of women, yet when its laws relating to women are examined it is obvious that the English consider women quite insignificant, unintelligent, and valueless."[11] He pointed out that when Englishwomen marry, they lose their "separate existence" and that "personal possessions, wealth, cash and property that were hers before marriage all belong to the husband after marriage . . . Her status is like that of a feeble-minded incompetent." In contrast, he stressed that women are honored in Islam, that their rights and authority are equal to those of men; that even after marriage Muslim women can own property, execute contracts, and control inheritance.[12] However, Sir Syed despaired that in practice, Muslim nations had fallen greatly behind the West in the actual conditions of women. "In India, there are perpetrated such unworthy and humiliating events that one can only cry out, May God have mercy on us!"[13]

Sir Syed's attitudes seem somewhat more concerned with defending Islam against the missionaries' charges than truly promoting the status of women. Indeed, he was against women attending his college at Aligarh.[14] But his religious arguments have become standard among Islamic feminists. Regarding polygamy, for example, he cited the relevant passage from the Quran that says, "Marry such women as seem good to you, two, three, four; but if you fear you will not be equitable, then only one."[15] He argued that since it is impossible for a man to love and treat more than one woman equally, polygamy must therefore be illegal and un-Islamic.

For his progressive Islamic interpretations (and no doubt because he continued to lionize the British), Sir Syed was roundly denounced by traditionalist *ulama*. He was even branded an infidel by clerics in the most conservative branches of Islam, the Deobandi and Wahhabi schools. By the end of his life, he shied away from the incendiary topic of women's rights in Islam.

However, the baton of women's rights was taken up with gusto by one of his own protégés, Mumtaz Ali (1860–1935), who made women's rights within Islam a particular focus of his work. Intrigued by the religious debates between Muslims and Christians, Mumtaz Ali studied the Quran and Islamic law at various *madrasas* (religious schools). Perhaps because of his expertise in Islamic law, he felt emboldened to tackle the sensitive issues of women's rights in Islam and was not so easily intimidated by the inevitable objections of heresy that so stung Sir Syed.

In his groundbreaking 1898 treatise on women's rights, simply called *Rights of Women*, Mumtaz Ali presented a compelling defense of women's equality before God. Relying extensively on the sources of Islamic law, the Quran and the Sunnah, he tackled a range of controversial issues, including inheritance, marriage, divorce, polygamy, girls' education, and *purdah*. He debunked the many Islamic reasons cited for male superiority, contextualizing those Quranic passages frequently cited for giving men authority over women. For instance, he argued that the passages stating that men should manage women's affairs and that the testimony of two women is equal to that of one man relate specifically to business matters where women might have had less experience than men due to social conditions, and rejected that they refer to any inherent inferiority of women.[16]

With regard to women's education, Mumtaz Ali cited the Quranic injunction that both Muslim men and women should seek knowledge. He argued that in God's eyes, this means men and women have equal intellectual powers. Anticipating the arguments of development economists a century later, Mumtaz Ali proclaimed that when women are inadequately educated and cannot raise children properly, the entire society suffers. "For the survival of the Muslim family and of Muslim civilization as a whole . . . the education of women to their fullest potential is necessary."[17]

On *purdah*, the seclusion of women, Mumtaz Ali argued that while modesty is appropriate, Muslims in India went far beyond what the religious texts intended and that the exaggerated restrictions were destroying family life. Again, he understood the dire social consequences of these customs—how isolation harmed women's health since they got no fresh air or exercise; when women fell ill, they could not be seen by a doctor; women were denied any experience of the outside world that could broaden their horizons. He concluded that extreme *purdah* "harms the entire society, as it promotes narrow-mindedness and mistrust, even among members of the same family."[18]

Mumtaz Ali was equally critical of common harmful marriage practices—in particular child marriage and marriage without consent of both parties. He argued that when children were married off at a young age, they were effectively incapable of making a choice, which is required by the Quran. Moreover, child brides became child mothers, which was injurious to their health and that of their children. This section of *Rights of Women* reads like an advocacy brochure from any number of NGOs working against child marriage in twenty-first-century India. He also made a strong argument for a woman's right to initiate divorce, a right he claimed is clearly permitted within sharia. He advocated for reform in divorce law to recognize this right, a change that did eventually occur in India, but not until several decades later.

In late-nineteenth-century India, where women's subordination was deeply rooted in custom and tradition, Mumtaz Ali's defense of women's rights within Islam was clearly ahead of its time. His ideas were too radical even for Sir Syed, who turned apoplectic upon reading a draft of the *Rights of Women* manuscript and threw it in the garbage. Out of respect for his mentor, Mumtaz Ali did not publish the treatise until after Sir Syed's death in 1898. Not surprisingly, his ideas were rejected by the conservative *ulama*. Although it caused quite a stir among intellectual elites when it was published, *Rights of Women* failed to have any broad impact during Ali's lifetime. But his progressive interpretation of the Quran provided an intellectual foundation for other Islamic modernists and for Islamic feminism today.

Nearly three thousand miles west of Delhi, a similar reform movement was taking shape almost simultaneously in Cairo. Egypt, like India, was experiencing the dislocations of colonialism. The intellectual milieu of late-nineteenth-century Cairo was dominated by several trends apparent in India at about the same time. Among urban, often foreign-educated Egyptian elites, there was an infatuation with all things European, including rationalist thinking, and a respect, bordering on awe, of Western technological sophistication. The British ruling class held a harshly critical view of Egyptian society and the apparent backwardness of Islam, and among the rapidly expanding ranks of missionaries, there was a disdain for Islam and in particular its mistreatment of women.

A group of Egyptian thinkers struggled to reconcile the challenges of modernity with their desire to remain loyal to and respectful of Islam. The result was the rise of Egypt's own Islamic modernist movement. As in India, Egypt's Islamic modernists found nothing wrong with Islam itself but only in how it had strayed from its original intent. Not only did they feel the need to defend against the Christian missionaries' particularly vitriolic attacks on the subject of women, but many of the modernists came to believe that the future of society depended on the advancement of women.

Although there were several important intellectuals behind Egypt's modernist movement, Muhammad Abduh (1849–1905) and Qasim Amin (1863–1908) were the two most prominent voices on the subject of women's rights. As a young man, Abduh studied Islamic law at al-Azhar, where he came under the tutelage of Jamal al-Din al-Afghani, one of the most renowned of all the modernist proponents, whose reputation spanned the Middle East. (Al-Afghani had lived and studied in India and was familiar with the ideas of Sir Syed Ahmed Khan.[19]) Later, working as a journalist, Abduh became a vocal advocate of reform. As the editor in chief of the government's official gazette, he returned again and again to the argument that the repressive practices of the day affecting women, particularly marriage practices, were a result of misinterpretations within Islam over the centuries and a muddling of corrupt practices with religion. Along the same lines as Sir Syed and Mumtaz Ali (and many Islamic feminists today), he argued that Islam was the first to grant women their rights, long before the West.

Abduh's voice was an important one—after all, he was a respected Islamic scholar who could argue knowledgeably about the religious texts. In 1899, he became Egypt's grand mufti—the state's most senior interpreter of Islamic law.[20] In that position, he continued to push for a rational approach to Islam as a critical step in its rejuvenation, and he promoted the practice of *ijtihad*—arriving at new interpretations of Islamic law through critical reasoning, rather than blindly following the views of past scholars. Abduh understood the need to reconcile Islam with modernity, to find authentic traditions on which reformers could build. Nevertheless, he was attacked by conservatives who were suspicious of his foreign contacts and travel and who questioned his progressive fatwas.

Abduh's friend and contemporary, Qasim Amin, is often referred to as a pioneer of Islamic feminism because he made women's rights in Islam such a central feature of his scholarship.[21] Without a doubt, his writings on this topic were sensational for the time and caused a lasting controversy. Born into an upper-class family, Amin studied law in France and returned to a rapidly changing Cairo. Foreigners were more visible across the city, wealthy families were hiring European tutors for their children (including their daughters), upper-class men were dropping traditional Arab dress in favor of top hats and waist-coats, some women were appearing in public unveiled, and several educated women were launching women's journals. It was a time of significant social dislocation among Cairene elites.

Qasim Amin dropped a literary bombshell into this combustible social mix with his publication of *The Liberation of Women* in 1899. The book was a passionate plea for women's emancipation, which Amin called a "patriotic duty." From his perspective, only by elevating the position of women could Egypt hope to throw off the shackles of colonialism. "The evidence of history," he wrote, "confirms and demonstrates that the status of women is inseparably tied to the status of a nation."[22] Much like Mumtaz Ali, who had published his *Rights of Women* a year earlier in India, Amin in *The Liberation of Women* carefully constructed religious arguments to reconcile Islam with modern views on women. He condemned polygamy. He made the case for a woman's right to divorce, and he was strongly in favor of girls' education. He also made note of the social and economic costs of women's seclusion.[23]

None of these arguments were particularly new or even that radical. Abduh had made similar claims about divorce and polygamy a decade earlier. Furthermore, girls' education had already been conceptually accepted by the state with the first girls' primary schools in the 1870s, and the seclusion of women, which only affected the upper classes anyway, was already beginning to break down.[24] Yet, *The Liberation of Women* took Cairo by storm. It was denounced by the traditional *ulama*, criticized in the press, and several conservatives wrote their own books rebutting Amin's positions.

The lightning rod for their criticism was Amin's attack on the veil.[25] His argument that the veil was the most obvious sign of Islamic inferiority to the West, and therefore had to go, thrust women's issues smack in the middle of a growing cultural divide between those wishing to adopt Western ways and manners and those wanting to preserve Islamic traditions. Amin's open contempt for how the lower classes clung to their customs highlighted the veil as a class issue. By adopting the language of European critics on veiling, Amin indelibly—and unfortunately—linked unveiling with Westernization and colonialism. Conservatives began to defend the veil not so much on religious grounds, but because they resented what they felt was blind imitation of Western ways. Even some women denounced Amin's call to unveil on the grounds that once again, men were simply telling women what to do.[26]

Unwittingly, *The Liberation of Women* helped launch the veil as a key symbol of resistance—resistance to Westernization, to colonialism, and to attacks on Islam. The more reformers tried to rip the veil off women, the harder conservatives clung on, deepening the veil's symbolic appeal and linking it to a broader struggle over class, culture, and politics. This is a struggle that every Muslim society continues to grapple with today.

In 1999, Egypt's Supreme Council for Culture celebrated the one-hundredth anniversary of the publication of *The Liberation of Women*, under the patronage of First Lady Suzanne Mubarak, wife of Egypt's authoritarian leader Hosni Mubarak. Inside the conference halls, secularists lauded Amin's stand against veiling, while outside more than 80 percent of women in Egypt had adopted the headscarf, many in protest against the perceived secularism of their own government. One wonders how different the evolution of women's rights in the Middle East over the course of the past century might have been had Amin and other reformers focused less on that cultural third rail—the veil—and more on improving the status of women in society through better access to health, education, and employment.

Religion Wins

Over the course of the twentieth century, women's rights and status gradually advanced across the Middle East, imposed top-down on skeptical populations by authoritarian leaders determined to modernize their countries. For the most part, these leaders viewed religion as an obstacle to their reform agenda. They treated Islam with suspicion, if not downright hostility, as they chipped away at the entrenched power of religious authorities. In recognition that women were critical to their reform and development efforts, they expanded female education and extended legal and political rights to women. Raising the status of women was also a visible sign of progress toward a secular, "Westernized" ideal—a way to prove that their societies were "civilized." As such, they leaned heavily on that seeming shortcut to female modernity, eliminating the veil, sowing the seeds for decades' worth of Islamic backlash.

The most famous secular nationalist leader was Mustafa Kemal Atatürk (1881–1938), who seized control of the long-failing Ottoman Empire in the aftermath of the First World War. Atatürk quickly abolished not only the seven-hundred-year-old Ottoman Dynasty, but also the Caliphate, the religiously inspired rulership of Islam that had led Muslims since the time of the Prophet. In 1923, Atatürk established Turkey as a republic and spent the last fifteen years of his life as its first president, unapologetically pursuing a series of iron-fisted reforms intended to push the country into the modern world—"for the people, despite the people," as he famously quipped.[27]

Atatürk's reforms included closing Islamic courts, recognizing equal rights for women, and replacing the religiously based sharia with civil law and a penal code modeled after those in European countries. Coeducation was established throughout the country. Women in Turkey were granted the right to vote in 1934, well before the full political participation of women in many Western countries. By the mid-1930s, there were eighteen women elected to the national parliament, and Turkey boasted the world's first female Supreme Court justice. Atatürk's own family was set before the new nation as a paradigm of modernity. After a brief two-year marriage, he divorced his wife in 1925 and went on to adopt several daughters whom he raised to be iconic trailblazers for women. Sabiha, his most celebrated daughter, became a fighter pilot in the Turkish military.

Rapid decolonization after World War II gave rise to a string of secular nationalist leaders across the Muslim world—Habib Bourguiba in Tunisia, Gamal Abdel Nasser in Egypt, Abdul Karim Qasim in Iraq, Muhammad Reza Shah Pahlavi in Iran, Ayub Khan in Pakistan, Sukarno in Indonesia—who modeled themselves after Atatürk. Soon, urban elites in these countries were wearing Western dress and pulling their children out of traditional religious schools to attend modern schools with Western-oriented curricula. Because the reforms grew from this pro-Western culture, women's rights became closely associated with an agenda of Westernization and secularization. The still-powerful religious class and the majority of the population, who continued to hew closely to their religious and cultural traditions, resented and resisted reforms for women.

Despite the state promotion of secularism, the powerful ideology of Islamic fundamentalism was gaining traction among Muslims. Islamic fundamentalists like Hassan al-Banna (1906–1949), the founder of the Muslim Brotherhood in Egypt, and Syed Abul-Ala Maududi (1903–1979), the founder of Jamaat-i-Islami in India, sought to reinvigorate Islam as a means of rolling back Western colonialism. Unlike the Islamic modernists earlier in the century, who were impressed by Western technological superiority, the fundamentalists fiercely rejected the West, its technology and innovations, and believed that modernity was an evil force that destroyed people's spirituality. To them, Islamic reform required a return to the "fundamentals" of the faith and a more literal interpretation of the texts.

When al-Banna founded the Society of Muslim Brothers in 1928, he had two priorities: first, to force the British out of Egypt; and second, to create a society in which everything would be guided by religion. Sharia would be the law of the land, and the Quran its only constitution.[28] While al-Banna believed that Islamic government could not be imposed, he thought it would be embraced by the people once they started living a true Islamic life. The Brotherhood was there to show them the way.

The Muslim Brotherhood began with an agenda of spiritual and moral reform, but it quickly evolved into a popular, grassroots political movement with strong anticolonial credentials. Like Muhammad Abduh and other modernists, al-Banna called for the defense of Islam through internal reform, but with a much more virulently anti-Western agenda. Rather than finding inspiration in the lofty spiritual and philosophical tenets of Islam that appealed to Abduh, al-Banna was drawn to a legalistic interpretation of Islam focused narrowly on traditional sharia. Conservative Islam today remains sharia-obsessed, particularly with regard to women and family life, with an emphasis on restricting women's role to the realm of the private sphere. To Islamic fundamentalists, Western-style feminism represents moral corruption.

Partly by dint of al-Banna's charismatic personality, and also by providing social services to the disaffected lower classes, the Muslim Brotherhood grew rapidly. Al-Banna's simple slogan, "Islam is the solution"—the solution to all problems—drew crowds. By the 1940s, the Muslim Brotherhood had more than a million members and sympathizers in Egypt and had spawned similar organizations in other Middle Eastern countries. Threatened by the popularity of the movement and the increasingly radical tendencies of some Brotherhood members, the Egyptian government disbanded the Muslim Brotherhood in December 1948. Within weeks, a member of the Brotherhood assassinated the Egyptian prime minister, and al-Banna himself was then killed, presumably in retaliation. Yet despite the premature death of one of its most influential leaders, political Islam was by then firmly on its way to becoming a global movement.

For nearly a century now, secular nationalist governments across the Islamic world have attempted, unsuccessfully, to stamp out political Islam by banning its organizations, like the Muslim Brotherhood, and imprisoning their leaders or assassinating the most troublesome, like al-Banna. But so far, that approach seems only to have energized the movement. Several decades ago, the Muslim Brotherhood began to espouse nonviolence and support parliamentary democracy. While many remain deeply skeptical of the Brotherhood's real commitment to political pluralism, by most assessments, free and fair elections would today deliver a political majority in Egypt and in other countries across the region to the Muslim Brotherhood.[29]

In recent decades, Islamism across the Muslim world has been resurgent, propelled partly by a message of social justice, partly by the failures of secular nationalism, and largely by its popular opposition to authoritarian, corrupt governments. The success of the Islamic Revolution in Iran in bringing down the U.S.-backed Shah encouraged Islamists. So too did jihadi resistance to the Soviet's godless communism in Afghanistan.

Across the broader Middle East, outward signs of Islamism, particularly the veil, have become widespread. Whereas in the 1960s and 1970s, Western-style miniskirts were common in cities like Cairo and Tehran, by the 1980s headscarves were again the norm—in some places forcibly imposed by fundamentalist or radical regimes, in others donned freely as a religious or political statement. The spread of satellite television (giving Islamist organizations a mass-media reach), the ongoing struggles in Palestine, Iraq, and Afghanistan, the rise of Hamas and Hizbullah, and America's war on terror continue to energize Islamism.

The advance of political Islam poses a conundrum for women. On the one hand, Islamist movements today actively solicit the participation and support of women. Nothing serves their purpose better than to have women out in front, promoting the Islamist cause and defying secular critics who contend that the Islamists want to send women back to the Stone Age. Nevertheless, the Islamist agenda remains deeply concerned with limiting the role of women in society, both as a point of contrast with secularism and as a symbol of women's purity. Signature Islamist issues include enforcing female modesty through veiling and gender segregation, and implementing sharia, especially in the area of family law. In those Muslim countries that have advanced women's rights through progressive civil law, the Islamists' narrow interpretation of sharia inevitably means greater restrictions on women's legal rights, particularly with respect to marriage, custody, divorce, inheritance, and mobility.

Islamists are trying to impose their restrictions on women, however, at a time when globalization and modernization are working in the other direction by inexorably expanding female opportunities. Girls' education for the middle and upper classes increased rapidly in the postwar decades. Today, girls' schooling is pushing out into poorer, rural areas, even in countries with relatively low enrollment rates. Women are entering the workforce in larger numbers, and also becoming more active politically. By the close of the twentieth century, several Muslim-majority countries—including Indonesia, Pakistan, Bangladesh, and Turkey—had elected women leaders. Increasingly, Muslim women who want to live within their faith are questioning the legal restrictions of sharia demanded by the Islamists. Despite, or perhaps because of, rising religiosity, more and more of these women are open to the egalitarian message of Islamic feminism.

Male Supporters

Islamic feminism today is part of a new modernist movement determined to contextualize Islam—to understand it within the context of the twenty-first century. Interestingly, some of the most influential Islamic feminist thinkers are men. Perhaps safe in their maleness, they can afford to take more intellectual risks than the women. The scholar Khaled Abou El Fadl, for example, readily refers to himself as a feminist and has been known to encourage his wife to lead him in prayer.[30] He writes frequently about the need for an "Islamic Reformation," a process that he believes must emphasize women's rights. Abou El Fadl, who holds degrees from Yale, the University of Pennsylvania, and Princeton, has also studied Islamic jurisprudence with distinguished scholars in Kuwait and Egypt and earned the *ijazat* (certificates) to qualify as a sheikh. He has issued a number of high-profile fatwas in favor of women's rights, including one that defends women leading prayers.[31] Like other Islamic feminists, he argues that it is the misinterpretation of the Quran that has led to repression of women, not Islam itself.[32]

Likewise, the Sudanese scholar and law professor Abdullahi Ahmed

An-Na'im argues that Islam promotes liberal values, including unequivocal support for women's rights.[33] In his book *Toward an Islamic Reformation*, An-Na'im makes the case that while men and women may have differences, "such differences . . . do not justify legal discrimination. This principle could not have been appreciated nor implemented in the context of seventh-century Arabia, but it can be appreciated and implemented today."[34]

Tariq Ramadan—the controversial grandson of Hassan al-Banna, founder of the Muslim Brotherhood—also frequently speaks in praise of Islamic feminism, which he defines as going back to Islamic sources and using Islamic principles to act "against any kind of discrimination."[35] He relies on none other than Muhammad himself to emphasize Islam's progressiveness. In his book *In the Footsteps of the Prophet*, Ramadan retells the story of Muhammad's life, portraying the Prophet as a great trailblazer for women, steadfastly reforming customs and practices in their favor. Ramadan emphasizes the critical role that Muhammad's first wife, Khadijah, played in supporting Muhammad mentally, emotionally, and financially in the early years of Islam.[36]

The hadith Ramadan includes in his book about Muhammad are instructive. He relays several stories of how Muhammad, left only with daughters after the deaths of his infant sons, respects, educates, and includes those daughters in his affairs. He emphasizes the way Muhammad listens to women, granting one her request for divorce, agreeing with another that it is her decision, not her father's, regarding who she should marry. Time and again, Muhammad is shown as relying on the advice and wisdom of the women in his life.

It is easy to take issue with Ramadan's version of Muhammad as a feminist. He glosses over Muhammad's many wives and other difficult points, such as his beloved wife Aisha being only nine when they married. Ramadan, like other Islamic feminists, clearly has an agenda. He aims to show that Islam is open to interpretation and finds much in the life of Muhammad that supports the full empowerment of women today.

The Islamic feminism of scholars like Abou El Fadl and Ramadan echoes the arguments of nineteenth-century reformers, but Islamic feminism today is profoundly different. It is not a conversation confined to a small group of male intellectuals, but one that is taking place across mass media and within every segment of society, with women very much in the lead. Today's gender jihad is gaining a foothold in even the most traditional, conservative Muslim societies, led by ordinary and extraordinary people. It is also a conversation that, finally, is beginning to move beyond the veil. Today's Islamic feminists focus on education, health, income generation, political voice, and legal rights, particularly in the all-important arena of family law, as their levers for change.

Activists Spreading the Word

Zainah Anwar flashes her megawatt smile and lets out an uncensored laugh. "The game is up," she confidently explains to me over coffee at a hotel in downtown Kuala Lumpur. "Muslim women today are studying the religion for themselves. They are organizing and networking across borders to put a stop to the use of Islam to perpetuate discrimination against women."[37]

She should know. As one of the founders of Sisters in Islam (SIS), a Malaysia-based organization that uses Islamic arguments to press for women's rights, she has long been on the forefront of efforts to take contemporary Islamic feminism out of the halls of academia and into the trenches of social activism. Today, activists are successfully using Islamic arguments to reform discriminatory laws, to change centuries of patriarchal customs and practices carried out in the name of Islam, and to promote change in sensitive areas like women's reproductive health and family law. Some work locally while others have formed organizations to work across borders, transferring ideas and strategies that have been effective in one context to another. These activists are now connecting with each other and forming a truly international movement.

Strong-willed and indomitable, Zainah grew up in Malaysia in a patriarchal household. She attended religious schools but admits to being a disobedient child and says she was chastised in school for asking too many questions, for being too talkative and high-spirited. "I never acquiesced in silence," she recalls. "I always had an answer." She remembers exasperating her mother with her endless questions and counterarguments. Required to help her mother with "girl chores," she often snuck away to climb trees instead. Her mother would go looking for her by searching for Zainah's abandoned sarong at the base of a tree.

Zainah's curiosity and questioning led her down the path of journalism. She got a full scholarship from the Malaysian government to study journalism at Boston University and, still on scholarship, she completed a master's degree in 1986 at the Fletcher School of Law and Diplomacy. When she returned home after five years abroad, she was appalled by what she witnessed in Malaysia's sharia courts. Malay women, who were well educated and highly visible in the workforce and public sphere, were being told by the *ulama* that all sorts of discriminatory behaviors were justified in the name of Islam. As she explained to me years later, this interpretation of Islam was quite different from the one she was exposed to as a child. "Perhaps because of what I felt was a solid religious understanding and background, this gave me the courage to start questioning all these things."[38]

Malaysia at the time seemed a showcase of Islamic modernity. Under the technocratic leadership of Prime Minister Mahathir bin Mohamad, the country was politically stable and economically thriving, although rising Islamist power was a concern for the government. To keep the Islamists at bay, Prime Minister Mahathir sought accommodation with the religious establishment, but this approach only emboldened conservatives to push for more restrictive sharia laws at both the state and federal levels. (In Malaysia, sharia courts operate alongside civil courts, hearing cases related to religion and family matters for the 60 percent of the country that is Muslim.)

Through a local legal-aid clinic, Zainah Anwar met many women whose cases were floundering in the sharia courts. "Whenever they complained that their husbands were beating them up, [the women] were told that, 'Oh, in Islam he has a right to beat you.' And when they complained that he had taken another wife, they were told that, 'Oh, in Islam it is his right.'"[39] Upset by this injustice in the name of Islam, she and a small group of other concerned women began turning to the Quran itself to determine whether the scriptures supported such treatment of women. "I was brought up to believe that God is just. How can God be God if he is not just to women?"[40]

In 1987, Zainah and some like-minded friends began informal weekly meetings in her home, reading the texts. "We learned to differentiate between the universal values that the Quran was trying to promote and the context that was specific to seventh-century Arabia," Zainah recalls.[41] In 1988, Zainah's little group held their first public meeting in conjunction with the Association of Women Lawyers to discuss their ideas more broadly. By 1990, they had formally launched SIS. Soon, they were debating conservative religious leaders and Malaysian politicians over Islamic law and women's rights. In the ensuing decades, Zainah and the work of SIS have inspired a generation of Muslim women activists around the world.

Not surprisingly, outspoken Zainah has developed enemies over the years. (Its harshest critics refer to SIS as Satan in Islam.) Unlike some of the activists working within an Islamic framework who carefully maintain their credibility by donning the headscarf and making nice with the mullahs, Anwar is willing to be far more confrontational. She defies convention by publicly refusing to marry, claiming she does not want "to be a slave to a man,"[42] a stance that enrages many traditional Malays; she also declines to wear the headscarf, explaining simply, "I grew up in a tradition where women didn't wear hijab." Her religious critics routinely swipe at her lack of "Muslim credentials," and point to her background and lifestyle as irrefutable proof that she is trying to impose Western-style secular feminism on Malaysia.

Asked about her choices, Zainah readily admits that they limit her personal appeal, and perhaps that of SIS, but insists that ultimately this struggle will not be won on her personal credentials. "Those who are ideologically committed to an Islamic state and sharia law will use any strategy to undermine those who challenge that ideology and the right they have to speak on Islam . . . Many of these Islamic activists don't know Arabic. They are engineering or medical graduates, and they don't have an Islamic background or an Arabic background."[43] Still, having a certain degree of religious credibility is important to SIS, since the group roots its arguments in religious discourse. So it is not surprising that early on, SIS engaged with reformist scholars like Abdullahi Ahmed An-Na'im and Fathi Osman.

In 1988, just as SIS was taking shape as an organization, Amina Wadud, the American Islamic scholar now best known for publicly leading Friday prayers, coincidently moved to Malaysia and started teaching at the International Islamic University Malaysia in Kuala Lumpur. Anwar and Wadud soon began collaborating. Sisters in Islam benefited immediately from Wadud's scholarship, her command of the religious texts, and her ability to cite sources in Arabic. In return, Wadud found a supportive audience for her own reformist message. SIS helped spread the message of Wadud's groundbreaking 1992 book, *Quran and Women*. Although Wadud later moved back to the United States to teach, she remained a key member of SIS.

SIS also became an important contributor to Women Living under Muslim Laws (WLUML), a transnational organization started in 1984 by women from various Muslim countries, including Algeria, Morocco, Sudan, Iran, Mauritius, Tanzania, Bangladesh, and Pakistan. Although WLUML marshals religious arguments as a tactic to overturn discriminatory laws, it is not a faith-based organization itself. In fact, it is a decidedly secular group that would prefer that religion be kept a private matter. WLUML recognizes, however, that in religiously charged societies, religious arguments are a tactical necessity.

One of WLUML's primary aims is to share information and scholarship as a way of demystifying Islamic law. Over the years it has collated Muslim laws from a multitude of countries, highlighting the huge diversity across legal systems to show that the laws are not divine. WLUML's website is a smorgasbord of briefs, dossiers, and manuals providing information, in six languages, on a broad range of topics. The site offers one-stop shopping for activists seeking to defend a sharia case, launch a training program for women to learn their rights within Islam, or simply to change the mind of the local mullah. WLUML's network, now spanning seventy countries, has been instrumental in helping to knit together the work of activists like Zainah Anwar and SIS with other Islamic feminists around the world.

In 2008, Anwar stepped down as the executive of SIS but continues to work closely with the organization. Support for SIS and its egalitarian message remains strong in Malaysia even in the face of rising extremism and the religious pandering of politicians. Among its victories, SIS counts the inclusion of Muslims in the country's Domestic Violence Act after repeated attempts by Islamists to exclude Muslims from the law's jurisdiction. SIS has also successfully marshaled resistance to the government's implementation of Saudi-style "moral policing" and is deeply engaged in reviewing Malaysian family law. It promotes examples from other Islamic countries to develop a model law based on the principles of equality and justice. A SIS writer contributes a column in a leading Malay newspaper for women to become more aware of their rights under Islamic family law. Anwar says that SIS's greatest contribution in Malaysia is the fact that it has "opened the public space for a public discussion, a debate of Islam."[44]

For all its successes, SIS still needs to strengthen its legitimacy among the conservative Muslims that it hopes to influence, and shake its perceived association with Western elites. As the organization works to develop a grassroots presence, Anwar looks for inspiration across the Java Sea to Indonesia, a sprawling country of more than 240 million people—the most populous Muslim country in the world.

Indonesia is home to some of the most effective Islamic women's organizations in the world today. They are viewed as completely homegrown and have a grassroots following to show for it. As such, they represent a gold standard in Islamic feminism—highly credible, decidedly nonelite, and far removed from the "tarnished" world of Western, secular feminism. Islamic feminism in Indonesia is not a radical notion or fringe movement. It is firmly in the mainstream. It is no coincidence that Indonesia is also one of the more moderate Muslim countries, especially when it comes to women's rights.

Confident Islamic Feminism, Indonesian-Style

Sitting on a folding chair on the conference-hall stage, Dr. Siti Musdah Mulia is beginning to seem frustrated. Her round, sunny face, usually marked by a broad smile, is now almost scowling. For hours, she has listened patiently as various Islamic scholars have debated the ins and outs of Islamic law and its application here in Banda Aceh, Indonesia.

It is 2007, less than three years after a massive tsunami ripped through this province, killing hundreds of thousands of people. In the wake of the devastation, hard-line conservative Islamists pushed to implement sharia across the province as they warned the traumatized population that the disaster had been caused by lax morality.

Not everyone in Aceh is happy about the increasing assertiveness of the sharia police who patrol the streets to enforce women's dress codes and to regulate moral conduct. They blame the sharia police and their public canings for driving away tourism and development in this deeply impoverished area. In response to the problem, a local Islamic university organized this conference to discuss the challenges of implementing sharia. Mulia is one of the guest speakers, flown in from the capital, Jakarta, where she is an official in the Ministry of Religion.

Finally, it is Mulia's turn to speak. As she walks to the podium, she intuitively adjusts her colorful headscarf, tied Malay-style. In her bright batik prints, Mulia stands out in an otherwise gray and bearded crowd. Addressing the segregated room—women on one side, men on the other—she expresses her frustration with the general direction of the conference. She reminds the audience that sharia is not merely a legal issue but also a pressing social and economic issue that needs attention. Poised and confident, she speaks about sharia in Aceh as an Islamic scholar, as a women's rights activist, and as a local Indonesian. "Whether unrelated men and women spend time alone together *should not* be the most important aspect of a discussion regarding sharia in Aceh," she scolds the audience.[45]

Her comments cause a commotion. Muhammad Ahmad Imam, a professor of Islamic law at al-Azhar University in Cairo, jumps up from the men's side of the room and grabs the microphone. Speaking in rapid Arabic, he assails Mulia's credentials as a scholar and her grasp of Islamic legal jurisprudence. "You have no idea what Islam is about!" he shouts at her.

While most of the Indonesians in the audience quickly put on their headsets to follow the tirade in translation, Mulia looks on calmly. She speaks fluent Arabic, having studied it since she was a young girl. Never one to be intimidated, Mulia calmly stares at her challenger. "Why is controlling women's freedom and dress always the first place to start whenever a region begins to implement sharia in Indonesia? Surely issues such as health and education for the underprivileged would be a more useful place to start? Isn't that more Islamic?"

Mulia is used to standing up to clerics, and speaks with a scholarly authority that buttresses her arguments. In fact, her whole life has been dedicated to studying Islam and promoting openness within the faith. The first woman in her country to receive a Ph.D. in Islamic political thinking and to serve as the head of research at the Central Board of the Indonesian Council of Ulama, Mulia's impressive religious credentials enable her to be a powerful voice for women's rights. From her perch in the Ministry of Religious Affairs where she is a researcher and lecturer, she challenges conservative elements in society and needles her government bosses. She is Indonesia's quintessential Islamic feminist.

Mulia grew up in a traditional Indonesian household and attended a *pesantren*, an Islamic boarding school. Her grandfather was a cleric and forced a very strict interpretation of Islam on his family. Mulia remembers, painfully, the tightly controlled environment of her childhood. Her parents did not permit her to have any contact with men. She was not even allowed to laugh out loud. If she socialized with a non-Muslim, she was made to shower afterward. Years later, when she left Indonesia to visit other Muslim countries, she began to realize that "Islam had many faces."[46] There were other ways to understand Islam beyond her grandfather's rigid orthodoxy.

Exposed to critical thinking in her postgraduate studies, she decided that much of what she had previously learned from her strict upbringing had to be reevaluated. Like so many other Islamic feminists, her careful study of the texts convinced her that Islam at its essence is progressive when it comes to women's rights. She has since written several books on the rights of women, focusing particularly on the sensitive issues of marriage, polygamy, domestic violence, and divorce. Although she continues to wear the headscarf, she does so as a matter of personal choice, insisting that Islam does not require it.

In 2004, Mulia caused a firestorm of controversy when she produced a detailed counterpoint to Indonesia's Islamic legal code. The 170-page draft recommended prohibiting child marriage, outlawing polygamy, allowing interfaith marriage, and permitting women to initiate divorce. In the face of violent protests, including death threats against her, the minister of religious affairs canceled the project. But even then, Mulia remained remarkably unperturbed. In the midst of the controversy, she told a journalist with the *Jakarta Post* that "conservative people used to annoy me, but now I pity them. Their narrowmindedness is due to limited access to knowledge and the opportunity to see the other side." Later in the same interview, she explained that the *ulama* like to claim that religious teachings—particularly with respect to marital laws—are final; there is no need to tinker with them. But she says that "none of it is a fax from heaven. Why be afraid? God won't get mad. He's very wise."[47]

Mulia's critics are powerful and vocal, to be sure, but she also has strong supporters across Indonesia. Several high-level, moderate politicians stand behind her. She is in great demand as a speaker, and numerous young Indonesian women look to her as a role model. Her international profile is also growing. In March 2007, she received an International Women of Courage award from U.S. Secretary of State Condoleezza Rice. (She initially hesitated in accepting it, worrying that it would open her to fundamentalists' accusations that she is a "Zionist agent working to destroy Islam."[48] But, encouraged by her colleagues, she chose to travel to Washington to collect the award.)

More important than international recognition, however, is the fact that the powerful Nahdatul Ulama (NU), the largest Muslim organization in the world, stands behind her. The NU has nearly 40 million members, the vast majority of whom are simple farmers living in rural areas and small towns across Indonesia. Nahdatul Ulama, meaning the "awakening of the *ulama*," was established in 1926 by religious leaders wanting to unify Indonesian Muslims against the threats of secular nationalism and communism and the rise of puritanical strains of Islam among rival religious groups. The NU's original purpose was to serve as a religious, social, and educational organization, although it has also operated as a political party.[49]

The backbone of the NU is its network of about 8,000 *pesantren*, Islamic boarding schools, which have educated millions of Indonesian boys and girls. The NU's religious leaders, known as *kyai*, are respected members of their villages who not only run their local *pesantren*, but also serve as community leaders and advisers on a range of social issues.[50] According to a 2007 poll, more than 80 percent of Indonesia's population supports the NU and its tolerant agenda.[51]

As early as 1940, women within the NU established its first women's association, the Muslimat NU, for women over forty, to improve the welfare of Muslim women. A decade later, a sister organization, Fatayat NU, was formed for women twenty to forty years old. These groups have local leaders in more than fourteen thousand villages across the Indonesian archipelago, giving them unsurpassed social reach at the grassroots level, which they actively flex.

Early on, Muslimat and Fatayat were instrumental in getting the NU's *ulama* to drop their opposition to family planning. Using arguments from the Quran, the NU *kyai* issued a fatwa in 1969 encouraging family planning. After that, Muslimat and Fatayat moved wholeheartedly into the field of family planning, running clinics and birthing centers, and promoting reproductive health programs. Between 1971 and 1997, birth rates in Indonesia dropped in half, from 5.6 to 2.8 births per woman, slowing the country's population growth.[52] Without the endorsement of religious leaders, the government's family planning initiatives would not have been nearly as successful. (With a population greater than 240 million people, Indonesia is still the fourth-largest country in the world.)

In recent years, the NU women's associations have been increasingly active in using religious arguments to press for greater gender balance on a number of fronts across Indonesia. Their efforts succeeded in forcing a comprehensive review of the texts used in *pesantren* to remove misogynist passages and revise gender stereotypes. They were instrumental in getting parliament to pass a bill in 2004 making domestic violence a crime. They are working to outlaw polygamy and expand reproductive rights for women, while simultaneously resisting government efforts to make women wear hijab. They have also lobbied hard against the practice of *muta*, or temporary marriage, which often involves a poor girl and a man seeking a short-term "wife." (*Muta* is legal is some Muslim countries.) Maria Ulfah Anshor, the outspoken head of Fatayat, denounces such marriages as "religiously sanctioned prostitution."[53] Remarkably, the NU women's associations are pursuing these controversial issues at a time of increasing conservatism across Indonesia.

The strength of Indonesia's Islamic feminism movement here is that it is not just the preserve of women. Some of its strongest proponents are men, like former President Abdurrahman Wahid, who led the NU before his political ascendancy. After he stepped down as Indonesia's president, he established the Wahid Institute, which focuses on promoting tolerant and progressive interpretations of Islam.[54] One of the Wahid Institute's advisers is another popular male Islamic feminist, KH Husein Muhammad, known fondly by his many female admirers as "Gender Kyai."

Among the many organizations that Husein Muhammad is involved with is RAHIMA, the Centre for Training and Information on Islam and Women's Rights Issues. RAHIMA promotes women's rights in Islam through public campaigns and research, including disseminating classical texts in Arabic and local languages that argue for women's rights. But the jewel of its programming is its training sessions for *pesantren* students and leaders. Gender Kyai, true to his nickname, uses these training sessions to push his progressive ideas about women and Islamic law into the minds of the religious leaders who wield such influence in their local communities.

Although Indonesia and Malaysia, like the rest of the Muslim world, have experienced rising Islamic fundamentalism, grassroots support for Islamic feminism has helped keep extremism at bay in these countries. Certainly, their more open, pluralistic, and democratic societies have been critical factors in this difference, fostering both active women's groups and diversity within Islamic intellectual thought. Given these seeming prerequisites for success, therefore, what hope does Islamic feminism have in the far more authoritarian Middle East? When I hold up examples of influential Islamic feminists from Asia, like Dr. Musdah Mulia, my Arab and Iranian friends dismiss them as somehow inauthentic. Islamic feminism in the Middle East will have to be homegrown, it seems. Luckily, there are promising signs that it is gaining a foothold.

Going Mainstream: Islamic Feminism
on Middle East Prime Time

On camera, Dr. Heba Kotb adjusts her pale blue headscarf around her broad face and resumes her assured pose, leaning forward, elbows resting on the table, fingertips together. Her bright diamond rings flash in the studio light as she gestures with her hands, answering the next caller's question. Her voice does not waver as she dispenses advice on masturbation (she is against it for women), oral sex (fine, if both parties agree), and the use of sex toys (fine too, as long as no one gets hurt). Kotb is a certified sex therapist whose popular show, *The Big Talk*, is beamed across the Arab world on a private Egyptian satellite channel.

Known today as the "Dr. Ruth of the Muslim world," Kotb frequently refers to herself as a scientist, and it is with scientific detachment that she imparts her wisdom and encourages her viewers to have more sex, "wherever, however, whenever." Having sex, she proclaims, is "a way to please each other in our world and to please Allah."[55]

True to the tactics of Islamic feminism, Kotb gets away with her taboo-busting talk because she carefully positions her arguments within Islamic discourse. She bases most of her sexual insights on the Quran, specifically on the chapter known as "The Cow," which she says obligates men to give pleasure to women—in effect, it mandates foreplay. (I have read the chapter, and I would say this is a stretch, but when I asked a few Muslim friends, none of whom I would describe as Quranic experts, they immediately identified the foreplay chapter: "Oh, you mean Surah 2:223!")

Kotb's own website, a montage of girly pink flowers with a happy-face icon composed of two sperm cradling an egg and pulsating background music, refers to sex as a "gift from God."[56] She encourages married women brought up in conservative, religious environments to throw away their inhibitions regarding sex, reminding them that Muhammad's wife Aisha used to call *him* to bed.[57] Based on Kotb's reading of the texts, as long as the couple is married, anything goes, except anal sex and intercourse during a woman's menstrual cycle. She brings Islamic clerics on her show to provide religious context for a wide range of sexual topics. Nothing is off-limits: On-air discussions jump from female orgasm to technical expositions on the merits of various sexual positions. She reminds her viewers that Islam encourages the enjoyment of sex within marriage.

Kotb acquired her "sexpert" credentials in the United States, where she went to study surgery but became intrigued by a world she had known nothing about growing up in Cairo. She abandoned her surgery degree and instead got a Ph.D. in clinical sexology at Maimonides University in Florida. Returning to Cairo, she became Egypt's first licensed sexologist and her reputation quickly spread. After years making guest appearances on widely watched networks like al-Jazeera, she launched her own program in 2006.

Somewhat prim and perfectly proper in her hijab, Kotb is hardly a liberal. She frequently and openly denounces homosexuality on her show, calls it an "illness," and compares homosexuals to drug addicts and alcoholics. She boasts that she has been able to "cure" thirty to forty of her patients of their homosexual tendencies.[58] Others criticize her for being so clearly patriarchal—after all, her bottom-line advice for women is to keep their husbands happy.

By Western standards, *The Big Talk* is decidedly tame, but Kotb's heady mix of sex, religion, and women has rocked the Arab world, where open talk about sex is still off-limits. While some conservative clerics have denounced her for bringing sex out into the open, most of her callers thank her on-air for doing just that. By couching her arguments within the Quran, Kotb has been able to push the sexual envelope in ways almost unimaginable even a few years ago.

The big point of *The Big Talk* is that, according to the Quran, women should get pleasure from sex. This is a radical notion in a country where female genital mutilation (FGM) is widely practiced on religious and traditional grounds exactly to prevent female sexual pleasure. FGM has been banned in Egypt since 2002, and fully criminalized since 2007, but it remains a deeply rooted practice that will take more than laws to change. In Upper Egypt, studies show that more than 85 percent of girls aged ten to fourteen have been cut even years after FGM was outlawed.[59] Kotb's prime-time brand of Islamic feminism is encouraging women to learn more about their bodies, and is demystifying sex—for men and women; both are important prerequisites for changing social attitudes and mores, not just in Egypt but across the region. Kotb is a popular figure across the Arab world and regularly lectures in other countries, even in conservative Saudi Arabia.

Over the past decade, the explosion of satellite television has resulted in open discussion of many women's issues that have long been unmentionable. It has pushed the debate over women's rights within Islam out of the halls of academia and into people's living rooms. Popular cable shows in most Muslim countries now regularly feature leading Islamic authorities debating back and forth about the religious justifications for this or that restriction on women. The front-runner of this phenomenon is al-Jazeera, the upstart cable channel based in Doha, Qatar, which was started in 1996 with a $150 million grant from the Emir of Qatar.

Originally staffed by many BBC World Service veterans, al-Jazeera introduced a level of openness and debate unprecedented in the Middle East. Although the network has been vilified in the United States for its anti-American views (Washington has twice bombed al-Jazeera stations, once in Afghanistan and once in Iraq), it has played a significant role in opening up political and social debate across the Middle East, including the touchy subject of women's rights.

One of the most popular features on al-Jazeera is the phone-in show *Sharia and Life*. The host is Sheikh Yusuf al-Qaradawi, a paunchy, octogenarian religious scholar cum Islamic televangelist who, by virtue of his prominence on al-Jazeera, is one of the most recognizable Muslim clerics in the world today. Born in Egypt in 1926, al-Qaradawi studied at al-Azhar. A Quranic wunderkind, he apparently memorized the entire text by the age of ten. By his early twenties, he had run afoul of the Egyptian government for being associated with the Muslim Brotherhood and spent a decade in and out of prison. In 1961, he decamped to Qatar where he established himself as a religious leader. But his worldwide appeal did not take off until he launched *Sharia and Life* on al-Jazeera in 1997.

During his ninety-minute program, Sheikh al-Qaradawi gives his interpretation of Islam on a wide variety of subjects, including sex in marriage. (A forerunner to Kotb, al-Qaradawi argued in a titillating episode that, with consent of both partners, just about anything goes.)

Millions of Muslim viewers—from New York to Riyadh to Kuala Lumpur—tune in to watch. Al-Qaradawi also maintains a website, islamonline.net, where he issues fatwas and offers advice to his followers. His Friday sermons, delivered from his mosque in Doha, remain remarkably fiery despite his old-man frailty. Tapes of his sermons are available around the world.

If nothing else, al-Qaradawi sparks controversy. Often referred to as a "reformer" or a "moderate alternative" to radical Islamists, al-Qaradawi urges Muslims to engage with the modern world. He has spoken out against al-Qaeda, and was one of the first to condemn terrorist attacks in the bombings in London and the events of 9/11.[60] But al-Qaradawi has also publicly supported the use of violence, including suicide bombings, against Israeli and American soldiers and civilians in Palestine and Iraq. Some blamed al-Qaradawi for the rash of grisly beheadings that plagued Iraq after the U.S. invasion because he issued various fatwas sanctioning violence there against U.S. forces. Since 1999, al-Qaradawi has been banned from entering the United States, and a few in the United States and Europe have called for his prosecution as a terrorist.

When it comes to women, al-Qaradawi offers a mixed bag of religious rulings. He insists that women must veil, and he does not think much of their leading mixed congregations in prayer. (He denounced Amina Wadud's actions.) Yet, he is a strong proponent of other rights for women. He constantly talks about the need to educate girls. Three of his four daughters hold a British Ph.D.—one in nuclear physics, one in organic chemistry, and one in botany. (His fourth daughter has a master's degree in biology from the University of Texas.)[61] He also advocates for women's participation in political affairs. He has issued fatwas saying that women should be able to vote in elections—a direct challenge to the Saudi ban on women's suffrage. He is not against the mixing of sexes as long as there is "respectful" behavior on both sides. In a part of the world where attitudes toward women tend toward deeply conservative, it is no surprise that al-Qaradawi is described as a moderate on women's rights.[62] Despite his tarnished reputation in the West, he has opened important space for discussions on women's rights within Islam.

Others have rushed in to take advantage of that space. The hit show *Kalam Nawaem* on the pan-Arab network Middle East Broadcasting Company (MBC) is an all-female talk show styled explicitly after the American show *The View*. It features four Arab women from across the region—a Palestinian actress, a Lebanese journalist, a London-based Egyptian woman, and a high-profile Saudi single mother who is the only one on the show who wears a headscarf. Chatting informally on comfortable sofas, they boldly address a range of sensitive social and political issues, including many women's issues.

Translated roughly as "sweet talk," *Kalam Nawaem* takes on such subjects as sexual harassment, polygamy, domestic violence, and a mother's right to pass on her citizenship to her children. (In several Arab countries, citizenship can only be passed on by the father.) In one groundbreaking episode, a Saudi female doctor demonstrated a breast exam on a plastic model as a way of drawing attention to breast cancer. While this type of demonstration is routine in the West, talking about breasts, even medically, was taboo-busting for *Kalam Nawaem*. Although the show's popularity is partly driven by the women's give and take, and their polite disagreement with each other, they are as a group generally more liberal than most of their viewers. Still, the show represents an important milestone in legitimizing debate and respectful disagreement on women's issues. Interestingly, nearly 40 percent of *Kalam Nawaem*'s viewers are men—the show for them is a rare window into the world of women from which they are mostly excluded.

Sheikh al-Qaradawi may have launched Islamic televangelism, but the suave and charming Egyptian preacher Amr Khaled is taking it to new heights. Hugely popular in the Middle East and among European Muslims, particularly women, Khaled is a rock-star televangelist who has been described as a Muslim cross between Oprah Winfrey and Billy Graham. Despite his lack of formal Islamic training (he worked formerly as an accountant), he has won millions of followers with his charisma and sex appeal. His sermons, carried on YouTube and multiple Arab satellite stations, are watched in more than 20 million homes across the Middle East and Europe. His Facebook fans number more than 230,000. His website at times draws more visitors than Oprah's, and *Newsweek* has counted him as one of the fifty most powerful people in the world.

In striking contrast to the aging, bearded, robed al-Qaradawi, Khaled is relatively young and fit, wearing designer suits or jeans and sporting a neatly trimmed mustache. He offers a "feel good" take on Islam—make money, be happy, and you will please Allah. He regularly discusses the positive impact Islam has on people's lives and communities, calling on his viewers to return to their faith and reject the message of misguided extremists such as Osama bin Laden. The fact that he speaks colloquial Arabic with a healthy dose of Egyptian slang helps draw in young people, as does his personal story. Born into a middle-class secular family in Egypt, Khaled worked as a number cruncher for a large multinational corporation when he felt a calling to give his life more meaning. As a "born-again Muslim," Khaled turned his energies from self-discovery to spreading the word. When a friend once asked him to stand in as a preacher at an event in Egypt, he wowed his audience and never looked back.

Many critics see Khaled as a conservative force, drawing his largely professional, middle-class audience away from secularism and toward Islamism. People credit (or blame) him for the steep rise in the number of women donning hijab, since he strongly advocates that women should wear the veil. However, he also speaks the language of Islamic feminism, preaching a strong message of women's empowerment. He urges women to wear the veil *and* be active in the public sphere. He strongly opposes those who say women cannot be political or social leaders, and denounces gender injustices in the name of Islam. "Women in the Arab world face very great oppression and, unfortunately, this oppression is in the name of Islam, but Islam is innocent. This injustice is due to old traditions and wrong ideas that wear the guise of Islam. Who says a woman cannot be a president of a state? Who says a woman cannot be a judge? Who? Who says not allowing women these rights are ideas or rules of Islam? Unfortunately, some traditional sheikhs defend this idea using flawed logic."[63]

Khaled has also spoken out on numerous occasions against practices such as "honor killings" and forced marriages. He does not pretend to be a scholar, and does not concern himself with parsing the texts. Indeed, scholars like Tariq Ramadan and Khaled Abou El Fadl have criticized Amr Khaled for glossing over the hard questions of modern

Islam with which they struggle constantly.[64] Yet if he is taken at face value, Khaled preaches an important message of women's rights, along with healthy doses of moderation and tolerance. Importantly, his millions of fans across the Middle East, particularly young people, are taking in this version of Islamic feminism.

Following in Amr Khaled's footsteps, a new generation of "satellite sheikhs" is also gaining popularity across the Middle East. The Saudi preacher Ahmad al-Shugairi is one such rising star (his Facebook fans only number about 25,000). In 2004, at age thirty, he started his own show, *Khawater* (or "thoughts"), which is especially popular among young people, even in conservative Saudi Arabia. Like Khaled, al-Shugairi favors jeans and T-shirts and speaks in a folksy, colloquial Arabic. He insists that Islam should simplify not complicate life and urges his followers to view Islam as an "ethical guidebook" rather than just a harsh set of medieval rules.[65] He also encourages women to wear the headscarf, but insists that they be treated with equality. His message, like that of Islamic feminism broadly, appeals to those trying to find moderation in Islam.

Storming the Gates of Religious Authority

The women stream into the village courtyard, mingling and chatting, slowly filling the benches arranged in a large square. The hot Moroccan sun is just poking over the ancient town walls of brick and mud. Despite their long coats, dresses, and headscarves, the women seem largely immune to the rising heat, although the shady side of the courtyard fills up first. They quiet down with anticipation as the new preacher enters the square. The preacher holds a Quran and begins by leading the assembled group in a simple prayer.

The new preacher is a woman. Known as a *murshida*, or religious guide, she is part of an ambitious experiment spearheaded by Morocco's reformist leader, King Muhammad VI. The idea of training women as preachers is central to the country's "religious restructuring" launched by the king in the wake of the May 2003 suicide bombings.[66] The attacks in Casablanca, Morocco's economic center, killed forty-five people, wounded dozens more, and deeply unsettled the country. It focused attention on how extremism was taking hold among the nation's disaffected youth. (A majority of those arrested in Europe on terrorism charges in recent years have been Moroccan.)

The idea of women preachers had been floating around Rabat for several years, but the shock of the 2003 bombings put the initiative into higher gear, and the king decided to take a chance. He broke with tradition that year and invited a woman to give the annual Ramadan lecture at the royal palace.[67] The woman's presence, amid imams from all over the world, stunned Morocco's religious establishment and signaled the more ambitious changes to come.

The program, not surprisingly, met with resistance. A rumor in the beginning that the women would lead prayers in mosques nearly sank the initiative. After heated debate over the permissibility of women leading prayers, the High Commission for Religious Knowledge in Morocco issued a fatwa saying that women cannot lead prayers in a mosque for men or women, although they could do so in the private sphere under certain conditions. This seemed to defuse the issue.

Ahmed Koutas, an official in Morocco's Ministry of Islamic Affairs overseeing the program, put a positive spin on this outcome. "These *murshidat* play a role far more important than the role of the imam. They go with women into their houses. They see their problems, their social problems. They guide them in every step of their lives. So leading women in every field is much better than just leading prayer."[68]

Although Morocco's more radical Islamist groups have denounced *murshidat* as "contrary to Islam" and have been harshly critical of the government's heavy hand in the program, one of the main Islamist opposition groups, the Justice and Development Party (PJD), has been supportive.

The explicit hope of the government is that the *murshidat* will help take the edge off Moroccan extremism by promoting a more tolerant version of Islam in the poor villages and urban slums that are fertile ground for jihadi recruiters. After a year of intensive religious studies alongside male candidates, the *murshidat* are sent to prisons, schools, and hospitals to talk with disaffected youth. During the day, they do administrative work in their mosque, and minister to people in the evening, often in their homes.

The first class of *murshidat* graduated in the spring of 2006, so it is still too early to tell how effective they will be in combating extremism. But so far, they have been well received by their communities. Women especially feel that the female preachers are good listeners who understand and relate to their problems better than the male imams. The *murshidat* dispense not only religious instruction but also act as social workers, giving advice on a range of family issues. They are serious and dedicated women with a mission to promote the "true face of Islam." Samira Marzouk, a short woman with olive skin, dark, heavy eyebrows, and a quick smile, was in the first class of fifty graduates. On graduation day, Samira beamed when discussing her role and how proud she was to be a *murshida*, but she clearly carried the weight of high national expectations on her shoulders. "It's a tough responsibility, not only because we are part of the first group, but also because Moroccan society as a whole is looking at us, and waiting to see how well we will do . . . We are part of a big mission."[69]

Ahmed Koutas in the Ministry of Religious Affairs expects to see the trend of women preachers spread. "The change *has* to come. Now it's time to make a change not just in Morocco, but in all the Arab countries, in all the Muslim countries. People are looking for a religious life that does not conflict with modern life."[70] Indeed, other Muslim countries are watching Morocco's program with interest and some already are following in its footsteps.

In 2005, Turkey launched a similar program. Until then, the state-controlled Diyanet, or Office of Religious Affairs, did not allow women to become Islamic jurists. Pressure from the Justice and Development Party (AKP), the moderate Islamic ruling party, which has a strong following of devout, active women, forced the Diyanet to change its position. In 2005, it appointed more than 450 women as *vaize*, or female preachers, and also allowed them to become deputy *muftia*, or Islamic judges. The *vaize* cannot lead mixed congregations in prayer, but like the Moroccan *murshidat*, they travel across the country teaching and advising on religious matters, particularly on women's rights and issues related to the family. While there remains some resistance from conservative Muslim men (and from women too), the program is very popular. Women continue to flock to theology classes and in several

Islamic studies programs actually exceed the number of male students.[71]

Turkey has also embarked on a controversial project to reexamine the hadith. As part of the AKP's continuing efforts to reconcile faith and modernity, the Diyanet has brought together hadith scholars at Ankara University's divinity school, which some have described as a "hotbed of liberal Islamic thinking."[72] Experts suggest that the results could help diminish discrimination against women by minimizing or even deleting some of the more misogynistic hadith.[73] In the face of conservative criticisms, the Turkish government sought to distance itself from suggestions that it was "rewriting" the Quran or the hadith. But the project could make it easier for women to break ground in ways like the *vaize*.

Not one to be left out of anything, Dubai is also getting in on the female-preacher business. In the spring of 2007, the Dubai Department of Islamic Affairs and Charitable Activities hosted a two-day training course for female preachers that attracted more than two hundred women. Egypt, too, began a *murshidat* program in 2006.[74] Cairo's prestigious al-Azhar has been at the forefront of women's Islamic scholarship since Nasser opened a women's faculty at the university in 1962, allowing a few women to begin their religious studies. The dean of the women's faculty today, Souad Saleh, was one of the first female graduates. Souad—who refers to herself as a "female Islamic activist" rather than an Islamic feminist—is a powerful voice for women's justice within Islam. Riding the wave of religious broadcasting that Yusuf al-Qaradawi and Amr Khaled made popular, Souad launched her own show, *Women's Fatwa*, on a government-owned Egyptian satellite station in early 2006. As the name implies, the show consists of Souad sitting at a gilded desk on the set imparting her religious rulings on a wide range of subjects.[75] She often points out that Islam provides women with many more rights than they usually enjoy in practice.

Souad has far less reach than megastar Amr Khaled. With the explosion of religious shows in the Middle East (in the past decade, the number of channels devoted to religious programming has gone from one to more than thirty), she has to compete not only with the male televangelists, but also with a growing cadre of self-appointed sheikhas who have no formal religious credentials but who draw an audience through their personal magnetism. Some of these women are faded actresses or singers who have jump-started a second career by taking the veil and hosting shows directed toward women about Islam. The fact that Souad has impressive religious credentials and most of these other women do not is probably lost on the average viewer seeking advice on a social problem. Yet, Souad is an important trailblazer for women within the world of religious authority. As the highest-ranking woman at al-Azhar, her delivery of fatwas, regardless of what they say, is a small step in breaking down Islamic orthodoxy.

In Iran, too, women are moving up the ranks of religious authority. Women have been attending religious seminaries for thirty years (although a very small number of women were able to attend even before that). A handful of women who trained in Qom's seminaries have even attained the rank of *mujtahideh*, a Shia female cleric given the authority to employ *ijtihad*, or independent reasoning. These women tend to be deeply conservative, and have kept a low profile within the Islamic Republic. But now some of them are beginning to speak out.

An interesting case is that of Zohreh Sefati, who is married to a grand ayatollah. Always covered in her black chador, which she clutches near her face as if the light of day will melt her, Sefati appears as conventionally orthodox as they come. On almost all issues related to women's rights, she takes a position in line with her conservative male counterparts. Over the years, she has generally been absent from public discussions on social issues and focused solely on her own scholarly work. In recent years, however, she has begun to step out into the public eye, giving interviews to both domestic and international newspapers and launching her own website. Having helped open the Women's Theology School in Qom in 1970, she is now more vocal in encouraging women to turn to religious studies in Iran.[76] Sefati's position within the most deeply religious circles of Iran is a source of pride for many Iranian women. Although she is conservative, she is challenging the patriarchal system simply by taking on a more public role. She is also quietly protesting Iran's ban on a woman becoming a high-ranking cleric, or *marja-i taqlid*, that can serve as a "source of imitation" for Shia followers.

Some Islamic scholars point out that women preachers are not a new phenomenon at all. In fact, there is a very old tradition of women preachers and jurists, dating back to the time of Muhammad. Aisha, the Prophet's young wife, is considered to be one of the first and foremost Islamic scholars who taught both men and women. She was also an important source for many of the hadith. During the first few centuries of Islam, women continued to follow Aisha's path. Many gained prominence and became religious teachers, scholars, and even legal jurists. Women continued to be active in these fields until roughly the sixteenth century, when states began to formalize their religious education programs and women were largely excluded.[77] Although some continued to study the Quran at the local mosque, few were able to do serious scholarly work on religious issues, and even fewer were able to become authorities. Women became marginalized from centers of Islamic learning, and from all official positions of religious power. By modern times, women's voices were all but gone from traditional Islamic circles. Today, however, this trend is slowly reversing itself.

The larger question, of course, is to what end? How will women as Islamic religious leaders be different than men? Certainly in Morocco, the government hopes that women preachers will be less susceptible to extremist tendencies, that they will help promote a more moderate and tolerant form of Islam. Already in Morocco and Turkey, the *murshidat* and *vaize* are taking on controversial issues such as domestic violence and honor killings, taboo subjects in many Muslim societies. But that is a far cry from dissuading a teenager from killing himself and others in a suicide bombing. To expect women religious leaders to be the antidote to the strain of nihilism running on the fringes of Islam today is to expect too much. But already reformist women are helping their societies find ways to integrate Islam with the demands of modernity.

Progressive and flexible interpretations of Islam have been around since the beginning of the faith, but they have waxed and waned in influence over the centuries. These male and female Islamic scholars, activists, and religious leaders are each playing an important role in challenging the rigid orthodoxy prevalent in many countries today. Over time, that should translate into real gains for women. Skeptics might say that a man does not refrain from beating his wife or committing an honor killing simply because a local religious leader tells him that it is against Islam, yet if such actions are widely perceived to be un-Islamic, existing laws are more likely to be enforced. This in turn creates both a legal and social deterrent.

One of the most notable and tangible success stories for Islamic feminism was Morocco's reform of its *mudawana* (or family code) in 2004. For years, women activists in Morocco had struggled to overturn many of the discriminatory aspects of their family code, the set of laws relating to marriage, divorce, custody, inheritance, and women's rights generally that had so bothered Fatima Mernissi. According to the *mudawana*, girls could be married at the age of fifteen, men could simply divorce their wives by declaring it out loud, polygamy was freely permitted, and men acted as the legal guardians for their wives. Many of these laws were justified using Islamic texts. Moroccan women who protested the family code were labeled *kafirs*, or unbelievers. They were attacked as being anti-Islamic and anti-Moroccan.

Undeterred, women activists began a formal campaign in 2000 to reform the *mudawana*. Wary of being labeled Western agents, the women were careful to showcase the local authenticity of their campaign by collecting signatures from ordinary Moroccans who supported reforming the laws. At the same time, they turned to Islam to bolster their case. Poring over religious texts, working closely with reform-minded clerics, and studying historical scholarship on the issues, the women were able to show their supporters and critics alike that Islam supports the equality of men and women—even within the sacred realm of the home. Within a year, their campaign had caught the attention of young King Muhammad VI, who had ascended the throne in 1999 upon the death of his long-serving father.

The signature campaign was a huge success. By 2003, various women's groups had collected an eye-opening one million signatures from Moroccans all across the country affirming their support for *mudawana* reform. Armed with both grassroots support and backing from the king himself, the women pushed a series of changes through parliament in 2004. Under the reformed *mudawana*, the age of marriage is now eighteen, divorces must be settled in courts, polygamy is greatly restricted, and women are given much greater financial guarantees in marriage and divorce.

Although the circumstances in Morocco were special because of the king's strong support, the reform of the *mudawana* was groundbreaking in that it demonstrated the potential for change for Muslim women around the world. It provided a model combining grassroots support and Islamic justification on which to base real political and social gains. Women's groups across the Middle East have been inspired and mobilized by the example, immediately working to organize similar campaigns.

The rise of Islamic feminism in countries as diverse as Indonesia, Turkey, Morocco, and Egypt demonstrates the growing appeal and importance of the movement. However, the ideals of Islamic feminism reveal their true strength when examined in the context of those Muslim countries where conservative Islam runs strongest: Iran, Pakistan, Afghanistan, Saudi Arabia, and Iraq. Although the differences among these five countries are vast—indeed, some Saudis I interviewed were distressed at the notion of their country being juxtaposed with Afghanistan—all of them share a common characteristic: They use rigid interpretations of Islam to reject important universal human rights and political and social reforms. More particularly, they use Islam to justify discrimination against women.

In all of these conservative societies, one can find Islamic feminists working to change public attitudes toward women and to repeal discriminatory laws. Of course, there are secularist feminists who have bravely worked on the front line of these issues for decades. These two camps—the Islamic feminists and the secular feminists, long wary of each other—are now finding ways to work together to promote, in more effective and sustainable fashion, a gender jihad for women's economic, political, and social empowerment.

PART II

CHAPTER 3

REVOLUTIONARY SISTERS: IRAN

The Prophet said that women totally dominate
men of intellect and possessors of hearts,
But ignorant men dominate women,
for they are shackled by the ferocity of animals.

—RUMI, Sufi Persian poet (1207–1273)

The video opens with Dr. Zahra Rahnavard sitting at her desk, working diligently through a stack of papers. It then cuts to her striding purposefully down a hallway, greeting colleagues. Her long black chador, the cover worn by devout Iranian women, billows out behind her, but little touches of femininity are apparent too. She wears a flowery headscarf under the chador, her cheeks are rosy with blush, and pink cuffs peek out from under her black sleeves. Her demeanor exudes confidence and her message of professionalism and determination is clear.

"A regime that does not have women's leadership will undoubtedly become a violent regime," Zahra asserts (in Persian) to the camera. "Women's presence in positions of power and leadership makes for a healthy society. It will create equality. It will create a gentle society. It will elicit enthusiasm."

The provocative nine-minute video, shown on Iranian state television, was made as a campaign promotion for Mir-Hossein Mousavi, Iran's former prime minister and the leading reformist candidate in the 2009 Iranian presidential election. Dr. Zahra Rahnavard, a professor of political science, a sculptor, a poet, an author of fifteen books, and a political and social leader in her own right, is Mousavi's wife. In 1998, she became the Islamic regime's first female university chancellor.

Unlike her husband, who is soft-spoken and known to mumble at times, Rahnavard is eloquent and commanding. "Women are here. We have expectations. And we want to participate in our own future," she states firmly.

Later in the video, Zahra sits at a conference table, joined by two other high-profile Iranian women. One is Massoumeh Ebtekar, Iran's first female vice president under former reformist president Mohammad Khatami. Ebtekar also wears the black chador but with a bright green silk headscarf underneath. Green, the color of Islam, is the color associated with Mousavi's reformist campaign. The other woman is Fatemeh Motamed-Arya, one of Iran's most acclaimed actresses. Fatemeh is wearing a simple purple headscarf over her red coat—defiantly showing her hair in the front. In a free-flowing, talk-show-style format, these articulate power women discuss issues relevant to all Iranian women: gender discrimination in the workplace, lack of female political leadership, and violence against women. Prominently displayed on the table are several Iranian books on women's rights.

The video was brilliantly crafted to appeal to Iran's female voters, and in particular, young women voters. Early in his campaign, Mousavi made a conscious decision to reach out to women of all backgrounds. Who better to represent him to this important demographic than his spirited wife? The central role that Zahra Rahnavard played in Mousavi's campaign against the incumbent president, hard-liner Mahmoud Ahmadinejad, was groundbreaking in many ways. Not only did she appear in public, hand in hand with her husband—a first for any Iranian politician—she also led Mousavi's rallies in his absence and delivered moving speeches.

Mousavi and Rahnavard's campaign aimed at women shows how important women have become in Iran's political and social landscape. Over the past thirty years, the women's movement in Iran has gradually expanded beyond its once-narrow base of secularists and leftist intellectuals to include many daughters (and sons) of the revolution—those who believed in the ideals of the Islamic Republic and were fervent supporters of Ayatollah Ruhollah Khomeini—traditional women like Zahra Rahnavard. In recent years, women of all backgrounds have joined together to confront the real discrimination they collectively face from the regime and their society. Along the way, their demand for greater rights for women has become inextricably intertwined with the country's broader reform movement.

In the aftermath of the 2009 presidential election, millions of Iranians, many wearing Mousavi-inspired green, took to the streets of Iran's major cities to protest the official results, which delivered a landslide victory to the incumbent, President Ahmadinejad. Women from all walks of life, with so much to lose or gain, were very much out in front: old, young, secular, traditional, wealthy, and poor. When security forces fatally shot Neda Agha Soltani, a twenty-five-year-old bystander, her tragic death was recorded by a mobile phone and beamed around the world. Neda, the young, beautiful Iranian woman, instantly became the face of justice and freedom in Iran, while the regime of Ayatollah Ali Khamenei and Ahmadinejad became symbols of oppression. Protesters across the country, including chador-clad women, religious men with beards, and street peddlers, were soon holding up the picture of the bloody, martyred Neda. "I am Neda" became the women's chant as they defiantly took to the streets.

While some have characterized the political conflict in Iran as a showdown between secular reformers and the theocracy, the reality is a more nuanced contest over what form of Islam Iranians want—the inclusive, more democratic, and woman-friendly reading of Islam associated with Mousavi, or the rigid, authoritarian Islam associated with President Ahmadinejad and Supreme Leader Khamenei? The rise of Islamic feminism and the notion that women's rights and Islam can be compatible has thrown critical intellectual weight behind the former and provided grounds for challenging the religious legitimacy of the latter.

To be clear, "Islamic feminism" as a label has been disparaged by all sides in Iran. In a country where bashing the "Great Satan" is official background music, juxtaposing the Western term "feminism" with "Islam" remains politically incorrect. As one activist explained to me, "using the word 'feminism' in any form means less support for our work."[1] Moreover, three decades of theocracy have left many Iranians weary of "Islamic" anything. Today, many of Iran's women activists long for feminism unencumbered by Islam. But the reality of the regime forces them to appeal to Islam as a tactic. Some prefer the term Muslim feminists to differentiate themselves from the Islamic theocracy they reject. Others call themselves "indigenous feminists." Regardless of these distinctions, which continue to evolve, Iran has emerged as ground zero of efforts to use Islamic discourse to promote rights for women.

Islamic feminism has in many ways helped bridge divides that have long existed between traditional, religious women and their secular counterparts. Some Iranians have come to Islamic feminism from the right. These are the daughters of the revolution—women from traditional families who were inspired by Ayatollah Khomeini, educated by the mullahs, and mobilized by the bloody Iran-Iraq War—who gradually began to feel betrayed by the failure of the theocracy's rhetoric of "Islamic justice" to live up to the reality for women. Others have come to Islamic feminism from the left—intellectuals and activists who recognize that in the religiously charged environment of the Islamic Republic where the premise of the regime cannot be questioned, religious arguments are essential to promote social change. They have turned to Islamic jurisprudence and *ijtihad* to promote reforms. Islamic feminism has been an important means of building bridges and finding common ground between traditionalist, conservative women and more progressive, secular women in Iran who in the early years of the revolution viewed each other with such disdain and mistrust.

Islamic feminism in Iran has also been an intellectual stepping-stone for some traditional women (and men) who have made the personal journey from maintaining deeply conservative Islamist views to supporting full-blown secularism. It has helped ease them through this transition, which often comes at great personal cost. Many of Iran's women activists, beaten down over decades by their country's authoritarian, Islamic system, insist privately that only a separation of mosque and state will permit a full dismantling of the country's "gender apartheid," as Akbar Ganji, one of Iran's leading dissidents, refers to the state of gender affairs in his country today. But they recognize that such a secularist system is not on the horizon. In the meantime, using religious arguments is simply practical and results in incremental improvements for women. As one activist said to me, "The mullahs want people to think that nothing can change. But that is not true. By not antagonizing religion, we can make changes. We can find daily solutions to our problems."[2]

Perhaps most important, by providing arguments that make social and legal changes for women more compatible with religion, Islamic feminism encourages women's empowerment at the grassroots level where traditions run deepest. It helps make the notion of women active in public life acceptable to average Iranians, not just elites.

Iran is a country of paradoxes, especially with respect to women. Although the revolutionary mullahs imposed some of the most regressive gender laws, denying women many basic legal rights they had had under the Shah, they also promoted female education and, over time, allowed women access to most types of professions, including medicine, engineering, and law, and even traditionally "male" jobs like police, taxi drivers, and pilots. Today, women make up the majority of university graduates. They have open access to reproductive healthcare. Prenatal care and safe delivery in maternity centers and hospitals are near universal. They are active in government. These glaring contradictions have inadvertently created fertile ground for Islamic feminism, with more and more Iranian women and men demanding an end to gender inequalities on religious grounds. Historians may well look back at this time as the tipping point for women in Iran—and more broadly for Shia women around the world—when mainstream opinion came to accept a woman's right to justice and equality. When the current repressive regime finally loses its hold, Iran will undoubtedly emerge as the most progressive environment for women in the region.

Daughters of the Revolution

The Institute for Women's Studies and Research (IWSR) is housed in a villa on a quiet side street in an upscale, leafy neighborhood in north Tehran. Although various offices and meeting rooms have been carved out of the interior, the building's original parquet floors and ornate moldings are hints of a more elegant past. French doors open onto an overgrown garden and a sweet smell of honeysuckle wafts through the windows on the hot breeze.

I am meeting with Monir Amadi Qomi, a cofounder of the institute and its longtime director. Amadi Qomi is a short, stout woman with thin, plucked eyebrows. She wears a brown jungle-print scarf beneath her black chador, secured tightly under her chin by a silver brooch. A large, stern photograph of Imam Khomeini looms over us.

It is the spring of 2007 and well over a hundred degrees outside. It is not much cooler inside where a lone fan in the corner stirs the air. I am sweating profusely under my hijab and the long black coat I am wearing. Since the revolution, a strict Islamic dress code has been in place for women in Iran—no exposed hair and only long, loose-fitting clothing to cover the body's contours. I had to cover my hair for my visa photo—something not even the conservative Saudis require. (I had my visa photo taken at my local drugstore in New York. Nahid, the salesperson, happens to be an Iranian exile. When I explained to her the reason for my headscarf, she took pride in making sure it was just right for the picture.)

A month before my arrival in Iran, President Mahmoud Ahmadinejad's conservative government launched a "spring-cleaning" initiative to crack down on women not sufficiently covered. Some three hundred women were arrested. Although on the streets I still see women wearing tight-fitting Capri pants, high-heeled shoes, and flimsy scarves pushed halfway back on their heads in defiance, I am taking no chances. So here I am perspiring under my coat and scarf. Amadi Qomi, in contrast, somehow looks perfectly comfortable in her chador.

Bookcases line the walls of her office. I notice an interesting collection of documents in English on the shelves—World Bank and UN publications, an Equality Now annual report, research papers from various international NGOs on microfinance, family planning, and human rights. A few young women, also wearing black chadors, move quietly about the villa, bringing Amadi Qomi messages and serving tea as she talks about Imam Khomeini.

"Before the revolution, eighty-five percent of Iranian women were repressed by religion and tradition. After the revolution, Khomeini gave women a voice. He energized us and liberated us. He made us believe that we were empowered, that now was the time to seize our educational and economic opportunities," Amadi Qomi waxes on enthusiastically under the intent gaze of Khomeini's picture.

A teenager at the time of the revolution, Amadi Qomi—like many young women from traditional families—was inspired by Khomeini. She recalls proudly the role that she and her friends played marching in demonstrations against the Shah. Khomeini knew that without women's support, the revolutionary groups would never gain the critical mass necessary to force the government to step down. He called upon women to leave the confines of their homes to support the protests—an act previously considered blasphemous in traditional families. A group of chador-clad women even joined in the infamous demonstration in Jaleh Square on September 8, 1978. When the Shah's troops fired indiscriminately on the crowd, killing hundreds, the event came to be known as the Black Friday Massacre. The bloodshed marked a critical turning point in the revolution. After the massacre, hundreds of thousands of Iranians took to the streets to protest the despotism of the Shah, whose control over the country was gone. Within months, the Shah and his family had fled Iran. On February 1, 1979, Ayatollah Ruhollah Khomeini returned triumphant from exile.

The slide toward religious absolutism soon began. In April 1979, Khomeini held a referendum asking the people to vote for or against an "Islamic Republic." Many were seduced by Khomeini's charisma and promises of Islamic democracy and justice. Others hoped that an Islamic state would bring prosperity. Some 90 percent of eligible voters—more than half of the country's population—voted in favor of the new regime. With this as his mandate, Khomeini declared himself Vali-i-Faqih or "Guardian Jurist," a controversial idea Khomeini had long supported based on the broader theory of Vilayat-i-Faqih or "Guardian of Islamic Jurisprudence." According to the constitution, the Vali-i-Faqih would serve as the country's supreme leader. Although he would leave day-to-day decision making to elected officials, he would have responsibility for ensuring that the laws and functions of the state were compatible with Islam. Khomeini now had the final say on all matters. Liberals and conservatives warned darkly about a return to despotism.

Flexing its Islamic credentials, the new regime began rolling back the Shah's relatively progressive laws for women. As one of its first moves, Khomeini's office in April 1979 rescinded the existing Family Protection Act. Although unevenly enforced under the Shah, these laws had stood out in the region as a progressive benchmark for women, providing equal rights in divorce, custody of children, and marriage settlements; raising the marriage age of girls to eighteen; and restricting polygamy. Over the next few years, Khomeini instituted sweeping legal changes for women. The regime barred women from becoming judges, ordered them to observe Islamic dress code when working at government offices, and, eventually, to wear the veil in public at all times. New laws reduced the age of marriage for girls to nine, allowed polygamy to become less restrictive, and made divorce again easier for the man and more restrictive for the woman. The new Islamic penal code also fell hard on women. A woman's life and her testimony in court now counted for only half that of a man's. Stoning was reinstated as a punishment for adultery.

Despite debate at the highest clerical levels over the religious validity of some of these decrees, any public questioning of the new restrictions on women was labeled as counterrevolutionary, or even worse, anti-Islamic. For educated, professional women, the legal changes were devastating, and they protested by the thousands in the streets. As the human rights lawyer and Nobel Peace Prize winner Shirin Ebadi has described it, the new laws "turned the clock back fourteen hundred years, to the early days of Islam's spread, the days when stoning women for adultery and chopping off the hands of thieves were considered appropriate sentences." She recalls in her memoirs how the new laws infused her with a "boundless rage."[3]

For the majority of women who came from traditional backgrounds, however, the new legal environment was hardly momentous. They lived in a world of rigid social and religious conventions, which had budged little despite—or perhaps because of—the Shah's more liberal tendencies. The public realm, including formal education, was mostly off-limits to them. At the time of the revolution, a third of girls were married by the age of thirteen,[4] and female literacy hovered around 30 percent.[5] Although the Shah's modernization programs emphasized girls' education, conservative religious leaders, particularly in more rural areas, warned that education for girls was a tool of Westernization and preached against it. Female literacy in rural areas barely broke 5 percent.

So it is not so surprising that women like Monir Amadi Qomi looked to Khomeini as a liberator. Although he systematically dismantled women's legal rights in Iran, those rights had mostly lived on paper for girls from traditional families. At the same time, Khomeini spoke directly to these previously invisible masses. With his flowery, religious rhetoric, he inspired them and mobilized them. "If women change, society changes," he liked to say.

Khomeini was nothing if not politically astute. He understood that women's mobilization was important for deepening and consolidating the revolution. After Iraq's invasion of Iran in 1980, women's greater involvement in public life became a matter of necessity too. Like American and European women during the twentieth-century world wars, Iranian women during the Iran-Iraq War were pulled into the workforce in larger numbers. As the brutal conflict dragged on, women even provided military logistical support, serving as nurses and drivers on the front lines.

The greatest anomaly of the revolution—indeed, some may say its undoing—is that the Islamic takeover made formal girls' schooling acceptable to even the most conservative families. Now that society was Islamized—with girls wearing hijab and schools and many public places segregated—how could a father say no? For girls like Monir Amadi Qomi, this truly was liberating.

"I come from a very religious family," Amadi Qomi explains to me. "My father is very conservative. He didn't want me to continue in school beyond the age of twelve. 'It is not right for girls,' he would say. I had a constant struggle with him, but I persisted." After the revolution, Amadi Qomi was able not only to convince her father to allow her to stay in school, but also to go to university, the first woman in her family ever to do so. She was accepted to the University of Tehran where she studied biology and theology.

"I broke the ground for the other women in my family," she says. "I have three sisters and they all went to university after me. Only my brother didn't attend university. Now, looking back, my father says he wishes his son had been a girl too."

"Be Happy for the Birth of a Girl"

By the mid-1980s, loyal foot soldiers of Khomeini like Monir Amadi Qomi were beginning to question the restrictions imposed on their lives in the name of Islam. "We expected to have a better position in the Islamic Republic. We expected to have more opportunities. But the government didn't match the vision of Khomeini. It continued to oppress women," Amadi Qomi says, referring to the legal restrictions that relegated her and her revolutionary "sisters" to an inferior status. Like most Iranians of the revolutionary generation, she still reveres Khomeini for what he seemed to represent—a step forward for Islamic justice and social equality. She conveniently manages to absolve him of the regime's turn toward despotism. Indeed, as disillusion with the corruption and hypocrisy of today's ruling mullahs has spread through the population, many Iranians seem wistful for Khomeini.

Yet, the inherent contradiction of Khomeini's position on women— one that encouraged their active participation in society, but restricted their legal rights on Islamic grounds—needed explanation for his millions of female followers who were beginning to feel deceived by the revolution. "We began to think that maybe the issue was a conflation of tradition and religion," Amadi Qomi explains simply.

As she sips her tea, she recalls a childhood conversation. When she was nine, she overheard her aunt expressing disappointment to her mother about the birth of another daughter. She was confused and asked the older women why they were so upset about the birth of a girl. Aren't boys and girls equal? No, she was told emphatically by her mother, they are not. Boys are far superior to girls. Later, as she made her way through university, this exchange weighed heavily on her, but she found clarity within Islam.

"The Prophet himself defended the rights of women," she insists. "One of his first social campaigns was to stop female infanticide." She then tells me, "When Muhammad's son, Ibrahim, died, people tried to commiserate with him by saying how terrible it was that now he had no successor. But the word of God came through Muhammad, 'Be happy for the birth of a girl.' Muhammad's daughters would be his successors." Amadi Qomi decided that her aunt and mother must have been misguided by traditional thinking, not by Islam.

"Imam Khomeini always told us that women are important and should participate in society," she continues. "He issued fatwas on behalf of women. For example, he clearly gave women the right to leave the house without their husband's permission. But after the revolution, other rights were taken away from us."

In the mid-1980s, Amadi Qomi joined forces with several friends who were likewise frustrated that the revolution had marginalized women. They decided to write directly to Khomeini to complain. "We sent a letter to the Imam to tell him that our situation is now worse than under the Shah," remembers Amadi Qomi. "We fought the last regime and expected to have a better position, but little by little we came to realize that the new government would not allow us to play our role."

"We insisted in the letter that the issue is a mixing of tradition with Islam, which suppresses women. We proposed starting a research organization that would work to disentangle religion from tradition."

Amadi Qomi proudly recalls Khomeini's response. "He not only approved of our concept, but he sent us 15,000 toman [about $500 at the time] to get the organization going." Islamic feminism had found an official foothold in Iran.

In 1986, the women formed a group that would become the Institute for Women's Studies and Research. They started out meeting on benches in parks around Tehran, but Amadi Qomi's father eventually donated the basement in his house to the fledgling organization. "With the help of God," she says, "we were able to raise additional funds."

The timing of the new organization was propitious, coinciding with the end of the Iran-Iraq War in 1988. Bankrupt, isolated internationally, and traumatized by the death of hundreds of thousands Iranians and the emigration of hundreds of thousands more of the country's skilled middle class, Iran began to take a much-needed pragmatic turn. The regime backed down from its aggressive policies to export the revolution and turned its attention inward toward the rebuilding of the country.

Khomeini's death the following year led to further national soul-searching. The bland, mid-level cleric Ali Khamenei, who succeeded Khomeini as supreme leader, was not even an ayatollah at the time of succession. With little of Khomeini's religious authority and none of his charisma, Khamenei had no hope of filling his predecessor's slippers. With Khamenei at the helm, it became harder for many in the revolutionary generation to sustain their religious zeal.

Just months after Khamenei's accession, Akbar Hashemi Rafsanjani, the "pistachio king" who amassed huge wealth from his ties with Iran's business class and his extensive land holdings, was elected president and began to steer the country toward more free market policies. Quietly, women were allowed back into some professions from which they had been excluded, but where their technical expertise was much needed. For example, beginning in 1992, women were again allowed to practice law and permitted to sit as assistant judges in courts hearing divorce cases.

The most obvious policy U-turn regarding women was undoubtedly in the area of family planning. Throughout the war years, the clerical establishment had exhorted women to strengthen the country by producing babies. Khomeini himself called on women to bear children to become "soldiers for Islam," claiming he wanted an army of 20 million people. Contraception was outlawed. By the mid-1980s, Iran had one of the highest fertility rates in the world, with women having on average six children. Between 1979 and 1986, the country's population zoomed from 34 million to 49 million.[6]

Faced with the challenges of postwar reconstruction, government planners began to warn that the population surge was a potential demographic time bomb. In 1988, the regime held a conference on reproduction and development to ready the public—and the broader clergy—for a comprehensive family planning program. Ayatollah Khomeini reintroduced the subject of birth control (the Shah had invested in family planning prior to 1979) and the government announced that not only would it permit contraceptives, but it would provide them to couples for free. Within a year, mullahs across the country were calling for smaller families in their Friday sermons and issuing fatwas encouraging the use of all types of contraception.

"Imam Khomeini was very influential in convincing the *ulama* that a big population is not necessarily good," explains Amadi Qomi approvingly. "Rather, a healthy, strong population is better. He relied on *ijtihad* to show that times change. During the time of the Prophet, there were many wars and a big population was important. That is not true today."

The Institute for Women's Studies and Research took up the challenge of family planning and found an open door. It began working with UNFPA, the UN's family planning and reproductive health division, promoting women's reproductive health by doing research and training women's health workers in the provinces. During the 1990s, many of the health workers trained by the institute went on to become grassroots activists, working on a range of women's issues throughout the country.

Iran's fertility rate dropped steadily throughout the 1990s, hitting 1.2 percent in 2001 and .8 percent today, lower than that of the United States. This is the fastest decline in fertility a country has ever recorded. It is also a tantalizing demonstration of how the power of Islam, when allowed, can be harnessed so effectively by women's groups.

Flush with its success on family planning, Amadi Qomi's institute set about raising broader social awareness of women's issues and bringing them to the table of policy makers. "Since many of the restrictions on women were implemented in the name of religion, we were interested in deepening our understanding of Islam, particularly what Islam tells us about the role of women in society. We started Quranic study groups, focusing on the differences between Islam and patriarchal traditions on which many laws are based," she recalls.

When I ask Monir Amadi Qomi to assess what impact her institute has had over the years, she comes up with a list of incremental changes, including better divorce and child-custody terms for women. She notes that they have been holding training sessions for judges and the heads of family courts to spread more progressive interpretations of sharia, and have made some gains. "Some policy makers, the men, even attend our training sessions now."

Leaning back in her chair, she looks out the window, still contemplating the question. "There are two different views of Islam—the closed view and the open view," she explains. "When the more open view comes to power, we can do more. When the political system is dominated by the closed view, as it is now, we have more trouble approaching our goals." Amadi Qomi chooses her words carefully. After all, even though she describes herself as the head of an NGO, she is effectively a public employee—her institute survives at the discretion of the government.

"I am disappointed with the government [of President Ahmadinejad]," she slowly admits. "Frankly, it is too conservative. It is against women." Amadi Qomi sighs. "Due to the pressures of today, we are refraining from working on those subjects that are seen as more political—those relating to sharia—and focusing on those that are less controversial. Our focus now is on creating employment opportunities for women. The biggest challenge is that women all graduate from university, but there are no jobs for them. Our institute is focusing on helping women achieve economic independence. We would like to see more privatization, a greater shift of resources away from the government and into the private sphere. This will be to women's benefit."

In the meantime, Amadi Qomi and her institute keep working to "sensitize society to the issues of women" as she puts it. Her mild— some might say acquiescent—brand of Islamic feminism is helping to establish the idea among even the most conservative segments of society that an expansion of women's rights is compatible with Islam.

Islamic Feminism Lite

A few days after my visit to the Institute for Women's Studies and Research, I meet with Massoumeh Ebtekar in her office overlooking City Park in downtown Tehran. I have been forewarned about Ebtekar's shrill anti-Americanism and tendency to pontificate (she keeps a strident blog in English, called "Persian Paradox," where she denounces America's misguided ways). But she welcomes me politely and strikes a subdued, if at times defensive, tone.

Massoumeh is wearing her signature sky blue *maghneh*—a hoodlike covering that slips over the head—underneath her black chador, keeping her hair carefully covered. I keep thinking she looks strangely like a nun wearing a blue wimple under her habit. A trailblazer of sorts, she was once the most high-profile woman in Iran when she became the Islamic regime's first female vice president and cabinet member in 1997. But now she is several years out of the limelight. After the 2005 election of hard-liner President Ahmadinejad, her star faded along with Iran's reform movement. She bided her time as a member of Tehran's city council, and aligned herself with Mousavi in the 2009 presidential election, hoping for a political comeback.

Just as we sit down, several women are ushered into Ebtekar's office. She stands to greet her friends, kissing them on both cheeks. The room has suddenly become a coffee klatch of Islamist power women, each with a more impressive job description than the next. One is the anchor of a popular morning television program. Another is the former deputy mayor of a major district in Tehran and now the head of the city's environmental initiatives. All of them wear conservative black chadors. Ebtekar enthusiastically introduces them to me, clucking over their credentials like a proud mother hen. After nearly a week of meeting with Iranian officials, I am used to this. There is a constant need to deflate the stereotype of the helpless, chador-clad woman for the unwitting American. A few more minutes of small talk, more tea, and pistachio nuts, and the other women leave. Finally, we begin our conversation.

In some ways, Massoumeh Ebtekar's story follows the arc of the Islamic Revolution itself. Raised in a middle-class, intellectual Iranian family, she grew up with a heavy dose of politics at the dinner table. Discussions raged on issues of poverty and class, Cold War rivalries between communism and capitalism, and despotism at home. Across the country, Iranians harbored deep resentments against the United States for its role in the 1953 coup d'état against the popular Prime Minister Muhammad Mossadeq (a resentment that still runs strong today). They despised the ruling Shah as a corrupt and sycophantic tool of America.

Like many young Iranians in the 1970s, Ebtekar was influenced by Dr. Ali Shariati, a charismatic, religious intellectual whose message blended elements of Marxism and Islamic social justice. Shariati is credited with (or blamed for) stirring Islamic revivalism across the country and making Iranians receptive to Ayatollah Ruhollah Khomeini's message of Islamism. Inspired by Shariati and Khomeini, Ebtekar marched in the streets and supported the revolution passionately.

When a group of her university friends took over the U.S. Embassy in the fall of 1979, she became their spokeswoman. Calling herself "Mary," she appeared daily at press conferences and soon was known as "Tehran Mary" in the Western media. I have watched the news clips of Ebtekar as a young nineteen-year-old addressing a phalanx of the world's journalists, her hijab tightly fastened under her chin. She is eerily poised as she defends the actions of the hostage takers, with only a slight quaver in her voice. "The West has a different conception of the word 'hostage,'" she drones into the microphone, reading from a prepared text in her American accent—a holdover from her childhood years living in a Philadelphia suburb while her father studied at the University of Pennsylvania. "They think hostages are a group of innocent people captured by terrorists. First, these are not innocent people. They are spies. They were preparing to destroy our country."[7]

Ebtekar's constant propagandizing in her perfect but steely English made her particularly distasteful to the hostages, who saw her as a Tokyo Rose–type turncoat.[8] She has never apologized for her involvement in the embassy crisis. Rather, she has tried to explain it away. "It was a difficult ordeal. [The Americans] were hostages of the Iranian people. We were hostages of those circumstances. There is no question of that. It was difficult circumstances for the students. Maybe some of the students went too far sometimes. We can't deny that," she admitted in a 2004 interview.[9]

The embassy takeover changed the course of the revolution, putting the country firmly on a radical path. The student hostage takers became national heroes. Some of the young men went off to the front to fight against Iraq. Others joined the Pasdaran, the Revolutionary Guards—Iran's elite military unit that reports directly to the supreme leader. Ebtekar married one of her fellow hostage takers, had children, and returned to her studies to complete a Ph.D. Over time, like other daughters of the revolution, she was forced to address the glaring contradiction of her support for a regime that now reduced women to legal subservience. In the mid-1980s, she worked with Monir Amadi Qomi to found the Institute for Women's Studies and Research and began to delve into what Islam really means for women. Nevertheless, she continued to toe the party line, leading various government initiatives for women.

In 1995, Ebtekar was chosen to represent Iran at the United Nations' Fourth World Conference on Women. Delegations from nearly two hundred governments and over two thousand nongovernmental organizations gathered in Beijing to develop a unified "Platform for Action" to improve women's rights globally. For Iran's government of conservative mullahs, Ebtekar was a perfect choice to represent the Islamic Republic at an international women's conference—well educated, articulate, and forceful, and yet an ardent supporter of the regime. Her role in the takeover of the U.S. Embassy in 1979 gave her gold-plated revolutionary credentials.

At Beijing, Ebtekar gave a speech defending the gains women had made under the Islamic Republic, especially in education. She interspersed her remarks with strident condemnations of the Taliban in Afghanistan and the "fossilized Islamic values" they used to oppress women. Some in the audience groaned with despair, offended by the Islamic Republic's attempts to present itself as a defender of women's rights. A few walked out in protest. For many in the room, watching a chador-clad woman use Islamic arguments to denounce oppressive practices against women was simply too rich.

Islamic arguments for women's rights, however, were very much present throughout the conference. Indeed, Beijing was in many ways a "coming out" of Islamic feminism. Benazir Bhutto, prime minister of Pakistan at the time, gave an opening address reminding the audience that Islam forbids injustice, including injustice against women, and warning against misogynist interpretations of Islam. Several scholars gave lectures showing that feminism is a deeply rooted concept within Islam, highlighting the Prophet Muhammad as a great defender of women's rights, and debunking some of the more repressive Islamic practices as rooted in patriarchal tradition, not religion. The Pakistani scholar Riffat Hassan, whom we will read more about later, delivered a scathing attack on how Islam is practiced in many conservative societies today. She caused a sensation among Muslims by questioning the authenticity of some of the hadith that are most oppressive toward women. She also angered many secular feminists by insisting on the need to engage with religion.

The Beijing conference revealed a deep rift between women from conservative religious backgrounds and secular women's rights groups—a rift that was all too apparent in Iran itself. Some of the more ardent secularists wanted nothing to do with religion—any religion—and felt that religious discourse had no place at the conference. Put simply, women's rights are human rights, as then First Lady Hillary Clinton insisted in her keynote address. But for many women at Beijing, their reality was religious law. Appealing to international human rights standards was simply not sufficient in their context, and sometimes even hurtful. The forceful presence of many Muslim women scholars and activists, working within an Islamic framework, pushed discussion of Islamic feminism into the mainstream for the first time. It helped launch a contemporary debate, involving women from Islamic countries around the world, about gender issues and more broadly, reform within Islam.

Beijing was also a watershed moment for Iran's emerging women's movement. Some conservative Muslim countries like Saudi Arabia chose to boycott the conference. Iran, however, seeking to improve its image in the world, sent a huge delegation of nearly a hundred people. Handpicked by the government, the delegation included journalists, women from religious groups, and representatives from some fifteen "nongovernmental organizations." (None of these NGOs were really "non" governmental. Some were created by the government solely for the purpose of attending Beijing and were soon dismantled after the conference. All of them were largely funded by government contracts.) They also sent ten male "minders" to watch the group. Monir Amadi Qomi, who was also at the Beijing conference, recalls how the organizers cleared out the whole embassy. "All of us slept there so that they could keep an eye on us better. They were afraid of what we might do and say!"[10]

On a tight leash, the Iranian delegates, led by Ebtekar, hewed closely to their official script, drumbeating audiences with statistics on the impressive health and educational gains women had made under the Islamic regime, yet also insisting on the centrality of motherhood and denying the need for equality in politics, law, or society between men and women. Iran sided with other conservative Muslim countries and a group of Catholic states led by the Vatican (dubbed an "Unholy Alliance" by its critics) to take a hard line against sexual and reproductive rights for women and homosexuality.

It was impossible, however, for the dynamism of the Beijing conference not to affect the Iranian representatives. The Iranian delegation's exposure to thousands of women's rights activists from around the world, and especially to the cutting-edge scholarship of Islamic feminists who were questioning all forms of patriarchy within an Islamic context, forced many of them to reconsider their positions. Some went on to become leading women activists in Iran, using increasingly progressive interpretations of Islam to challenge the regime's restrictions on women.

In the aftermath of Beijing, Ebtekar increasingly gravitated toward the reformist thinking that began to gain traction in Iran in the 1990s. In the 1997 presidential election, the then little-known candidate Muhammad Khatami touched a national nerve with his calls for change. Sporting elegant chocolate-colored robes and a neatly trimmed beard and promising to promote freedom of speech and rule of law, Khatami was the anti-mullah's mullah. Women in particular supported him, and he was overwhelmingly elected. To meet women's high expectations, he appointed Ebtekar as his vice president for the environment.

"My becoming vice president in Iran," Ebtekar tells me proudly, "broke all sorts of barriers for women. When President Khatami made it known that he would like to appoint a woman to be his vice president, he sent an emissary to Qom to convince the *ulama* that there are no religious constraints to this. He warned them that women's expectations were high and had to be met or else there would be a big backlash. Khatami told the clerics that there could be two outcomes. Either a woman as vice president would fail and put an end to the women's agenda, or she would be successful and there would be no problem." Ebtekar leans back confidently in her chair, the expression on her face leaving no doubt that she views her tenure as vice president as a great success.

"My appointment also paved the way for Megawati to become president of Indonesia, the largest Muslim country in the world," she declares. She can see from the puzzled look on my face that I am not following this leap, so she explains. "Megawati's party wanted to nominate her as a vice presidential candidate, but the clerics protested, saying Islam did not allow it. The party pointed to the fact that the clerics in Iran had allowed me to become vice president, and the *ulama* in Indonesia dropped their objections. When [then President] Wahid was forced from office in 2001, Megawati became leader with little protest from the *ulama*." Ebtekar says that Megawati relayed this anecdote to her at an international conference some years later.

As an Islamic power mom, Ebtekar seems to be a walking example of Islamic feminism, but she herself rejects the label. "I don't agree with the term," she insists, as we continue talking in her office. Outside, the sky has turned black and an impressive thunderstorm lashes the windows. "Feminism is a Western phenomenon, and inside Iran, this is not a good term. I prefer to call it an 'Islamic campaign for women's advancement.' Men and women are equal before God, but this is very different than the egalitarian approach in the West. In Iran, family is central. We don't want to emphasize the individual too much because that will rip apart the family." I brace myself for another lecture about Iranian family values, but Ebtekar answers her ringing cell phone and I am spared.

"Islam must face modern challenges and the requirements of a new generation," she continues, picking up the conversation. "In order to apply Islamic principles to modern times, we need *ijtihad*. Conservatives feel that if we emphasize the dynamic qualities of our religion, we will lose our principles. They don't agree that we need to adjust ourselves to the reality of highly educated women entering the workforce. They think they can ignore reality. We reformists believe that we need to apply the dynamic quality of Islam to recognize the reality of social change."

"There is no doubt we have gone backwards [under Ahmadinejad]," Ebtekar concludes. "But the reform movement has forced so many changes and created so much awareness in the hearts and minds of people that we cannot go backwards. In the long term, reform is the only viable political alternative. We will find a way to stick to our reformist principles and adhere to our religion."

As a politician, Massoumeh Ebtekar adopts the language of reform, but her reluctance to fight for equality—legal equality—for women for so many years discredited her in the eyes of many Iranian women activists who have suffered so much to make legal change happen. To remain in good standing with the regime, Ebtekar when I met her seemed stuck in some version of Islamic feminism "1.0"—heavy on the Islamism, light on the feminism, whereas many in the country's women's movement have moved on to versions "2.0" and beyond—a commitment to principles of equality tactically supported by Islamic arguments. For her refusal to cross the regime's red lines, Ebtekar is often disparaged as a government toady. But others in the women's movement are willing to cut her some slack. "Ebtekar is not an activist," one dedicated reformer explains to me. "She is not brave. But she is a politician who works under the table. For change to happen, we need some of those too." With her decision to stand by reformist candidate Mousavi so publicly, however, Ebtekar took on greater political risks. On her blog, she insists that the 2009 presidential election results were fraudulent and that the actions of the regime in response to the people's protest were "illegal." In the turmoil of 2009, she—like many former revolutionaries—picked sides and came down openly on the side of women's rights, democracy, and freedom in Iran while staying true to her Islamic values.

Islamic Jujitsu

While women like Monir Amadi Qomi and Massoumeh Ebtekar were beginning to dabble in the tenets of Islamic feminism, others began applying Islamic discourse to push open doors for women in very practical ways. One of the most high-profile early initiatives was that of Faezeh Hashemi, the younger daughter of then President Ali Akbar Hashemi Rafsanjani. In the early 1990s, Faezeh Hashemi emerged as an outspoken advocate for women's sports. An athlete herself, stylish and even glamorous (she was known to prefer Chanel under her chador) yet careful to respect "Islamic values," Faezeh appealed to both conservative and more progressive women who looked to her as a role model.

At the time, women in sports were a deeply controversial topic in Iran. Conservatives were driven crazy by the very notion of women

WALLED LAKE CITY LIBRARY
WALLED LAKE, MICHIGAN

breaking a sweat, not to mention the association of women and sports with the Shah's regime. Physical education for girls was very much part of the Shah's modernization plans, and the training of female athletes to compete internationally was part of his nationalist agenda.

Initially after the revolution, women in Iran were banned from all sports on the grounds that men might see them exercising. Once hijab and gender segregation became mandatory in 1981, the mullahs begrudgingly allowed women to participate in sports again, as long as they were in separate facilities. A few women-only clubs emerged, but the pickings were slim.

When Faezeh Hashemi took up women's sports as her cause, it fit with her father's broader shift toward pragmatism for the country. He appointed her as head of the country's women's sports organization, and she used that position to push for more facilities for women—from swimming pools and tennis courts to driving ranges for golf. She even championed women's cycling despite the fact that traditionalists are particularly bothered by the idea of women riding bicycles. Battling conservatives, she established bike paths for women in Tehran's parks.

In 1993, Faezeh Hashemi oversaw the first all-women Islamic games in Tehran. Muslim women from twenty-four countries participated—including sprinters from Gabon and Ping-Pong players from Indonesia. The athletes had to wear hijab to conform with the regime's Islamic dress code, even though many of them did not wear the headscarf at home. All men—even coaches—were excluded from those events where the athletes could not be fully covered, like swimming and basketball. Faezeh Hashemi's advocacy of women's sports, however, and the popularity of the games, helped normalize fitness as an acceptable activity for women in Iran.

Walking through Tehran's many parks, it is common to see women jogging and exercising in public, albeit wearing a headscarf over their tracksuit. Girls exercise in their school yards as part of their daily school routine. Sports like paintball, tae kwon do, jujitsu, snowboarding, and race-car driving are especially popular among young Iranian women today. Saudi Arabia, in contrast, continues to deny girls any physical education in school. The only athletic outlets for Saudi women are a few exclusive private clubs that cater solely to women. In

Pakistan, radicals have resorted to violence to stop women from running in races—even when they are fully covered wearing *shalwar kameez* and segregated from the men.

In Iran, the mullahs long ago lost that fight. A woman's right at least to participate in sports (as long as she is covered) is now firmly grounded and accepted. Faezeh Hashemi and others successfully challenged the religious arguments that were used to exclude women from sports, highlighting stories from Muhammad's own life that recount him running (and losing) a race against his wife Aisha.[11]

Slowly, Iranian women are even becoming internationally competitive in sports where the dress restrictions do not unduly hinder them. Three Iranian women—one each in rowing, archery, and tae kwon do—qualified to compete in the Beijing Olympics in 2008, a direct result of Faezeh Hashemi's championing of the cause fifteen years earlier. Despite their huge popularity, the national women's basketball and volleyball teams have yet to compete outside of Iran because the dress code is too restrictive to be competitive, but it is probably only a matter of time.

Activists in Iran have since moved on to fight restrictions on women as spectators at sporting events. Iranian women (although, curiously, not foreign women) are banned from attending the country's wildly popular soccer matches held in public stadiums. Women's groups have protested and even stormed the stadium gates, risking arrest and police beatings to make their broader point against gender segregation.

Gaining access to public sporting events is an issue that appeals to younger women in particular, and they have formed the Women's Access to Public Stadiums Campaign to push for policy changes. Bending to their pressure, conservative president Mahmoud Ahmadinejad announced in 2006 that women would now be allowed to attend the games on the grounds that their presence would be "morally uplifting" and make the men behave better. Several hard-line clerics overruled him, insisting that Islamic law prevents women from looking at the bodies of male strangers, although of course the women can watch the games on television. The inanity of these rules and restrictions just serves to further alienate average Iranians from the clergy, and makes the women more determined than ever.

Meanwhile, one of the most popular sports figures in Iran today is Laleh Seddigh, a glamorous brunette race-car driver who has won national championships against an all-male field of contenders. In between studying for a Ph.D. in sports management, she also competes in international events such as a rally race in Morocco and the Middle East Formula 3 Series Championship in Bahrain. Laleh, a single woman in her early thirties, has her own website, a MySpace page, and, purportedly, a Hollywood film about her life in the making.

After making a name for herself on the subject of women's sports, Faezeh Hashemi moved on to politics, running a highly visible, well-organized campaign for parliament in 1996. Largely based on her appeal to women and students (she was endorsed by *Zanan*, a popular women's magazine, and appeared on its cover), she was elected to the fifth Majlis with the second highest number of votes in Tehran. (Rumor has it that in fact she got the highest number of votes, but to save face, the mullahs manipulated the results to put a conservative cleric ahead of her.)

Although Faezeh Hashemi's election raised expectations among women reformers, her track record in parliament was less than impressive. High-energy and outspoken, she remained an important symbol for women, but was either unwilling, or unable, to exert leadership on women's issues. She did, however, stand up against two regressive bills proposed by the ironically named Women's Commission. One sought to impose Taliban-like gender segregation in hospitals, meaning female patients could only be seen by a female doctor. In rural areas with few female healthcare workers, this could have been catastrophic for many women. The other bill tried to curtail the vibrant debate on women's rights taking place in the press by banning feature stories on women. Only Faezeh Hashemi and one other woman in parliament voted against the legislation. All the other female parliamentarians meekly signed the bills.[12]

Faezeh's political career stalled when it became clear to her support base that she was unwilling to break with the conservative establishment that her powerful father represented. In the 2000 election, with many people hungering for deeper changes, she declined to align herself fully with the reform movement. She lost key support from women and students and was unexpectedly voted out of office. In recent years, Faezeh has become more outspoken on the need for reform, and remains a vocal supporter of women's rights. She publicly campaigned for reformist candidate Mousavi and led protests against the 2009 election results. After speaking passionately at an election protest, she was briefly detained by the authorities. That the government dared to arrest Ayatollah Rafsanjani's daughter reflects how deep the cracks in the regime have become.

Women's Journals: The Voice of Islamic Feminism

Women's journals in Iran look much like a Persian version of women's magazines found on newsstands around the world: recipes for favorite meals, advice on child rearing, tips for sewing the perfect wedding outfit, good housekeeping suggestions. But alongside how-to and advice columns, Iranian women's magazines have been promoting their own quiet revolution. Over the past twenty years, they have become a hotbed of Islamic feminism—disseminating international scholarship, giving voice to the ideas of progressive religious authorities, challenging government restrictions in the name of Islam, and confronting— at times even mocking—social mores. For this they stand accused of undermining national security and the government regularly shuts them down.

At first, the Islamic regime welcomed the genre and helped establish some of the first women's journals as a way of trumpeting Islamic family values. One of the earliest, *Payam-i-Hajar* (Message of Hajar), started in 1980. Its articles focused on the good Muslim woman's family obligations and justified the Islamic Republic's regressive family laws. The magazine's editor was Azam Taleghani, daughter of the late Ayatollah Taleghani, who, for a time, rivaled Khomeini in popularity. Azam herself was active in the Islamic cause during the 1970s, and for that spent time in the Shah's prisons. After the revolution, trading on her famous family name, she was one of three women elected to the first parliament, where she strongly endorsed the Islamist agenda.

Azam Taleghani soon began to resent the regime's restrictive attitudes toward women, its enforced gender segregation, and its institutionalization of women's inequality. During the Iran-Iraq War, she started a volunteer organization called the Women's Society of Islamic Revolution to teach war widows and those with husbands fighting at the front some basic economic skills to be able to support their families. Her work with the destitute led her to quip derisively that "poverty and polygamy are the only things that poor women have obtained from the revolution." She came to believe that women's role in the revolution and their paid and unpaid work during the war qualified them for a greater role in society and a greater political role in the regime.

By the 1990s, Azam Taleghani emerged as one of Iran's most active Islamic feminists, challenging narrow religious interpretations that hindered women's roles. She was a powerful voice for Islamic feminism at the UN's 1995 Beijing conference. Her magazine *Payam-i-Hajar* also changed its tone and began to promote Quranic reinterpretations to expand women's rights—a first for women's magazines in Iran. In particular, the magazine launched religious arguments against polygamy, in favor of women's right to enter the mosque to pray, and for equal rights to inheritance. It also pushed the notion of women's political leadership. Based on women's active roles in the early history of Islam, *Payam-i-Hajar* maintained that they should be allowed to assume all political leadership positions in the Islamic Republic.

Practicing what she preached, Azam Taleghani boldly declared herself a candidate for president in the 1997 election. This was an act of protest, considering that Article 115 of the constitution is broadly interpreted as excluding women from holding that position. But Taleghani exploited the ambiguity of the wording in the constitution. In the law, women's exclusion hinges on the word *rejal*, which means "statesman" in Persian. The word is borrowed from Arabic, where it clearly denotes a male. But in Persian the word is gender neutral, and Iranian experts have long been tied up on its exact meaning.

Taleghani's candidacy was an embarrassment for the conservative regime. Her famous family name and her conservative Islamic credentials gave her quest a level of legitimacy that few other women could have achieved at that time. She was careful to maintain those Islamic credentials by staying within important boundaries. She did not challenge the prevailing Islamic framework, and she never appeared in public without being fully covered by her long black chador, with only her oversized eyeglasses providing just a glimpse of her face.

Tenaciously, Taleghani made the rounds of Qom's seminaries, taking her appeal to the highest religious authorities. Arguing theology with theology, she eventually got several clerics to go on record supporting her position that a woman could indeed be president of Iran. The logic was laid out in detail in *Payam-i-Hajar*. Eight other women joined her quest by declaring themselves candidates as well. In the end, the powerful Guardian Council rejected them all, but it has not been able to squash the idea of women as national leaders. In the 2001 presidential election, forty-seven women registered as candidates to continue pushing the point. In the 2005 elections, nearly one hundred women ran for president. In 2009, forty-two women declared themselves as candidates. In a small sign of progress, the Guardian Council this time conceded that there is in fact no restriction on women standing for president. However, it still rejected all the women candidates.

As *Payam-i-Hajar* began flexing its intellectual muscles, other women's magazines followed suit. In the early 1990s, Massoumeh Ebtekar edited the journal *Farzaneh* (Wise). Featuring the writings of well-known Islamist women, the magazine offered up a predictable government line: It criticized Western feminism and lauded the gains that women had made under the Islamic Republic. It also railed against the Western stereotype of Iranian women as being helpless creatures. At the same time, the journal began to press some of the ideas of Islamic feminism, making distinctions between Islam and patriarchal traditions and questioning the authenticity of various religious rulings used to oppress women. *Farzaneh* helped legitimize the genre of women's magazine, although its tentative tone was soon eclipsed by other, more provocative women's journals.

The standard-bearer of Islamic feminist thinking soon became the magazine *Zanan* (Women) edited by the indomitable journalist Shahla Sherkat. It also became the voice of the reform movement. Like others who came to Islamic feminism from the right, Sherkat was a devout supporter of the revolution who found herself increasingly at odds with the conservative regime. Her first brush with trouble came in 1987 when she landed in court for writing an article about a young girl at a beach on the Caspian Sea who was beaten by the police for not covering her hair appropriately. Although the charges against Sherkat were later dropped, the experience led her to question the sanctity of the regime's rules regarding women.

Shahla Sherkat went to work for a conservative government weekly paper that focused on women's issues, where she rose to become managing editor. But in 1991, she was dismissed from her position because the more modernist views she wanted to promote were beginning to clash with the rigid party line. The following year, she launched her own magazine, *Zanan*. She shared office space with other leading reformers, including the political philosopher Abdolkarim Soroush, who would become Iran's most famous dissident intellectual. Significantly, *Zanan* was privately funded, making it the first independent magazine to focus on women's issues.

In her inaugural issue, Shahla announced that *Zanan* would examine Islamic jurisprudence and how it relates to women. In particular, the magazine would explore modernist interpretations of Islam and their impact on family law, women's political and social participation, and criminal punishments. The early years of *Zanan* were touch and go. Vigilante groups ransacked its offices. Making payroll every week was a challenge. Shahla was frequently summoned to the Iran Press Court, where she had to defend some of the magazine's more outspoken articles. But the publication survived financially, and for an independent, it even thrived. Its staff grew to thirty.

Before long, *Zanan* was not only a leading voice on gender issues in Iran, but was at the forefront of international efforts to reread the Quran in a more egalitarian light. The magazine published the work of many international scholars like Fatima Mernissi, Leila Ahmed, and Ziba Mir-Hosseini. Its writings were soon a central part of the expanding Islamic feminist conversation around the world. It even managed to get clerics within Iran to consult for the magazine and publish articles taking progressive positions on issues of Islamic jurisprudence relating to women.

The magazine also became an important bridge to more secular female reformers who had come to believe that if they wanted to see change in Iran, they would have to achieve those changes within an Islamic framework. One of *Zanan*'s earliest and most prolific contributors was Mehrangiz Kar, a lawyer who advocated for the dismantling of legal barriers to women. Although Kar is avowedly secular, she sometimes referenced Islamic arguments to bolster her positions. The secular human rights lawyer Shirin Ebadi, a close friend of Shahla Sherkat's, was also a frequent contributor to *Zanan*. Ebadi had come to realize that to win cases, she had to draw on principles and precedents in Islamic law.[13]

Zanan became increasingly involved in the evolving political debates within Iran. The magazine is credited with helping to elect Khatami in 1997. It certainly played a role in mobilizing women to vote and promoted Khatami by publishing an in-depth interview with him and putting him on the cover of the magazine when he was still considered a dark-horse candidate. Khatami's election undoubtedly encouraged *Zanan* to push the boundaries of its reformist agenda much further.

The reform movement in Iran exposed deep fault lines within society. Intellectuals and even rival religious leaders began to question openly the very notion of religious absolutism on which the Islamic Republic was founded. Women and student groups became increasingly vocal in their demands for reform. Not content with simply a more relaxed social environment, they wanted to see changes to the country's legal system, which still defined women as minors, imposed harsh punishments, and left women vulnerable to highly disadvantageous family laws. Demands from the women's movement for more progressive interpretations of Islam began to blur with calls for democracy and human rights.

Benefiting from the more open media environment under Khatami, *Zanan* began mixing social and political commentary along with its practical health and business advice to readers. It published in-depth articles on sensitive subjects like domestic abuse, the spread of HIV and prostitution, the failure of the legal system to protect women, and divorce and child-custody rights for women. Its provocative covers garnered international attention. *Zanan* not only increased awareness of women's issues among its readers, but it also raised expectations for change. It was highly critical of the conservative women in parliament who continued to side with traditionalists and vote for legislation designed to restrict women. It encouraged its readers to consider that women's interests are not necessarily served simply by electing women to parliament. Rather, they have to elect women willing to push for reform.

As Shahla Sherkat and her fellow reformers learned, however, this era of Khatami-inspired openness was uneven at best and proved to be relatively short-lived. Conservatives were not about to stand back and lose control. The Revolutionary Guards and paramilitary Basij used brute force to suppress the growing street demonstrations. The all-powerful Guardian Council used its veto power to block reform efforts within parliament. In the run-up to the 2004 elections, the Guardian Council issued a hard blow to the reform movement by rejecting nearly 2,500 reformist candidates. With almost all reformist candidates banned from reelection, the major reform parties called for a boycott of the parliamentary elections. Conservatives easily won back control.

Disillusioned and threatened by the regime, some of the leading reformers sought refuge overseas. The following year, Mahmoud Ahmadinejad, running on a populist platform and emphasizing pocket-book issues, beat out former President Rafsanjani to become president. To validate his hard-line credentials, Ahmadinejad cracked down on women's dress and tightened up on gender segregation. A joke began to circulate in Tehran that when Ahmadinejad combs his hair in the mirror, he takes care to separate the male lice to one side, females to the other.

The faltering of the reform movement signaled the beginning of the end for *Zanan*. Although the magazine survived for three years under the conservative backlash of Ahmadinejad, its luck ran out in 2008. The government shut down *Zanan*, claiming that the magazine was a "threat to the psychological security of the society" because it showed Iranian women in a "black light."[14] *Zanan* had continued to promote progressive interpretations of Islam, and in one of its last publications, argued that laws codifying unequal treatment of women in Islamic countries lacked religious justification and could be changed. Although *Zanan* has been silenced, the debates over women's role in Islam that it amplified continue unabated. The regime's harsh response is a sign of how threatened it is by the movement's potential for countercultural change.

The Women's Mufti

Ninety miles south of Tehran, past the enormous cemetery of Beheshteh Zahra and the golden mausoleum of Ayatollah Khomeini, is the holy city of Qom. Dusty and flat, the city is a jumble of mosques and seminaries, its skyline dotted with minarets and domes. Long a center of Shia scholarship and home to Iran's clergy, Qom is the beating heart of the Islamic Republic. Its scholars conjured up the theological foundations of the 1979 revolution. Today, its religious schools continue to train the country's next generation of spiritual as well as political leaders.

The atmosphere of the city is solemn and serious, a big change from bustling Tehran. Even the air feels thick and somewhat restricting. The high, forbidding walls protecting the shrine of the sister of the eighth Shia imam reflect the dour character of the city. Women all wear the black chador instead of the fashionable bright scarves seen on Tehran's streets. Men wearing clerical robes and turbans whiz by on their motorbikes. Some wear black turbans, signifying their status as a *sayyid*, or descendant of Muhammad.

Qom seems an unlikely place to find an outspoken defender of women's rights. And yet, sitting among his books in his seminary, Ayatollah Saanei easily fits that bill. Saanei openly challenges many of the regime's restrictions on women. (In the aftermath of the contested 2009 election, he has also challenged the very legitimacy of the regime itself.) Saanei believes that women should be allowed to hold any job, including that of a judge (from which women have been barred since the revolution), president, or even supreme religious leader. He argues that Iran's restrictive family laws need to be revised. He says that a woman's testimony should be valued the same as a man's. (Despite the efforts of countless lawyers and activists, the regime still values it at half.) He has ruled that women can lead prayers while men pray behind them, and that they have the right to abortion on grounds of "compassion." He has also issued a fatwa condemning discrimination based on gender.

"How can we say Islam is a religion of justice if its laws consider women and non-Muslims unequal to Muslim men?" he demands.[15]

Ayatollah Saanei is no run-of-the-mill religious leader. One of ten clerics in Iran to be granted the title of grand ayatollah, the highest religious authority in Shiism, Saanei is revered by his many followers. He was a protégé of Ayatollah Khomeini, who referred to Saanei as a son. He prominently displays framed photos of Khomeini along with the late leader's words of praise for his former student on the walls of his reception room at his seminary. During the early years of Iran's revolution, Saanei served as a prosecutor for the state and as a member of the all-powerful Council of Guardians. But by the mid-1980s, having looked into the abyss of religious absolutism, he withdrew from government, his views taking a decidedly more moderate direction than those of Iran's hard-line leadership. Over the past two decades, the aging cleric, with his signature white turban and wispy beard, has held forth in Qom, issuing a stream of increasingly liberal rulings on women's rights within Islam, earning the devotion of reformers and the distinction of being referred to as the "women's mufti."[16]

Despite the progressive tone of his rhetoric, Ayatollah Saanei is still very much a product of his background and position. Central to all of his arguments is first and foremost a strict adherence to the Islamic texts themselves. Although he proclaims frequently that men and women are equal, he holds two exceptions, divorce (only men can initiate divorce) and inheritance (men are entitled to double the share of women), because on these points he says the Quran is clear. "In all other rights they are equal."[17] He also supports mandatory veiling for women and segregation of the sexes. There is no mistaking Saanei for a liberal. Nevertheless, as a leading religious figure in Iran, his arguments for women's equality carry weight among Shia that few others can match. He readily admits that his views are still in the minority in Qom, but believes that over time reforms will trend his way. "My thoughts will find their place in today's world," he insists.[18] Saanei's outspoken defense of the reformists in the 2009 election, and his public condemnations of the regime's harsh crackdown on the protesters, have caused his currency to soar, building support for his Islamic counter-narrative.

In Qom, Grand Ayatollah Saanei is the most senior "women's mufti," but he is certainly not the only one. Ayatollah Muhammad Kazem Mousavi Bojnourdi, recognizable in his *sayyid*'s black turban, wire-rimmed glasses, and thick, salt-and-pepper beard, has been even more "radical" in his reading of the texts in favor of women. He argues for example that veiling should not be compulsory, saying, "Hijab is ineffective when observed out of pressure and intimidation. It is only valuable when one believes in the concept."[19] As the director of law at the Imam Khomeini Research Institute in Tehran, Ayatollah Bojnourdi advocates for human rights in an Islamic framework, and has represented his country at various high-level international conferences and UN delegations. His mantra is that Muslims must keep pace with the times to avoid reaching a dead end, a view in stark contrast with the ruling clerics' literalist readings of the Quran.

Ayatollah Bojnourdi was a close adviser to Iran's reformist President Khatami, particularly on women's issues. Some have suggested it was Ayatollah Bojnourdi who encouraged President Khatami to allow women to take leadership positions in his cabinet, insisting that women should be allowed to hold high positions of office given the equality of men and women in Islam. Like Ayatollah Saanei, Ayatollah Bojnourdi has provided important theological and intellectual support to reformers and has been a vocal supporter of Mousavi and his reformist campaign.

Other religious scholars have been even more confrontational with the regime on issues of democracy and women's rights. The reformist cleric Mohsen Kadivar is one of the strongest proponents in the Islamic world on the need for *ijtihad*. He argues that sharia in particular must be revised to fit the modern age, since much of sharia law is "not among the firm issues of the Quran." When it comes to women, Kadivar believes that they should have political and financial rights equal to men, that women can become presidents, governors, and judges if people elect them, and that they should enjoy equal rights in marriage, divorce, and custody.[20]

Kadivar speaks with some authority. He spent seventeen years studying Islamic law and philosophy in a seminary in Qom. In the late 1990s, Kadivar began teaching philosophy at a university in Tehran, packing his lectures with young people eager to hear his reformist message. His theological critiques of religious absolutism helped energize the reform movement under Khatami. Kadivar has been in and out of jail for his views, and is currently teaching in the United States, but his ideas still resonate strongly with those seeking change within Iran. Kadivar, too, has denounced the regime's crackdown on the election protesters and refers to the government of Ahmadinejad as an "Iranian Taliban."

Perhaps Iran's most famous intellectual dissident today is Abdolkarim Soroush. His deep religious values prompted him initially to support the Islamic Revolution. He actually helped close down the universities in the early years to rewrite their curricula along "Islamic" lines. However, like so many of his peers, Soroush began to see the dark side of the regime and became a vocal dissident—first by starting an intellectual newspaper in Iran (alongside Shahla Sherkat's *Zanan*) that criticized the regime, and later through his writings as an exile. While his support for women's rights has not been as direct as many activists would like, he has always included women's rights in his broader appeal for a true Islamic democracy in Iran. Many Islamic feminists, including Shahla Sherkat and Ziba Mir-Hosseini, have found inspiration in Soroush's writings.

Clearly, there is a broad spectrum of views represented by Grand Ayatollah Saanei on the one hand and Soroush on the other, but together they represent an intellectual challenge to Iran's conservative mullahs. They provide an alternative reading of the texts, which allows Iranians to find compatibility between Islam and the modern world in which they actually live, even on the thorny issue of women's rights.

Although Soroush and Kadivar live in exile, their ideas remain hugely popular and influential, especially among students and women. In the aftermath of the contested presidential elections in 2009, reformers in Iran have looked to them for intellectual guidance more than ever. Their interviews and statements were widely circulated on Facebook, YouTube, and Twitter within Iran. With 60 percent of the country under the age of thirty, this is precisely why the regime finds them so threatening. They represent a legitimate Islamic alternative to the current repressive system. They represent a bridge between what exists now, and the Islamic democracy that Iranians have been searching for since the revolution.

Pushing the Limits

Mahboubeh Abbasgholizadeh is a revolutionary daughter who dares to cross the red lines. She has paid for it by being in and out of Iran's notorious Evin Prison. Inspired and mobilized by Khomeini, she was once a passionate revolutionary; then she became a soul-searching, self-described Islamic feminist, trying to reconcile the contradictions of her life under the Islamic Republic with her search for a tolerant, pluralistic Islam; then a Muslim feminist, rejecting the label Islamic as she began to question the Islamic regime itself. Now she calls herself simply a feminist, but one who understands the role that Islamic feminism plays in helping other conservative Iranian women (and men) make similar transitions.

"When I was a teenager," she admits to me, "I used to dream about Imam Khomeini. In my dreams, he called to me. He told me to join the revolution. Other girls my age dreamed about boyfriends, but I dreamed of the Imam." Mahboubeh settles back in her chair and sips her coffee. It is the winter of 2009 and we are chatting at a conference we are both attending outside of Iran. Because Mahboubeh has been arrested several times by the Islamic regime for her activism, it is difficult for her to meet with foreigners, especially Americans. A chance meeting outside the country is the only place we can speak.

A heavyset woman in her early fifties, Mahboubeh looks much younger than her years. Indeed, her round face and bob haircut make her look almost boyish. She is wearing a pink scooped-neck blouse over jeans. As she explains, she no longer wears hijab when she is out of the country. One of the charges brought against her by her interrogators the last time she was arrested was that she does not wear hijab when overseas. "If that's what they think already, then I see no reason to keep up the pretense. I stopped believing years ago that women must wear hijab to be good Muslims."

Mahboubeh married when she was nineteen—a "revolutionary marriage" as she describes it. Both she and her husband were devotees of Shariati and Khomeini and the ideals of the revolution. But in the early years of the revolution, when the full weight of the mullah's patriarchy came down on her and her friends, they began to struggle for a better understanding of Islam's meaning for women. She spent much of her time in the 1980s reading the Quran and seeking answers to tough questions: Are women second-class citizens within Islam? What are women's real duties within Islam? She started to explore these issues as coeditor of the journal *Farzaneh*, working closely with Massoumeh Ebtekar. In those years she called herself an Islamic feminist.

In 1993, Mahboubeh got divorced. The process, she says, was life-altering. "I touched it—the discrimination in the system," she says matter-of-factly. The 1995 Beijing conference was another turning point for her. She traveled to the conference as the country's NGO coordinator, a role that exposed her to a wide range of people and ideas. "Beijing really helped me to make the transition from Islamic feminism to just plain feminism." After she returned from Beijing, she explained to her coeditor, Massoumeh Ebtekar, how her views had changed. She could no longer stick within party lines writing for *Farzeneh*. "Ebtekar was very tolerant with me," she recalls. "She told me to keep writing, that I could write about my new (more progressive) views in *Farzaneh*, but I declined. I knew that I needed to find a new group, a new network." She began gravitating toward more secular groups.

In 2002, Mahboubeh founded an NGO training center to help civil society groups develop the skills and resources they need to be effective. Two years later she was arrested for the first time upon her return from an international conference. She was accused of sending out "propaganda against the state" and her training center was shut down. Undeterred, she began to throw herself wholeheartedly into efforts to overturn the regime's discriminatory gender laws. In 2006, she became very active in the Campaign to Stop Stoning Forever. Since the start of the campaign, several people have had their stoning convictions overturned, and others have been granted stays of execution. As important, the campaign has opened public discussion in Iran about the validity of stoning as a punishment.

At the same time, Mahboubeh became one of the founding members of the Meydaan Women's Group, an inclusive network of women activists in Iran dedicated to exposing the dangers of rising "neo-fundamentalism." The Meydaan network has its own website providing news on various women activists and helps coordinate various reform campaigns. The biggest women's initiative in Iran in recent years has been the One Million Signatures Campaign, an effort to bring men and women together to push for women's rights from the ground up.

In 2005, the women's journal *Zanan* ran an interview with the London-based scholar Ziba Mir-Hosseini, who discussed how women in Morocco had launched a broad-based signature campaign to petition the government to change the country's discriminatory family laws. Mir-Hosseini argued that the signature campaign was an important driver behind the progressive changes the government eventually made to the Moroccan family code (*mudawana*) in 2004. The success of the Moroccan women inspired a group of reformers in Iran to pursue a similar strategy.

Making their appeal as broad as possible, the women behind the One Million Signatures Campaign in Iran base their arguments for women's rights on both international and Islamic law. They have earned the support of various religious leaders in the country who express a more egalitarian interpretation of women's rights in Islam. The campaign focuses on raising awareness and building grassroots support to address women's legal inequalities in Iran. They take a face-to-face approach, listening to women's concerns and explaining why all Iranians should care about the inequality of the laws. Slowly, the campaign is spreading throughout the country with a network of activists in more than thirty Iranian cities and half the country's provinces. The government fears this peaceful movement and has sent thugs to beat up signature collectors. It has arrested more than fifty organizers, but still the campaign continues to gain traction.

In the summer of 2008, conservatives in the government of President Ahmadinejad tried to push through a bill perversely named the Family Protection Act, which would have made divorce laws even more favorable for men, and polygamy and temporary marriage easier. The leaders of the One Million Signatures Campaign, along with other women activists, brought together a diverse coalition to oppose the bill. Women within the Meydaan network made up 300,000 postcards that they handed out to people on the streets all over the country explaining the regressive nature of the laws. They mailed the postcards to every member of the Majlis. High-profile personalities like Laleh Seddigh, the race-car driver, and Nobel Prize winner Shirin Ebadi protested outside the gates of parliament.

The coalition, one of the broadest since the revolution, also included moderate politicians and clerics. Ayatollah Saanei was an important voice behind the women. On his website, he wrote that a second marriage without the permission of the first wife is "*haram*, a sin, a religious offence . . . contrary to the concept of justice prescribed by the Quran . . . I pray that such a decision that is oppressive to women will not be made into law . . . God forbid that the Majlis should add another problem to the existing problems of women."[21] The worst provisions of the bill were deleted.

The Meydaan network and the One Million Signatures Campaign insist that their goal is not to overturn the regime, but rather to change the country's discriminatory laws. The government, however, views these women's organizations with tremendous suspicion since it is convinced that the women activists are the vanguard of some type of "velvet revolution." Mahboubeh Abbasgholizadeh and others pay the price with prison time. In July 2009, Shadi Sadr, Mahboubeh's lawyer and close friend and a member of Meydaan, was violently pulled off the street in downtown Tehran in the middle of the day and shoved into the back of a car. She was held for nearly two weeks then released. This type of violent intimidation is a clear warning to other women activists that they are in the government's crosshairs.

Granddaughters of the Revolution

The cafeteria at the Foreign Ministry's School of International Relations is a sea of young women in black. Everyone is wearing a *maghneh* over a long matching coat. This is the official uniform for women working in government jobs. As I move through the food line, the short, heavyset cook behind the counter heaps *zereshk polo*—a rice and chicken dish—onto my plate.

I sit down at a long table with my three "minders." They are teachers at the School of International Relations, where they help train the country's diplomats. (While I was there, the school was full of Venezuelans. No one could explain to me what exactly they were studying.)

My minders have been assigned by the ministry to take turns accompanying me on all my meetings in Tehran. A dean of the school sponsored my trip to Iran. Since he helped me get a visa—no easy task given the diplomatic freeze between Iran and the United States at the time—he is now responsible for me in the country. When I first arrived, he warned me, for his sake and for mine, not to take any risks and not to have any meetings except those cleared by the ministry. Having no desire to see the inside of an Iranian prison, I abide by the rules.

At first, my minders were uncomfortable with me, clearly reluctant to engage in conversation. In fact, one of them later told me that she had begged her director not to be assigned to escort me. "I just don't want to get involved in politics," she had told him, to no avail. However, after days spent navigating the gridlock of Tehran together in the backseat of an old Paykan, the Iranian-built cars ubiquitous on Tehran's streets, the barriers broke down. Eventually, each of my minders asked me tons of questions about my life and about America, and shared intimate details of their own lives.

At lunch this day, the conversation among the women turns, as it so often does, to men. "I am never getting married," insists Maryam. "Why would I? All men treat their wives badly in Iran. They say nice things to you at first, but they don't really respect you. They only want one thing and once they get it, their true nature comes out." So much for love in the Islamic Republic I think to myself, quietly eating my *zereshk polo* while they talk.

Soheila pipes in that the real problem is the lack of eligible men for them. "I want to marry someone who is at least as well educated as I am, but few of the men I know have college degrees, let alone graduate degrees. And they don't speak good English." The women grimace in unison.

The conversation has hit upon a growing worry for the mullahs— the widening gender gap in Iranian higher education. Women are zooming past men. Today, more than 60 percent of the country's college graduates are women. All of my minders have master's degrees and one is working on her Ph.D. Not one of their brothers, in contrast, completed college. One brother is working for the family business. Another left school for a job in Dubai. Two other brothers are not working at all. Much to their sister's dismay, they sit at home killing time on their Sony PlayStations and surfing the Internet. The government has floated the idea of imposing quotas for women in higher education to keep their numbers down, but resistance from women's groups forces them to shelve the idea.

"I will only get married if my husband agrees to let me finish my Ph.D. and have a career," announces Nahid. "I want to be the Islamic Republic's first female ambassador. I would prefer to remain single and have a good career if he won't agree to this. I will insist that this goes in my marriage contract." The other women nod approvingly.

Interestingly, I find out later that Nahid is divorced and working as a single mother. Divorce rates in Iran are much lower than in Western countries (roughly a quarter of marriages end in divorce in Iran, compared with more than half of marriages in many Western countries), but divorce is on the rise. Nahid confides to me that she secured her divorce against her husband's wishes. When I express surprise, knowing how difficult it is for women to initiate divorce in Iran and aware of the intense social stigma still associated with it, she explains that her ex-husband has many problems. "I was able to argue to the court that he was unfit. This way, I got full custody of our child." Normally in Iran, to get a divorce a woman must show that her husband has neglected her financially or physically, or is a drug addict or abusive. Even then it is still difficult. Nahid just shrugs. "He still calls me, begging me to come back, but I won't," she says firmly.

Nahid, Maryam, and Soheila are in their twenties, born long after the passionate fervor of the early revolutionary years had cooled. Iran under the mullahs is the only life they have known. Daughters of traditional families, they are well educated and ambitious, and consider themselves devout. They are also the beneficiaries of the academic, professional, and social gains that women in Iran have made over the past thirty years. They assume they will get graduate degrees. They aspire to the top levels of government. They think nothing of traveling with friends within the country, and overseas for work. (The fact that they need their father's permission to leave the country is nothing more than paperwork for them.) They take their sports for granted. One is serious about her tae kwon do. Another likes to spend her free time doing target practice at an indoor firing range.

In their day-to-day lives, they face fewer of the heavy contradictions that confronted women in the early years of the revolution. I ask them how they feel about having to wear hijab, and at first they demur, insisting it is an important part of their identity. But then Soheila admits that while she chooses to wear hijab, she does not think it right that the government forces women to do so. The others nod in agreement.

Several times over the course of our conversations, they ask me about the Council on Foreign Relations, about my research. "What happens if you write something criticizing government policy? Doesn't the government punish your organization? Does it shut it down?" I explain, again and again, that my organization is independent of the government, that we receive no government money, and that the government cannot shut it down. But they seem to have difficulty fully understanding this concept. Finally, Maryam simply concludes, "You are very lucky for this."

A recurring theme among these young women, and others I spoke with in Iran, is their desire for greater personal freedoms. The country's strict social conventions, especially with regard to gender relations, weigh heavily on them. By way of example, Soheila regales me with a long story about her troubled love life. For three years in college, she secretly dated a fellow student. They would steal private moments together, meeting in the park or peeling off from a larger group during a hike in the mountains. He finally got up the courage to ask his family for permission to marry her, but his parents rejected her outright. Citing the fact that Soheila's mother does not wear the chador, only a headscarf, they determined that her family was not sufficiently religious. Soheila still seethes with indignation. "How dare they judge how religious I am or my family is based on what we wear! The chador is not mandated by Islam! We are just as religious as they are." The young suitor was quickly married off to another, more suitable girl, but he still pines for Soheila. He calls her on her cell phone, leaving plaintive messages. Now that she is dating someone new, an older man, she is considering changing her phone number. As if on cue, her cell phone rings while she is telling me this sad story. Her ring tone is Lionel Richie singing plaintively, "Hello! Is it me you're looking for?"

A few days later, sitting together in the back of a taxi, Soheila whips out her cell phone to show me photos of herself without her *maghneh*. "These are pictures I took just when I woke up, with no makeup on," she says somewhat apologetically. In the photo, she is lounging seductively on unmade sheets, her long auburn hair falling loosely over her bare shoulders. She looks like a young Sophia Loren. Another photo, this one a close-up, shows that indeed she is wearing makeup. In fact, she is remarkably coiffed for having "just awakened." As she is showing me the photos, she self-consciously pulls out more makeup and begins applying lipstick and blush in the back of the Paykan as we bump along in the traffic. "You must think it's strange that I am the religious one, yet I am the one wearing makeup, not you," she says to me, without a trace of irony. I suddenly feel as if I am in some strange Persian *Alice in Wonderland* where everything is upside down. "What makes you think you are more religious than I am?" I shoot back. She frowns, opens her mouth as if to say something, then clearly thinks better of it.

During our days together, Soheila, Maryam, and Nahid studiously avoid any conversation that could be construed as political, despite my attempts to draw them out on the subject. However, when I ask them who they admire in Iran, they all agree immediately that they look up to Shirin Ebadi, the country's courageous human rights lawyer. They like the fact that she speaks her mind, that she is known internationally, that she uses Islamic arguments to fight her cases.

Ebadi's appeal to these young daughters of the regime, who think of themselves as pious and rule-abiding, clearly confounds the mullahs. Ebadi is the country's conscience and she will not go away. No doubt the clerics would have locked her up long ago had it not been for her Nobel

Peace Prize and the international attention if gives her. (The mullahs like to think of themselves as better than the thugs in Myanmar.)

Nevertheless, the government of President Ahmadinejad stepped up its harassment of Ebadi. In the summer of 2008, after Ebadi agreed to defend seven Bahai leaders accused of "spying for Israel," the official news agency in Iran ran a series of articles attacking her, recycling the usual brickbat that she is a Zionist spy and claiming that she supports prostitution and sexual promiscuity. I can imagine Soheila rolling her eyes at the ridiculous charges. They may not be democracy activists, but one result of all their education is that they can think for themselves. In January 2009, thugs ransacked Ebadi's office in Tehran, and she and her staff were forced to flee to a secret location, fearing for their lives. During the disputed elections that summer, Ebadi was traveling overseas and was advised that it was too dangerous for her to return to Iran. At the time of this writing, she remains outside Iran, scolding the regime from afar. In return, the government has confiscated her Nobel money. Attacking Ebadi so publicly only further alienates the regime from young women like Soheila and her friends.

Before leaving Tehran, I was asked to stop by the bursar's office at the ministry where I was presented with a bill. Apparently, the authorities were charging *me* several hundred dollars for my minders—payable in cash only. Suddenly, I found myself uncharacteristically at a loss for words. I was not about to pay the government of Iran for keeping tabs on me, but on the other hand, I was hesitant to cause any trouble.

While I was struggling to come up with a response, Soheila took charge. "How dare you make these demands," she shouted, incensed. "She didn't ask for a minder, you stuck her with it!" Wagging her finger at the bursar, then scolding the other men who came in to see what the commotion was about, she dressed down everyone in the room in a Persian tirade. Eyes flashing, she picked up the bill and with great flourish, ripped it into tiny pieces and scattered them all over the bursar's desk. The men stood there agog for a few moments, then fell over themselves apologizing to me for any confusion. "They were mistaken," Soheila said flatly, and that was the end of that.

The Search for Islamic Democracy

As I am leaving the School of International Affairs, I bump into Dr. Mossaffa, a self-assured professor of human rights at the University of Tehran. She is on her way to a conference in Qom on human rights in Islam, and invites me to join her. The director at the Ministry of Foreign Affairs who is responsible for me wrings his hands. Very apologetically, he says no, I cannot go. Too sensitive. I settle for tea with Dr. Mossaffa instead. We sit chatting on a threadbare couch in the lounge.

"In Iran today," she explains to me, "you can't discuss the universality of human rights. In this environment, it is just not possible. You have to start with the similarities between Islam and human rights. The reality is that if you want to change laws for women in Iran, you must do so within an Islamic framework.

"We have made progress," she insists. "Ten years ago, the idea of a human rights conference in Qom was unthinkable. Today, when we have these discussions about the compatibility of Islam and human rights, the clerics all sit there nodding." As she talks, I keep mulling over the "Big Question." Will Iran ever be able to evolve toward the Islamic democracy that so many Iranians believed in and hoped for with the revolution? Is Islamic democracy achievable in Iran? Clearly, the country's constitution enshrining ultimate power in the hands of the supreme leader must be changed for that to happen.

The widespread protests following the 2009 presidential elections, involving millions of demonstrators, were only initially about the veracity of the election results. They quickly erupted into a broad-based pro-democracy movement. The regime may well be able to win the battle in the streets through sheer repression, but conservatives have lost the war for popular sentiment. By openly defying the Supreme Leader Khamenei and his paramilitary Basij forces, the reform movement has dealt a body blow to authoritarian Islam and its attendant rigid interpretations on women. However these events unfold, the regime has lost any pretense of moral authority. Every person marching in the streets, wearing a green bandanna, or shouting "God is great!" from their rooftops, is taking a stand for greater democracy, human rights, and women's rights.[22]

In the meantime, armed with education and a growing sense of empowerment, women in Iran will continue to challenge the restrictions imposed by the regime in a myriad of different ways. Some challenge the regime through their dress, wearing bright, tight clothes in defiance of the religious authorities. (Under Ahmadinejad, some twenty thousand women have been hauled in to the police for violating Islamic dress code. The government simply cannot stop them.)

Others have chosen the realm of sports or arts to express themselves and to push for greater equality. During my time in Tehran, I visited al-Zahra University, the women's university where Zahra Rahnavard became the first female chancellor. I was shocked by the graphic paintings on display in the art room. One sticks out in my mind: a naked woman with blood seeping out of her eyes and splattering on her bare breasts. When I expressed amazement to the director that such nudity is allowed, she explained that when it is by women, for women, anything goes. Film is another important outlet, with many popular Iranian films depicting strong female characters unapologetically calling themselves "feminists" on the screen. Indeed, many women activists are pouring themselves into filmmaking, documenting their struggles in the most accessible medium.

The success of the One Million Signatures Campaign and the Meydaan network in bringing traditional and secular women together gives the mullahs good reason to feel nervous about the women's movement. The fact that chador-clad grandmothers marched in the streets in support of Mousavi and threw rocks at the Basij militias shows how far disillusion with the regime has spread. Thanks in large part to Islamic feminism, women's activism in Iran is no longer the preserve of Westernized elites, but a countrywide grassroots force. No matter how many times the government tries to squash the women's groups, like dandelions in a garden, another one pops up somewhere else. By focusing on the gender equality demanded by Islamic justice, the women's movement in Iran is gradually changing minds. On so many levels, Iran's Islamic feminists are no longer arguing from a theoretical position, but are simply explaining and reflecting the reality of their lives.

CHAPTER 4

UNDER THE CRESCENT
MOON: PAKISTAN

*I don't believe that any true Muslim will make an attack
on me . . . because Islam forbids attacks on women.*

—BENAZIR BHUTTO, former prime minister of Pakistan, on her
return to Karachi, October 2007

Dressed in a deep purple *shalwar kameez*, her usual white headscarf draped loosely over her hair and a crimson-and-white *haar*, a traditional garland of flowers, around her neck, Benazir Bhutto stood at the podium and addressed thousands of her adoring fans. It was a Thursday afternoon in late December 2007 and Bhutto was speaking at a rally for her Pakistan People's Party (PPP) in Rawalpindi, the former British garrison town not far from Islamabad, the country's capital. After nine years of self-exile, Bhutto's every appearance was thronged by supporters.

On this afternoon, Bhutto delivered an impassioned speech pledging repeatedly to fight extremists in Pakistan and to improve the lives of the poor. Flanked by party loyalists, she whipped up the enthusiastic crowd, many of whom were waving her picture in the air along with the PPP's red, black, green, and white flags and banners that read "Welcome." After the speech, Bhutto made her way down to the street where hundreds of people rushed to try to get a glimpse of her—some reaching out to touch her—as she made her way to her bulletproof white Land Cruiser.

Bhutto's security guards whisked her into her car. They were rightfully concerned about various assassination attempts since her return to Pakistan a few months earlier. Her dramatic homecoming in Karachi in October had been marred by a suicide attack on her motorcade that killed 135 people and injured hundreds more, but miraculously spared Bhutto. She requested additional security from Pakistan's President Musharraf, but her requests had been denied. Driving away from the event in Rawalpindi, supporters again mobbed her vehicle. She stopped. Unwilling to disappoint her loyal fans, she appeared through the sunroof to continue waving to the people, one of her trademark campaign maneuvers. Suddenly, the sound of gunshots cracked the air and almost simultaneously, a suicide bomber detonated himself in the crowd, killing at least twenty bystanders. Bhutto slumped through the sunroof. She was rushed to the hospital but never regained consciousness. She was dead at the age of fifty-four. In tragic irony, she died just a few miles from where her father, Zulfikar Ali Bhutto, was hanged by General Zia-ul-Haq, who overthrew Bhutto's democratically elected government in a military coup in 1977.

In the fall of 2007, Benazir Bhutto returned to Pakistan vowing to take on Islamic extremism, restore democracy, and return stability to her troubled country. In numerous interviews, anticipating her martyrdom, she made clear that she was willing to lay down her life to "save Pakistan." Perhaps more than any other Pakistani politician at the time, she seemed to understand the existential crisis facing her country: how the jihadi monster created and sustained by Pakistan's intelligence service to advance its interests in India and Afghanistan could no longer be contained; how poverty was fueling extremism; how radical Islam was beginning to overwhelm the country's tradition of moderate Islam.

Benazir Bhutto's own life and tragic death epitomized the very contradictions at the heart of Pakistan. She was a scion of the Bhutto political machine, a third-generation left-leaning politician. Despite her populist views, she herself had been raised in feudal luxury. The Bhutto family, one of the largest landowners in Sindh, is known for its huge wealth and Western tastes. As a child, Benazir was taught by an English governess (English was her first language), attended convent schools (not unusual among upper-crust Pakistanis who seek the best education for their children), and graduated from Harvard and Oxford. She was groomed to be the consummate politician that she was. On the several occasions I met her in Washington and New York, she always greeted me warmly, as if we were old friends.

Benazir embodied the tensions between Pakistan's modern, educated, urban elite and the country's poor rural majority that elected her. The corruption of that elite, and their failure to deliver basic services and social justice to the poor, is what the Taliban is exploiting so successfully in Pakistan today. Benazir herself was dismissed twice as prime minister on corruption and mismanagement charges. (Her husband, Asif Zardari, Pakistan's current prime minister, is known as "Mr. Ten Percent," a reference to the kickbacks he supposedly demanded on various government contracts during his wife's time in office.)

Tragically, at the end of her life, Benazir seemed to appreciate that time had run out in Pakistan for "business as usual." She understood that her country had to confront extremism within and its root causes. She was struggling with the role that Islam can and does play in shaping the country's politics and multilayered culture, and in particular, its implications for women.

In her book *Reconciliation*, finished weeks before her assassination and published posthumously, Benazir writes passionately about Islam as a religion "committed not only to tolerance and equality but to the principles of democracy."[1] *Reconciliation* is a plea to rediscover the values of pluralism and peace within Islam. It is also an unabashed promotion of Muslim gender equality. "Islam prohibited the killing of girls and gave women the right to divorce, child custody, alimony, and inheritance long before Western societies adopted these principles . . . Thus, the message of Islam is pro–women's rights."[2] She explicitly linked extremists who close girls' schools with terrorism. "Actually," she wrote, "it is sexual discrimination, terrorism and dictatorship that are incongruent with the teachings of the Holy Prophet and the words of Allah." She called upon women in Islamic societies to join together to serve as the catalyst for economic, political, and social change. Benazir Bhutto, for all her faults and disappointments as a politician, was an articulate and passionate advocate for tolerant Islam. With her assassination, the world lost not only an important voice for Islamic feminism but its most iconic Muslim female leader.

Pakistan today is a teeming country of nearly 180 million people. With its unrelenting growth rate, it will be the fifth most populous country in the world within twenty years, topping 250 million people. It wears its arbitrary, British-drawn borders uneasily, sparring with Afghanistan to its west and facing off against a nuclear India in the northeast. A nuclear power itself, Pakistan has been led by a military dictator for more than half of its existence. Not surprisingly, it devotes huge resources to its military. Officially, 15 percent of its budget goes to military spending, although most analysts believe that actual military allocations are more like 30 percent. Unfortunately, Pakistan's military spending is at the expense of the development of its people. The government allocates only 1 percent of the budget to education. The results speak for themselves. More than half of Pakistan's adults are illiterate, and a full 40 percent of school-age children are still not in school. Although the country boasts a hefty roster of billionaires, 75 percent of its population lives on less than $2 a day. Despite various gestures toward land reform, entrenched feudal overlords continue to control about half the country's farmland.

Since the founding of Pakistan in 1947, the role of Islam in government has been a source of significant political friction. Historians to this day continue to clash over the intentions of Muhammad Ali Jinnah, the suave, well-dressed lawyer who spearheaded efforts to create an autonomous country for India's Muslims and who is widely recognized as the father of the nation. Did he intend Pakistan to be a secular country or a full-fledged Islamic state? Many Jinnah supporters insist that his vision was one of a liberal, democratic system that would be consistent with the principles of Islam, if not the letter of Islamic law. They point to the strong statements he made about the need for religious freedom. On the other hand, Pakistan's religious establishment was determined to forge an Islamic state where the Quran and the Sunnah would form the basis of all laws. Naturally, the *ulama* would have sole responsibility for interpreting and applying those laws. Jinnah's premature death from tuberculosis a mere thirteen months after independence left the issue of religion painfully unresolved.

The status of women in Pakistani society is one area where these tensions and contradictions come to a head. In the country that elected Benazir Bhutto as the Muslim world's first female head of state, feudal and tribal practices still control the lives of tens of millions of Pakistani women. *Purdah*, child marriage, and *karo kari*—the custom of raping, maiming, or even killing a woman suspected of having unsanctioned contact with a man—are not uncommon in the countryside. Girls are sold to pay debts to settle tribal disputes. Illiteracy among women is particularly severe. Pakistan has one of the largest gender gaps in literacy rates of any country in the world. The male literacy rate is around 65 percent while female literacy is less than 35 percent.[3] This thirty-point gap puts it on par with some of the world's poorest countries—Afghanistan, Yemen, and Mozambique.

Pakistan's local Taliban-driven insurgency plays on the country's class rifts and the grievances of landless peasants.[4] Its terror campaign is justified in the name of Islam, and women and women's rights are collateral damage. To showcase their religious credentials, the Taliban shut down theaters and shops selling alcohol; they ban Western-style clothing and music; they also brutally enforce strict codes of behavior for women. While none of this is new, over the past decade the battle lines have hardened as extremism has metastasized and spread.

Pakistan has no lack of highly educated, courageous women leaders who agitate for democracy, for the rule of law, for investments in education, particularly girls' education, and for women's political and economic rights. Traditionally, these women have come from elite, relatively liberal families privileged by the state. While their elevated social status has provided them with influence in society, it has also limited their impact beyond their urban, upper-class confines.

The forces working against such modernist women leaders are many, and deeply entrenched. Since the founding of Pakistan, women's groups have clashed with conservative religious leaders who emphasize a traditional role for women and "the need to protect women's honor"—positions that reinforce some of the more detrimental cultural practices toward women. Political events, too, have slowed women's progress in Pakistan. The spread of extremism, fueled by jihad against the Soviets in Afghanistan and India in Kashmir and the Talibanization of Pakistan's tribal areas, has given religious fundamentalists a megaphone. They use it to inveigh against women. Conservative *madrasas*, many of them supported by Saudi funding, reinforce puritanical views toward women among their male—and increasingly female—students. At the national level, influential Islamists have used their considerable political power to block attempts to roll back Islamic laws.

Against all of this, and often at considerable personal costs, Pakistani women's groups have fought back. They have been an important bulwark against the unbridled Islamization of society, contesting the self-appropriated right of conservative religious leaders to interpret Islam. Many women's groups, although secular themselves, recognize that women's empowerment depends on the promotion of a pluralistic and modern Islamic society. They are using Islamic arguments to encourage female education, economic empowerment, and a public role for women. Unlike in Iran, where Islamic feminism evolved out of a heartfelt conservative religious tradition, in Pakistan it is more often adopted tactically, at times uneasily, by secular groups that recognize that the Islamization of the country is part of the problem and requires a religious response.

"This Is No Way to Run a Revolution!"

The leafy suburbs of Lahore have the look and feel of an outer-London borough: wide tree-lined boulevards interspersed with cricket pitches and polo grounds. The country club requires tennis whites on the grass courts and serves full English tea in the afternoon. This is the soil that has grown Pakistan's women's movement—secular, elitist, leftist, and far removed from the country's downtrodden female half. Overcoming class differences has been an enormous challenge for the country's women's movement—a challenge that pioneers like Nigar Ahmad have struggled with for a long time.

"We've been bloody lucky," says Nigar, reflecting on the work of the Aurat Foundation. Aurat, which means "woman" in Urdu, is an organization she cofounded in 1986 to promote women's economic and political participation in Pakistan. "We have been able to try out lots of crazy ideas. Sometimes we landed in a heap, but we landed in one piece."[5]

A heavyset woman in her mid-sixties, Nigar moves slowly but speaks with passion. We are chatting on a warm March evening in 2008 in her home in an upscale neighborhood of Lahore. The quiet of the early evening is disturbed only by the occasional cacophony of tropical birds in the trees outside her windows. Over tea and spicy samosas, she looks back on her decades of work on behalf of women.

Nigar's personal story—from her early years as a leftist intellectual spouting ideas of socialist revolution to a humbled community organizer trying to achieve social change at the most local level—in many ways reflects the growing pains of Pakistan's women's movement itself. Along the way, Nigar dropped her Marxist rhetoric and learned to speak in terms more understandable and acceptable to local women. She and her ardently secular colleagues also came to appreciate the tactical benefits of couching their efforts in Islamic terms, particularly when dealing with sensitive social issues.

Nigar grew up in Lahore. A distinguished student, she studied economics at Cambridge University in England on a Commonwealth Scholarship in the 1960s. She returned to Pakistan in late 1971 as a self-described revolutionary. These were tenuous times for Pakistan. The country had just been through civil war, lost half the state when East Pakistan seceded to become Bangladesh, and suffered a humiliating defeat at the hands of India. Pakistan's senior military brass, which had ruled the country off and on since its founding in 1947, concluded that its interests were best served by passing the mess to a civilian government. (Faced with mass demonstrations, rising Islamic militancy, and a faltering economy, Pakistan's military made a similar decision to transfer power back to a civilian government in 2008 after yet another decade of military rule.)

In 1971, the leftist leader Zulfikar Ali Bhutto, founder of the Pakistan People's Party, was elected on an unabashedly populist platform. His slogan "*Roti, kapra,* and *makan*" (bread, clothing, and shelter) appealed to the oppressed and downtrodden, and his magnetism mobilized the masses. Bhutto's government also appealed to Pakistan's small but growing class of educated women. Bhutto broke down barriers by appointing women to several high-profile public posts, opening the foreign service, police force, and civil administration to women, and forming various committees to improve their status. His wife took on an active public role, representing Pakistan at international conferences.

Encouraged by these gains, women's organizations proliferated. Founded by educated, left-leaning women of the upper classes, many of them educated overseas, these organizations mostly focused on consciousness-raising among their own. They did research on the status of women in society and took on various advocacy projects.

"It was a very political time. Those of us educated abroad had been shaped by the 1960s," Nigar Ahmad remembers. "The film *Z* (a French-language thriller in which leftist idealists are crushed by a right-wing military junta) had a huge impact on me." Fresh out of graduate school, Nigar started teaching economics at Qaid-i-Azam University in Islamabad and working with various labor union groups to promote "the revolution."

"I was assigned to work with the women, the wives of the workers. My job was to 'counsel' them but really what I was instructed to do was tell the women that they should be supportive of their husbands and the 'workers' cause.' I was twenty-six and unmarried, and I would visit these women's homes. They were all illiterate and had crying babies and small children climbing all over them. I kept thinking, this is no way to run a revolution!"

Nigar went back to the men and argued that if you want a revolution you need to bring the women along. She demanded some materials to be able to teach the women during her visits. She was handed a copy of Lenin's *Imperialism: The Highest Stage of Capitalism*, in Urdu. "I tried to struggle, dutifully, through a few sessions with it, but it was ludicrous. I barely understood it myself," she recalls.

One meeting with the women stands out in her memory. "I was reading to a group of female railroad workers. A young woman began weeping. I thought to myself, 'Yes! I've really moved this woman.' But it turns out she was weeping because she was so upset that I hadn't begun with *Bismillah ar-Rahman ar-Rahim* [In the name of God the Merciful and Beneficent . . . the beginning of every Muslim prayer]."

This was the start of Nigar's own awareness. "I came to realize how alone all these women were, how no one cared about the miserable reality of their lives. I also realized that they were deeply religious and any efforts to work with them must take that into account."

At the time that Nigar Ahmad was trying to inspire female workers with Leninism in the 1970s, female literacy in Pakistan was in the single digits in many places. Outside of the major cities, girls' schooling remained the exception, not the norm. Tribal and feudal customs prevailed in the countryside, keeping girls secluded and ignorant. The country's conservative religious establishment, too, worked against an expansion of women's rights, invoking rigid interpretations of sharia to keep women in their homes. The country's upper-class, well-educated, secular women living comfortable lives in Karachi and Lahore had far more in common with women in London or New York than with those living a few miles from them in the countryside.

Under Zulfikar Ali Bhutto's leadership, the country got a new constitution—one that gave women more de jure rights than ever before. The constitution stated that all citizens are equal before the law and emphasized that there could be "no discrimination on the basis of sex." It also stated grandly that women should participate in all spheres of national life and even reserved ten seats for them in the national parliament. At the same time, in response to pressure from Islamists, the constitution strengthened the role of Islam in society, declaring Islam to be the state religion.

Pakistan's elite women were wholly unprepared for General Zia-ul-Haq, who seized power in 1977 as a self-described Islamic Puritan determined to "cleanse" Pakistan of moral corruption. General Zia quickly began a process of "Islamizing" the country, a situation that continues to reverberate across Pakistan and around the world. He explained his beliefs in a 1979 interview: "Islam is our only salvation . . . It comes before wheat and rice and everything else . . . I can import wheat but I cannot import the correct moral values."[6]

General Zia found much of his inspiration in the works and writings of Maulana Maududi, the conservative cleric who founded the Jamaat-i-Islami party in 1947. While Maududi's policies over the years blew with the winds of political expediency, he was uncompromising with regard to women. Maududi professed the inferiority of women and insisted on their complete segregation, in their homes if possible. He also called for their exclusion from public leadership roles. Over the years, Maududi tried to restrict women's right to vote, to abolish coeducation, and to segregate the workplace.[7] While Pakistan's early political elites were prone to dismiss Maududi and other *ulama* as somewhat irrelevant to the modern country they were building, they were also careful not to antagonize them. Already subject to criticisms from conservative clerics that they were merely ersatz Muslims, Pakistan's early leadership was constantly reaffirming its commitment to Islam, and courting the support of influential Islamist parties, particularly Jamaat-i-Islami. Compromising on women's rights was a quick and easy way to achieve this. It is a pattern that persists even today.

Maududi was sentenced to death in 1953 for his antigovernment provocations, but his sentence was eventually commuted. He remained intellectually active, and died in 1979 in Buffalo, New York, where he went to seek medical treatment for a kidney ailment. His Islamist views, however, got a second wind under Zia. General Zia made Maududi's writings compulsory reading in the armed forces. He also shared Maududi's restrictive views on women. Zia's government began to demand that women wear Islamic dress in public offices and made noises about enforcing the headscarf for girls in high school. Women were banned from participating in sports competitions. Rumors swirled about ending coeducation and even repealing the country's relatively progressive family laws.

A centerpiece of General Zia's efforts to Islamize Pakistani laws and society was the passing of the Hudood Ordinance. The Hudood Ordinance claimed to enforce sharia by imposing Quranic punishments for *zina* (extramarital sex), *qazf* (giving false testimony), theft, and drinking alcohol. The punishments included lashings, amputations, and even stoning to death.

While the Hudood Ordinance raised many questions, the most galling issue for women was that it made little distinction between adultery and rape. To mete out maximum punishment for adultery required four male witnesses in good standing, who actually saw the act of penetration, or a voluntary confession from the adulterers. Conceivably, this would confine punishment of adultery to only the most brazen public acts (resulting in the necessary four male witnesses). But the same level of proof was also required for rape. Unable to produce four male witnesses (who ostensibly must have been standing around watching the rape) or a voluntary confession on the part of the rapist, the female victim could in turn be accused of extramarital sex and punished.

Several high-profile cases revealed the discriminatory nature of these laws and punishments and began to mobilize the country's women's movement. One of the most notorious cases was that of Fehmida and Allah Bux, who were among the first poor souls to be found guilty under the new Hudood punishments. In 1981, Fehmida was a young girl from a middle-class family who made the simple mistake of falling in love with Allah Bux, a bus driver from a different community and a lower social class. She ran off and married him against her parents' wishes. Her parents pleaded with them to end the marriage, but they refused. So Fehmida's parents went to the police. They told them that their daughter had been abducted.

When the police caught up with Fehmida at Allah Bux's home, she was pregnant. The couple insisted they were happily married. They claimed they had entered into an oral marriage (not uncommon at the time) and had simply delayed registering it. They produced witnesses to corroborate their story. The authorities, under pressure from Fehmida's angry parents, refused to believe them. Since the couple was unable to produce a marriage certificate, they were deemed to be living in sin and subject to Quranic punishment. Fehmida was sentenced to a hundred lashes. Allah was sentenced to be stoned to death. To make public examples of these sinners, their sentences were to be publicly carried out at the Karachi Race Course grounds. The court's only nod to leniency was to suspend Fehmida's punishment until after she had given birth.

Another notorious case was that of Safia Bibi. The injustice of her situation particularly enraged women across the country. Safia lived in Sahiwal, a town in the fertile southeast corner of Pakistan's Punjab Province known for its famous cattle. A partially blind girl of eighteen,

Safia worked as a maid in the local landowner's home. She became pregnant after being raped by the landlord and his son. She told her parents, who went to the police. The judge, however, acquitted the landlord and his son due to lack of evidence. On the basis of her pregnancy, he convicted Safia of adultery and sentenced her to public lashings and imprisonment. Public outrage and international embarrassment caused the government to hastily sideline the case. Shortly thereafter, Lal Mai, another teenage rape victim, became the first woman to be publicly flogged under the Hudood Ordinance.

Religious conservatives cheered Zia's Islamization policies. They had strongly opposed the secular policies pursued by Zulfikar Ali Bhutto, Zia's predecessor, as a threat to Islam. They had burned Bhutto's effigy in the streets. The middle and lower classes, too, had never been comfortable with Bhutto's liberal socialism, and they viewed Zia's Islamization process mostly with acquiescence. Powerful industrialists and landowners had also deeply resented Bhutto. They seethed with outrage as he nationalized their manufacturing and agricultural industries. Consequently, they welcomed Zia's firm hand at the helm and accepted his Islamization policies as a way to restore order and tackle corruption.

Zia's Islamization plans were also assisted by geopolitical events. His decade of rule coincided with the Afghan jihad against the Soviets. Zia's military government quickly became the main conduit for funneling U.S. and Saudi weapons, money, and recruits to jihadi groups in Afghanistan, a foreign policy which at the same time enhanced his domestic agenda for Islamizing Pakistan. Islam became the rallying cry on both sides of the border.

Mobilizing Women—Creating a Movement

Ironically, the excesses of Zia's regime also led directly to the growth of the country's women's movement as women gradually mobilized to fight back against the discriminatory nature of his Islamization policies.[8] The backsliding of the Zia years was a wake-up call to women activists. As they mobilized to resist Zia's attempt to dismantle legal rights for women, they were also forced to acknowledge that those rights only existed on paper anyway for most women in the country. Various women's organizations set out to change that, adapting their message and their programs to begin working, finally, with the people.

"Women began mobilizing against Zia's restrictive policies," remembers Nigar Ahmad, "but there were not more than a few hundred of us. The Western media gave us a lot of prominence, made us seem bigger than we were, and forced the government to pay attention to us. But we were very limited. We would hold a demonstration here or there, write a pamphlet or two, but basically we were a few hundred upper-middle-class professional women. Our activism was very part-time and ad hoc. We didn't have any research and it was hard for us to respond."

Liberals across the country were shocked and galvanized by the Hudood Ordinance. Few had understood the severity of the new law or how easily it could be misused. A prominent lawyer took up Fehmina and Allah Bux's case and defended them both in the Supreme Court. Eventually, their case was dismissed, but not before energizing women's groups.

Angry at the new laws and recognizing that only a coordinated response would be sufficient to oppose the government's Islamization policies, the representatives of numerous women's groups in Pakistan came together to form an umbrella organization called the Women's Action Forum (WAF) in the fall of 1981. WAF opposed both the growing segregation of women and also the government's use of Islam to pass restrictive laws.

WAF's leaders were faced with a critical decision—the same decision that confronts would-be reformers across the Muslim world: to oppose repression only through secular logic and existing laws, or, tactically, to work within the framework of Islam itself. Somewhat reluctantly, they decided to add Islamic arguments to their arsenal. This was not an easy decision for the group. As two of WAF's founding members admitted, the urban upper-class women who were the backbone of WAF were often more conversant in Shelley and Keats than in their own traditions.[9]

The Women's Action Forum began reaching out to sympathetic *ulama* who disagreed with the hard-core Jamaat-i-Islami interpretations favored by Zia's government. It started Quranic classes for its members and invited religious experts to its meetings to share their perspectives on why some of the government's proposed sharia laws were in fact un-Islamic. This approach, while satisfying to the middle- and lower-class women, was resented by WAF's left-leaning upper-class women.

"Many of them were simply antireligious," remembers Dr. Riffat Hassan, one of Pakistan's leading female theologians who was invited to some of these early WAF meetings. "They were uncomfortable with me as a religious person. They would ask me to their meetings to explain what Islam says on various topics. But they were out of their comfort zone. These women knew what they didn't want but not what they stood for."[10]

Soon after the launch of the WAF, Nigar cofounded the Aurat Foundation as a full-time research institute on women's issues. Over time, Aurat has come to play an important role in bridging the deep class divisions in the women's movement in Pakistan. Nigar readily admits that as Aurat began to do research, they realized that their issues were not the ones most women in Pakistan cared about.

"We were adamantly against the idea of a separate women's university (a long-standing Jamaat-i-Islami demand, which gained ground in the early 1980s under Zia). We thought this would 'ghettoize' women. We argued that a separate women's university wouldn't prepare women for the mixed workplace. And with such low female literacy, Pakistan couldn't afford a separate women's university. But when we tried to rally poor women on this issue, they looked at us as if we were from another planet. They would say to us, 'We can't even send our daughters to first grade. We have no clean water.' It was clear we were talking at cross-purposes."

The Aurat Foundation received an initial grant from the Canadian International Development Agency and the Norwegian government to start working with existing community-based organizations. A turning point for the organization came when the United Nations Development Fund for Women (UNIFEM) asked Aurat to host a conference for rural women in 1992 as part of UNIFEM's series of Peasant Women's Summits across Asia.

The conference was a challenge for Aurat, since at the time it did not have a lot of rural contacts. As it held discussions in rural villages across the country in preparation for the summit, Nigar remembers being "shattered" by her confrontation with the harshness of rural life. "These women had ten or eleven children, and seven of them would die." Out of the Peasant Women's Summits came the idea of using radio programs to reach rural women with important news and information.

Nigar Ahmad describes the radio shows as transformative. Once a week, women would gather under the shady limbs of a tree in the center of their village. Some would sit on folding chairs holding babies in their laps. Others sat on mats on the ground, their bright *shalwar kameez* tucked under their legs. Their children would play games nearby. A cardboard box might serve as a table in the middle of the gathering. On it, a battery-operated radio would hum to life as the women tuned in to their half-hour radio show.

Ostensibly, the purpose of these programs was to teach the women farming techniques. Surveys conducted by Aurat across forty villages in the early 1990s showed that women were responsible for more than eighty agricultural activities. With very low levels of literacy and almost no formal schooling, the women were eager to access information and training to improve their productivity. The radio shows were accompanied by a book of colorful pictures reiterating important information on the agricultural cycle in graphic form.

The shows, however, went way beyond farming. They were witty, romantic soap operas that weaved together information not only on how to plant seeds, but also on a range of topics from healthcare and nutrition to family planning and domestic abuse. "The women got involved in the stories," says Nigar Ahmad. "They started speaking up and becoming engaged in a whole range of subjects."

The quick popularity of the shows demonstrated that radio was one of the best ways to provide women in rural villages with information. Aurat hired a leading drama scriptwriter to produce the programs and secured discounted rates from the Pakistan Broadcasting Corporation to transmit them. It also provided women in the villages with a cassette recorder to tape the shows so they would not miss an episode. By the mid-1990s, Aurat had nearly two hundred "listening centers" across the countryside reaching tens of thousands of women.

"We never wanted anything to sound radical, so we would have real characters using real language," recalls Nigar. "In one episode, we had the local *maulvi* [religious leader] saying that a woman is like the bottom of a man's shoe. This led to a discussion among some of the women on the show about sensitive issues like a woman's right to choose where to work, and who and when to marry."

The most important impact of the shows, however, was in raising women's awareness of their political rights. During the 1990s, a consensus emerged among women activists that increasing female political representation was critical for improving women's status in society. They lobbied to reserve a third of seats for women both at the provincial and national levels of government. Aurat and other groups launched a nationwide campaign behind the effort. For years, however, they were rebuffed by government officials who insisted that the goal was unrealistic—that there simply were not enough qualified women in the country to fill such an ambitious quota. Aurat knew otherwise. From its work with its "listening centers" across the countryside, it recognized that there were many capable, if not highly educated, women leaders in the villages. It kept up the pressure.

The meteoric rise of Benazir Bhutto in the 1990s, the first woman elected to lead a Muslim country, also helped the initiative. General Zia's sudden death in 1988 ushered in a renewed attempt at civilian government in Pakistan. The Pakistan People's Party, now led by thirty-five-year-old Benazir, rode a groundswell of support to victory. During the election, political opponents in the military and the Islamist parties tried to discredit Bhutto, portraying her as a morally corrupt Westernized woman. They dropped leaflets from airplanes in major Pakistani cities showing her and her mother wearing bathing suits.[11] Despite fatwas from various *ulama* saying that a woman could not be a head of state, she prevailed.

Benazir was an electrifying figure who inspired not only moderates across Pakistan, but also the country's women. Her government moved quickly to undo many of the restrictions of the Zia regime—she freed political prisoners, opened the media, lifted bans on student and labor unions, removed restrictions on NGOs, and began a process of economic deregulation and decentralization. She also took actions to roll back some of the limitations that Zia had imposed on women in the name of Islam. She again allowed women to participate in sports. She created a Ministry of Women's Development. She introduced women into the police force, appointed women to her cabinet, and emphasized the need for girls' education. But, ultimately, she failed to enact the substantive economic and social changes that the country desperately needed (and still needs).

During the 1990s, Pakistan experienced a decade of dysfunctional democracy as government alternated between Benazir Bhutto and Nawaz Sharif. Both were surrounded by clouds of corruption and let critical reforms languish. Neither was willing or perhaps able to rein in the military and intelligence service, which continued to arm jihadi groups for strategic leverage in Afghanistan and India. Both pursued a clandestine nuclear program. In 1996, Pakistan (led by Bhutto at the time) joined Saudi Arabia and the United Arab Emirates (UAE) to become one of only three countries to recognize the Taliban.

In style, however, the two could not be more different—Benazir Bhutto a secular, Western-oriented woman, Nawaz Sharif an Islamic conservative. In villages all over Pakistan, women put Benazir at the top of their list when asked whom they admired in the world. Although she accomplished little legislatively for women (she failed to make any headway on repealing the Hudood Ordinance, and despite campaign pledges did not introduce any significant legislation to improve women's social welfare), Bhutto's symbolism as a female leader, especially at the grassroots level, was powerful. Her electoral success put a dent in the perennial conservative Islamist charge that women could not be leaders. Her victories also encouraged activists to keep pushing for a quota to bring more women into politics.

In 2000, women's demand for a significant electoral quota was finally met. General Pervez Musharraf designated that 33 percent of seats in local councils, 22 percent in provincial councils, and 17 percent in the National Assembly would be reserved for women. Having just taken over the previous year in yet another military coup, Musharraf no doubt made this change partly to burnish his international reputation. Regardless, the challenge now fell to civil society groups such as Aurat to register women as candidates and voters. Aurat's radio network proved invaluable. Whole programs focused on explaining to women how to take advantage of reserved seats and what their rights were as voters. Not surprisingly, a disproportionate number of rural women candidates emerged from the ranks of the Aurat "listening center" managers—the women who organized the weekly sessions in the villages.

To ensure maximum participation among women, Aurat organized a Citizen's Campaign to train women candidates on the basics: how to register, how to run a campaign, how to meet and speak with voters. The campaign also helped tens of thousands of women get national identity cards, which are necessary to access many public services. Aurat recorded songs to encourage men and women to accept women's political participation. The lyrics promoted the notion of women as less corrupt than men, as more likely to demand good governance and to solve the village's problems.[12]

The results of the campaign went far beyond Aurat's expectations. In the 2001 elections, more than 70,000 women ran for local office, and more than 30,000 were elected. Women filled some 90 percent of the seats reserved for them—defying critics who warned that a high percentage of seats would go empty due to a lack of any qualified and willing women. More than half of the women elected were illiterate; they were overwhelmingly housewives with little professional experience; most were from families that did not own land and had never contested an election before.[13] They were, indeed, the previously disenfranchised.

The use of quotas in Pakistan to increase women's political participation is far from a panacea for women's rights. Tribal and patriarchal traditions still weigh heavily on women in office, limiting their ability to move about their constituency and meet with voters. Lack of education, early marriage, and the demands of large families also discourage a public role for women. Islamic extremists have been known to target female politicians in a bid to terrorize women into staying at home. Islamist parties like Jamaat-i-Islami, once harshly critical of women in politics, now take advantage of the quotas by putting conservative women in office who toe the Islamist line. But the dramatic increase in women's participation in government over the past decade has largely normalized politics for women, even in rural, traditional communities. It has also created a pipeline of local women leaders who, over time, have the potential to bring women's issues to the policy table. And as history has shown, it will be hard for Jamaat-i-Islami and other conservative Islamist groups to mobilize women, put them in parliament, and then expect them to stay mute. Inevitably, even the Islamist women begin pushing back on legislation that restricts their rights.

A Matter of Honor

In April 1999, an honor killing shocked Pakistani society and generated international headlines due to the sheer audacity of the case. Samia Sarwar, a twenty-nine-year-old woman and mother of two young sons, had recently fled an abusive marriage in Peshawar against her parents' wishes. She sought refuge in Lahore, where the noted human-rights activist and lawyer Hina Jilani took up her divorce case. Samia's family insisted on seeing her, but sensing danger, Samia refused. Finally, she agreed to meet with her mother, who was to hand over some papers necessary for her divorce. However, still suspicious, Samia insisted on seeing her mother only in Jilani's presence at the law office. When the mother arrived, she was accompanied by one of Samia's uncles and another man who served as the mother's driver. Hina Jilani refused the men entrance. The mother demanded that she needed her driver's help to walk, so the two of them entered the office together. As Samia rose to greet her mother, the driver took out a gun, put it to Samia's head, and pulled the trigger. She died instantly. The killer was shot dead while trying to flee, but the mother and uncle, taking an office assistant with them as a shield, escaped. According to the hostage's account, they all made their way to a nearby hotel, where they joined Samia's father. As they entered the room, he asked them if the "job was done."[14]

In the aftermath of the incident, members of the *ulama* and even some government officials insisted that the killing was in accordance with tribal and religious traditions. They heaped criticism on Hina Jilani, the lawyer, as a "misguided" woman, and called for her censure. Some of the most radical *ulama* issued fatwas labeling both Jilani and her sister, Asma Jahangir, who was the Supreme Court advocate and

chairperson of Pakistan's Human Rights Commission, as *kafirs* (unbelievers) and called for their murder. The Pakistani authorities declined
to arrest anyone in Samia's family.

In the United States, ABC's *Nightline* ran a segment on honor
killings ("A Matter of Honor"), with Asma Jahangir and Dr. Riffat Hassan, a prominent Islamic feminist, as commentators. Riffat Hassan,
raised in Pakistan but working as a scholar in the United States, was
moved by an outpouring of international support after the show, so
much so that she formed an organization to combat honor crimes in
her native land. Timing is everything: In October 1999, just as she was
contemplating her new organization, General Pervez Musharraf overthrew Nawaz Sharif to seize control of Pakistan.

Positioning himself as a moderate, technocratic leader, Musharraf
also began speaking out against honor crimes. At the time, Pakistan's
relations with the West were frayed. The United States had cut off all
aid and imposed sanctions in the wake of Islamabad's testing of a
nuclear weapon in 1998. Musharraf's coup created further diplomatic
isolation. His outspokenness on the issue of honor killings was not only
meant to increase domestic awareness of the problem. It was also a
convenient way to reduce Pakistan's isolation abroad.[15]

Encouraged by Musharraf's various public statements condemning
honor killings as "un-Islamic," Riffat Hassan decided to reach out to
the general about the need for gender justice in Pakistan. Five months
after the coup, she wrote the military dictator an open letter that she
published in *Pakistan Today*, a Pakistani-American newspaper. In it, she
beseeched Musharraf to focus on human rights, and specifically
women's rights, as a way to build the moral foundations of the country
and win the approval and respect of the international community.
"Pakistanis," she wrote, "never tire of saying that Islam has given more
rights to women than any other religion. Certainly, if by 'Islam' is
meant 'Quranic Islam,' the rights that it has given to women are,
indeed, impressive . . . Unfortunately, however, Muslim tradition, like
the tradition of other major religions of the world, developed in patriarchal cultures . . . and reduced women to the status of chattels."[16]

In her letter, Riffat Hassan argued that while the Quran appears
weighted in favor of women, in practice Islam has been used to oppress

women. She went on to cite numerous violations of women's rights within Islam: discrimination against the girl child, marrying off girls as minors ("even though marriage in Islam is a contract and presupposes that the contracting parties are both consenting adults"), and the difficulty for women to obtain a divorce (although the Quran "presents the idea of what we today call a no-fault divorce").

Somewhat to her surprise, Musharraf was receptive to her ideas, and invited her to meet with him. In September 2000, she found herself sitting across the table from the general in his official residence in Islamabad, drinking tea and discussing Pakistani society.

"Do you think culture can be changed?" Riffat remembers him asking her. She quickly replied, "Of course," and cited the example of Confucius, whose philosophy was incorporated into China's educational system. Within a generation it had changed the country.

Musharraf suggested she give up her teaching position in the United States to return full-time to Pakistan to launch a "movement" to promote moderate Islam. This was the start of a lengthy dialogue. Over the next few years, they had several meetings in which they discussed human rights, education, and the spread of extremism in Pakistan. "He was particularly concerned about what was coming out of the more radical *madrasas* in Pakistan. He suggested I host a television show, do workshops throughout the country."

Riffat Hassan was no doubt appealing to Musharraf as a voice of Islamic moderation. Since childhood, she had been fighting battles against patriarchy and tradition, usually coming out on top. Born in 1943, she grew up in a cultured, intellectual family in Lahore. In the 1950s, upper-class Pakistani girls were just beginning to venture out of the home for schooling. Riffat's father resisted and the two battled over this point. She watched with dismay as her older sisters were married off to cousins by the age of sixteen. "A turning point for me came when my second sister was married. I was twelve, and I saw how she was pushed into it, and all I could think was that in four years' time, I would be next."

Riffat the student had an ally in her young mother, who wanted to see her daughter have opportunities that were denied to her. Her mother supported Riffat's educational ambitions, and she stayed in school. "My mother was always telling me, 'You have to be successful, you have to be tough.' I was the horse who was going to win the Kentucky Derby for her."

When she was seventeen, Riffat went to England for university. Her father agreed to pay for one year of university, thinking this would satisfy his daughter. But the horse was out of the gate. Once in England, Riffat earned a scholarship, making her financially independent for the rest of her studies. She stayed to complete a Ph.D. in philosophy, writing her dissertation on the progressive Muslim scholar Muhammad Iqbal, whose insistence on the need for *ijtihad* influenced much of her later work.

After eight years of studying in the UK, Dr. Riffat Hassan returned home. Back in Pakistan, she found it difficult to get a job. "Men would question me, 'Why are you working? Don't you have a husband to support you?'" It was 1968, and despite a thin layer of progressive changes for women imposed at the time by General Ayub Khan, Pakistan remained a deeply patriarchal society. "All the prominent women working were *begums* (the wives of important men). They did respectable social work, but none of them came up on their own." Eventually, Riffat started working for the government as a researcher in Islamabad, but she is dismissive of those years. "The work wasn't really research at all. We wrote papers to prove to the outside world that Pakistan did not have an education problem or a healthcare problem."

During this time, Riffat Hassan married. "It was a marriage of choice. I like to make my own mistakes," she explains simply. The marriage was rocky from the start. By 1972, convinced that staying in Pakistan was a professional dead end and hoping that going abroad might salvage the relationship, she and her husband moved to the United States. Nevertheless, the marriage soon crumbled. Now with a baby daughter, Riffat accepted a teaching position at Oklahoma State University in Stillwater, Oklahoma. Ironically, it was here in the heartland of America that she experienced her awakening as a "Muslim feminist."

In the fall of 1974, Riffat Hassan became the faculty adviser for the Muslim Students Association (MSA), one of the best-organized Muslim groups in the United States. At that time, members of the MSA were predominantly Arab men from conservative Persian Gulf countries, many of whom were members of the Muslim Brotherhood. They shared uniformly traditionalist views on women and were irate at the thought of having to report to a woman as their faculty adviser. They tried to sideline Riffat at their annual conference by confining her to speak on the topic of "women in Islam." Little did the association realize what it had unleashed.

The more Riffat Hassan began to study the Quran, the angrier she became about the glaring disparities between the ideals of her religion and the realities of women's treatment in Muslim countries. "There is such a huge gap between what the Quran says, and what is done. I realized that so much of what had happened to me was simply because I was born in a Muslim country." Riffat Hassan decided to dedicate her life to promoting the ideals of Islamic feminism.

During the 1983–1984 school year, newly tenured at the University of Louisville where she was teaching religious studies, Riffat took a sabbatical to spend time again in Pakistan. She arrived in Lahore just as Zia's Islamization policies were beginning to register with women across the country. Shocking cases of rape victims being punished for adultery jolted upper-class Pakistani women into understanding their own legal vulnerability. Riffat argued that since the laws were based on religion, they had to be challenged from within the discourse. "I was probably the only Muslim woman in the country at that time who was interpreting the Quran from a non-patriarchal perspective."

Like other Islamic feminists before her, Riffat began a systematic study of the hadith. "I used to work with an Islamic scholar who always said that if you are on a train that gets derailed, you can only get it back on track at the point where it got derailed. For Muslims, we need to go back to the original texts. A lot of problems stem from the hadith. Some people simply reject them, but that's not right. So many details are found there. You can't reject or ignore them."

Riffat Hassan delved into the hadith to debunk the widely held view in Islam that men are "above" women. Soon, she became a leading voice in Pakistan against the traditional, Jamaat-i-Islami interpretations of Islam that underpinned many of Zia's Islamization policies. Although she resumed her academic position in the U.S., she returned regularly to Pakistan and through her writings continued to challenge conservative Islamic interpretations used to reduce women's status.

Musharraf's encouragement seemed to present a perfect opportunity to bring a more progressive interpretation of Islam into the Pakistani mainstream. Musharraf portrayed himself as a moderate leader full of liberal ideas. He promoted a policy of "enlightened moderation" as a means of combating the country's growing extremism. His tenure, however, was fraught with contradictions from the beginning. Within a year of seizing control, he had appointed himself president and then held a suspect referendum in 2002 to legitimize and extend his rule for five more years. Although he positioned himself as the United States' critical ally on the front line of global terrorism, he played a dangerous double game behind the scenes. His government continued to work with extremist groups, promoting the military's (and Islamists') agenda of securing "strategic depth" for Pakistan in both Afghanistan and Kashmir. After 9/11, that game became considerably more complicated for the general, but also far more lucrative. The U.S. poured billions into Pakistan as Musharraf delivered just enough—the arrest of a high-profile terrorist here or there—to keep the money flowing, while the military-intelligence establishment remained deeply entwined with radical Islamist groups.

Musharraf also cynically used the Islamist parties to bolster his own position. He barred his main opponents—Benazir Bhutto and Nawaz Sharif—from politics, thereby creating an unprecedented electoral opening for the Islamists. In the 2002 elections, a coalition of Islamist parties captured 20 percent of the seats in parliament and gained control of the provincial governments in both the Northwest Frontier Province and Baluchistan, their best showing ever. Musharraf was more than happy to present the Islamists as his primary opposition, a tactic sure to quiet U.S. pressure for further democratic openings.

Despite Musharraf's double-dealing, Riffat Hassan took up his challenge to return home to start a movement of moderates. In 2005, she established a government-backed research institute in Lahore to bring together progressive Muslim scholars. She called it the Iqbal International Institute for Research, Education, and Dialogue after Muhammad Iqbal. General Musharraf was listed as the "patron-in-chief" of the institute. He promised to provide the institute with an endowment and a building in Lahore.

The Iqbal International Institute set out an ambitious mission: to bring about a new Islamic Renaissance through the collaborative work of notable scholars; to work with Muslim masses, especially youth, to create enlightened, just, compassionate, and life-affirming communities; to develop leaders of Pakistan and the Muslim world who would be seen by global society as models of true enlightenment and civilization; and to engage in a reasoned dialogue with the West.

The institute adopted the motto of the nineteenth- and early-twentieth-century reformers: "Back to the Quran, forward with *ijtihad*." The goal was to create a beachhead of progressive Islamic thinking in Pakistan to challenge the radicalism spreading throughout the country. Seminars, meetings, and lectures would encourage dialogue. Teachers would be trained in Muslim ethics and human rights, including women's rights within Islam. The plan was to reach 5 million students by year five.

In the spring of 2006, the institute held its inaugural event at a hotel in Lahore. The speakers were three progressive Muslim thinkers—Dr. Fathi Osman, Dr. Aslam Abdullah, and Dr. Gamal Solaiman—all of whom live in the West, but had joined the institute as international resident scholars. Their presentations emphasized the importance of *ijtihad*, the compatibility of Islam, democracy, human rights, and the rights of women in Islam. Throughout that year, these and other scholars began promoting their ideas through television programs, working with schools and teachers, publishing articles, and giving talks and lectures. Riffat Hassan herself gave numerous lectures, including continuing to speak out against honor killings. The Pakistani press covered these events, and the institute seemed to be thriving.

Behind the scenes, however, the institute was troubled. Months of back-and-forth struggle for control of the organization ensued among various factions, and the promised endowment from the government never materialized. Over lunch at the Pearl Continental Hotel in Lahore in early 2008, Riffat looked back on that period with anguish. "Musharraf had no sense of detail, and there was no real follow-through. He seemed to want to just put a few progressives on television and be done with it," she said in retrospection. "We were promised the world, but nothing was delivered. The only money we received came in bits and pieces, and all of it from the ISI [Pakistan's intelligence service]. Our only government contact was the ISI."

"I warned her not to trust Musharraf!" her brother, the prominent international lawyer Farooq Hassan, interjected. Riffat nodded slowly and sighed. "It was not hard to figure out that we were being used," she explained, with considerable chagrin. By the summer of 2007, the government had decided to move the institute to the Islamic University in Islamabad, effectively shutting it down. "I know people are critical of me, and say that I was following Musharraf's agenda. But really, I thought he was following mine. I was deceived," she concluded.

So were many people. Musharraf was a consummate salesman who convincingly pushed his agenda of "enlightened moderation" while continuing to fuel the sources of extremism that today are so destabilizing to the country. Ironically, he may have understood Pakistan's critical need for cultural change better than most, but ultimately, he failed to lead that cultural shift. One of his greatest missed opportunities was with respect to honor crimes, the very issue that brought Riffat and Musharraf together in the first place. During his tenure, the sensational case of Mukhtar Mai came to light—a woman who was gang-raped on the orders of her village council to settle some (false) accusations against her younger brother. This time, the victim fought back, becoming a heroine. Rather than celebrating Mukhtar Mai, however, Musharraf sought to silence her. This, more than anything, should have given Riffat pause.

In Mukhtar Mai's own recounting, she was gang-raped one night in June 2002 by a group of village elders. After they had finished with her, they made her walk home half-naked in front of the staring villagers.[17] For several days, she considered suicide, the expected course of action for a woman so shamed and the only culturally acceptable way to return honor to her family. She begged her mother to buy acid for her, but her mother refused. After a few days, Mukhtar's mood changed to anger, and instead of suicide, she now wanted revenge. Her father insisted that she keep quiet. Her older brother threatened to kill himself in shame if she went to the police. Her mother, however, quietly supported her. "It is your right," she insisted. "Someone has to be the first drop of rain."[18]

Mukhtar filed a report with the police. They stonewalled her and made her sign her thumbprint to false statements, but she persisted. Her savior was none other than the local mullah, who took up her case, preaching in his Friday prayers about the injustice done to this woman. The international media picked up Mukhtar's story. Women's groups in Pakistan rallied to her cause, and she persisted through the corrupt legal system to victory. Eventually six of her attackers were arrested and convicted. A government minister appeared in her village, presenting Mukhtar with approximately $8,500 in compensation, a fortune for a peasant in her village of Meerwala, a poor, remote area in the southern part of Punjab.

Mukhtar decided to use the money to open the first school for girls in the village. "If I had bought a car or jewelry, after a few years, it would be nothing," she says. "But the school is still running. I'm helping to produce a nation."[19] She enrolled herself in the school, and now spends her time persuading parents in Meerwala to let their young girls attend. She has several hundred girls in classes. They are learning to read and write, and about their rights within Islam.

Mukhtar became an international celebrity and hero. Journalists called her the Rosa Parks of Pakistan. A documentary was being made about her life. Donations flowed in from around the world and she used the money to support girls' education and combat honor crimes. But her troubles continued. In March 2005, Punjab's high court overturned the conviction of five of her six attackers and reduced the sentence of the sixth. With her attackers on the loose and seeking revenge, she feared for her life. A hail of international criticism forced the central government to intervene, and a few months later the Supreme Court ordered her attackers to be rearrested. Her case has languished for years in legal limbo, adjourned again and again due to pressure from powerful tribal and feudal interests who resent her.

I met Mukhtar during one of her visits to New York. She has traveled to the U.S. on several occasions to be honored by various organizations for her courage. On the day we met, she had earlier rung the closing bell at NASDAQ, signing her name in the book in the way she learned to do by attending her own school. I was struck by how quiet and shy she is—she hardly seems like a revolutionary. But back home in Pakistan, and around the world, she is an inspiration to millions of women.

To Musharraf's government, however, she was an embarrassment. Musharraf criticized Mukhtar for airing the country's dirty laundry. He tried to impose a travel ban on her to prevent her from speaking in the United States, claiming it would damage Pakistan's reputation. He dismissed her efforts as little more than a moneymaking concern.[20]

In fact, Mukhtar Mai's courageous stand is a harbinger of the cultural change that Pakistan needs. Extremism will never be defeated when violent practices against women are tolerated by the legal system and broad segments of society. To eliminate honor crimes, local communities must band together and reject the practice. This requires the support of men and women, of the media, of the police, of schools and educational institutions. It also requires progressive interpretations of Islam that reject the practice and call for strict punishment. The time was not ripe for Riffat Hassan's comprehensive approach to the problem, but Islamic feminism is stirring in Pakistan, and that time will come.

Despite the challenging circumstances, Riffat Hassan remains determined. "I know that this can be done. I know that we can have a group of moderate Islamic scholars here in the heart of Pakistan working on the issues confronting Muslims worldwide—issues of tolerance, of modernity, of human rights and women's rights . . . Pakistanis are fed up with extremist thinking. They want another way to understand their religion in the modern world."

In the spring of 2009, another shocking honor crime dominated Pakistan's headlines, stirring outrage across the country and giving some credence to the notion that Pakistanis are indeed getting fed up with extremism toward women. A one-minute video, recorded on a mobile phone, captured a seventeen-year-old girl in the Swat Valley (a lush, scenic district in the northwest region of the country—an area some have called the "Switzerland" of Pakistan) being held facedown in a circle of nearly thirty bearded men. A black shroud covers her head and shoulders, and she is being repeatedly flogged by one of the men. Her bloodcurdling screams and calls for mercy send chills down the viewer's spine. Within days of the video's release, not only had everyone in Pakistan seen the shocking video, but the entire world had as well. The response was vociferous. Women's rights activists, politicians, and various religious groups publicly condemned the flogging.

Taliban leaders suddenly found themselves on the defensive. Some continued to bluster, justifying the beating by accusing the young girl of refusing to marry the man chosen for her. Others claimed that she had allowed a man that was not her husband inside her home. But as outrage grew, some Taliban sympathizers tried to distance themselves from the entire ordeal. They claimed the video was a fake or even a "Jewish conspiracy" designed to undermine a recent peace agreement that had given the Taliban the right to impose their harsh and unforgiving brand of sharia in the Swat Valley.

For nearly two years, the Taliban had been extending control over Swat as the government in Islamabad put up token resistance. Across the region, women were forced out of the public sphere and made to wear the all-encompassing burqa. The flogging of the young girl undoubtedly played a role in galvanizing Pakistani public opinion against the Taliban. Few wanted their own daughter to be next. Later that month the peace deal in Swat was scrapped by all parties. The government resumed fighting with greater urgency and with increased public support behind its actions.[21] Within months, the Pakistani army had regained control of the valley; women were soon back at work and moving around freely without burqas.

Just Think!

The television program opened with the requisite South-Asian music jingle and the name of the show flashed across the screen—*Zara Sochiye* ("Just Think" in Urdu). The host, sitting in front of a cool blue background, introduced the day's subject, Pakistan's controversial Hudood Ordinance. In a smooth voice, he assured the viewer that the show would not take sides, but would bring people together to discuss the matter with knowledge and integrity. Around the table sat a group of Islamic scholars representing a range of perspectives, from moderate to more conservative. Some were wearing a suit and tie. Others wore a traditional outfit, a thick cotton *shalwar kameez* underneath a khaki vest with a matching Jinnah cap, the fez-shaped hat made from fake karakul wool and named after Pakistan's founder.

The host of the show introduced the question of the day: "The Hudood laws are presented as divine laws, which cannot be touched. Do you agree?" Politely, the experts made nuanced theological arguments, but quickly a consensus emerged. The Hudood laws not only are man-made, but they are open to changes and improvements. While this might not sound like riveting television, *Zara Sochiye* became a media sensation in Pakistan in the spring of 2006 through its open discussions of the Hudood Ordinance.

The show was the brainchild of Mir Ibrahim Rahman, grandson of the founder of the Jang Group, one of South Asia's largest media conglomerates. At the end of 2001, Mir left his investment banking job with Goldman Sachs in New York to return to Pakistan to launch GEO TV, an independent satellite channel that his father had badgered the government for years to establish. At the time, Mir was twenty-eight years old. Overnight, he became one of the youngest CEOs in the television business.

On his flight home to Karachi, Mir wrote a memo to himself outlining what he hoped to accomplish by taking up the challenge of GEO TV. One of his goals was to stimulate critical thinking in his home country on a range of sensitive issues. High on his list was the Hudood Ordinance.

In Karachi, GEO hired more than two hundred journalists and producers, explicitly seeking out a diverse mix of talent—men and women, all ethnicities, class backgrounds, and political persuasions. "We were looking for real balance," explained GEO's president, the veteran Pakistani editor and journalist Imran Aslam.[22] The company was determined to project a nonelitist image and a range of views. GEO TV launched in August 2002, offering a mix of news, business, sports, and entertainment. Stealing viewers from the staid state-run television, its ratings quickly climbed. It soon captured a third of the market.

GEO's innovative shows, each pushing cultural and political boundaries in its own way, became hugely popular. One show offers political satire, skewering public figures in often hilarious and certainly unprecedented fashion. Another program, *Aalim Online* ("Scholar" Online) showcases mullahs debating the meaning and social implications of various Quranic passages. GEO has stirred controversy by addressing such sensitive issues as incest, birth control, and homosexuality.

In the spring of 2006, GEO's management launched a media blitz around the Hudood Ordinance. Another attempt to repeal the law was again working its way through parliament, and GEO saw this as its moment to help shape the debate. In May, it invited the esteemed Islamic scholar Javed Ahmad Ghamidi to discuss the Hudood Ordinance on air. Earlier in his career, Ghamidi had worked for nearly a decade with Maulana Maududi, the fiery, conservative founder of the Jamaat-i-Islami Islamist party. But over time Ghamidi came to espouse a more modernist interpretation of Islam and diverged intellectually from Maududi. For this he was ejected from the Jamaat-i-Islami in 1977. On GEO TV, Ghamidi—a member of the Council of Islamic Ideology, a constitutional body responsible for providing the Pakistani government advice on Islamic issues—noted that Islam does not advocate the jailing of women. He went on to insist that "the interpretation of divine laws in the Hudood Ordinance is totally against Islamic knowledge and wisdom."

The following month, GEO ran four episodes of *Zara Sochiye* focused on the Hudood Ordinance. Instead of having the women's rights activists who had long been on the forefront of challenging the Hudood Ordinance on the show, GEO invited Islamic scholars—some moderate, others more conservative—onto the program to debate.[23] The shows succeeded in publicizing the Hudood issues to a broad segment of the population. The debate among the scholars also helped debunk the notion that the Hudood Ordinance was divine. As Sohail Akbar Warraich, the law coordinator for Shirkat Gah, one of Pakistan's leading women's rights organizations, recalls, "The GEO debates exposed the rigidity in the *maulvi*'s thinking. On national television, they got caught up in their own contradictions and ended up looking silly."[24]

The Hudood Ordinance was somewhat of a litmus test for the Musharraf regime with regard to women's rights. The promotion of women's empowerment had, from the beginning, been an important component of the moderate, progressive reputation the general liked to cultivate. But in the face of strong resistance from conservative Islamist factions, he had shied away from backing any significant leg-. islative changes for women, aside from the 30 percent political quota for women, which Islamist parties fully used to their advantage.[25]

In 2002, the government's National Commission on the Status of Women convened a committee to review the Hudood Ordinance. In a much publicized report it published the following year, it urged the government to repeal the Hudood laws. The commission noted that in particular, the Zina Ordinance, which blurred the lines between rape and adultery, had been used against poor, illiterate rural women. Its final report stated that nearly 90 percent of women in Pakistan's jails were there because of ambiguities in the Zina Ordinance. Not surprisingly, the Islamist coalition (the MMA) denounced the commission's report, and the Musharraf government also quietly backed away from it. At the time, Musharraf had just secured the MMA's support for a package of constitutional amendments legitimizing the military's political control.

In 2004, PPP member Sherry Rehman introduced a bill calling for the repeal of the Hudood Ordinance. Musharraf did not support the bill, but did call for a debate on the issue, creating a new uproar among the Islamists in parliament. The bill was rejected.

In the spring of 2006, while GEO TV was doing its media blitz on the issue, the government prepared its own bill called the Women's Protection Act (WPA), which did not repeal the Hudood Ordinance but diluted its deleterious effects on women. Among other changes, it proposed adding rape to the country's penal code, allowing rape cases to be tried in civil courts, and no longer requiring four witnesses to prove rape. Also, those accused of extramarital sex could post bail to avoid languishing in prison.

Javed Ahmad Ghamidi, in his role as a member of the Council of Islamic Ideology, worked overtime to present the changes as fully consistent with Islamic law. Invoking his religious authority and relying on classical Islamic texts, Ghamidi produced numerous scholarly documents showing that the Hudood laws themselves were "un-Islamic." He appeared frequently in the media to promote his views.

Musharraf also worked to protect his liberal flank. In her memoir *Reconciliation*, Benazir Bhutto described how Musharraf contacted her in New York in the summer of 2006 saying that he wanted moderate forces to work together. The legislative fig leaf he held out to her was the Women's Protection Act. He asked for the PPP's support on the bill and she agreed. From this point, they began a process of dialogue through back channels that culminated in Benazir's return to Pakistan the following year. As she recounted in her memoir, "The passage of the women's bill gave momentum to the process of negotiations, although deep suspicions existed."[26]

Nevertheless, pressure from the Islamic parties to keep the Hudood Ordinance intact continued unabated. They threatened to resign from parliament if the Women's Protection Act were passed. To appease the Islamists, Musharraf appointed a group of conservative *ulama* to review the bill that summer. Not unexpectedly, this group insisted on significant changes to the pending legislation. Javed Ahmad Ghamidi resigned from the Council on Islamic Ideology in protest. He insisted that the *ulama*'s proposed amendments were not only against the injunctions of Islam, but that the group itself was a breach of the council's mandate to ensure that Pakistan's laws do not conflict with the teachings of Islam. Again straddling, Musharraf refused to accept Ghamidi's resignation.

Parliament narrowly passed the WPA in November 2006. The coalition of Islamist parties boycotted the vote, saying that the bill encouraged "free sex" and accusing the Musharraf government of caving in to foreign pressures. Many progressive groups also publicly denounced the act. What they sought was a complete repeal of the Hudood Ordinance, not simply a watering down of its regulations. But in private, they acknowledged that the WPA effectively took the teeth out of the Hudood Ordinance. Women's groups are now busy working with grassroots organizations to make sure that villagers understand the meaning of the act.

That the WPA disappointed both opponents and supporters of the Hudood Ordinance reflects the balance that Musharraf always claimed he was trying to find. In some sense, the legislation was a milestone. It was one of the few examples in recent times of an elected parliament in a Muslim-majority country rolling back laws that claim to be religious. Morocco's parliament did it in 2004 when it approved reforms to the personal status code—the *mudawana*. Yet it took more than two decades of efforts by women activists and strong leadership on the part of the country's reformist king. The passage of Pakistan's Women's Protection Act, although far less sweeping than Morocco's *mudawana* reforms, shattered the myth that angry mullahs would tear the country apart if any changes were made to the Hudood Ordinance. It also showed the limits of political Islam in Pakistan today. Not only did the Islamist parties, long a political bogeyman, fail to stop the passage of the bill, they did not even follow through on their threat to walk out of parliament.[27]

Perhaps more important than the actual legislation was the fact that the process sparked debate on a number of sensitive religious issues. For the first time since Zia-ul-Haq began his process of Islamization nearly thirty years earlier, there was an open public discourse on religious matters that engaged a broad cross section of society. The rise of independent media like GEO TV is helping to make average Pakistanis "just think," to question what is divine and what is man-made law that can be changed, to consider what are the values and essence of the religion they uphold.

Crossroads

In many ways, Pakistan is the most important battleground in the world today in the contest between moderation and extremism within Islam. With al-Qaeda and the Taliban operating in the tribal areas of the country with near impunity, suicide bombings alarmingly on the rise, increasing sectarian violence across the country, and Pakistani soldiers bogged down fighting extremists near the Afghan border, the headlines suggest that radicalism is gaining the upper hand. The jihadi monster nurtured by the Pakistani intelligence service has now morphed into numerous splinter groups, some of which are long beyond the control of their former masters.

Musharraf's crackdown in November 2007, when he suspended the constitution, effectively put the country under martial law and censored the media, putting any pretense of "enlightened moderation" to rest. Benazir Bhutto's assassination in December of that year removed one of the country's most articulate, and certainly best-known, advocates of tolerance.

Yet democracy is very much alive in Pakistan. Despite the violence and political chaos, the country went ahead with relatively clean elections in February 2008. An independent media continues to thrive in the face of government censorship. The courageous activism of Pakistan's independent judges and secular lawyers who have led a popular mass movement to protect rule of law in the country reflects the strength of Pakistan's civil society. So too does Pakistan's determined women's movement.

When Zia took over in a military coup in 1979, Pakistan's few women's groups were comprised of elite, liberal women with little in common with the vast majority of their countrywomen. Their efforts to roll back Zia's Islamization policies were easily characterized as culturally inauthentic, and indeed, they had little grassroots appeal.

Today, women's groups in Pakistan are building grassroots support by pursuing broader-based initiatives. Despite targeted violence against women seeking public office, more than eighty thousand female candidates ran for office in the last provincial elections in 2005, often encouraged and supported by NGOs like the Aurat Foundation.

Women's groups are also developing local networks to tackle sensitive issues like honor killings, domestic violence, and child marriage, many of them carefully couching their efforts in Islamic frameworks. As the case of Mukhtar Mai shows, while Islam is often used to justify mistreatment of women, it can also play a role in overturning deeply rooted cultural practices. After all, it was Mukhtar Mai's local mullah who critically supported her initial quest for justice.

Women's rights in Pakistan will continue to be a hotly contested cultural, political, and social arena where tribal, feudal, religious, and liberal secular interests clash. Islamic feminism is helping women and men work across these lines to encourage women's empowerment. Over the long term, their ability to promote moderate interpretations of Islam will impact not only the status of women, but the moral fabric of the country itself.

CHAPTER 5

REDIRECTING JIHAD:
AFGHANISTAN

I awoke from the Mullah's call to prayer
Oh, the Muslim prayer is better than sleep
I answered: Yes, without a doubt, but I
Just wish to finish my dream.

—SAFIA SIDDIQI, Pashtun poet and member of Afghanistan's
parliament, from her poem "Interrupted Dream"

A "Neutral" Quran

The women sit on the floor, shifting their weight from time to time to keep the blood flowing to their feet. As they move about, the plastic floor covering crinkles, bunching up under their blue burqas and black chadors. Through a small window, the rays of the morning sun begin to cut across the room, illuminating the dust floating in the air. Many of the women have walked miles from neighboring villages to attend this workshop in Jibril, a small town about forty-five minutes outside of Herat in the western part of Afghanistan. Their feet and skirt bottoms are covered in the countryside's ubiquitous brown dirt. It is summer and already the temperature is climbing in the crowded space. A lone fan in the corner strains to stir the heavy air. There is no furniture in the room, except for a large blackboard on one wall. Every inch of floor space is occupied by a shrouded figure. Although there are no men present, the women keep their burqas and chadors in place. Murmurs of expectation, tinged with suspicion, ripple through the crowd.

Sakena Yacoobi, a short, stocky woman wearing a flowered headscarf tied tightly under her chin, stands in front of the blackboard. She senses the women's nervousness and starts with a cheery "*Salaam Alaikum* [peace be with you]." The women mumble a greeting back. Sakena, a native of Herat, speaks local Dari with little trace of the nearly twenty years she has lived off and on in the United States. She is the founder and director of the Afghan Institute of Learning (AIL), a nonprofit organization that provides health and educational services to more than 350,000 women and children across Afghanistan. This morning, she is visiting AIL's women's center in Jibril. The center is a converted house AIL has rented in a newer section of town. It is surrounded by a high mud wall. A wiry, bearded older man guards the thick metal door, carefully monitoring the constant stream of humanity. A pile of worn shoes accumulates by the door. It is a mystery how people manage to leave with their own pair. From morning until night, each of the house's six rooms are packed with classes—literacy classes for the unread; tailoring, English, accounting, and computer classes to build job skills; health and hygiene classes for mothers.

The women in this room have gathered for a human rights workshop. Sakena starts by asking everyone to introduce themselves. The room remains quiet, so she jumps into the silence and runs through her own life story, dwelling on her years growing up in Herat so that the women can better relate. Eventually, she begins to draw out some of the other women in the room until almost everyone is volunteering personal tidbits.

Later, Sakena explains to me that these sessions always start out slowly. The women who come are curious but cautious, and it takes at least a day just to build some trust. I am not surprised. It seems quixotic to be teaching human rights to a group of rural Afghan housewives. Most of them are illiterate and have spent their whole lives doing the bidding of others. But Sakena insists that these sessions are among the most powerful and beneficial courses that AIL offers. "We call it a human rights workshop, but what we are really teaching is the Quran. These women can read very little so they have never actually read the Quran. Or if they can read, they don't understand the meaning of it. By working within our culture, and respecting our traditions, we are able to give them the tools they need to communicate—and negotiate— better with their husbands."

After warming up the group, Sakena turns the blackboard over to Fatima Makia, one of AIL's "master teachers" who has come from Kabul to run the workshop. Fatima grew up in Afghanistan, but like so many others, fled to Pakistan as a refugee in the late 1990s. She was twenty-seven years old and started teaching in Peshawar at a high school supported by AIL. There she met Sakena and after four years, she started working directly for AIL. Now, she travels all over Afghanistan training AIL's growing corps of teachers and instructors, mostly women, but some men too.

Today, Fatima focuses on the subject of orphans. Many of the women in the group are caring for orphans, the children of dead relatives or neighbors who have no place else to go. Some complain that their husbands beat the children and resent sharing their meager resources with them. Fatima recites Surah 4:10 from the Quran to the women: "Those who unjustly eat up the property of orphans eat up a Fire into their own bodies. They will soon be enduring a Blazing Fire!"

This passage unleashes a torrent of discussion for the rest of the morning, not only about Islamic obligations to orphans, but also about more sensitive subjects. From the complaints of the women present, domestic abuse seems to be an endemic problem. Fatima keeps the discussion moving and fills the blackboard with the women's ideas and statements. I am told this is no off-the-cuff process. Rather, she is following a program that has been carefully developed and tested by the Women's Learning Partnership (WLP), a U.S.-based nonprofit, in collaboration with various women's groups in Muslim-majority countries around the world, including Sisters in Islam in Malaysia. Fatima has even been to Washington, D.C., for training. Sakena Yacoobi was an adviser to the project and has tailored it for use in Afghanistan.[1] This, I realize, is how Islamic feminism is trickling down to the village level.

"I remember the first time we did one of these training sessions. It was in Peshawar, in 2001," Sakena excitedly recalls, her usual rapid-fire speech revving up another notch. "One of the women in the group was a mother so upset that her husband was marrying off their daughter to a much older man. He had told her she had no right to interfere in the matter, and she was very upset. We went through the Quran with her, showing her the various passages that say marriage must be consensual, that it is the daughter's right to choose. This gave her the courage to go home and speak with him. Based on the Quran, she got him to change his mind. Pretty soon, many people were coming up to us asking for help to resolve their family disputes too. These counseling sessions really began to change the women's lives."

Across Afghanistan, Sakena has seen the impact of AIL's classes on many women. She tells me about Najiba, a Tajik woman from the Kushk District to the north. Najiba's husband died in the war, and she was living with her parents-in-law and four brothers-in-law, two married and two single. With three small children of her own, she was forced to do all the housework and was regularly beaten. Her own children were made to eat scraps and wear rags. Her father-in-law announced one day that she would have to marry one of the single brothers, the one who beat her the most. She obeyed, and now has a child with him too. Her life was miserable.

Through a neighbor, Najiba had heard about the classes at the Afghan Institute of Learning and had snuck away from home to attend one of the sessions. "We were scared for her," remembers Sakina. "We urged her not to come if it was dangerous for her. For several days, she did not appear. Then she showed up again with a sister-in-law in tow. They had both come with the mother-in-law's knowledge. All the women in the house wanted to learn more about the Quran, what it says about their rights. Soon, the mother-in-law herself was coming, and all the sisters-in-law, bringing their children too, to the medical clinic. Najiba started taking literacy and sewing classes and earning some extra money. Her husband stopped beating her."

Sakena is well aware of the culturally sensitive line AIL is walking. "We only teach the Quran in a 'neutral' way," she insists. "We work with the local mullahs to make sure they have no objections to our materials. And we welcome the involvement of husbands too. All of us observe our culture and traditions ourselves. We go slowly, and very carefully . . . I don't want to criticize the work of foreigners, but when they come here and start teaching the women about their rights, the women often go home and criticize their husbands and their life just gets worse. We are helping the women learn how to negotiate with their husbands. The Quran is most helpful for that."

The twentieth century was particularly harsh to Afghan women. Decades of war and devastation, topped off by five years of gender brutality under the Taliban, left Afghan women with some of the worst human development statistics in the world. In parts of the country, female literacy is in the single digits. One out of eight Afghan women is likely to die in childbirth. Self-immolation is a common way for young girls, many of them child brides, to express their desperation. Afghan women must contend not only with dire poverty, but also with deeply ingrained customs and religious traditions that hinder their access to school, work, and healthcare. Various top-down attempts to improve the status of women, from the Westernizing efforts of King Amanullah in the 1920s to the crash-course social engineering of the communists in the 1980s, stirred up such cultural resistance that tribal leaders took up arms.

Under the internationally backed Karzai government, expectations for improvements in women's lives are again high. More girls are in school than ever before, the country's new constitution promises gender equality, and women comprise a quarter of the national parliament by dint of a constitutionally mandated quota, one of the highest levels in the world. Yet tensions over women's rights are strong and there is no doubt that Afghanistan remains a deeply conservative country. The resurgent threat of the Taliban looms largest over the country's women.

The challenge for Afghan women today is to break their cycle of one step forward, two steps back—to improve women's opportunities without creating a destabilizing backlash. So many of the current women leaders in Afghanistan have personally been through that cycle and are determined not to repeat it. They carefully cloak their work within Islamic arguments, acknowledging that their progress depends as much on progressive, women-friendly interpretations of Islam taking hold as it does on any national laws or edicts. The ability of people like Sakena Yacoobi to help spread a "neutral" understanding of the Quran to rural areas where 80 percent of the population lives may ultimately be the key to building long-term, sustainable change for Afghan women.

Winds of Change

Sakena Yacoobi was born in 1950 into a middle-class Shia family in Herat, a provincial city marked by minarets and strong Persian influences. Her youth coincided with Afghanistan's "golden years"— a period remembered wistfully as one of peace if only limited progress. King Zahir Shah presided over the country from Darulaman Palace, a hulking neoclassical building on the outskirts of Kabul that King Amanullah built in the 1920s. After Amanullah was ousted in the wake of his short-lived modernization attempts, one of his former army commanders eventually seized control of the country and a *loya jirga* (grand assembly) of tribal elders granted him the title of king. When he was assassinated in 1933, his nineteen-year-old son Zahir Shah became king and remained Afghanistan's titular ruler for the next forty years.

Sakena's father was a self-made businessman with unusual ideas for his eldest daughter. "Starting when I was only four years old, my father took me to the mosque. This was just not done back then. Fathers only took their sons to the mosque, not daughters. But there I was, with all my boy cousins, and me the only girl. Maybe he did it because I was his firstborn, and his second child died. I was the only one for a while. Maybe it was because he was orphaned at the age of five. He did everything on his own and became successful. But he couldn't read or write and he suffered for that. He insisted that I learn."

Herat in the 1950s was feeling the winds of change blowing from Kabul. In 1953, Muhammad Daoud Khan, a cousin of the king, was appointed prime minister. Over the next ten years, he initiated a series of reforms in an attempt to modernize the country. Playing the United States and Soviet Union off each other, Daoud began a flow of foreign aid to Afghanistan, which led to the building of schools, roads, and dams and the training of military officers by both the Americans and the Soviets. In the 1950s, less than 10 percent of the population and less than 2 percent of women could read or write.[2] Sakena's father made sure his daughter was among that small group of literate women.

By the age of seven, Sakena knew every Arabic book there was in the mosque. The mullah told her father he did not have anything else to teach her. So she went to school. Soon, she became her father's secretary, doing all his paperwork after school. In the late 1960s, Sakena completed high school in Herat, finishing first in her class. "All during that time, people tried to make me marry. My father told me that if I wanted to marry I could, but if I wanted to keep studying, don't marry. I said I want to study!"

At the time, women were very much the symbol of change in Afghanistan. In 1959, Prime Minister Daoud appeared on a public stage with his wife and daughters unveiled, courting outrage from religious and tribal conservatives. Daoud was boldly repeating history. Some three decades earlier, King Amanalluh had attempted to modernize his country by decree, leading with the role of women in society. Amanulluh's final undoing came when he tried to discourage veiling by having his beautiful young wife publicly remove hers. Within weeks, he was swept from power.

Daoud reckoned he had a firmer grip on the situation, since he controlled the army and was able to squelch resistance to his social changes without much violence. Indeed, the 1960s in Afghanistan were a period of rapid gains for women, at least in more urban areas like Kabul and Herat. Even though Daoud was removed from power in 1963 (in the wake of aggressive foreign policy moves toward Pakistan, which backfired), the steps he started to improve women's status in society continued. In 1964, a new constitution accorded equal legal rights to men and women and also elevated secular civil law over sharia.[3] The first parliament, elected in 1965, included four women out of 216 members.

Sakena benefited from these new openings for women. She pursued her studies and took the exams for medical and engineering school in Kabul. With no place to stay in the distant city, however, it was not feasible for her to continue her education. Toc Dunlap, an American Peace Corps volunteer who was teaching English in Herat and was friendly with Sakena's family, encouraged Sakena's father to let his daughter go to the United States. Sakena soon found herself living with the Dunlap family in Michigan. It was 1971.

In the fall of 1972, Sakena started at the University of the Pacific in Stockton, California, on a partial scholarship. Her parents sent her some money, but she was also working as many as four jobs to support herself—night shifts at hospitals and in convalescent homes, tech jobs in laboratories, anything to earn money. "I was premed," she remembers. "I wanted to become a doctor, an obstetrician. My mother had sixteen pregnancies but only five of her children survived. So many women in Afghanistan die during pregnancy too. I knew I had to become a doctor."

Back home, Afghanistan was beginning its long descent into chaos. In 1973, Daoud, the former prime minister, felt frustrated by his exclusion from power. He ousted his cousin King Zahir Shah in a coup, ending the monarch's forty-year reign. Relying on his influence with the army and support from the People's Democratic Party of Afghanistan (PDPA), a communist party comprised of elite intellectuals, Daoud embarked on a period of even more rapid reforms. Just as King Amanullah's reforms energized his conservative opponents, Daoud's opponents began to rally behind Islamist groups that advocated a return to Islamic values and the creation of an Islamic state. The cleavage of Afghanistan had begun.

Sakena completed her B.A. in biology in 1977, and started a master's degree in public health, but her window of opportunity to continue her studies in the United States was closing. Although she dreamed of becoming a doctor or getting a Ph.D. in public health, her home country was disintegrating. In 1978, Daoud lost control of the reform process he had started. He was killed in a military coup instigated by the communist party that had become increasingly radicalized. Over the next year, the communists accelerated land reforms deeply unpopular with tribal groups and pressed ahead with highly controversial social reforms. The government tried to limit bride price (the money paid by the groom's family to the bride's family), and eliminate child marriage by establishing a minimum age of marriage. In the countryside, girls and boys were put together in classrooms, and male teachers from the cities were sent to teach girls.[4] Faced with domestic revolt, Afghanistan's communist government increasingly had to rely on force—backed by the Soviets—to push through its social reforms. Rising Islamist opposition in Afghanistan, combined with concerns about Ayatollah Khomeini's Islamist takeover in neighboring Iran earlier that year, worried the Soviets about their long-term interests in Afghanistan. On December 25, 1979, they invaded.

Sakena's family in Herat, like millions of other Afghan families, became scattered. "My father was afraid," she recalls. "There were so many bad things happening in Afghanistan that he permitted my sisters to marry at a young age. Both of my sisters were sent to marry relatives in Iran. My brothers stayed with my parents in Afghanistan, but it was very hard. So I made a decision to try to bring them all to the U.S." Sakena finally finished her master's degree in 1981. Working a variety of healthcare jobs and teaching at D'Etre University in Grosse Pointe, Michigan, she managed to save enough during the 1980s to bring her parents, siblings, and various in-laws to America. Once they were all settled in Michigan, she announced that she was going back to help her country. Her father encouraged her. "He knew how much I was needed in Afghanistan. He agreed that it was the best use of my education."

Sakena arrived in Pakistan in 1992 as a consultant for the International Rescue Committee (IRC). After the last Soviet troops had left Afghanistan in 1989, the situation inside the country only deteriorated as the mujahideen commanders turned their guns on each other. With the fighting moving to the cities, the flow of Afghan refugees to Iran and Pakistan became a flood. Sakena went to work in Peshawar, the Pakistani border town that by then had morphed into a sprawling Afghan refugee camp. There, she started a variety of teacher training programs geared toward girls' education. She remembers the challenge of getting these initiatives up and running.

"In the Kohat Mountains, about two hours from Peshawar, the first thing I did was find the mullah in the refugee camp. I asked him to be the teacher. He thought I was a crazy woman! But there were few schools in the camp and none for girls so finally he agreed. For three months I trained him to be a teacher. We started out with one tent for twenty students. Within three months, we had seven tents and three hundred girls studying. The mullah's wife and daughters and daughter-in-law, all four of them, also became teachers.

"Together with two other trainers, we wrote a manual to improve teaching quality. The only style any of the teachers had known was rote memorization. Our manual taught all the teachers how to be interactive, how to use question-and-answer with the students, how to work in a group. Within a year, we had fifteen thousand students—boys and girls through the sixth grade, all Afghan refugees. The reason I was so successful in getting the kids in school was because I respected the local culture, I was very sensitive to the local culture."

Funding for Sakena's work through the IRC, however, began to decline as the international community lost interest in Afghanistan. With the Soviets gone, Afghanistan was no longer a key battleground in the Cold War being waged by heroic mujahideen. It was just a messy civil war fought by thuggish warlords. By 1995, funding for her programs had evaporated. Sakena returned to the United States still determined to help her poor country. With $20,000 of personal savings, she founded the Afghan Institute of Learning to promote education in Afghanistan. "I knew that if people get a good education, they will think, they will ask questions, they will not just be sheep following other people." She persuaded Toc Dunlap, the former Peace Corps volunteer and her longtime mentor and supporter, to run AIL's umbrella organization in Michigan.

AIL started out with two schools in Pakistan for Afghan refugees, most of them women. The core of its program was teacher training. "People thought that I was crazy that I wanted to spend so much time on teacher training, but now, ten years later, everybody wants teacher training. Because everybody realizes that if you don't have a good teacher, you don't have good students, and if you don't have good students, you don't have good civil society," Sakena says. In addition to teacher training, AIL was soon offering a range of courses from leadership and management workshops to life skills and reproductive health classes. With strong community support it expanded quickly, and within five years, Sakena was again reaching fifteen thousand students.

At the same time, the Taliban was extending its reach across Afghanistan. Beginning in late 1994, the Taliban gained control of the south of the country. They took Kandahar, the nerve center of Pashtuns, with almost no resistance. After years of fighting and chaos, many people welcomed the order the Taliban imposed. Their puritanical customs were not so foreign in Kandahar. But the Taliban set about purifying broader Afghanistan and ridding it of Western influences. Men could no longer wear Western clothes, only the traditional *shalwar kameez*. To reflect the tradition of Muhammad, they were not allowed to shave their beards. They had to wear turbans. The Taliban banned music, dancing, and any representation of human or animal forms.

Taliban puritanism was particularly strident with respect to women. They closed girls' schools, forbade women from working, and demanded the wearing of burqas. To enforce their strict rules, they created a Saudi-like Department for Promotion of Virtue and Prevention of Vice. Wahhabism had gained influence in Afghanistan not only through significant Saudi funding of various mujahideen groups in the 1980s and 1990s, but also through Saudi support of Afghan universities, *madrasas*, and mosques and through aid to refugee camps in Pakistan.

The Taliban met with greater resistance in Kabul and Herat, where their strict rule was more onerous and where there were a considerable number of girls in school as well as professional women. Taliban restrictions on women posed deep hardship in the cities. Moreover, their ban on women working decimated the ranks of teachers, including those for boys' schools. Afghanistan's meager educational system collapsed. Surreptitiously, AIL operated girls' schools in several of Afghanistan's cities—in Kabul, in Jalalabad, in Herat. Again, Sakena developed a training manual, this one to assist teachers who had multiple grades, sometimes from first through eighth, in one makeshift classroom.

"The Taliban never shut us down because they never found out about us," says Sakena. "I worked closely with each community. They had to choose the teacher. They had to identify the house where she would teach. I also made a contract with every teacher to set the rules. No men could ever come to the house except the teacher's father or husband. If other men started coming to the house, the Taliban could get suspicious." Students also had to vary their arrivals and departures to avoid scrutiny. And Sakena was strict with the teachers. "I insist that they wear hijab. We are Muslims. We wear a hijab all our lives. It is not a new thing. I asked the teachers, what do you want? Education? Or not to wear this hijab? They all said education, so I tell them to cover themselves. Make sure you are always covered, at any meeting, wherever someone could see you. Because I insist on wearing the veil, some people, especially in Pakistan, thought I was part of Hizb-i-Islami [a puritanical Islamist party led by the warlord Gulbuddin Hekmatyar].

My God," she says, a look of disgust passing across her face, "I don't have anything to do with those people!"

During the Taliban years, AIL was not only providing crucial services to thousands of Afghan women and girls, it was also a veritable proving ground for a generation of future women leaders. Several AIL employees now run their own social service organizations or hold political positions in the government. The most prominent AIL veteran is Habiba Sarabi, a hematologist who spent the Taliban years working in refugee camps in Peshawar and undercover in Afghanistan. She joined AIL in 1998 as a teacher trainer and became its general manager. In 2002, President Karzai appointed Sarabi as minister of women's affairs. In early 2005, she was appointed the governor of Bamiyan, the country's first female governor. Sakena herself has turned down several requests to join the government. "I can do more outside the government, running AIL," she insists.

After the fall of the Taliban, AIL quickly expanded its programs within Afghanistan, setting up women's centers in various provinces that have become hubs for all its educational initiatives, including health education. "Everywhere we go, we work with the community. In Herat, I went to see Ismail Khan. Many people said I was crazy to go to him, but I wanted his support." Ismail Khan was the leading mujahideen commander of the Herat region who immediately resumed power after the fall of the Taliban. A staunch religious conservative, he reportedly maintained a secret "morality police" while he was governor. The morality police would pick women up off the street who were not wearing a burqa or were seen with a man. Sometimes, they were taken to hospitals to have their virginity checked.[5] Sakena assured the governor that all the girls in her schools would be covered, that no men would be allowed into the centers. "If we followed his rules, he would leave us alone. And we got to educate the girls. We started out with basic literacy classes, but now we are teaching them about reproductive health and also their rights, their rights according to Islam."

Today, AIL has more than forty women centers in operation. Each one has a mini–health clinic that provides some community access to doctors and nurses. In the winter of 2008, I visited one of AIL's health clinics in Parvan Province with Sakena. The clinic, built about five years earlier with AIL funds on land donated by the local community, is on a small lane off the main road that runs north out of Kabul. On any given day, the clinic's courtyard is crowded with women and their children waiting to see AIL's doctor or midwife. First, however, they must file through the "classroom" where AIL health workers impart important information on cleanliness, nutrition, and family planning. "We use the Quran here too," Sakena explained when I questioned her on the sensitivity of distributing condoms and birth control in these conservative villages. "We teach the women the passages in the Quran that emphasize cleanliness and health. We explain that using condoms prevents disease and using birth control helps space pregnancies and maintains the mother's health. We encourage the women to bring their husbands and we explain it all to them too."

AIL has also trained more than fifteen hundred teachers across Afghanistan. In 2002, it started a women's college in Pakistan for Afghan refugees. "It's not sophisticated, but it is good training," explains Sakena, somewhat apologetically. "We offer computer science and nursing degrees. We have graduated several classes already and our graduates quickly get jobs, especially the nurses. Many of them work in Pakistan, but more and more are going back to Afghanistan too." One of these graduates is Nooria Nuri, a twenty-five-year-old midwife who now manages AIL's health clinic in Parvan. During my visit, I watched her work efficiently across the clinic's various rooms, managing the constant flow of patients. In her clean white lab coat, she exudes professionalism. Many of the women have walked miles with their children for this brief interaction with modernity.

AIL's budget hovers around a million dollars a year, raised from various international sources including American Jewish World Service, the UN's Population Fund (UNFPA), and the Global Fund for Women. However, essential in-kind donations bring its effective budget closer to $3.5 million per year. Abbott Labs and Direct Relief provide AIL with medicines, and the local communities where it works all provide land and labor.

Still, AIL operates on a shoestring. In several AIL schools I visited with Sakena, the students are crammed into tiny classrooms with no desks and few supplies. But the teachers are dedicated and strive to meet Sakena's high standards of excellence. In one classroom, Sakena stopped to berate the local mullah who was teaching the Quran to a group of boys. "Quranic studies are important," she explained, "but I don't want the boys to mindlessly memorize! I want them to understand what they are learning. The mullah must teach critical thinking skills along with the text." Sakena remains determined. "My next challenge is to teach the men, because no matter how much we teach the women, if the men don't change, we won't get anywhere."

"We Will Continue on Our Way"

Safia Amajan adjusted her burqa, the long, billowing covering she always wore when leaving her home. She straightened the garment carefully so the mesh grille was positioned in front of her eyes, allowing her to see at least directly in front of her. Although it was the fall of 2006, nearly five years since the Taliban had been overthrown, few women in Kandahar, Safia's hometown, dared venture outside without the burqa. The custom is deeply ingrained in Kandahar, the cultural heart of ethnic Pashtuns where Pashtunwali—the traditional code of Pashtuns based on honor (particularly female honor), tribe, and revenge—regulates daily life. Moreover, the resurgent Taliban was again threatening women who defied their strict codes. Safia was already a target of Taliban ire for her work as the provincial minister of women's affairs in Kandahar. For years, she had been a tireless advocate for women's rights, even secretly running a school for girls in her Kandahar home during the Taliban years while she raised her own four children. Now a grandmother in her fifties, she was overseeing the reestablishment of girls' schools and opening vocational training centers for women. More than a thousand women were learning commercial baking and tailoring skills in these centers and selling their goods at market.

Lately, Safia had been receiving "night letters" slipped under her door anonymously and other threats singling out her work with women and her own public role. She had asked the Afghan government to provide personal bodyguards and official transport, but her request had been rejected. On this September morning, a taxi was idling outside, ready to take her to her office, and she said good-bye to her seventeen-year-old son. It was early, just seven in the morning, and the street was still quiet. As she stepped outside, two men on motorcycles raced down the street, kicking up a cloud of dust. With the surge of drug money in the Afghan economy, young men on motorcycles are a common sight even in small villages. These two had machine guns over their shoulders and they unloaded several rounds into Safia's burqa-clad body. She crumpled to the ground beside the taxi and died instantly.

Hundreds of supporters packed the mosque for Safia's funeral, including the provincial governor and various tribal leaders. They spoke admiringly of her courage, her determination, and of her faith. Several noted that Safia was a *hafiz*, a person who has memorized the entire Quran. They denounced her killers as un-Islamic. One female parliamentarian from Kandahar who attended the funeral summed up the feeling of many who were there. "The enemies of Afghanistan killed her," she said, "but they should know it will not derail women from the path we are on. We will continue on our way."[6]

Assassinating women leaders has been a favored Taliban tactic to sow fear across the Afghan population and to dissuade women from taking on public roles. But intrepid women like Safia Amajan persist despite the threats and intimidation. The fact that nearly 30 percent of Afghanistan's parliamentarians are women is a remarkable development since the days of the Taliban. Today, Afghanistan has one of the highest levels of representation for women in parliament in the world. But it was only through the use of quotas that Afghan women garnered such a relatively high level of political representation. Polls show that nearly 70 percent of Afghans overall say they support women's right to hold public office, and that support has increased in recent years. But not surprisingly, there are deep gender and urban/rural differences on this point. Urban women overwhelmingly support women's right to vote and hold office, but support for a public role for women declines significantly—among both men and women—in rural areas where more than three-quarters of the population live.[7]

The idea of a quota for women in parliament surfaced early in the process of drafting a new constitution. While the notion generated some lip-service support as a way to redress some of the wrongs inflicted on women by the Taliban, many Afghan leaders were hostile to the idea. But a group of determined Afghan women, supported by the international community, were not going to let the opportunity slip away. As a first step, they secured a quota for women delegates to attend the constitutional *loya jirga*, the "grand assembly" held in December 2003 to debate and approve the country's new constitution. This was critical to make sure that women's voices were at the table.

For two weeks, 500 Afghan delegates (including 116 women) argued over a number of key issues, including how strong to make the central government, the role of Islam in the constitution, and women's rights. The advocates of a political quota for women organized a petition. Like seasoned backroom negotiators, they worked the *loya jirga* tent, trading favors and cutting deals to gain support. They got male delegates from minority parties to support women's rights in exchange for women's support on sensitive ethnic issues. They persuaded women delegates to put aside their ethnic and partisan loyalties to come together on this issue. Eventually, they collected signatures from over 150 delegates. They also worked behind the scenes to gain the support of key power players like the U.S. ambassador at the time, Zalmay Khalilzad, and the UN Special Representative Lakhdar Brahimi. "The ambassador's female assistant made time on his schedule for the women to see him. The women delegates were deeply divided on all the issues. But on this [getting the quota for women], they came together," says Rina Amiri, political affairs officer for the UN's Afghan mission at the time.[8] "Before they met with Khalilzad and Brahimi, they were trying to hold onto just one seat per district for women. After that meeting, with [Khalilzad and Brahimi's] support, they were able to push for two."

With a little over a quarter of the national parliament now constitutionally reserved for women, would conservative Afghan society allow women to take advantage of this opportunity? Simply registering men and women to vote was a daunting task in the impoverished, war-torn country, where the majority of people were illiterate and deeply suspicious of government. Numerous tribal and religious leaders, particularly in the conservative Pashtun areas in the south and east of the country, boasted that they would not allow women even to register to vote. The quotas, however, changed the political reality.

Minority groups, like the Hazara in central Afghanistan and Tajiks in the north, quickly realized the upside of getting out the women's vote—it would boost their numbers. They made a big push to register women voters. Soon, other political leaders began to understand the importance of the women's vote. Even conservative Pashtun leaders began encouraging women to vote. They urged the mullahs in the countryside to preach in their Friday prayers that the Quran allowed for women's political participation. In the presidential election on October 9, 2004, a remarkable 75 percent of eligible voters cast ballots. More than 40 percent of them were women.[9]

Attention quickly turned to the parliamentary elections to be held the following year. With women now guaranteed two seats per district, the immediate challenge was finding female candidates willing to stand for election. Critics of the quota had from the outset warned that there were too few qualified women to run for, let alone serve in, parliament. As usual, they underestimated the women. From across the country, women of all ages and backgrounds answered the call. Some came from the elite, some from working-class families. Some of the candidates had stayed in Afghanistan during the country's dark years. Others had fled as refugees and now were returning home. Many of the women were in their forties and fifties—they had come of age during the relatively liberal 1970s or under the firm hand of the Soviets in the 1980s. But a surprising number were in their twenties and thirties, more often than not products of refugee camps in Iran and Pakistan. All of them, given the chance, wanted to be part of the historic change that was the new Afghanistan.

Poetry in Parliament

Safia Siddiqi stood a bit stiffly on the stage in a dusty meeting hall in Jalalabad, a city on the eastern edge of Afghanistan near the Pakistan border. She was a lone female face in a sea of dour, turbaned men. With a dark brown scarf covering her hair, and a beaded shawl flung around her shoulders, she moved to the microphone, opened a book—her book—and began to read a poem in *Pashto* to her attentive male audience. The poem, called "Rain Drops in Blue Skies," is one of her most popular. As she recited the poem in a voice clear and confident yet full of emotion, some of the hard, weathered faces in the audience appeared visibly moved. Although officially this was a *mushaira*, a poetry reading, for Safia Siddiqi it was also an unofficial campaign stop. It was the spring of 2005, and Safia was running for parliament. She took every opportunity to appeal to her constituents' sense of Pashtun honor and cultural pride, to put herself in the limelight, and to read some poetry. "The people demanded it," she told me some years later, remembering her campaigning. "The men especially liked my 'Rain Drop' poem. I recited that one a lot."[10]

Safia was born in a small village just outside Jalalabad in Nangarhar Province, a lush valley that was once an oasis of flowers and fruit gardens in the midst of Afghanistan's rocky desert. She grew up in an educated family of judges and scholars, although she herself did not attend a formal school until she was fifteen. There was no school for girls in her village, but as a child, she would sit on the roof of her home and strain to hear the teachers in the nearby mosque teaching the boys. "My grandfather donated the land for the mosque so it was adjacent to our *kila* [the large, walled compounds of wealthy Pashtuns]. There were as many as fifty boys sitting in the courtyard of the mosque, learning from the mullah. I would sit on our rooftop and listen and in this way I memorized the poems."

Later, her younger brother started in school and her father would help him with his homework in the afternoons. Safia remembers sitting in on those sessions and in this way learning to read. She was a quicker student than her brother and soon her father had outsourced the homework help to her, even though she did not attend school. When her father took a judgeship in Kabul and moved the family there, Safia helped make ends meet by working as a seamstress. She herself finally started school when a family friend asked her to apply to the school where he was a teacher. Self-taught, she passed the tests for seventh grade, and within months had moved on through the eighth and ninth grades. "I didn't enjoy it very much. The other students were younger, and I was big," she remembers. "So I waited for enrollment in the tenth grade. In the meantime, I sewed clothes for tourists and made more money than my own father."[11]

Encouraged by an uncle, Siddiqi also started writing poetry, pouring her teenage heart out in traditional verses. Her early poetry was inspired by the tragic death of a bride and groom in a village near her own in Nangarhar, killed in a Soviet bombing raid. "Writing poetry was not acceptable for women. It is considered romantic, like singing. But my uncle pushed me. He would give me prizes for my poems. From the beginning, I was a very good declaimer, and he would come listen to me recite my poems."

In between writing poetry and stories, making money and plowing through high school, Safia Siddiqi managed to pass the entrance exams to law school with honors. An eligible suitor appeared at this point, handsome and educated, and her parents begged her to marry. But the suitor made it clear that he had no interest in Safia attending university, and she refused the proposal. She credits her poetry with saving her from this early marriage. Her father had come to recognize her special talent. Rather than force her into marriage, he allowed her to attend university.

She studied law at Kabul University. In 1987, she published her first collection of verse, *Dupatta* (Scarf), which earned her considerable local recognition. Even at that young age, she began dreaming of becoming a lawyer, of running for parliament. Although she recalls those years fondly, her anticommunist family was coming under increasing pressure from the Soviet-backed government. In 1988, her father decided to send her and her brother to Pakistan and soon she found herself a refugee in Peshawar.

"From Afghanistan, Peshawar looked like heaven, but it was really hell," she remembers. She was forced to scramble for survival and to wear a burqa for the first time in her life. "All the women in Peshawar were forced to wear burqas by Hizb-i-Islami [the virulently anti-Western Islamist organization of Gulbuddin Hekmatyar, known for fighting against Soviet forces in Afghanistan]. The only jobs we were allowed to hold were as nurses and tailors. I felt threatened by Hizb-i-Islami in particular. They criticized me because my book of poetry had been published by the communists in Kabul."

Safia started working as a seamstress in a shop funded by the Danes and was quickly promoted to manager. Taking advantage of some of the classes provided by aid organizations for Afghan refugees in Peshawar, she learned English. She tried to keep a low profile, since she feared the Taliban, the communists, and the fundamentalist mujahideen parties in Pakistan. But she could not help getting involved. She was drawn in particular to working with women's groups. She became an unofficial spokeswoman for various women's causes and even traveled overseas representing Afghan women. The highlight came when she was included in a delegation of Afghan women to attend the UN's International Women's Conference in Beijing in 1995. As is true for so many women leaders around the world today, Safia's activism took a leap forward after Beijing. Upon her return, she started her own women's organization in Peshawar.

These were busy years. Somehow, Safia also found time to complete a master's degree in literature and another in business administration, as well as produce a second edition of poetry called *Unread*. Published in 1997 during Taliban times, the cover of this book is deceptively simple: cool mountains and a lazy river surrounded by a pink border. Inside, the poetry is powerfully raw and emotional.

Safia Siddiqi's rising prominence, as she anticipated, earned her enemies and soon the threats started. Heeding the advice of friends, she sought asylum in Canada and for a few years lived a more predictable, if not mundane life. She even married a fellow Afghan refugee. But she missed her country and felt helplessly far from the crisis. When the United States toppled the Taliban after 9/11, her decision to return to Afghanistan was not hard. She quickly landed a job with the newly created Ministry of Women's Affairs in Kabul.

Within a year, Safia Siddiqi emerged as one of Kabul's more high-profile women, serving as deputy chair of the constitutional *loya jirga* held at the end of 2003. (She was appointed to the position after women's groups complained they were being shut out of leadership positions.)[12] A year later, Safia was running for parliament from her home province of Nangarhar, carefully treading her way through conservative Pashtun country.

Across Afghanistan, campaigning for the women candidates was like navigating a minefield, every action a broken taboo. Each female candidate had to feel her way forward carefully, finding out through sometimes painful trial and error where the red lines were, what society was willing to tolerate with regard to women in politics. In Kabul, the unspoken parameters were looser, and several women jumped right into the fray, plastering their local districts with billboard-sized posters of themselves, holding town hall meetings, and appearing on television and radio shows. In rural areas, the female candidates were more circumspect, quietly calling upon tribal elder and religious leaders to appeal for their support.

Safia Siddiqi has natural political instincts, tacking with the wind depending on which audience she was addressing. In the Nangarhar countryside, she solicited village elders and invoked their sense of Pashtun pride. She recited the Quran and her Pashto poems at every opportunity while avoiding all talk of women's rights and human rights. These topics aroused suspicions among her rural male—and female—constituents. In more urban Jalalabad, she took a bolder stance, speaking with women about the need to improve education and job opportunities, and appearing in startling campaign posters draped in the Afghan national flag. She even campaigned in the marketplace hanging out of the sunroof of her SUV. "That was my husband's idea," she remembers. "He got out and directed the car through the crowds. I just remember looking at the sea of men all around the car."

During the election, Safia Siddiqi was in center stage, just where she loves to be, with all its attendant drama. Determined to win, she pulled out all the stops. She even campaigned, quite imprudently, in her competitor's hometown and came under attack from gunmen. She survived (the attackers narrowly missed) and came out a winner. When the final results were tallied, Safia placed third in a field of fourteen candidates. She makes a point of telling me that the man who placed first did so by paying $40,000 of bribes to secure the top spot. She spent only $18,000 on her campaign, funded out of her personal savings. "The men all spent many times that amount. One commander spent more than $3 million to get elected," she says. By winning the support of a substantial number of men, Safia even came in ahead of a popular local mujahideen commander.

Against the odds, women secured seats ahead of male candidates in a quarter of Afghanistan's thirty-four provinces.[13] Some men openly admitted they voted for certain women because of their attractive looks and despite their lack of political experience. (A few of the "hottest" female candidates saw their campaign posters become bestsellers.) Many voters, though, said they supported female candidates simply because they were not mujahideen with blood on their hands. Defying expectations, the women elected were generally well educated. Fifty percent of them hold a university degree versus only 40 percent of the men.[14] (By one count, some 20 percent of the men elected were illiterate.)[15] The women also brought to parliament quite a different set of professional experiences. While many of the men had spent the prior decade shouldering AK-47s in the mountains, the women had been working for the UN and running social-service agencies—a more relevant set of skills for the new government, some might argue.

The reality is that the quota opened doors for some of Afghanistan's most talented, skilled, and educated human capital, which the country desperately needs to rebuild. Without the quota for women in place, far fewer women would have dared to put themselves out there to run, and far fewer would have been elected. Indeed, women would have won less than 8 percent of the seats in parliament on their own, and in nearly two-thirds of the provinces, no women would have been elected without reserved seats.[16] The use of the quota shaved several decades off the time that it would have taken to get women into politics in any meaningful way in Afghanistan.

For Safia Siddiqi, getting elected—despite the assassination attempt—was in some ways the easy part. Now she had to work alongside some very conservative men, many of them with a strong jihadi orientation. A big part of her day-to-day challenge was fighting a rearguard action against troglodyte colleagues in parliament. Safia got a taste of how tenuous her situation could be when in early 2006, just months after she was elected, she joined President Karzai on a delegation to a major donor conference in London.

While she and another woman in the delegation were negotiating aid packages, back home in Kabul conservative legislators denounced them for breaking Islamic law by traveling without their husbands. "As

Muslims, we have a strong book, the Holy Quran, and we believe in the Quran, we don't believe in the constitution. We have given women the right to educate themselves, to take part in government, to participate in political life. But there are special rules," warned Hajji Ahmed Farid, a religious scholar and parliamentarian.[17] Hajji Farid happens to be Safia Siddiqi's brother-in-law.

When we discussed the incident, Safia was reluctant to criticize her brother-in-law on the record, saying only that "some men in society don't respect the work of women." She described how Hajji Farid argued strenuously during subsequent debates in 2007 that women should not be issued their own passports. Instead, he wanted them to travel as minors on their husband's passport. Many female parliamentarians pushed back hard, arguing against a narrow interpretation of *mahram*, the sharia-dictated requirements for male chaperones. They feared slipping back into Taliban-like restrictions on women. Safia made the point over and over again in the press that the precedent being set was important not only for the women in parliament, but for all Afghan women.

In the end, parliament passed legislation allowing women to get their own passports, although processing the application requires the permission of a male guardian. "You know," Safia told me, "the irony is that Hajji Farid's daughters are being educated outside the country, in Pakistan. His family is Canadian-Afghan. His mother lives in Montreal. They all have their own passports."

For the trailblazing women in parliament, success for now seems to be measured by holding onto their gains, by not slipping backward, and by surviving. Several female parliamentarians have been the targets of assassination attempts. Safia herself narrowly escaped a tragic attack in November 2007. Traveling with a parliamentary group to tour a sugar factory, her car pulled over to put air in a tire. She was just minutes behind the rest of her delegation when a suicide bomber struck, killing at least forty people. The blast left six Afghan MPs dead, including the popular opposition leader Mustafa Kazimi, who was probably the target of the attack, and scores of onlookers, mostly women, children, and tribal leaders. Safia, along with her then seven-month-old son who she often took with her on provincial visits, arrived unscathed on the bloody scene only minutes later.

"I was walking fast across the parking lot to catch up with the delegation," remembers Safia. "One man, running, overtook me. He was killed. The attack was devastating. It was much worse than the attack on me in Nangarhar [when she was campaigning]. That attack was just against me. This attack killed so many people. I lost many friends." A week after the explosion, she miscarried a baby. Adding to her devastation were the rumors that swirled around her after the attack. Some within parliament began questioning whether it was simply luck that delayed her, or whether there was a far more sinister explanation. Rumors of suspicious cell phone activity just before the attack dogged her. "I am a woman and a mother," she insists. "I have devoted my life to a free Afghanistan. How could I be a part of such a terrible suicide bombing? If I had been two minutes earlier, my baby would have been waiting for me in the car for the rest of his life. To make rumors is easy, but they should check my cell phone records. There were no calls." She fingers the small silver canister she wears around her neck that holds a tiny, indecipherable, rolled-up Quran inside. "It keeps me safe," she says.

Getting to Zero

Shukria Barakzai breezes through Afghanistan's parliament like a movie star, lighting up the building's gloomy hallways with her glamorous smile. While many of the female members of parliament wear tightly wrapped headscarves, Shukria is usually seen with her signature sunglasses nestled in her thick dark hair, a gauzy scarf thrown on top almost as an afterthought. She favors bold-colored scarves or jazzy prints like leopard skin or panda-bear black and white.

Born in 1972, Shukria was trying to complete her studies at Kabul University when the country was plunged into civil war. As the fighting escalated, it became too dangerous for her to stay in school. She dropped out, married, and started a family. Later, confined to home by the Taliban, she set up a clandestine school for girls and worked as a teacher during those grim years. She finished her own degree only after the Taliban were toppled in 2001.

Shukria knew that her role in the new Afghanistan was to help improve the dire situation for women. In 2002, she launched a women's magazine, *Women's Mirror*, as a way of bringing attention to critical gender issues and encouraging women to take part in the country's fledgling civil society and democracy. Under her editorial direction, the magazine focused on topics such as violence against women, child marriage, and women's health—or lack of it—in Afghanistan. She also lost no opportunity to speak out against warlordism and the political thuggery that had destroyed her country.

In 2003, Shukria was appointed to the constitutional *loya jirga*, where she became an outspoken proponent for women's rights and fought hard to ensure that women received a guaranteed number of seats in parliament. She then turned around and took advantage of that quota, running for—and winning—a seat representing Kabul. Her wealthy businessman husband also ran for parliament at the same time (for another seat) but lost, a point that seems to give Shukria quite some satisfaction. "He spent half a million dollars on his campaign but didn't get even half the votes I got," she likes to boast.[18]

One of the more sophisticated members of parliament, Shukria speaks five languages (English, French, Urdu, Pashto, and Dari) and can often be found translating documents for her male colleagues, even her former Taliban colleagues. Once flogged by the Taliban moral police for visiting a doctor without a male escort, now she works burqa-less alongside former Taliban leaders and other elected Islamists.

Indeed, Shukria's assigned seat in parliament was initially next to that of Abdul Rasul Sayyaf, the notorious mujahideen leader who now wields enormous power from inside the government. The two could not be more physically different—she charismatic and winsome, he hulking and dour behind his long gray beard. They are also true political opposites—she an outspoken critic of warlords, he one of Afghanistan's most brutal strongmen. At first, they chatted and traded notes, but it went quickly downhill from there. "Yes, we had fun in the beginning," she says with only faint sarcasm. "But of course our views are very different. I was always raising the red card to object to his statements, and after a while he got tired of me and moved his seat to the other side of the chamber."

Parliament has been a frustrating experience for this resolute, gutsy woman. A tireless advocate for women's issues, Shukria is often out in front, debating, exposing, insisting, cajoling. But she bemoans the lack of support she gets from her female colleagues. Despite the relatively high number of women in parliament due to the quota, the women members are a fractious lot—divided by regional differences, ethnic loyalties, and political allegiances far more than they are united by gender. They represent the full gamut of political views within a parliament that itself is divided and weak. They have yet to constitute a voting bloc, although they have managed to come together on a few issues, like better treatment for women in prison and for widows.

Shukria insists that the women's presence in parliament is definitely more than just tokenism. At a minimum, women members are using the public stage to keep women's issues on the agenda and help break down deeply rooted stereotypes through their work. Many of the female MPs vow to support greater rights and opportunities for women, including improving girls' education, women's health, and income generation, and also to take on more sensitive issues like child marriage and domestic abuse. But the gap between aspiration and facts on the ground is huge. As Shukria explains, "Women in Afghanistan are starting at minus twenty. We are just trying to get to zero." She insists that the Afghan people want change, and she is trying to be a bridge between government and civil society. She has been working strategically with the Ministry of Interior to get more women in the police force and working with the Ministry of Education to change stereotypes of women and girls in the textbooks.

In one small victory, Shukria worked with the Ministry of Finance to get a line item in the budget to measure funding for women and track how many women are in government. She recalls what a battle even this was. "Minister of Finance Ahady said to me, 'Ms. Barakzai, that type of thing is for a modern country, not for Afghanistan.' But I said no, that is unacceptable, and I pressured him. In 2008, we got a report showing the number of women in government. It's only twelve percent, which is too low. But at least we are measuring it now," she tells me proudly.

In recent years, Shukria has actively campaigned against polygamy—something with which she has painful firsthand experience. In 2004, after twelve years of marriage, her husband and the father of her three children took another wife. She only found out about it indirectly, through friends—an added humiliation. Shukria urges women not to become second wives. She also notes that the Quran demands that men treat all their wives equally and requires that the first wife give permission for subsequent marriages, practices rarely followed. As part of her campaign against polygamy, she has taken on the sensitive issues of forced marriage and child marriage, still common practices across Afghanistan.

In the spring of 2009, Shukria Barakzai, working with other progressive female parliamentarians, fought a pitched battle over a controversial piece of legislation called the Shia Personal Status Law. As originally proposed, the law intended to roll back the age of marriage for Shia girls to nine, and also allowed for *muta*, or temporary marriage, a custom many women feel simply legitimizes prostitution. By dint of the female parliamentarians' efforts, those elements were removed (the marriage age was set at sixteen), but two troubling clauses remained: women could not refuse their husband sex (seeming to legalize marital rape) and women needed a husband's permission to leave the home (a Taliban-like restriction). Pandering to conservatives in the run-up to the 2009 presidential elections, President Karzai signed that version of the bill. Shukria and other women activists took their complaints to the international media and a firestorm of protest ensued. Several NATO countries threatened to withhold troops from Afghanistan if the law was implemented. Emboldened by the international response, women activists led protests in the streets, holding firm in the face of violent counterdemonstrations. A few months later, the law was revised, removing some, but not all, of the controversial provisions. (The new version still allows a man to withhold food and shelter from his wife if she does not submit to his sexual demands.) Shukria Barakzai well knows this was only a partial victory. "We need a change in customs, and this is just on paper. What is being practiced every day, in Kabul even, is worse than the laws."[19]

Shukria is aware that she is a role model and very much in the vanguard of the fight for democracy and women's rights in Afghanistan. But at times she cannot help but sound beleaguered. "I thought parliament would be a great place for change. But the vote is always with the majority, and the majority is against me," says Shukria with some resignation. "I can't touch progress." She admits that she is unlikely to run again in the next parliamentary election (scheduled for 2010). "I think I can do more as a journalist, a political leader outside of parliament, building up an independent party."

Shukria, however, is hardly defeated. "I want to be president," she says simply. "I will run for president, not in the next cycle, because I will not be old enough, but sometime in the future. I know I am on the assassination list. But I don't care. I would be proud to die for my country." When I demur, mentioning her three young daughters, she shoots right back. "I love my country and my people even more than my girls. Maybe in the future my children will be proud of their mother and understand that I am working for my beliefs on behalf of all the children of Afghanistan."

It Takes a Village

National leaders like Shukria Barakzai make some Afghan women proud, but three-quarters of Afghans live in villages and pay little attention to what goes on beyond their local council. Women have traditionally played almost no role in the running of village affairs, but through an innovative initiative called the National Solidarity Program (NSP), that is gradually changing. Indeed, the NSP is one of the most powerful engines for women's political empowerment in Afghanistan today, creating sustainable changes for women at the grassroots level. The idea behind the NSP is a simple one, but for Afghanistan, revolutionary: Local villages can and should take responsibility for their own development.

Ashraf Ghani, Afghanistan's finance minister just after the fall of the Taliban, was one of the key visionaries behind the NSP. During the decade he spent at the World Bank prior to returning to his home country, he had become familiar with a successful community development initiative in Indonesia where villagers directly voted on and managed local projects. Not only did schools and water pumps get built, but local governance improved significantly. Ghani knew that Afghans had little reason to trust their long-dysfunctional government and believed that community-led development was the only way forward.

He brought Scott Guggenheim, the World Bank expert who had designed the Indonesian program, to Kabul and they got to work creating a similar initiative for Afghanistan.

Quickly, they joined forces with Samantha Reynolds, an undaunted Englishwoman who had spent the previous decade setting up community development projects across Afghanistan under the auspices of UN-Habitat. Amazingly, despite Taliban restrictions, many of these projects were led by Afghan women, for women. Initiatives included health clinics, schools, and home-based businesses. Still, Reynolds remembers what a challenge it was to get women involved in the beginning. She credits the intervention of a local mullah in the northern town of Mazar-e-Sharif with breaking down the barriers. She said to him, "Islam grants women so many rights. Why can't we meet with the women?"[20] On a Friday morning in 1995, at the end of an all-male session, Reynolds finally got her wish. The mullah promised to include women.

"The *muezzin* crackled into life over the frozen mudscape of domes. It turned out he was not calling people to prayer; rather he was using the mosque's loudspeaker to invite all the women in the neighborhood to the meeting. Before we knew it, the room was filled with blue shrouded figures," recalls Reynolds.[21] When the Taliban gained control of most of the country the following year, the women's initiatives had to go underground. But even during the worst of the Taliban's excesses, the community programs continued to function. Interestingly, the UN-Habitat community centers were largely unscathed during the turmoil, reflecting the degree of community ownership and protection they enjoyed.

Recognizing that UN-Habitat had already laid a solid foundation for a community development initiative, the World Bank expanded upon those experiences to develop the National Solidarity Program. At the heart of the NSP are community development councils (CDCs) which are democratically elected through secret ballots at the village level. Once in place, the councils receive block grants from the Ministry of Rural Rehabilitation and Development, which they decide how to use. The grants average $31,000 per village, a considerable sum by rural Afghan standards.[22] Not surprisingly, the money comes with some strings attached: The council has to be transparent and accountable in its decision making, and women have to be part of the process, both in terms of voting for and serving on the councils.

Clare Lockhart, who worked as Finance Minister Ashraf Ghani's deputy in the early years of the NSP, remembers the resistance of village leaders to the idea of including women in the councils. "The men complained that it was against their traditions, against their religion, to have women on the councils. To solve the impasse, we proposed that the men let the women set up their own councils, and we would split the money—evenly. They quickly decided that it would be much better to have women on the council rather than have to share the money!"[23]

Sayed Sawayz tells a similar story. Sayed worked with Samantha Reynolds at UN-Habitat as a provincial manager and stayed on as it evolved into the NSP. He remembers working with a local commander in Bamiyan who had ruled the town in Taliban times. "He agreed with just about all of our NSP goals for his village, except he refused to allow women to participate. He was worried that women wouldn't elect him. We insisted, but he quoted the Quran, trying to make the point that women were not allowed out of the house. But we quoted the Quran right back to him. Our workers were all trained in the relevant passages from the Quran and the hadith to make the case for women's participation. The local mullah had no choice but to agree with us. The commander relented. However, he was not elected and he was angry. He went around to all the other villages nearby, saying that the NSP was trying to promote Christianity. He caused an uproar. I had to go out there [to Bamiyan] myself, and go through the manuals with village leaders and show them how we were using the Quran. In the manuals, we took the Arabic quotes from the Quran, we translated them and put them into context. These people are uneducated and we had to interpret for them. The men calmed down, but still they resisted women in the NSP. They said, 'Women tell us what to do in the home, so we don't want them in the *shura*.' But we persisted. Without the Quran on our side, we would not have won."[24]

Starting in the summer of 2003, the NSP began to roll out across the country. By 2008 it was up and running in nearly 80 percent of Afghanistan's thirty thousand villages all across the country.[25] The secret balloting for the councils has produced a whole new crop of rural leaders. On average, those elected are younger (under thirty-five), more literate, yet poorer than traditional leaders—a profound change for Afghanistan, where age and wealth have defined village leadership for centuries.[26] Elected leaders are getting training in financial accounting, project management, and conflict resolution. The World Bank estimates that projects completed by the CDCs are on average 30 percent cheaper than those constructed by foreign organizations. At a national conference for council leaders in Kabul in November 2007, Finance Minister Anwar ul-Haq Ahady noted that an NSP-built school costs on average $100,000, whereas schools built by foreign organizations cost $250,000.[27] Villagers feel they really own the projects and are therefore willing to donate their labor and find deals in local markets for materials.[28] And because they are locally owned and managed, they tend to benefit from much better security.

The inclusion of women has also been unprecedented. For the first time, women in rural villages are part of the decision-making process. In every community financed by the NSP, women must identify at least one project per community.[29] They tend to favor literacy and income-generating projects. While male priorities still get the lion's share of the funding, women are learning to speak up and be heard. In some cases, foreign donors fund the women's priorities on top of the regular allocations to give the women additional leverage.[30] The process has brought village women together in other ways. Many are now meeting in groups for the first time and even setting up savings schemes.

In some conservative areas, not surprisingly, it remains a challenge to get women involved in the local councils. Mixed meetings are not allowed, so the women meet separately and feed their suggestions into the men's group. In several elections, the women running for the councils would not use their own names so they ran under fictitious names, which, not surprisingly, created all sorts of confusion. But women are making progress. At the 2007 national conference for development councils, fully a third of the delegates were women. For many, it was the first time in their lives they had left their village.

The NSP, however, has been chronically underfunded. In Indonesia, the success of the program hinged on the communities' ability to apply for follow-on grants once a project had been completed. According to Scott Guggenheim, who oversaw these programs for the World Bank, it took four or five grant cycles before responsive government began to emerge in Indonesian villages.[31] Afghanistan's program has not had the funds both to expand to all the villages (and there is understandable pressure from villagers to do so) and to provide follow-on grants. Yet existing councils in thousands of villages are likely to dissolve without additional projects to manage. Despite the billions of dollars the Bush administration spent propping up the Karzai government and fighting insurgents in Afghanistan, it neglected one of the few programs popular among Afghans with proven results. It provided NSPs with only $10 to $15 million a year, less than 15 percent of its total budget.

In 2009, Washington approved a sizable increase in funds for NSP, allocating $70 million a year to the program. The hope is that a stronger NSP program will help stabilize the country. Gradually, the NSP is now being expanded into the more hostile southern and eastern parts of the country, which will pose even larger challenges for including women in the process. The World Bank's Scott Guggenheim is optimistic that NSP will bring progress for women into the heart of Pashtun country, albeit slowly. "Demand for the NSP is high in the south and east of the country, but to be successful, the program must have a 'light touch.' It must take its lead from the villagers. Some will say 'no' to women in the *shura* councils, but some will say yes, and over time, change will happen."[32]

Sharia Tensions—the Battle for a Song

Just after the dinner hour one cold January night in 2004, Kabulis sitting around their televisions—those lucky enough to own one and to have electricity at that moment—were shocked to see a woman appear on the screen and break into song on the Afghan state channel. Wearing a shiny red dress and a simple headscarf, the popular performer sang a well-known Pashtun ode about Afghanistan's beautiful mountains. The grainy video, shot in the 1980s, marked the first time a woman had sung on television since the mujahideen had ousted the communists from government in 1992. Although female singers, some in relatively scanty outfits, had been common on television during the communist years, the mujahideen put an end to that in the name of Islamic values. The Taliban went even further, banning all television and nonreligious music. Many of those television sets Kabulis were watching that night in 2004 had spent years wrapped in plastic and buried in backyards.

Although women had recently begun to appear on television as newscasters—conservatively dressed, veiled, but with their faces showing—singing was another matter. Allowing women to sing, even older, dignified women rendering traditional songs, crossed some conservative threshold. The issue immediately became a test of wills between reformists and religious conservatives, with both sides referring to the country's new constitution, adopted only days earlier, to back up their positions. Moderate officials insisted that images of women singing were in keeping with the new constitution, which grants equal rights to men and women, even on television. The minister for information and culture vowed that such broadcasts would continue. But the Supreme Court, which at the time was dominated by conservatives, protested the broadcast, citing a constitutional clause that states that no laws can run contrary to the beliefs and provisions of Islam. In their view, Islam does not allow for women singers. Various mujahideen commanders grumbled publicly that they did not fight an Islamic war for twenty years to end up with women singing on television.

The tension between these two constitutional clauses—equal rights between men and women and no law contradicting the beliefs of Islam—was destined to erupt in conflict. The fact that it took only a few days to do so after the constitution was approved was no surprise given how central women's status is to both the jihadis and the reformers. Indeed, the clause elevating Islam in the constitution was the compromise the mujahideen leaders demanded in return for accepting the strong presidential system Karzai and the international community wanted over the more decentralized parliamentary system that they favored. The broad, open-ended provision that no law could be "contrary to the beliefs and provisions" of Islam gives religious leaders significant sway over the making of policy. Both sides are well aware that which "beliefs" and whose "provisions" are adopted become all important in establishing legal precedence.

At the highest levels, it is not even clear who has ultimate responsibility for interpreting Afghanistan's constitution. One article of the constitution seems to give responsibility to the Supreme Court by stating that the court can review whether laws are in "compliance with the constitution." Yet, another article calls for an independent commission to supervise the implementation of the constitution. Several influential mujahideen leaders in parliament hold that the Supreme Court should only determine "compliance" with the constitution, while the independent commission should interpret the constitution. This tussle will no doubt continue for years as part of the larger power struggle between the presidency and influential warlords-cum-parliamentarians.

On one level, the stakes are high because Afghanistan's judicial system is in such a shambles, with rampant corruption and high levels of illiteracy and incompetence among judges. (More than half of Afghanistan's judges have no higher education.) As a result, the Supreme Court is dragged into even minor legal issues. Moreover, the constitution calls for the Supreme Court to exercise authority over lower courts all the way down to the district level. Over the long term, Supreme Court decisions should play an important role in charting the direction of the country. But given the realities of Afghanistan's conservative society, reformists recognize the narrow line the Supreme Court must walk. Its challenge is to encourage gradual legal reforms while still being seen as the guardian of Islamic values. Otherwise, a destabilizing backlash is likely to ensue. Issues involving women's role in society—what is acceptable within sharia and what is not—are likely to be among the most sensitive flash points.

For decades—since well before the rise of the Taliban—Afghanistan's judiciary has been dominated by influential *ulama*. Many received their training in Pakistani religious schools, often under the intellectual sway of the conservative Islamic theologian Maulana Maududi, the founder of Pakistan's Jamaat-i-Islami party. During the years of resistance to godless communism, Afghanistan's Islamic judiciary was seen as the keeper of the country's Islamic soul. After the fall of the Taliban, Islamists—notably the powerful mujahideen leader Abdul Rasul Sayyaf—were determined to keep it that way. They stacked the Supreme Court with retrograde religious figures who faithfully resisted all reform efforts.

The interim chief justice, Faisal Ahmad Shinwari, the former head of a religious school in Peshawar, was particularly conservative. Under his direction, the court issued bans on women singing on television, tried to bar a presidential candidate for questioning whether polygamy is in keeping with the spirit of Islam, and upheld the marriage of a nine-year-old girl, even though Afghan law at the time set the marriage age at sixteen.[33] Shinwari spoke out against coeducation and ordered the arrest of an Afghan journalist who suggested that, in some cases, the Quran was open to interpretation. He also filled the judiciary at all levels with unqualified mullahs and established a "fatwa council" of questionable legality within the Supreme Court to issue religious edicts.

Karzai came under significant international pressure to revamp the Supreme Court with better-trained, more professional judges. The slate he presented to the new parliament in 2006 was a great improvement, replacing every member of the court—except Shinwari. Some say Karzai renominated Shinwari as chief justice because he wanted to maintain Sayyaf's support, and that he did so knowing that parliament would reject Shinwari. (Both Shinwari and his deputy chief justice, Abdul Malik Kamawi, have been members of Sayyaf's militia group, the Ittihad-i-Islami, since the 1980s.)[34] Karzai might have also bargained that by keeping the elderly, white-turbaned Shinwari with his strong Islamic credentials and filling the court below him with professionals, he would actually have had an easier time overhauling the judiciary. Regardless, parliament did reject Shinwari in May 2006. The question of the chief justice was nothing less than a showdown between fundamentalists and intellectuals. In this instance, the intellectuals won. The new Supreme Court, comprised of nine judges who hold nonrenewable ten-year terms, is now filled with technocrats with experience in both civil law and Islamic jurisprudence. It is headed by Abdul Salam Azimi, a U.S.-educated judge with moderate views who wears Western suits and ties. "He is so smart," gushes Shukria Barakzai, the parliamentarian, who performed the Hajj with Azimi and his wife in 2003. "I have learned about Islam in a new way from him." Many people today in Afghanistan credit Azimi with vision and integrity and view him with great hope. His court is certainly more professional, although it lacks the Islamic credibility that Shinwari's court enjoyed.

Strengthening the legitimacy of the Supreme Court is only part of the broader process of judicial reform that is needed in Afghanistan, where at least 85 percent of justice is still administered outside the official court system. Local *jirgas* settle most disputes not only because the regular courts are incompetent, but also because people are often illiterate and find unwritten customary law easier to understand and implement. The *jirgas'* verdicts tend to be more enforceable. Yet, the country will never be able to develop a sustainable, modern economy, nor consolidate democracy, without establishing the rule of law across the country and protecting the political and economic rights of all Afghans, men and women alike. But it is a long way from that goal.

Judicial reform is particularly important for women, who fare poorly not only in the court system but also in the *jirga* process. Nearly 80 percent of the women in prison have been convicted of *zina*, engaging in sexual activity outside of marriage. Rape victims, if they dare speak out, are often then arrested for *zina*. Several women leaders in Afghanistan are hoping that better training for judges and for mullahs—not only in civil law but also in more progressive interpretations of Islamic law—will help lead the way on women's rights.

Rahala Salim is one of the few women who has served as a judge in Afghanistan—no small task in a country where conservative opinion believes women cannot be judges. (Shinwari, when he was chief justice of the Supreme Court, gave his explanation for why women cannot serve as top judges: "If a woman becomes a top judge, then what would happen when she has a menstruation cycle once a month, and she cannot go to the mosque?")[35] Not surprisingly, Rahala was appointed a judge in the 1980s by the communists, one of about fifty women assigned to the bench during that period, almost all of them in Kabul. Fired from her position by the Taliban, she spent those dark years quietly teaching Islamic law to a group of about seventy women. From her study of Islamic jurisprudence, Rahala believes there are various ways to interpret the Quran and that sharia can and should be conducive to women's rights. "We have to know the real sharia. We have to be able to point to passages in the holy Quran and say, 'Here, read this,'" she insists.[36]

Now a member of parliament, Rahala is often called upon to provide her legal expertise to policy debates. She also continues to try to pry open the gates of religious authority for women. She has been working with mullahs from her district to allow her to address families in the mosque—how else, she argues, can she communicate with her constituents? Many mullahs are now allowing women to attend the mosque to hear from Rahala, their representative. "It was the first time that women saw the inside of the mosque," she explains. She is working with these same mullahs to get their approval to send girls to school.

Mahbooba Huquqmal is probably the best-known female legal expert in Afghanistan. Once the dean of the Law and Politics Faculty of Kabul University, she too was unceremoniously dumped by the Taliban. Since then, she has championed women's legal rights through her nonprofit organization RAWZANA, and through the various government positions she has held. One of her main priorities has been to promote more moderate interpretations of Islamic family law. Like a true Islamic feminist, she argues that a "correct" understanding of the Quran would never allow such practices as polygamy, wife beating, and child marriage. Her efforts include reaching out to legal experts and women activists from Muslim-majority countries around the world to learn from their experiences. In this way, she is bringing Islamic feminism into policy debates in Afghanistan.

In May 2003, Mahbooba hosted a conference in Kabul on Islamic family law in conjunction with Women Living Under Muslim Laws. WLUML has since been actively involved in promoting Islamic justifications for reform of sensitive family laws in Afghanistan. Mahbooba also hosts a radio show in Kabul devoted to exploring women's rights in Islam, inspiring a younger generation to stand up for their rights within Islam.

Getting the Mullahs on Board

The men file into the conference room, a rented space in a nondescript, single-story building in central Qala-i-Naw, a provincial capital in northwest Afghanistan. Outside, snow is falling and the men stamp their feet on the mat to loosen the mud and ice from the boots they are wearing under their *shalwar kameez*. Almost all of them sport white turbans and long beards, some jet black, others salt-and-pepper gray in keeping with their age. They congregate by the beverage table in the back of the room, heaping spoonfuls of sugar into small cups of bitter green tea.

Nilofar Sakhi stands a bit nervously in front of the group, the only woman in a roomful of fifty men—teachers, mullahs, and other elders of the community. Her long dark hair is carefully swept up under her headscarf, but this does little to diminish her attractiveness. A poster tacked to the wall advertises the Women's Activities and Social Services Association (WASSA), an organization that Nilofar started after the fall of the Taliban. This morning, the elders have assembled to debate a recent WASSA newsletter, which went out to several thousand village leaders in the region. The newsletter has sparked quite a controversy by publishing the views of several Islamic scholars who challenge conservative interpretations of sensitive passages in the Quran. The subject of these controversial passages? Women.

Nilofar is there simply to moderate the discussion. She welcomes everyone and introduces the first loaded subject—the suitability of women as leaders. One mullah stands and announces that while women can be leaders in some respects, everyone knows that they cannot lead Friday prayers. This automatically disqualifies them from high leadership positions like being president. Moreover, since women are "half-minded" they can never be real leaders.[37] A murmur of approval ripples through the audience and he sits down. A young scholar from the Sharia College in Herat who has accompanied Nilofar to the meeting stands next. He respectfully acknowledges the mullah's comments but then offers another interpretation of the texts. Nilofar sits quietly in the corner and lets the mullahs hash it out. "We [at WASSA] don't give our own views on the Quran. We bring in religious scholars and sharia experts to do that."[38]

When WASSA first started getting involved in sharia debates, Nilofar received threatening letters slipped under her door at night. But she also heard from tribal elders and mullahs across the region praising her work and asking for WASSA's assistance to get literacy classes and other workshops going for the women in their villages. "Eighty percent of Afghans live in villages," Nilofar says to me later. "They think this way. We must engage them and work with them, because if we don't, we'll be like tiny pockets of reason surrounded by fundamentalist thinking and not getting anywhere."

Nilofar was born in Herat but moved in 1980 to Quetta, Pakistan, where she grew up as a refugee. Her father believed in education for all his eight children, but Nilofar was the best student among them so he chose her to attend private school. She went to St. Joseph's Convent Girls' High School in Quetta (the most rigorous school around, she explains) and on to the University of Baluchistan, where she got a bachelor's degree in biochemistry. Like so many ambitious young Afghan women, Nilofar desperately wanted to become a doctor, but life as a refugee was tough. "There were too many distractions. I got good grades, but not good enough to secure one of the few 'Afghan seats' in medical school." Instead, she started teaching English at a community center and working as a program officer for the Aurat Foundation, the Pakistani-based organization mentioned earlier. Aurat at that time had several programs in place to assist Afghan refugees. These were the Taliban years, and Nilofar's work with Aurat brought her into contact with many Afghan women leaders running social-service organizations in Pakistan. "My father kept pushing me all the time, saying 'You must go back to Afghanistan to work for women and your country.'"

After the fall of the Taliban in 2001, that is exactly what she did. Within three months, she had registered her own organization (WASSA) in Kabul and moved back home to Herat. "That's when my problems started. I had to negotiate with Ismail Khan [Herat's strongman governor]. I had to meet with him so many times. Yes, he deserves credit for keeping the peace and rebuilding Herat, but on human rights he was a disaster. We had no freedoms. He was always polite speaking to me, and came across as a gentle personality. But we got nowhere with him. He would have liked to shut down all the women's groups, but he knew that that would cause an international uproar. So instead, he just stonewalled us."

That experience convinced Nilofar that to have any real impact, she would have to engage conservative attitudes, not ignore them. "You cannot ever be against religion in Afghanistan. You must work through it." WASSA was soon reaching out to mullahs and scholars in the area to begin a dialogue—one based on the Quran—that tries to separate religion from oppressive cultural practices. Over tea with me in Kabul one cold afternoon in early 2008, Nilofar assesses WASSA's impact at a local level. She tells me the story of a mullah outside of Herat who worked with her organization.

"At first, the mullah was totally against girls' education. He is a young guy, educated in Pakistan. So often it is these young men who are most conservative, more so than their fathers, no doubt because of their Pakistani *madrasa* education," she muses. "Over the course of a year, we convinced him to allow his sister, who was the only educated woman in the village, to be a teacher for girls. He agreed but only if the students came to her. He provided a one-room building in his compound, and we [WASSA] started holding literacy classes for girls there in shifts.

"After several months, the demand for the classes had increased so much that we asked the mullah to start teaching too. He saw the positive impact it was having, he saw how his people wanted it, so he agreed. Then, we convinced him and his sister to attend WASSA training sessions in Herat to prevent violence against women. [A large proportion of WASSA's work focuses on challenging the view that domestic violence is religiously sanctioned.] Not only did he go to those sessions, but he later agreed to allow his sister to travel to California for training. Up until that time, he had insisted on two *maharams* [male escorts] for his sister to travel to Herat. But he said if WASSA was taking her to California that was okay. She didn't need a male escort."

In the end the mullah's sister did not make it to California due to visa issues, but she and her brother are still teaching literacy to local girls. WASSA is no longer funding the classes, but the mullah and his sister keep them going. They collect about fifty afghanis (about fifty cents) per student per month, which more than covers their costs. They have made a small business out of it. "It is challenging, but not impossible, to work with mullahs," concludes Nilofar. "Afghans want change," she insists. "But you always have to be sensitive to religious issues." For inspiration, she remembers the words of the great change agent Mahatma Gandhi: think internationally, but act locally.

A Long Road Ahead

With little competitive advantage in the global economy, Afghanistan is likely to remain one of the poorest countries in the world for a long time. Resurgent Taliban activity continues to undermine security, especially in the southern and eastern regions of the country, and the unbridled growth of the narco-economy adds to widespread lawlessness and corruption. Women face the added constraints of deep gender biases that continue to hinder their access to education, healthcare, and employment, and perpetuate the cycle of poverty. There are, however, signs of progress.

Today, a higher proportion of Afghan girls attend school than ever before in the country's history. Although more girls are still out of school than are in school, the next generation of Afghan mothers will be better educated than any previous generation. Polls show that a strong majority of Afghans—both male and female—supports girls' education. Despite Taliban efforts to sow fear and derail girls' schooling, girls' education is expanding in most parts of the country.

Afghan women are also becoming more aware of their rights, not only through state-led educational initiatives, but also through privately run programs like those led by AIL and WASSA, and through the efforts of independent media. There are now several radio programs targeted toward women that help spread ideas of democracy and human rights. The ongoing process of judicial reform and extension of rule of law into the countryside will also be to women's benefit.

The inclusion of women in government at both the local level through the NSP and through quotas at the national level is bringing women's voices to the table in an unprecedented fashion. A woman's right to hold public office is now widely accepted, and several women leaders, like Habiba Sarabi, the governor of Bamiyan Province, are among the country's best-known and most popular politicians. Women leaders in civil society and in government have chalked up some successes over the years in pushing along improvements for women, and just as important, in protecting against backsliding in sensitive areas like family law.

One of the most positive indicators to come out of Afghanistan in recent years is a steep decline in infant mortality. A 2007 Johns Hopkins study estimated that infant mortality declined from 165 per 1,000 births in 2001 to 135 per 1,000 births in 2006, translating into 40,000 fewer infant deaths per year. (To put that in perspective, wealthy countries like Sweden and Japan have infant mortality rates less than 3 per 1,000 births.) The main driver of this improvement is women's increased access to medical care through the use of mobile clinics in rural areas, a significant expansion of trained midwives at the community level, and more female healthcare workers in general. Women receiving prenatal care increased from only 5 percent in 2003 to 30 percent in 2006. The rate is even higher today. While Afghan women still have one of the highest rates of maternal mortality in the world, the trend is now finally in the right direction.

Women's gains in education, political voice, and healthcare are critical for improving their status in Afghan society. But changing deeply ingrained cultural and religious biases is also important and requires a careful reframing. Afghan women have experienced the downside of cultural whiplash too many times in the past century. As a result, many of today's leaders are understandably moving cautiously. They have tried not to become mired in the inevitable culture wars—for example, whether women can sing on television—and have moved to distance themselves from provocative issues like the suitability of Afghan women participating in beauty contests.

Ultimately, they understand the need to respect the Islamic fabric of their country. Just about all the Afghan women leaders I have interacted with over the years—whether of deep faith themselves or personally more secular—acknowledge the need to work with and through religious leaders to secure change for women. Many reform-minded Afghan men also have a vested interest in promoting progressive interpretations of Islam. But for Afghan women, who have had their rights denied in the name of Islam, the stakes are even higher. Today, they are important contributors to, and beneficiaries of, the global Islamic feminism movement.

CHAPTER 6

CHANNELING KHADIJAH: SAUDI ARABIA

Khadijah believed in me while others rejected my call. She affirmed my truthfulness when people called me a liar. She spent her wealth to lighten the burden of my sorrow when others had forsaken me.

—THE PROPHET MUHAMMAD (570–632),
honoring his wife Khadijah

The ballroom looked much like any generic conference setting, although this being Saudi Arabia, the chandeliers were a bit more ornate, more garish, than usual. The noticeable exception was a six-foot-high barrier down the middle of the room and the attendants ushering the women in their black *abayas* to one side, men in their cool white *thobes* to the other. There was to be no public mingling of the sexes in this conservative Muslim society.

It was February 2005. Outside the frigid air-conditioned business center, the Red Sea sparkled along Jeddah's corniche, and families picnicked under the palm trees in the hot desert weather. All the women on the beach, still fully covered, must have been sweltering under their long black robes.

Inside, a mostly Saudi audience with a sprinkling of international journalists and business executives gathered to discuss the Middle East's employment crisis. How would the region, with 60 percent of its population under the age of twenty-five, create the 80 million new jobs it needs over the next fifteen years? The issue for Saudi Arabia is particularly acute. Unemployment among its youth is extremely high, approaching 30 percent for men and even higher levels for women. I had been invited to speak about the potential of small business development in the kingdom, and the segregated audience listened politely to my comments. Then I took questions.

From the women's side, there was dead silence. I wondered if they had any idea what I was talking about. On the men's side, a few hands went up in tepid response. The first to stand was a young man who identified himself as an employee of Saudi-American Bank. Why, he demanded, would anyone start a business when so many of them fail? When I tried to explain the high-risk, high-reward nature of start-up businesses, he interrupted. The real issue, he insisted, is that there is simply nothing left to invent. With that he sat down. Well, I thought, so much for entrepreneurship in the kingdom.

As the last of the white-robed men filed out across the gleaming marble lobby, a group of anonymous, veiled women—"black moving objects" as they are derisively called—waited diffidently off to the side. Might it be possible, one asked, to have a few minutes of conversation? We arranged some chairs in a semicircle, and they waited mutely until the last man had left the room. Then, as if on cue, they threw off their headscarves and got out their notepads. As they thrust their business plans toward me, the questions flew.

"What's the difference between venture capital and angel financing?"

"How can we connect with investor groups in the United States and Europe?"

"I see from your speaker's bio that you worked for [the consulting firm] McKinsey. Can you help get me a job in their Dubai office for the summer?"

They were students from the local private women's colleges in Jeddah. With their *abayas* off, they looked and spoke much like a group of ambitious business students anywhere. They got particularly excited when I explained that in the United States, women-owned small businesses were the fastest-growing segment of the U.S. economy and the strongest engine of job creation.

"That's what we all want to do," one young woman explained. "We want to start our own businesses. It's the only way for us to gain some independence. We all want to be modern Khadijahs!" As our conversation progressed into the afternoon, with plans for landscape businesses, fashion design, and specialty food companies flying around, I began to get the sense that the future of Saudi Arabia might just rest on the black-shrouded shoulders of these Islamic feminists.

Saudi Arabia is a country of contrasts, no more so than with respect to women. Saudi women are internationally recognized doctors. They are prominent businesswomen running global companies. They are Ph.D. economists and scientists. They are deans of colleges and heads of university departments. They are journalists and newscasters. Yet none of these women can drive in their home country or vote in a local election. Saudi women enjoy fewer legal rights than women in any other country in the world today. Every several years, Freedom House ranks Arab countries in terms of economic, political, social, and judicial freedoms for women. Saudi Arabia consistently scores worst in each category, in most cases by a lot. The Saudi state treats women as legal minors their whole lives, requiring a father's, then a husband's permission for many basic activities. Yet despite, or perhaps because of, the considerable restrictions on them, Saudi women are very much in the forefront of social and economic change in the kingdom. By dint of their academic, professional, and economic successes, they are quietly breaking down their country's pervasive discriminatory policies and social attitudes. They are also challenging the puritanical interpretations of the Wahhabi religious establishment that are used to justify restrictions on women in the first place.

Puritanism runs deep in the kingdom. As the custodian of the Muslim holy cities of Mecca and Medina, Saudi Arabia considers itself to be the spiritual heartland of Islam. Yet the version of Islam it clings to, and promotes worldwide, is an austere school of thought called Salafism, often referred to as Wahhabism in the West.[1] Salafis idealize the time of Muhammad and his Companions (the pious ancestors, or Salafs) as the "golden age" of Islam. Salafis seek to cleanse Islam of any foreign notions, innovations, or ideas that have seeped into the religion. They tend to reject Shiism and Sufism (since their veneration of Muslim saints smacks of polytheism), and common Muslim practices such as worshiping at Muslim shrines.[2] They also take a very narrow approach toward women, seeking strict gender segregation and measuring piety by female modesty and seclusion in the home. Women going to universities, learning critical thinking skills, and setting forth in the global economy pose no small challenge to Salafi asceticism.

Salafism is closely intertwined with Saudi Arabia's history—and that of its ruling family, the Sauds. In 1744, the clan's leader, Muhammad Ibn Saud, a direct forefather of today's ruling al-Sauds, joined forces with Muhammad Ibn Abdul Wahhab (the eponymous "Wahhabi"), a conservative religious leader determined to purify Islam. They formed an allegiance—Muhammad Ibn Saud would be the political ruler, while Muhammad Abdul Wahhab would lead in religious matters—to wage jihad on those unbelievers who refused to reform.[3]

Ibn Saud and Abdul Wahhab's forces scorched the countryside for several decades in their quest to make Muslims follow their puritanical version of Islam. The massacres committed by their fighters across Arabia are notorious. As far north as Karbala in present-day Iraq and deep into Yemen in the south, they forced the inhabitants of conquered towns to adhere to Wahhabi beliefs and practices or die as infidels. Not surprisingly, the movement came under considerable criticism for the brutality of its ways. Muhammad Abdul Wahhab's own brother denounced him, claiming that he was "an ill-educated, intolerant man who was ignorantly and arrogantly dismissive of any thoughts or individuals that disagreed with him."[4] The Ottomans—titular overlords of Arabia at this time—eventually tired of the troublesome Wahhabis, especially after they began attacking pilgrims on their way to Mecca, cutting into Ottoman taxes collected from the Hajjis. They sent an army to defeat the Wahhabis, bringing an end to the first Saudi state in 1818.

Subdued, but not totally defeated, the descendants of Abdul Wahhab and Ibn Saud sustained the alliance, making several efforts to regain dominance. In the early twentieth century, they were finally successful. In 1902, accompanied by a small band of loyal fighters on horseback—just sixty-three in all—Abdul Aziz Ibn Saud, the future founding king of Saudi Arabia, stormed across the desert and took Riyadh by surprise.[5] From there, he began a thirty-year drive to conquer all of Arabia. His core group of soldiers was supplemented by the particularly brutal Ikhwan, a tribal force motivated by religious passions that raided and plundered their way across the Arabian Peninsula in the name of jihad. Supported by the Ikhwan, by 1932 Abdul Aziz had crushed all tribal resistance, married his main rivals' daughters to cement the new order, and crowned himself king of the new state. Saudi Arabia was literally formed in the crucible of religious fanaticism.

Today, women's reform efforts are a critical part of the country's broader, struggling reform movement. Women are pushing for educational changes, for economic changes, even for legal changes. Their ability to succeed is clearly a vital social issue—one that will shape Saudi public opinion over the long term, not only on women's rights, but also on related issues of workplace reforms, attitudes toward globalization, economic integration, and religious extremism. Given the deeply entrenched religious establishment in the kingdom, women reformers are careful to couch their efforts within Islamic discourse. Since Saudi Arabia's monarchy takes the Quran as its "constitution," the case for women's rights in Saudi Arabia is inseparable from women's rights within Islam.

Women's role in Saudi Arabia is also a long-term economic issue. Women now comprise more than 60 percent of all Saudi college graduates, but only 5 percent of the workforce. Tradition, regulation, and discrimination keep women at home. The added burden of not being able to drive to work, in a country with limited public transportation, makes working especially difficult for nonelites. Windfall oil revenues certainly undermine any sense of urgency for reform, but the country's underlying demographics—Saudi Arabia has a persistently high birthrate—puts large demands on state resources. Indeed, when oil prices collapsed in the 1980s, GDP per capita fell from a high of $18,000 in 1981 to less than $6,000 in 1988. Propped up by rising oil revenues, it rebounded to about $20,000 in 2008, putting Saudi Arabia on par with Portugal and Estonia. But with rising costs of living driven by a high inflation rate (Saudi inflation in recent years has topped 7 percent), many Saudis today claim they need two incomes to make ends meet.

The kingdom's reluctance to unleash the productive energies of women is undoubtedly costly, not only in terms of wasted capabilities, but also with respect to the resources devoted to maintaining gender segregation. One outspoken member of Saudi Arabia's Shura Council uses economic arguments to agitate for women driving. In his role as a public official, he complains that a million foreign chauffeurs in the country shipping home annual remittances of more than $4 billion is simply bad for Saudi Arabia's economy.[6]

Benefiting from rapidly rising educational levels, women are quietly pushing for changes throughout society. They are moving into new professions and working discreetly alongside men; they are taking on high-profile roles in the media, and bringing public scrutiny to topics that were formerly taboo; they are nudging the government to address the country's gross legal inequalities. Well aware of the potential for backlash, they are moving slowly but purposefully forward, leading the way for change within an Islamic framework.

Shattering Walls

Dr. Haifa Jamal al-Lail leans forward in her chair, explaining her "small is beautiful" principle. "It is so important that we get it right. We are developing the next generation of leaders, so our emphasis is not just on the girls' technical skills, but also on their critical thinking and analytic abilities."[7] Dr. Haifa, as she is widely known, is the dean of Effat University, Saudi Arabia's first private women's college, which in 2009 became accredited as a university—again, the first for women. The university is small, with only about a thousand undergraduates, but its ambitions are large. "If we can produce students here with big ideas, then they will have a big impact on our country . . . The walls for women in Saudi Arabia will shatter," she insists, "but in time."

Outside Dr. Haifa's office, four busy assistants field calls and dart back and forth with stacks of papers and cups of cardamom-spiced coffee. When I entered her office, I was surprised to see Dr. Haifa with her auburn hair falling to her shoulders. We had met several times over the years, and yet until now I had only seen her in public, always with a headscarf wrapped tightly around her face and under her chin, never a wisp of hair showing. Even at a ladies-only session in her home the previous year, where all the other Saudi women were relaxing in jeans and tank tops and loose hair, Dr. Haifa had cautiously kept her headscarf in place. "She never lets her guard down in public," another prominent Saudi woman had told me. "Given her position, she can't afford ever to make a mistake, ever to step out of line. She is always conservatively dressed and careful in what she says."

Dr. Haifa's measured cautiousness, her willingness to stay within some perceived set of unwritten rules, aggravates her critics. "She's nothing more than a government toady," sniffs one particularly out-spoken Saudi journalist, who dismisses her with a wave of his hand. Not fair, I think, as I look around Effat. Dr. Haifa is at the forefront of a social revolution in the kingdom, one that its deeply entrenched, con-servative religious establishment continues to resist. It serves her and her mission well to showcase her piety.

Occupying several city blocks on the outskirts of Jeddah, Effat is surrounded by high, imposing walls, not only to sequester the girls within, but to keep out the prying, meddlesome eyes of critics. The college was the dream of Queen Effat, beloved wife of King Faisal and the person for whom the college is named. Faisal, son of the founding ruler Abdul Aziz, became king in 1964 when he seized control from his older brother Saud. At the time, Saudi Arabia was still a largely rural society of just 5 million people with a strong Bedouin desert culture. It had remarkably little infrastructure, few paved roads, no modern trans-portation or communications, and little semblance of modern govern-ment. Ministry budgets were allocated as royal gifts.[8]

A deeply conservative and pious man himself, King Faisal was also a shrewd political operator. He positioned himself as an Islamic modern-izer able to bring technology and economic development to the king-dom while preserving Islam. One of the first acts of his new government was to institute a series of reforms both to satisfy growing U.S. pressure and to squelch rising domestic dissent. He abolished slavery, which was still widespread in the kingdom, and introduced new technologies such as television. Faisal needed the *ulama* to legitimize his reforms, and he rewarded moderate religious leaders who were willing to endorse his modernization programs.[9]

One of the most significant changes Faisal made was to expand education and, also important, to initiate girls' public education in Saudi Arabia. (In the early 1960s, Saudi female literacy was less than 2 percent.)

Conservative religious leaders vehemently resisted Faisal. They understood that letting girls go to school was to start down a slippery slope from which there was no return. To assuage their concerns, Faisal made girls' schooling publicly available, but not compulsory. He also gave the religious authorities control over girls' education (whereas boys' education was administered by the Ministry of Education). To lead by example, he sent his own daughters to school and publicly attended graduation ceremonies at girls' schools.

Primary and secondary schooling for girls quickly became mainstream, and by the 1980s, Saudi girls were routinely attending college. When a royal decree granted permission for private higher education in 1997 (an important change, since private colleges have more leeway on curriculum and pedagogy), it was fitting that Faisal's widow, Queen Effat, secured the first license to open a private women's college. She tapped her daughter, Princess Lolwah (an elegant and imposing woman who in profile looks remarkably like her father), to get the college up and running. The ailing queen lived just long enough to see the college open in 1999 with thirty-seven students.

The college's low-rise, 1950s-era concrete buildings were originally built to house the Dar al-Hanan school, the first private K–12 girls' school in the kingdom, which Queen Effat opened in 1955, and which Dr. Haifa attended. While Effat's physical campus has a distinctly outdated, 1950s feel to it, inside it is easy to sense the boldness of the experiment. All courses, even Islamic studies, are taught in English, a radical step in Saudi education. The introduction of English language in public schools has been strongly resisted by religious conservatives, who view it as a corrupting foreign influence. But as one Effat College professor explained to me, "The girls must learn English to be well prepared for the global job market." They defend teaching Islamic studies in English too, saying that their graduates must be able to explain their religion in English. Several professors also note that there simply are not enough texts in Arabic to teach their courses.

Another innovation was making physical education mandatory. At first, this was resisted by most of the students, for whom exercise was a foreign concept. But it gradually caught on, and the students now proudly show off their Olympic swimming pool and gymnasium. The girls' basketball team is hugely popular.

Effat's distinction is not only in what the students are learning, but how. One significant departure from the Saudi norm is that male professors are in the classroom, face-to-face with the female students. When the college first opened, male teachers lectured to the students through video from another room, as is usual practice in the kingdom. Soon, the male teacher was face-to-face in the classroom, and only the few female students uncomfortable with this arrangement were in a separate room watching by video. Now, everyone has adjusted to the face-to-face teaching (the proverbial slippery slope in action). "We're preparing our girls for an integrated workplace," explains another professor.

The emphasis of the teaching methodology is on fostering open-mindedness among the students. In every class, the girls are forced to form their opinions about a range of issues, including ethical, moral, and sexual issues. "We have no taboos," says another teacher. The students are encouraged to think for themselves, to push back on conventional wisdom, even to challenge the teacher.

As a way of opening minds, Effat regularly screens foreign films without censorship. Religious conservatives believe movies are a bad influence. Consequently, there are no public movie theaters in the kingdom, although Saudis have access to foreign films via the Internet and DVDs. Several malls contain movie theaters, built by hopeful real estate developers, but the public ban remains in place and the theaters stay dark. Films are even banned from being shown on the national airline. On the ten-hour flight from New York to Riyadh, the only "video" shown is that of the plane's direction with respect to Mecca, so passengers can pray appropriately. Behind its high walls, Effat is using foreign films, and other international media, to encourage more open discussion and debate.

Effat started out with a traditional curriculum, offering an "early childhood" major. Numerous Saudi princesses attended the college to train as nursery and kindergarten teachers, socially appropriate work for women in the kingdom. But quickly, the college added more business and technical majors. It has formed several international affiliations to bring world-class degrees to Effat: business administration programs in conjunction with Georgetown University in Washington, D.C., and Instituto de Empresa in Madrid; a fashion design academy in coordination with Canada's LaSalle College; a "Women in Technology" program in conjunction with Microsoft. This last program was encouraged by the U.S. State Department through a small grant under the auspices of its Middle East Partnership Initiative (MEPI). Although the funding was small, Dr. Haifa insists that the symbolism of that early grant was important (American higher education still enjoys considerable prestige in the region).

Effat's most ambitious program to date has been its partnership with Duke University to launch the first engineering program for women in Saudi Arabia. Duke has provided curriculum support, helped design laboratories, and mentored faculty. As Dr. Haifa explains, "This has been big work, persuading people in Saudi Arabia that women can and should do engineering. Those in the business community said to us, 'Why teach the girls engineering? We won't hire them.' Others who are more sympathetic to our goal said, 'Why don't you call it something else, so people aren't so against it?' But I like the word engineering—I am not hiding anything!"

When I ask Dr. Haifa about the origins of the program with Duke, she explains that Effat approached seventeen top American universities about forming a joint engineering program. Only three responded, and only Duke responded with passion. Duke's dean of engineering at the time was a woman, and Dr. Haifa believes that made a difference. The dean, Kristina Johnson, later told me that she took on the project as a way to "do some good in the world." She was influenced by a Ph.D. thesis she had read by an African student at Duke that correlated a stable middle class with having a critical mass of women with engineering, math, and science degrees. Dr. Johnson, tall and thin with short-cropped light hair, is the physical opposite of Dr. Haifa, yet they shared the same drive to get the program established. Dr. Johnson acknowledged to me that a male dean might not have pursued the relationship, because it was slow going and the benefits for Duke were not at all obvious at the time.

Dr. Haifa credits her own mother with creating in her a passion for education. Raised in a traditional family, her father died when she was only eight, but her mother kept the family together and instilled in each of her four boys and four girls an appreciation for learning. Social change, notes Dr. Haifa, starts within the family. She was raised in a segregated household—not unusual in Saudi society. "Today, I can sit with my male cousins with just a headscarf on—that's a big change from my youth," she says. When Dr. Haifa got engaged, she was working as a teaching assistant at King Abdulaziz University. She inserted a clause into her Muslim marriage contract allowing her to complete her education. With that permission in hand, she went off to the University of Southern California, where she earned both a master's degree and a Ph.D. in public policy, a first for a Saudi woman.

On the subject of sharia, Dr. Haifa is again careful. "Our whole country is built on sharia. I don't want to lose that base. I believe in sharia. Yes, sharia says that women need a male guardian's permission, but only in some things, not in everything. I believe in the simplest form of sharia. The way I run my life is that I smile when I see people, I wear modest clothing—long pants and long sleeves—beyond that, it is up to the individual. That is my own interpretation."

After completing her Ph.D., Dr. Haifa returned to King Abdulaziz University, where in short order she became dean of the Girls' Section, overseeing fifteen thousand students and eight faculties, and reporting directly to the president of the university. "My husband, a businessman, has always been supportive of me," she says, noting that he was a hands-on father who helped raise their daughter Nora. In July 2001, Nora was killed in a traffic accident in Jeddah. She was only seventeen. "It's made me stronger, more determined," Dr. Haifa says quietly.

When Princess Lolwah approached Dr. Haifa about Effat College, she readily took up the challenge of helping design a totally new educational experience for women in Saudi Arabia. She started out as a part-time consultant to the college's first dean, an American educator, but soon took over as dean herself.

Dr. Haifa recognizes that Effat could be little more than a footnote for women's progress in the kingdom. Tuition is high and scholarships are few, restricting the innovative educational experience to a small class of mostly elites. "I know people complain that we have small classes. But that is our strength, not a weakness," insists Dr. Haifa. "We are teaching a new way of learning, with a focus on critical thinking skills. Diversity is central to our mission. We have succeeded in building a diverse, international faculty. We are working on diversifying our student body."[10]

She also reminds me that the elitist nature of Effat does not diminish the challenges her students face as trailblazers. She tells me about visiting one of her young Effat graduates who was pursuing a Ph.D. at an American university. "She started crying when she saw me, saying it was so hard to be all alone so far away, to have to do everything for herself. She wanted to quit and come back to Saudi Arabia. I told her she can't return without her degree. She would be a failure. I also pointed out to her that the Saudi government is paying her tuition and that she won't get this chance again."

Effat undoubtedly occupies important ground in breaking down barriers and showing what is possible. It is not alone. Dar al-Hekma College, another private women's college—this one backed by the Jeddah business community—also opened its doors in 1999 with a similarly ambitious agenda to provide world-class education to Saudi women. Dr. Saleha Abedin, a vice dean of Dar al-Hekma and one of the masterminds behind the college, tells me proudly that several of her students have been accepted for graduate work at top-notch universities like the London School of Economics and Columbia University. "You know, we provide one of the few Saudi degrees that are recognized internationally," she says. Then, shaking her head sadly, she continues, "It's a shame, really. The men here are getting left behind."[11] The head of recruiting for a global consulting firm based in Dubai seems to concur. He tells me that his firm would never consider graduates from any Saudi universities, except these innovative women's colleges. "They are the only college students in the kingdom who are being taught to think for themselves," he says.

Permission to Talk

On the morning of March 11, 2002, a fire broke out at a girls' high school in Mecca. One of the students had snuck a cigarette in the hallway and dropped the butt in the trash to avoid detection. Within min-utes, smoke began to fill the corridors. Panic ensued and the students and teachers rushed for the exits. Ambulances and fire trucks quickly arrived at the scene, along with the *mutawa*, Saudi Arabia's dreaded religious police tasked with enforcing morality by the Big Brother–sounding "Committee for the Propagation of Virtue and Prevention of Vice." As the firefighters attempted to enter the building, eyewitnesses say that the *mutawa* tried to stop the men from rushing to the girls' aid, admonishing that "it is sinful to approach them."[12] Witnesses also claim the *mutawa* forced some of the girls who escaped the burning building to return because they were not appropriately covered. In the chaos of the blaze, many of the girls, not surprisingly, had neglected to don their *abayas*.

"We told them that the situation was dangerous and it was not the time to discuss religious issues, but they refused and started shouting at us," one of the rescue workers told a Saudi journalist.[13] Eventually, the police arrived and forcibly overrode the orders of the *mutawa*. They bashed open the doors to the school and easily extinguished the fire. But it was too late to prevent tragedy. Fifteen schoolgirls had suffo-cated or burned to death and more than forty were injured.

The next day, a courageous newspaper editor in Mecca published the story, knowing it was the type of explosive article for which he could be jailed. The authorities let it run. Immediately, all the major papers followed, aggressively attacking the interference of the *mutawa*.[14] As word of the fire spread, there was intense public revulsion that the *mutawa*'s obsession with gender segregation and Islamic dress codes led to some of the deaths. The *mutawa*'s role in the fire prompted average Saudis to question openly how such intolerance had come to dominate their Muslim traditions.

Tensions over the role of women in Saudi society had been festering since the 1960s when King Faisal started down the path of moderniza-tion with the introduction of girls' education. Faisal's brothers who succeeded him as king continued his modernization programs but struggled to balance conservative and progressive forces in the coun-try.[15] The sudden influx of oil wealth in the 1970s and subsequent expo-sure to Western materialism pulled at the very fabric of Saudi society, where the vast majority of people remained deeply traditional and conservative.

Inevitably, friction between traditional values and modernization was felt most keenly in the changing role of women. With rising educational levels, women were beginning to assume a more active role in society, studying abroad in freewheeling cities like Beirut and London, going on vacations to Europe and the United States. Some from elite, more Westernized families were mingling with men in public, at restaurants and cafes, and even appearing on television unveiled. They were also taking jobs in greater numbers in all-female offices. In the late 1970s, there was open debate about allowing women to drive to get to work more easily and reduce their dependence on foreign drivers. At the same time, religious conservatives were putting ever greater importance on women's domesticity and seclusion as symbols of the nation's Islamic identity and piety. As in other conservative societies, women's traditional role represented a red line in the modernization debates for the *ulama*.

In 1979, a group of religious extremists took over the Grand Mosque in Mecca, demanding to rid the country of foreign influences and a return to their idealized notion of Muhammad's premodern life. They wanted an end to Western-style universities, to radio, television, and sporting events, to gambling, and to the presence of Westerners in the kingdom. They also strongly opposed women working. They were scathing in their attacks on the corruption and consumerism of the royal family and its deals with the West. The Saudis retook the Grand Mosque, but the event deeply traumatized those in the royal family who were aware that the extremists' demands struck a sympathetic chord throughout society.[16] Earlier that year, the Islamic Revolution had swept away the Shah's monarchy in Iran, fueling the ruling al-Sauds' insecurities. The Soviet invasion of Afghanistan barely a month after the attack at the Grand Mosque provided more grist for the *ulama* that Islam was under siege—from Shia extremists in neighboring Iran, from the godless communists in Afghanistan, and from pernicious Western influences inside the country undermining Saudi Arabia's traditional culture and mores.

Saudi Arabia's leader at the time, King Fahd, responded to these crises by cleaving more closely to religious conservatives. Known for his extravagance and debauchery, Fahd essentially acceded to the demands of the Grand Mosque terrorists in an effort to bolster his own wobbly credibility. Saudi leaders calculated that their survival depended on slowing down and even reversing recent liberalizations, especially with respect to that easy target: women. Soon, women were banned from appearing on Saudi television. The *mutawa* began to enforce dress codes more strictly. Sheikhs issued numerous fatwas restricting everything from women's ability to travel and study abroad to their right to run businesses. The sheikhs even banned the wearing of high heels (the sound of heels clicking on the floor is too enticing) and singing publicly (women's voices are too seductive).

The return of hardened jihadi fighters to Saudi Arabia in the wake of the Soviet retreat from Afghanistan in 1988 only ratcheted up extremism in the kingdom. Saddam Hussein's invasion of Kuwait in 1990 and the ensuing Gulf War was another watershed. The arrival of half a million U.S. troops on Saudi soil deepened the crisis of legitimacy for the Saudi monarchy. Dissident religious leaders known as the "awakening sheikhs" began denouncing the royal family in fiery sermons and on widely distributed tapes—harping on the monarchy's incompetence and corruption, and how the reliance on "infidel" troops was defiling the holy land of Mecca and Medina.

During the 1990s, divisions within Saudi society hardened. Under pressure from religious authorities, the government tried to suppress the communications revolution, banning the Internet, satellite television, and mobile phones from the kingdom. It was a lost cause. Before long, various princes had gone into the satellite television and mobile phone businesses, and rooftop satellite dishes became ubiquitous. As dissident preachers ratcheted up their vitriol against the monarchy, *Baywatch*, beamed in by satellite, quickly became one of the most popular shows.

In unprecedented public petitions to the government, the "awakening sheikhs" demanded a rollback of Western influences, the creation of a true sharia state, an Islamic army to wage jihad, and a greater role for the *ulama* in running the country. Their message resonated with a segment of the country's increasingly disaffected youth. The most radical fringe had returned from Afghanistan and was adrift in society. One of these was Osama bin Laden. The Saudi response was to exile bin Laden and some of the more radical preachers from the country and to jail others. The banned dissidents continued to agitate and motivate from abroad.

One area where the government chose to be responsive to the dissidents' demands was with respect to women's morality—a seemingly low-cost capitulation. The *mutawa* increasingly operated with impunity. Its ranks swelled with young men wearing their easily identifiable Salafi devotion on their sleeves—long beards and shorter garments above the ankle, in the style of Muhammad. With murky authority and oversight, the *mutawa* strictly enforced gender segregation. Women, including foreign women, were beaten and jailed for the slightest indiscretion, and the public was cowed into submission.

The girls' school fire in Mecca was a jolt to public consciousness, especially since it occurred just six months after the shock of 9/11 when the world learned that fifteen of the nineteen terrorists that day were Saudis. Although some Saudis actively denied Saudi complicity in the 9/11 attacks, there was a grudging acknowledgment that domestic realities inside Saudi Arabia shouldered some of the blame. The trauma of the *mutawa*'s role in the girls' school fire struck a national nerve and helped pry open the door to unprecedented introspection.

In the wake of the fire, Mecca's Civil Defense Department issued a report directly blaming the *mutawa*'s obstructionism for the high number of casualties. While many Saudis had long criticized in private the zealotry of the *mutawa*, this was the first time the organization had been so publicly rebuked. Critics began demanding wholesale changes to girls' education, which since the time of King Faisal had been controlled by conservative clerics through the autonomous General Presidency for Girls' Education. Within weeks, the cleric in charge was fired and the department was merged into the Ministry of Education, a move that reformists had long sought. Moreover, the walls around a whole host of taboo subjects began to crumble, including the fundamental question of the role of Salafi thinking in fostering extremism.

When terrorists—later identified as al-Qaeda affiliates—implemented a series of car bombings in Riyadh in May 2003, these nascent reform discussions took on a greater sense of urgency.

One prominent Saudi columnist, Hussein Shobokshi, sensing an opening around the time of the Riyadh terrorist bombings, published an article in the Arab press imagining a future of women's rights and democracy in the kingdom. He wrote the piece as a bedtime fable to his young daughter, musing that when grown, she might become a lawyer, be able to pick him up at the airport, chat with him about his meeting with the female social affairs minister, discuss their plans to vote in an election, and catch the finance minister on television openly presenting the national budget. The article created enormous buzz, with people cheering Shobokshi for taking on so many sensitive issues. Others attacked him. What seemed to upset conservatives the most was the notion of women driving, working as lawyers, and mingling with men.

"Know your limits or you will be punished by God and by his followers on earth," warned one email. Other emails wished cancer on Shobokshi, and called him a goat, a cow, and an infidel for trying to steer the country away from Islam.[17] Shobokshi's article had crossed the line, and for this he was fired.

Yet, the door to greater introspection had been opened another crack. Those most determined to push through it include a handful of intrepid female journalists. One of these women journalists is Sabria Jawhar, a self-described "trailblazer" and the first woman to become a bureau chief of a major Saudi daily newspaper.

The first time I met Sabria was in early 2005. At the time, she was a rising reporter with the *Saudi Gazette*, one of the country's leading English-language newspapers. We arranged to meet in a Starbucks in downtown Jeddah. She brought along a male colleague as her escort, an American writer hired by the *Gazette* to teach the craft of investigative journalism to its Saudi employees. Sabria was one of his star pupils.

We ordered coffees and sat in the purple velvet club chairs in the Starbucks lounge. Sabria was wearing not only the requisite long black *abaya*, but also a full *niqab*, the veil covering her nose and lower face, leaving only her dark eyes showing—conservative dress even by Saudi standards. To drink her latte, she slightly lifted her veil with one hand and sipped discreetly behind it. When she shifted in her chair, I could see that she was wearing camel-colored slacks and a pair of sensible shoes under her *abaya*. She spoke with traces of an American-Euro accent, but she told me that she had only left Saudi Arabia a few times on family trips.

During that first meeting, Sabria explained to me that journalism was her calling. Raised in a traditional family in Medina, she had attended a local university and went on to get a master's degree in linguistics from King Abdulaziz University in Mecca. She worked as a high school teacher for a year, but in 2002, she applied for an internship with the *Saudi Gazette*. She was the only woman to make it through the program. "I became a journalist to make a difference," she says. "When I started as a journalist, I felt sorry for my country. I wanted to tackle the really critical issues—terrorism, women's rights . . ."[18] As a woman, she brought a perspective to the pressing issues of the day that her male colleagues simply lacked.

Sabria remembers her reaction upon hearing about the girls' school fire in Mecca. "I was extremely angry about it. I had just been living in a girls' dormitory in Mecca, doing my master's degree. We were treated like prisoners there! I was in my mid-twenties, but I could only leave in the care of my brother with written permission from my father. One time, my [designated] brother couldn't come to get me, and we had to jump through numerous bureaucratic hoops to get permission for another brother to get me. What if I was sick? What if there was a family emergency? Once, we did have a small fire in our dorm, and when the firemen arrived all of the female students were locked in a corridor while the firemen went upstairs. It was nonsense!"

Sabria quickly began working her way up at the *Gazette*. She became one of the first, and still few, Saudi female journalists to cover hard news. Her beats eventually included the Ministry of Foreign Affairs and Ministry of Interior. "I had a very supportive editor in chief who gave me opportunities," she recalls. A few months after our first meeting in early 2005, she won a fellowship to study journalism in Korea and went off to Seoul for the summer. Later, I see from the blog she keeps, which she calls "Sabria's Out of the Box," that she started traveling the world on her own. Her blog's icon is a drawing of a *niqab*-clad woman springing out of a jack-in-the-box.

Sabria's reporting is helping to bring women out of the shadows. She writes about Saudi women's general frustration with their lack of rights and openly takes on the sensitive issues. Since Hussein Shobokshi was fired in 2003 for his musings, more open journalism has been gradually tolerated in the kingdom, nudged along by King Abdullah himself. In June 2003, Abdullah (then crown prince, but the country's de facto leader since King Fahd had become incapacitated by a stroke in 1995) initiated the "National Dialogues," a series of meetings to coax along greater openness in society.[19]

The third such National Dialogue, held in June 2004, focused on the hot-button issue of women. The three-day meeting was the first time women's rights had been publicly addressed in the kingdom. Half of the seventy participants were women, many of them leading professionals and activists. During the session, there were heated exchanges among participants on issues such as the legal rights of women, women's concerns in the workplace, and girls' education.

At one point during the session, a woman read from a state school textbook that called women "weak creatures in need of guardians," provoking a strong reaction from others in the room, who argued that women were already afforded more rights than they "are entitled to."[20] In the end, participants gave the crown prince a list of recommendations calling for the creation of a women's commission in the government. They also asked the government to make a concerted effort to disentangle cultural traditions from the religious tenets regarding women's rights, and to push for more balance between sharia and the realities of everyday life.

Critics dismiss the National Dialogues as little more than window dressing, but Sabria Jawhar disagrees. "The National Dialogues have been a big change," she says. "They gave us permission to talk . . . We all agree on the need for change; now it's just a question of pace. Saudi Arabia is a young nation. We still have people who don't know how to read. We need to take it step by step. Saudi women work in the shadows. We don't want to live in the shadows anymore . . . We need equality for women, as long as it falls within the sharia."

Even Hussein Shobokshi marvels at how much more open discussions on women's rights have become since the National Dialogues. When I met with him in his office in Jeddah a few years later, he laughed ruefully about the article that got him fired. "That article wouldn't even cause a stir today," he noted, adjusting the plaque on his desk that reads "Winners Never Quit. Quitters Never Win."[21]

Permission to talk, however, does not necessarily translate into change, and many Saudis express frustration with the slow pace of reforms. When it comes to women's issues especially, progress seems to be limited to two steps forward, one step back, frustrating those who seek real change. Sabria Jawhar is one of them. "Change in Saudi Arabia is not a choice," she insists. "Either we change ourselves or change will come against our will, against our culture and traditions. We need faster, more structured and planned change."

When Abdullah became king in August 2005 upon the death of his brother Fahd, he made numerous public statements about his commitment to tackle the kingdom's serious challenges, and raised hopes in particular for women. In an important symbolic move, he included women in his delegation on his first trip abroad as king. He immediately appointed his daughter Adila to lead a commission on women's issues. Rumors flew about women finally being allowed to drive. But nothing so bold happened. The pace of change remains slow, at times even imperceptible to the outsider.

By 2006, Sabria began to run headlong into the *Gazette*'s glass ceiling. She had become a bureau chief, the first woman to achieve that role in a Saudi daily newspaper. But the *Gazette* had a new editor in chief who was not as supportive as his predecessor, and he began to chip away at Sabria's responsibilities and freedom of movement. With no explanation, Sabria was told she could no longer use the *Gazette*'s conference room to meet male guests. She could only meet with female guests in the ladies' section of the office, a career-limiting restriction for a journalist. Then, the editor hired a newly minted Ph.D. as a consultant who would act as deputy editor. "It was humiliating. Why should the consultant be signing off on the paper when that was my job as bureau chief?" For Sabria, the final straw came when the paper discouraged her from traveling overseas. With her rising profile, she began to be invited to international media events, but her editor refused to allow her to attend them in an official capacity.

At the end of August 2007, Sabria resigned from the *Saudi Gazette* to pursue a Ph.D. She is studying applied and educational linguistics at Newcastle University in Great Britain. "To be honest," she tells me over tea at the local Starbucks in Newcastle in May 2008, "I would have preferred to study international relations or politics, but those degrees are not eligible for the government scholarship I have."[22] In 2005, King Abdullah announced a new scholarship program to fund five thousand Saudi students to study abroad in four-year programs, complete with living expenses. However, the government only funds engineering and science degrees, and "safe" subjects like linguistics. Sabria also tells me that she would have liked to go to the United States to study, but had heard too many stories about Saudis unable to finish degrees they had started at American universities because of visa issues.

When we meet at the Newcastle Starbucks, Sabria is wearing an attractive beige pantsuit covered by a long jacket and a matching head-scarf. I ask her about her decision to wear a simple hijab here in New-castle rather than the full face-covering *niqab* as she does when in Saudi Arabia. She explains that her interpretation of religion just requires her to cover her hair and dress modestly, as she does this afternoon. But when she returns to Saudi Arabia, she fully intends to wear the *niqab* again. "It's my choice to wear the *niqab*. I wear it to show respect to my family and my culture of Medina. My family would not say no, I couldn't take it off. But I wear it because I want to tell those Saudi women who wear the *niqab*, and for 99 percent of them it's not their choice, that they can make it *even* wearing the *niqab*. The *niqab* shouldn't be a hindrance. It shouldn't prevent them from following their dreams. It shouldn't veil their minds."

Sabria as a Ph.D. student is every bit as determined as Sabria the journalist. "I am taking a leave from journalism to gain new experi-ences, to be in touch with new cultures, to improve my English, and to be able to return to journalism even stronger," she says. "My dream is to be the first editor in chief of a major newspaper, or the first female ambassador or minister. I am preparing myself for when the time comes. I will be ready."

Driving in Circles

Nothing reflects the forward-backward nature of women's rights in the kingdom more than the perennial driving issue. For years now, some Saudi observers have speculated that women's right to drive is just around the corner, but like a desert mirage, that right seems always to remain in the distance. In his first television interview as king in October 2005, Abdullah opened the door a crack on women driving, saying to Barbara Walters in an interview, "I believe strongly in the rights of women . . . I believe the day will come when women drive. In fact, if you look at the areas in Saudi Arabia, the deserts and in the rural areas, you will find that women do drive. The issue will require patience. In time, I believe it will be possible."[23] But later, when pushed on whether he would issue a royal decree permitting women to drive, King Abdullah demurred. "I cannot do something that is unacceptable in the eyes of my people," he said.

Nevertheless, rumors began to fly that a pilot program would soon be put in place. The Saudi information minister announced in 2006 that there is nothing in the law preventing women from obtaining driver's licenses. In 2007, several Shura Council members again proposed that women should be allowed to drive for practical reasons, arguing that there are no grounds within the Quran for denying women this right. Various women have formed groups petitioning officials for the right to drive. They have gained the support of several Saudi princesses. Conservatives, however, hold the line, claiming that women driving would lead to their socializing with men, removing their veils, and causing an increase in traffic accidents because women are "weak and easily alarmed." So the debate rages and nothing happens.

The driving issue embodies the perils for women of pushing for change too quickly. Every Saudi woman knows the story of that group of intrepid—some might say foolhardy—women who tried to force the issue in 1990. On the morning of November 6, 1990, just three months after Saddaam Hussein invaded Kuwait, a group of nearly fifty Saudi women gathered in the Safeway parking lot in downtown Riyadh. Their chauffeurs drove them there, but once assembled, they had their drivers get out and each took the wheel of her own car. The fleet of Mercedes, Cadillacs, and BMWs moved out into the traffic. For a good forty minutes, the women drove around downtown Riyadh in convoy, most of them clearly unveiled, drawing attention to their public protest for the right to drive. This was in fact the first political demonstration by Saudi women against the many restrictions they face in society.[24]

For the most part, the women were daughters and wives of eminent Saudis, including several high-level government officials and members of important Saudi clans, and they had their family's support. Some of them were inspired by the recent heroism of their "Kuwaiti sisters" who drove their families to safety across the Saudi border in the face of Iraq's invading army. Others noted that American servicewomen were driving cars on the U.S. base in Dhahran. All of them thought the time was right to push the driving issue, which had been percolating for well more than a decade. Just a few months earlier, King Fahd had urged the government to accept female workers in medical and social services to free up Saudi men in anticipation of the war with Iraq.[25] Driving was just the wedge issue on the much broader topic of women's rights. These educated, mostly liberal women figured that the dislocations of the Gulf War created their opportunity. They figured wrong.

After a few laps around the center of the town, the driving procession was finally halted by the *mutawa*. When the police arrived, the women were taken to the local station and released to their male guardians. At first, they thought they had scored a tremendous victory. They were praised by supporters, and the governor of Riyadh, brother to the king, assembled a commission that immediately announced that the women had not in fact broken any laws—there was no official ban against women driving, just the weight of custom. For a few short hours, they were heroes. But the backlash was fierce and unrelenting.

One of the women, a university professor, told me years later that she realized she was in trouble when she arrived at her office and found notes on her door calling her a "whore" and an "infidel." Harassing phone calls and public denunciations in the press and at mosques across the country followed. Clerics called them "harlots" and blamed "secularist American" ideas for their public impertinence. The *mutawa* branded them "fallen women." Those women working in the public sector were fired from their jobs by royal decree. All of them had their passports revoked and were confined virtually to house arrest. The leading religious authorities, including the grand mufti, quickly issued fatwas formally banning women driving on the grounds that it contradicts Islam by degrading their dignity.

Saudi women, for obvious reasons, are reluctant to be skewered on the driving issue again. Many protest publicly that they do not really care about driving, that it is not important to them. When Karen Hughes, then U.S. undersecretary of state for public diplomacy, suggested in a town hall meeting at Dar al-Hekma College in 2005 that Saudi women should be able to drive to "be full and equal participants in society," several students stood up and defended the driving ban, claiming they liked to be chauffeured around town. Offline, some of them admitted that of course they would prefer to have the freedom to drive, but driving is not the issue they want to push. Journalist Sabria Jawhar was at the meeting and later summed it up this way: "We don't need to be told to spread our wings as if we are in middle school, and we are all too aware of our right to drive a car."[26]

Rather than incite the wrath of the religious conservatives in society over driving, most Saudi women seem to prefer to focus on getting ahead through education and jobs. Still, a few continue to push the issue. On International Women's Day in March 2008, a gutsy Saudi women's rights campaigner, Wajeha al-Huwaider, drove her car along the highway. She posted a videotape of her civil disobedience on YouTube, calling for an overturn of the ban before the next International Women's Day in 2009. That day came and went, and the ban remained in place. Slowly, however, attitudes are changing. The subject of women driving is no longer taboo, but is openly debated. Wajeha al-Huwaider, far from being slandered for her driving like an earlier generation of women, has achieved quasi-celebrity status. A 2007 Gallup poll showed that a slight majority of Saudi men (55 percent) support a woman's right to drive. At some point, that majority will become so comfortably large that the driving issue will dissolve under its own anachronistic weight.

Channeling Khadijah

Madawi al-Hassoon meets me in a hair salon she owns in one of Jeddah's trendiest malls in the fancy al-Hamra district. It is the end of the day, and the salon is packed with women getting pedicures, haircuts, styling, makeup, and all sorts of other treatments. Madawi herself is in the middle of a hair treatment. Her long dark tresses are swept up on top of her head and marinating under a shower cap. I know Madawi has adult children, but she looks many years younger than she must be. Her dark eyes and dramatic, Cleopatra-like eyebrows accentuate her beautiful face. Madawi reigns over the salon like a queen, greeting everyone and discreetly directing her staff.

Wearing just a long white terrycloth robe, she thinks nothing of taking my arm and steering me out of the salon to stroll confidently around the mall, showing me the different shops and her other enterprises. This floor of the mall is "ladies only" so perhaps it is not surprising that it has a definite sorority feel to it. Gaggles of Saudi girls, sporting a full array of fashion-forward *abayas*—including Goth-*abayas* with skulls and crossbones down the front—gather at the cafes, texting on their cell phones constantly. Most malls in Saudi Arabia have a ladies-only area sealed off from men where women are free to remove their *abayas* as they shop, or in Madawi's case, even stroll in a bathrobe. Signs at the entrance warn against using cell phones to take pictures of uncovered women. Since it is around Valentine's Day, almost every shop in the mall has a red dress prominently, some might say defiantly, displayed in its window. Celebrating Valentine's Day is forbidden in Saudi Arabia since it smacks of idolatry, and the *mutawa* have been known to enforce a strict anti-red code by smashing red-clad mannequins.

Madawi is one of Jeddah's more prominent female entrepreneurs. She runs a string of upscale salons and boutiques selling home furnishings, fine objects, and antiques, which she started in the mid-1980s. Born in Jeddah, she learned business at the feet of her father, who started out cleaning mosques but later moved into drilling wells for drinking water. "King of the Wells, they used to call him," she recalls proudly.[27]

When Madawi was still young, her parents moved the family to Cairo for their children's education. "My parents wanted the same schooling for their [twelve] girls and boys, which wasn't possible at that time in Saudi Arabia." She remembers her parents always encouraging her to have a career, never speaking about marriage. Later, she went to the University of San Francisco for two years, but did not finish her degree. Instead, she returned to Saudi Arabia to become the director of a girls' secondary school. In the early 1980s, she got married, but quickly divorced. "He was against me having a career," she explains simply. Madawi then took a job with a Saudi bank, which sent her off to London for some training. Within a few years, she had become the first female director and branch manager of the al-Rajhi Financial Company.

"It was a big deal that a woman was working in a bank," she recalls. "When I started, women were not welcome in banks, and banks were just beginning to open all-women branches. I knew a lot of wealthy women that I attracted to al-Rajhi, but soon my clients were questioning why we needed a women's bank. Why not just have one bank? Today, women can transact most business in any bank. Things have changed a lot since then." Madawi remarried, had a son and daughter, and started her first business selling antiques. "I used to go to London for the auctions, and I was able to expand into home accessories, reproductions, and furniture. I also started opening salons," she explains.

Madawi is clearly part of Jeddah's more liberal elite. As a successful businesswoman, she has a lot of "firsts" to her credit, and has been instrumental in breaking down barriers. Taking advantage of the post-9/11 dislocations in the kingdom, Madawi and others pushed their case for fewer restrictions on businesswomen with the relatively open-minded Prince Majeed, then the governor of the province of Mecca. With the prince's blessing, they started a Saudi businesswomen's committee within the Jeddah Chamber of Commerce and Industry (JCCI). At the end of 2004, the committee became the Khadijah Center, named after Muhammad's first wife, who was a powerful businesswoman herself. Princess Adila, daughter of King Abdullah, became the head of the center. Today, the Khadijah Center occupies a full floor of the Jeddah Chamber, has its own budget and staff, and provides research and training for women-owned businesses. "I'm known as the 'mother of the Khadijah Center,'" Madawi boasts.

Madawi treads carefully, acutely aware that her views on women's empowerment are out of step with a majority of Saudi society. One of the first times we met, in the home of Dr. Haifa, the dean of Effat College, we discussed the recent National Dialogue on women. "We all know the stereotypes, that Riyadh is more conservative and Jeddah more liberal," she said, relaxing on a couch wearing a tight T-shirt over a pair of blue jeans. A large rhinestone belt with a picture of the Mona Lisa on the buckle completed her outfit. "Before the National Dialogues, we had never talked openly about the big issues. It was shocking to face reality. The National Dialogues showed that elite intellectuals are a real minority. We need to open many doors. We have a long way to go. Before, I was very optimistic that women would move forward quickly, but the National Dialogues made me realize that I am way ahead of my people. They . . . well . . . *they* are victims of negative education."

This conversation occurred in 2005, and Saudis had gone to the polls for the first time in municipal elections that had just been held in February in Riyadh. To the great disappointment of many, women had not been allowed to run or vote. "I respect that women didn't vote. I wanted it, to be sure, but I respect my people. It's too fast for them. I need to work hard to be respected. Next time, I'm sure we will vote," said Madawi.

At first, the government's position on whether women would be able to run in the 2005 municipal elections was unclear (no doubt due to internal disagreements). Several women took the initiative to declare themselves candidates before they were disallowed. One of the first women to throw her hat in the election ring was Fatin Bundagji, a tall, bubbly woman with the easygoing confidence of a natural politician. She insists, however, that she was an accidental candidate.

"I hadn't decided about running in the election," she recalls, "but then Sabria Jawhar wrote an article for the *Saudi Gazette*, naming me as a candidate. She said I was running when I wasn't. I immediately called her and said 'Sabria, what are you doing? You've misquoted me.' And she explained that when she interviewed me, I was so enthusiastic about the elections that she just assumed I was a candidate. Once everyone was talking about it, I thought why not?" Fatin quickly got organized and put together an impressively detailed platform that won accolades for its local practicality. She started speaking out on issues such as recycling, consumer rights, waste disposal, and the significant challenges facing Saudi youth.

After deliberating—some might say obfuscating—for several weeks, the government's final position was that logistics made women's participation impossible. Given cultural constraints, there would have to be separate voting areas, women would need ID cards (which most do not have), and women would not be able to campaign among men. But many Saudis saw these reasons as mere excuses. Sabria Jawhar was unequivocal in her support for women's participation in the elections. "I'm not convinced by those arguments of logistics," she said. "ID cards? That should have been the impetus to get women ID cards. Lack of facilities? They should have asked women to volunteer [at polling stations]. I know many would have done so."[28]

Later in 2005, prodded by the business community, the government allowed women to run in a series of chamber of commerce elections around the country. Madawi al-Hassoon made headlines by declaring herself the first female candidate for the JCCI elections. "Working under the guidelines of our religion, we men and women can cooperate and achieve remarkable results," she told the *Arab News*.[29] Madawi came out of the gate fast, campaigning first as an independent and then joining a group of eleven men (their twelfth man dropped out in the final stages and they chose her as a replacement). She says she knew that her slate was bound to lose to that of the powerful businessmen Saleh Bin Laden and Mohamed Jamil. Those men were instrumental in pushing for the elections in the first place and had included two women in their group. But Madawi wanted to run a "good fight." Indeed, her slate did lose, but she made a strong showing. "I came in thirteenth in terms of votes—the first twelve got elected," she says a bit wistfully.

After the elections, Madawi was appointed as an "at-large" member to the chamber of commerce along with another woman, joining the two who had been elected. She became a media sensation and was interviewed repeatedly by the local and international press. "I was dubbed the 'Star of the Election,'" she crows proudly. "I'm an antiques dealer, so I know that this chair I'm sitting in will be valuable someday!" In a more somber moment, she acknowledges that the elections were stressful. "If one thing went wrong, I could have been killed. I tried to sidestep the question of religion. When asked, I would give a big smile and say, yes, people are entitled to their opinions, but then I would remind them of Khadijah." In all of her interviews, she was careful to emphasize that she is not a feminist. "While women need rights, those rights are different from men's rights." On one Beirut news show, the moderator started out the segment by asking why Eve must attack Adam. What has he done wrong? Madawi was quick to respond. "No, no. Saudi Adam has done nothing wrong! He elected me, he encourages me, he loves me!"

"We cannot provoke them," Madawi says, referring to religious conservatives. "The only reason the chamber of commerce election was successful is because it did not provoke. I can do my job because I have the right clothes of Islam, my look is suitable for Islam, and I respect differences." In public, Madawi is always carefully covered. When I asked to take her photograph in her salon, she quickly put on her *abaya*. "I don't want to give them any reason to talk about me," she explained.

As chamber of commerce members, Madawi and the other businesswomen have been instrumental in identifying legal and institutional constraints that impede women's participation in the workforce and in business. One area of focus has been to promote acceptable religious rulings and to disentangle old traditions unrelated to Islam from the law.[30] In 2007, Madawi and some of the other women in the JCCI held a courageous meeting to discuss the nuances of *khulwa* (the state of an unrelated man and woman being in seclusion, a no-no for conservative Muslims). As Madawi explains, *khulwa* is a critical issue for women in Saudi Arabia. "Conservatives claim that whenever a man is with a woman, even in a crowded business meeting, it is *khulwa* when in fact it is not. They use this to justify segregation. We want people to understand and debate these points. We are told all the time in Saudi Arabia that we women have so many rights within Islam. Well, yes we do. We are now simply asking, politely, to clarify those rights, to write them down on paper so we can keep track of them."

Khulwa might seem like an esoteric issue, but in the winter of 2008, it took center stage in the kingdom in a much-discussed case. In February, a woman known only as Yara in the press—an Arab-American woman born in Libya but raised in the United States—was arrested by the *mutawa* in a Starbucks in Riyadh in the middle of the afternoon. She had gone there with a colleague to finish some work after a power failure interrupted the Internet service in their offices. For the crime of sitting in Starbucks with a man other than her husband, the thirty-seven-year-old businesswoman, U.S. citizen, and mother of three was detained in prison for hours, strip-searched, and denied permission to call her husband, who was frantically searching for her.

The case stirred fierce debate within Saudi Arabia, with reformers condemning the actions of the *mutawa* and with conservatives lashing out about immoral behaviors. In its own defense, the *mutawa* posted a statement saying, "It's not allowed for any woman to travel alone and sit with a strange man and talk and laugh and drink coffee together like they are married."[31] "Not allowed by whom?" Madawi demands to know. "Of course women are allowed to travel alone, with permission, and Yara had the permission of her husband. The whole case is simply preposterous!" While incidents like this occur from time to time in the kingdom, what is new is the ability of the press to report on them, the willingness of men and women to speak up about them, and the broader societal debate about religious interpretation on such matters as *khulwa*.

Another sensitive topic the women in the Jeddah Chamber of Commerce have taken on is the requirement that female businesses have a legal male guardian, or *wakil*, to conduct their business. Although this law has officially been changed on paper, it is still the de facto expectation. Many bureaucrats simply refuse to deal directly with women business owners. A further obstacle is licensing. Women businesses are often licensed under the category of "tailor," since women sewing is socially acceptable, even though the business is actually marketing or public relations (or in fact, just about anything). Madawi's salons are licensed as boutiques. "Salons are just too much for the *mutawa*. They forbid them, although there are hundreds of them throughout Saudi Arabia. It's like the driving issue, just ridiculous," scoffs Madawi.

Madawi was also instrumental in the Jeddah Economic Forum (JEF), an annual conference put on by the Jeddah Chamber of Commerce that, during its nine years, became one of the largest and best attended business events in the Middle East. Most importantly, it was a window into Saudi Arabia. It was through the Jeddah Economic Forum that I received several of my visas to travel to the kingdom. Otherwise, my early visa requests languished without approval. The JEF also provided the relatively more open and liberal business community in Jeddah an opportunity to break down barriers, particularly with respect to incorporating women into the business world.

When the Jeddah Economic Forum started in 2000, women were decidedly not included. Madawi al-Hassoon and other businesswomen in the Jeddah Chamber of Commerce pressed for a role. Gradually, change happened. In the early years, some women were invited to sit in a separate balcony section for a few of the sessions. If they wanted to ask a question, they had to write it on a piece of paper and pass it via courier to a man sitting in the main conference room.

In 2003, the forum held a special one-day session just for female attendees. Princess Sara bint Abdul Mohsen al-Angari, wife of the powerful Prince Abdul Majeed, then the governor of Mecca, opened the women's conference. Many of the notable women of Jeddah were in attendance. Princess Lolwah spoke about the future of Saudi businesswomen. Dr. Haifa Jamal and Madawi al-Hassoon were two of the coordinators. Hewing carefully to acceptable social standards, the coordinators made known that they would adhere to strict Islamic codes. As Madawi told a reporter at the time, only by observing these rules of gender segregation were women able to participate.[32] The following year, the JEF included women in the main meetings, but kept them strictly segregated behind a six-foot-high barrier that divided the conference room.

In 2004, in a groundbreaking development, Lubna Olayan, a leading Saudi businesswoman who is CEO of Olayan Financing Co., a major private investor in the Middle East (and around the world), gave a keynote address at the conference in front of both men and women.

During her talk, in which she called for greater economic and political rights for women, her loose headscarf slipped backward, exposing some of her hair. This picture appeared on the front page of many Saudi newspapers, causing a firestorm. Saudi liberals held their breath, concerned they had pushed too far too fast and fearing a repeat of the 1990 driving incident backlash. The grand mufti issued a statement denouncing calls for women's rights, and specifically lambasted the conference for violating the rules of Islam by mixing unveiled women with men at the forum. Eventually, however, the controversy passed. As Lubna Olayan told me later, it was a good thing that the press was under the control of the government in this case. "Crown Prince Abdullah was able to put a stop to it. Had it [the debate in the press] continued, it would have been bad for women," says Olayan. She more than weathered the storm, and within a few months was appointed to the board of Saudi Hollandi Bank, the first woman to become a director of a Saudi company (the Olayan Group is a major investor in the bank). She has since gone on the board of the multinational company WPP and was also named one of the 100 Most Influential People by *Time* magazine in 2005. "Some in the business community criticized me to curry favor with the religious conservatives, but then they turn around and ask me to get jobs for their kids. I just hate the hypocrisy," she says.

By 2006, the incorporation of Saudi businesswomen at the Jeddah Economic Forum was pretty much complete. That year, the barriers dividing the conference rooms in half were still in place, but seemed perfunctory. Their height had been reduced by a few feet, allowing men and women to see each other over the top. Women moved through the gaps in the barriers to mingle with the men on the other side. At one point I saw Sabria Jawhar, the journalist, push through to the other side to gain an interview with a senior Saudi minister.

Perhaps the most significant sign of the changing times was that Nahed Taher, the first female CEO of a Saudi investment bank, delivered a keynote talk on a leading financial issue—the role of public-private partnerships—devoid of any discussion of the role of women in society. As she addressed the packed audience, her black scarf was only casually draped over her head, exposing her long blond hair. No one in the audience seemed to care, or even much to notice. Taher, who holds a Ph.D. in economics from Britain's University of Lancaster, served as the chief economist for the National Commerce Bank for several years in Jeddah, but seeking a new challenge, she left NCB to form Gulf One and quickly raised a $10 billion fund to invest in infrastructure projects. She moved through the Jeddah Economic Forum like a rock star, stopping to chat with various ministers, private investors, and corporate chieftains, no longer even bothering with her headscarf. Businesswomen like Taher and Olayan, with international personas and huge financial clout, can afford to push the boundaries further than most women.

In 2009, the Jeddah Economic Forum was abruptly canceled, just weeks before it was supposed to be held. The official reason given was that the organizers had yet to secure a license for the conference, an astonishing excuse in light of the international dignitaries—including various current and former heads of state—who had attended the event in the past. Some speculated that the conference was canceled due to the unfolding global economic crisis. Others questioned if it was due to mismanagement and infighting and the expansion of a rival business conference in Riyadh. Not a few Saudis wondered if the Jeddah conference organizers had gone too far, too fast, in the mixing of the sexes. Perhaps it was a combination of all of the above. Even if the cancellation of the conference signals some backsliding, the forum achieved some real gains of greater openness and integration. It played an important part in slowly but gradually normalizing a public business role for Saudi women.

Engines of Change

Despite much talk of reform, Saudi Arabia remains a deeply conservative, religiously infused monarchy, and there is no indication that this will change any time soon. Hopes of political reform—inspired by the 2005 municipal elections—have faded. Another round of municipal elections (in which women were promised that they would be allowed to run) was scheduled to be held in 2009. In the spring of that year, King Abdullah quietly extended the term of the municipal councils, postponing any elections for two more years while the government "better prepared" for them. Intrepid civil society activists continue to call for a transition to constitutional monarchy, but their demands seem quixotic at best.

Other types of reforms, however, are slowly proceeding. King Abdullah is widely viewed by his countrymen as a pious, uncorrupt leader who understands the need to break away from the most radically zealous elements of Saudi Arabia's recent past. Bringing women into the mainstream of society appears to be a key element of his efforts. Of course, women's rights are a social flash point and he proceeds carefully. So while he allows the sensitive driving issue back on the table—indeed, encourages a more active debate—he will not force through any provocative changes. Instead, he seems more willing to focus on women's long-term advancement through education and economic opportunities.

In October 2007, the king laid the cornerstone for a new science and technology university bearing his name. "I pray to God to make this university a house for wisdom, a forum for scientists, and a ray that lights the road of the coming generations with science," he said at the dedication ceremony.[33] Attempting to bring modern science to the kingdom was in itself a big step. The whole of the Arab world had fewer patents issued in 2006 than did MIT alone.[34] But equally important was the decision to enroll both men and women—the first public coeducational university in the kingdom.

In a significant departure, King Abdullah University for Science and Technology (KAUST) has been managed by the oil company Saudi Aramco, which provides a level of professionalism and internationalism that is simply not present in other government bodies. This arrangement has the added benefit of moving KAUST out from under the conservative tentacles of the Ministry of Education. By early 2008, KAUST had signed partnerships with Berkeley, Stanford, and the University of Texas at Austin to help pick faculty and develop curriculum over the next five years. Aware that its American university partners were concerned about academic and personal freedoms in the kingdom, KAUST guaranteed them that it would be operating on the basis of nondiscrimination regarding race, religion, and gender, even giving the American partners a thirty-day, no-penalty cancellation clause in their contracts. To jump-start its female enrollment, it also tapped some of Effat's top engineering students as future graduate students. KAUST is covering their remaining tuition at Effat and funneling them right into its graduate programs.

With great fanfare, King Abdullah celebrated KAUST's opening on September 23, 2009, remarkably on time. He invited more than 3,000 Saudi and international dignitaries, including heads of state and Nobel laureates, to attend the ceremony. Inside the lecture halls of the university, 500 male and 500 female students attended classes together, albeit on separate levels. KAUST is chipping away at the kingdom's intense gender segregation, a key component of the country's strict Wahhabi code. Yet even KAUST's incremental approach is not without its critics. Within days of the inauguration, Sheikh Saad bin Nasser al-Shithri, a top cleric in the Saudi Board of Senior Ulama, publicly criticized the university's coeducation policy on the grounds that it violated sharia. Al-Shithri faced a storm of criticism for his comments from columnists and various liberal forces, and King Abdullah himself demanded the sheikh's resignation. Coeducation will no doubt continue to face strong resistance throughout the kingdom.

Undoubtedly, the greatest urgency for the king is to steer his country away from the violent religious extremism that has led to global and domestic terrorism. In recent years, the government has deployed reformed extremists inside Saudi prisons to "reeducate" and deradicalize jihadi terrorists. Some of the "awakening sheikhs" of the 1990s who were most virulently against the royal family and actively promoted jihad have publicly renounced terrorism, no doubt with considerable government inducement. Counterterrorism experts remain skeptical about these jihadi volte-face, with good reason. Some of these "reeducated" terrorists have been released from Saudi prisons, only to show up fighting with new terrorist cells in Yemen and Iraq.

Nevertheless, the Saudi government continues to try to vaccinate its youth against the ideology of militant groups like al-Qaeda by promoting more moderate religious scholars. One of the more popular of such scholars is Sheikh Obeikan, a prominent member of the kingdom's Council of Senior Islamic Scholars. Obeikan has denounced suicide bombings and issued fatwas against jihad. He has lent some support to the right of women to drive and even to travel without a *mahram*, a male guardian, if she feels safe. His rulings have encouraged debate over whether the government should ease *mahram* restrictions. Proposals such as allowing women over thirty-five to travel unaccompanied are now under consideration.

In 2005, Sheikh Obeikan received me graciously in his home, an enormous stone villa in the north of Riyadh richly appointed with deep blue oriental rugs, crystal chandeliers, and gilt furniture. Over gourmet dates and Arabic coffee, he explained his views through a translator. "There are those who want to return to the time of 1,400 years ago. This is wrong. We need to direct people to the right Islam."[35] Obeikan could never be mistaken for a liberal—he demands strict adherence to sharia—but he also supports legal, educational, and social reforms. "Women," he tells me, "must stay within the rules. But I accept new ways." He waxed proudly about his own daughter who works as a teacher.

Judicial reform may present one of the most important opportunities to improve women's rights in the kingdom. Currently, Saudi Arabia has no written penal code. Judges do not follow procedural rules and their sentences are arbitrary, varying widely. They often do not provide written verdicts, even in death-penalty cases. Trials are closed to the public, and it is not unheard of for judges to deny individuals legal representation. It is very difficult for women to receive justice in court, particularly with respect to domestic violence and rape cases. In October 2006, a woman who had been gang-raped was sentenced to one hundred lashings for out-of-wedlock sex. She publicly complained about her sentence but when her case came up for review a year later, the judge arbitrarily doubled her lashings to two hundred and sentenced her to six months in prison. He also banned the woman's lawyer from the case and confiscated his professional license. Embarrassed by a firestorm of international condemnation, King Abdullah quickly pardoned the woman, a disappointment to those who wanted to see the courts actually work through her case and rule in her favor. Around the same time in the fall of 2007, the king also announced a major judicial overhaul, promising new specialized courts and training for judges and lawyers, but very little has happened in this regard.

Instead, shocking legal cases keep occurring. In the spring of 2009, an eight-year-old girl was secretly sold by her father as a bride to a forty-seven-year-old man to settle the father's debts. Distraught, the mother tried to get the court to grant the child a divorce, but twice the judge upheld the contract. The case exposed deep social divisions in the kingdom between traditionalists who see nothing wrong with child marriage and reformers who want the widespread practice banned. (The country's chief cleric, Grand Mufti Sheikh Abdulaziz al-Sheikh, endorsed the practice; Sheikh Obeikan ruled that girls below the age of eighteen must not be allowed to marry.)

The story sparked headlines in the kingdom and international denunciations. Eventually, the case was resolved as they so often are in Saudi Arabia—quietly, behind the scenes. After direct intervention by the governor of Qassim Province, the husband voluntarily dissolved the marriage contract, forgoing the bride price he had paid to the girl's father. Although this left the legal ruling in place, many Saudis vowed to change the laws. Members of the Shura Council announced they would discuss establishing a minimum age of marriage for girls. Officials in the justice ministry too agreed that the laws needed to be changed. While an actual change in law could take years, the domestic debate on this previously taboo subject was unprecedented.

The journalist Hussein Shobokshi tells me that he hopes for a domino effect in his country, with women's rights being one of the first dominoes. "If Saudis can learn tolerance for women, then they can also learn tolerance for other Muslims, and even other religions."[36] His new project is a privately funded television channel in Jeddah that hopes to take on many of the most sensitive social issues in the kingdom, including some of the difficult legal cases on the front lines of the country's culture wars, like that of Yara's arrest for sitting with an unrelated man in public. "Even though women can't drive in Saudi Arabia," he insists, "they are our engines of change in society."

Can Saudi Arabia achieve a soft landing, moving away from extremist thinking and engaging the modern world while still retaining its identity? "The royal family and the Wahhabis are like Siamese twins," warns Zaki Yamani, the kingdom's famous oil minister, who ruled OPEC in the 1970s and 1980s. "If they are separated, one will die, but it is not clear which one."[37] Conservative forces are not going down without a considerable fight. Jarring cases like that of Yara's arrest in Starbucks send a chill down many reformers' spines. A few weeks after that notorious incident, I saw Madawi al-Hassoon in Jeddah and her usually smiling face clouded over at the mention of it. "It is disgraceful that my society could treat a woman like that," she said indignantly.

Many Saudi women continue to push firmly but gracefully forward, trying to change the system from within. Fatin Bundagji, the thwarted politician, remains undeterred. She started her own civil society organization, "Save Corniche Jeddah," which focuses on improving Jeddah's fragile and failing environment. By latching onto the environment, she has found a "safe" set of issues through which to pursue greater government transparency and accountability. "We petition the members of the municipal government and demand explanations for why this or why that. We are using Facebook and other new media to get the youth involved, to get them politically active. I think we are helping to lay the foundations of democracy in our country. You know, Allah has plans for all of us. Perhaps it was for the best that I couldn't run for the municipal elections." (Her Facebook group, "Save Corniche Jeddah," had fifteen hundred members in 2009.)

Some of the Saudi reformers I speak with look not to freewheeling Dubai, but rather to Qatar as their role model. Under its reformist emir, Sheikh Hamad bin Khalifa al-Thani, and his indomitable wife, Sheikha Mouza, Qatar has managed to maintain its Wahhabi piety while also embracing modernism and globalization. Sheikha Mouza is the ultimate Islamic feminist, traveling the world calling for women's rights within an Islamic framework and impressively championing modern education at home in Qatar. But the task of reforming the Qatari principality, with a population of just two hundred thousand citizens, pales in comparison to the Saudi challenge. Change is undoubtedly happening within the kingdom, as I have seen in my successive trips there—albeit too slowly for some, and too fast for others. The hope of the next generation of women lies with today's trailblazers like Dr. Haifa, Sabria Jawhar, and Madawi al-Hassoon, who are navigating the edges of society while slowly transforming their country.

CHAPTER 7

DAUGHTERS OF ZAINAB: IRAQ

A veil does not protect a women's chastity. An education does.
—JAMIL SIDQI AL-ZAHAWI, Iraqi poet (1863–1936)

Zainab bint Ali—granddaughter of the Prophet Muhammad and one of his last surviving direct descendants—walks at the head of the line of prisoners. Her hands are shackled and her clothes are ripped and bloodstained. It is the year 680, forty-eight years after Muhammad's death, and civil war has split the Muslim community. As Zainab staggers along the dusty road to Damascus, her mind wanders back to the numbing events of the past few weeks.

In a heroic but doomed effort, Zainab stood shoulder to shoulder with her brother Hussein on the plains of Karbala, supporting him in his fight for the right to lead the Muslim people. For nearly a week, Hussein and his small band of loyal followers repulsed the advances of the Caliph Yazid's army of thousands, dispatched from Damascus to destroy the challengers. But after the Umayyad soldiers surrounded them and cut off their water supply, their fate was sealed.

Zainab had worked tirelessly, tending to the wounded women and children. Almost all the men in the group had been killed in the fighting. The few survivors were weak and dying of thirst. The end was near. When morning came, Hussein summoned his last strength to mount his white steed. He would die with honor. Zainab came to his side for a quiet farewell. She watched stoically as he spurred his horse onto the battlefield, slashing bravely at his opponents with his sword.

Hussein was quickly overwhelmed. The Umayyad soldiers knocked him to the ground with their lances and trampled him with their horses. Unable to ignore her brother's cries, Zainab ran to help him but he called her off. His time was at hand. She stood motionless as the triumphant Umayyad general walked over to her brother lying crumpled in the dirt. She turned away as the general unsheathed his sword and severed Hussein's head. Zainab sank to her knees, sobbing as she mourned her brother and her own two sons who were also killed in the siege. The soldiers took Zainab and the other survivors as prisoners. They put Hussein's head on a spike to carry it with them back to the Caliph Yazid.

Now Zainab must make the seven-hundred-mile trek to Damascus, watching her beloved brother's head wither in the broiling sun. As an added humiliation, she is made to walk with her head uncovered, for all the townspeople to gawk and stare at her along the way. Exhausted from days of forced marching with little food and water, she nevertheless walks with proud determination as she enters Damascus. She holds her head high and ignores the taunts and jeers from the crowds lining the streets. Although she is tethered like an animal to the other prisoners in the group, she somehow exudes a sense of dignity.

The caravan of prisoners, some walking, some riding bareback on camels, approaches the gates of the palace. They pass under the ornate archways and enter the outer courtyard. Hussein's head is removed from the spike and placed on a golden tray—a gift for the Caliph. A hush falls over the court as the bedraggled prisoners are led before Yazid, who looks uncomfortably insignificant on his lavish throne.

The other prisoners bow their heads meekly, but Zainab refuses to submit. She glares fiercely at the Caliph with her beautiful, still-defiant eyes. Yazid orders the others in the group to reveal this woman's name.

"Why are you asking them?" she demands as she steps forward. "I will tell you. I am Muhammad's granddaughter. I am Fatima's daughter. Ask me, Yazid!" Wearing dirty clothes still stained with her brother's blood, Zainab clenches her fists in rage and spits her words at him.

"Is this your justice that you keep your own daughters and slave maids veiled while the daughters of the Prophet of Allah are being paraded from place to place exposed? You have dishonored us by unveiling our faces! Your men take us from town to town where all sorts of people, whether they be residents of the hills or of riversides, have been looking at us."

Standing before Yazid and his court, Zainab recounts the entire story of the Battle of Karbala. Her impassioned speech continues for nearly an hour. With not a trace of fear, she denounces Yazid for his arrogance and greed. She accuses him of desecrating Islam, and shames him and those around him for their treatment of the Prophet's family and for their hypocrisy.

"O Yazid, you are striking the lips of Imam Hussein with your stick in front of this crowd while these very lips used to be kissed by the Prophet of Allah, and yet your face reflects pleasure and happiness!"

Yazid twitches nervously on his throne. As Zainab's speech reaches its crescendo, he looks around the court and sees his officials with tears streaming down their faces. Enraged, he tries to silence Zainab, but she keeps on speaking. Finally, he commands his soldiers to take this brazen woman away. He orders her to be put to death.

One of Yazid's advisers intervenes. He begs the Caliph to show mercy to Muhammad's granddaughter and warns him not to create another martyr. Disgusted, Yazid reluctantly agrees. Zainab is sent to the palace prison as Yazid storms out of the courtyard.

The roots of this internecine warfare—Muslim against Muslim, Caliph against the Prophet's family—extend back to the succession struggle that began immediately after Muhammad's death in 632. One of Muhammad's closest companions, Abu Bakr, emerged as Caliph, but some believed that Ali, Muhammad's devoted cousin and son-in-law, husband to Muhammad's beloved daughter Fatima, and father to Zainab and Hussein, should lead. Ali and his partisans reluctantly accepted Abu Bakr and bided their time. A quarter century later, Ali finally became leader of the growing Muslim community. But his rule was cut short when an assassin killed him with a poisoned dagger. The Caliphate was then seized by the Umayyads in Damascus.

Hussein's stand at Karbala was a last attempt by Muhammad's direct descendants to wrest control away from the tyrannical and increasingly corrupt rule of the Umayyads, now led by the incorrigible Yazid. With a reputation for drinking and debauchery, Yazid felt threatened by the moral influence that Muhammad's family still wielded over the people of his empire. He ordered his troops to show no mercy to Hussein's impetuous challenge.

The massacre at Karbala cemented the split between those Muslims who supported the direct succession of the Prophet's family—the partisans, or "Shiat" of Ali, or Shia as they became known—and those who supported Abu Bakr and the establishment of the Caliphate. (They became known as Sunni, a word derived from the Arabic for "one who follows the traditions of the Prophet.") In the hearts of many Shia today, the battle of Karbala is synonymous with the Shia struggle against tyranny and injustice. Hussein's martyrdom is reenacted with passion and vigor by Shia worldwide on the day of Ashura to commemorate Hussein's death.

Zainab's stirring speech at Damascus is also legendary among Shia. She is revered for her courage, her eloquence, and the learned ways she fought oppression with words instead of swords. On YouTube today, there are literally hundreds of renditions of young women reciting Zainab's famous speech before the cruel Yazid. Some versions feature girls as young as eight who have memorized long passages of Zainab's words. They cry and beat their breasts as they reenact Zainab speaking truth to power. Her appeal as a female icon is so strong that she crosses over sectarian divides—even many Sunni Muslims revere her and the power of women that she represents.

It is the Shia, however, who are truly passionate about Zainab. They name their daughters after her. They flock to her shrine in Damascus. They give her a starring role in their Ashura celebrations. During the postelection demonstrations in Iran in 2009, women protesters carried banners in the streets calling forth the moral authority of Zainab while denouncing Ahmadinejad as a modern-day Yazid.

With the rise of Shia power in Iraq after the American invasion, the presence of Zainab bint Ali is as strong as ever in Mesopotamia. The overthrow of Saddam Hussein sparked a revival of Shiism that had long been suppressed by the secular, Sunni Baathists. The pilgrimages of millions of Shia to Karbala, fifty miles south of Baghdad, to pay homage to Ali's family are a potent sign of this revivalism. For decades, such pilgrimages were tightly regulated or even outright banned under the Baathists, who feared the religious fervor—and political opposition—of the Shia.

After years of war, Iraq today remains a stew of sectarian hostility, tribalism, and rigid identity politics. Jihadi terrorism and ethnic cleansing have brutalized the country. Although violence has significantly declined in recent years, Iraq is still far from stable and unified. The improvement in security seems to have had little impact on the underlying political drivers of the conflict. The American "surge" strategy of empowering Sunni Arab tribes has sustained the ambitions of recalcitrant Sunnis who still cling to the hope that they will regain their privileged position, even as Shia leaders see hegemony within their grasp. Meanwhile, Kurds remain committed to their long-cherished goal of an autonomous Kurdistan. Each group vies for control over Iraq's significant oil reserves. The hope for the country is that political compromises can settle these deep divisions, averting a return to civil war and geographic dismemberment.

If power sharing can be achieved, the throbbing issue of religion still has to be resolved. After years of brutal suppression, the newly empowered Shia are determined to give Islam a central role in Iraq's reconstituted state. The country's constitution enshrines Islam as the state religion and as a basic source of legislation, but much ambiguity remains. For starters, what form of Islam will prevail, and who will be responsible for interpreting it? Who will decide how Islam influences the country's legal system? How will tensions be resolved between sharia and other clauses of the new constitution that guarantee equality before the law? Is Iraq headed toward Iranian-style theocracy? Or might Iraq emerge as a vibrant democracy, where Islamic parties compete in fair elections alongside secular groups, and freedoms and human rights are protected?

The stakes are high for everyone, but particularly high for women. Iraq was once a model of progressiveness for women in the region. Under the secular Baathists, women had relatively high levels of education, as well as workforce and political participation (albeit within a rubber-stamp parliament), and they benefited from favorable personal status laws. But the elevation of sharia within the constitution makes many secular Iraqis fear an erosion of women's rights. The chaos and lawlessness of recent years gave rise to religious and tribal vigilantism, with women often the target. In parts of Iraq, religiously motivated violence and the threat of violence forced women to cover themselves, led to de facto segregation in public areas, and pushed girls out of the classroom. In some places, extremist fundamentalism pushed women out of the public sphere altogether.

The future of Iraq remains starkly uncertain, but it is unlikely that the genie of religious politics will be put back in the bottle for some time. Religious discourse will be a significant factor going forward on numerous fronts. It will undoubtedly shape the role of women in Iraq— namely, by influencing what rights and status they will hold in society. Among religious Iraqis, that discourse is clearly more conservative regarding women than the authoritarian secularism it replaced. But it is not immutable.

Although in recent years, *abaya*-clad women have marched in Iraq's streets demanding sharia, they also proudly discuss their rights within Islam. They want a public role in the rebuilding of their country. They want jobs and education. They demand their place in parliament. They are pushing for more progressive interpretations of Islam that allow them to keep their faith and enjoy their rights. As part of Iraq's religious awakening, women are flocking to mosques and demanding education in Islamic jurisprudence. They want to understand the rules and have a say in making them. Islamic feminism is beginning to stir along the banks of the Euphrates River as Iraq's conservative, traditional women find their inner Zainab.

Sharia Tensions

On a hot, muggy day at the end of July 2005, I met with a group of Iraqi women leaders in Washington, D.C. The State Department had brought them from Baghdad for "democracy training"—a worthy although idealistic endeavor given the rising tide of violence then sweeping the country. The group was comprised of prominent female politicians, bureaucrats, and a few civil society leaders, all of whom were active in pushing for women's rights in Iraq. Over the course of the week, they made the rounds on Capitol Hill, met with President Bush and other high-level officials in the administration, and gave numerous interviews to the press. These smart, brave, well-educated, Western-oriented, secular women were to be the face of the "new" Iraq supposedly emerging from the rubble of Saddam Hussein's brutal dictatorship.

As I made my way to the windowless conference room, my mind kept turning to the draft of Iraq's new constitution that I had sitting on my desk. Although it was only a draft—the final version would not be presented to the Iraqi National Assembly for several more weeks— many important compromises had already been made. One glaring compromise was between religion and women's rights. The constitution included a clause guaranteeing men and women equal rights before the law, but in another article it also clearly stated that no law could be passed that contradicts the "rulings of Islam."

I wanted to understand how these Iraqi women felt about this development. "How will you deal with sharia in your new constitution?" I asked. Their reaction was fierce.

"We will never allow sharia in our constitution!"

"Iraq has been a secular country. It must remain a secular country!"

"We cannot have religion in politics!"

Their vehement denials surprised me. Iraq's Shia power brokers had long made clear their desire for an Islamic state. In the earliest discussions of the country's new legal framework, Grand Ayatollah Ali al-Sistani—the most revered Shia cleric in Iraq—announced that "The religious constants and the Iraqi people's moral principles and noble social values should be the main pillars of the coming Iraqi constitution."

In January 2005, Shia political parties drew closer to their ambitions when, in a coalition called the United Iraqi Alliance (UIA), they won the most votes in the country's first post-Saddam election. Conservative Shia parties now dominated the government. With polls showing that a majority of Iraqis endorsed sharia, it seemed there was never any real question of whether Islam would be in the constitution. The only debate was over how much weight it would get.

I politely pointed out to the Iraqi women leaders that every recent draft of the constitution I had seen included important provisions for religion. They continued to shake their heads, saying "no," in part out of denial and in part out of frustration. Now that the United States had helped midwife an Islamic state in Iraq, these secular Iraqi women had been largely sidelined in their own country. Although they had the ear of influential Americans, outside of the Green Zone they had been marginalized. Secular activists would continue to play an important role in keeping women's issues on the agenda. But the new constitution confirmed that secularism was officially dead in Iraq. Gains for women going forward—for better or worse—would depend in large part on the acceptance of more progressive interpretations of Islam.

The intention of Iraq's conservative Shia leaders to assert sharia over a whole range of legal questions became readily apparent soon after the U.S. invasion. The most blatant reach for religion occurred on December 29, 2003. Behind closed doors (and when many key U.S. officials were absent on home leave), the U.S.-appointed Interim Governing Council (IGC) slipped through Resolution 137, replacing Iraq's personal status law with sharia. At the time the IGC passed Resolution 137, the council was headed by Abdulaziz al-Hakim, the hard-line Shia cleric who for many years led one of Iraq's most powerful Shia parties, the Supreme Islamic Iraqi Council.[1] Leadership of the Governing Council rotated among Iraq's various political groupings, and al-Hakim had only days left on his term. His parting gift was to try to extend sharia to matters relating to marriage, divorce, custody of children, inheritance, and all other areas of personal status.

Resolution 137 would have effectively placed family affairs in the hands of the clerics. The decree implied that each Islamic community—Shia or Sunni—would be free to impose its own rules on sensitive matters like divorce and custody. Some feared an Islamic free-for-all would exacerbate rising sectarian tensions.

As word spread about the religious coup, women's groups and secularists were particularly concerned. For nearly fifty years, Iraq's personal status law had provided women with some of the broadest legal rights in the region. The law, first enacted in 1959, included several progressive provisions loosely derived from various schools of Islamic jurisprudence. It set the marriage age at eighteen and banned forced marriages. It prohibited arbitrary divorce and allowed women to divorce abusive husbands. In the event of divorce, custody of the children did not automatically go to the father. The law also restricted polygamy, making it almost impossible. The code required men seeking a second wife to get judicial permission, which would only be granted if the judge believed the man could treat both wives equally. It also required that men and women be treated equally for purposes of inheritance.

Religious leaders were unhappy with the personal status code from the beginning, not least because it imposed a unified standard on Iraq's population without allowing for differences among its various religious sects. Shia clerics, in particular, viewed the code as another aspect of unwanted Sunni oppression. Over the years, pressure from religious leaders diluted some of the more progressive elements of the 1959 personal status law, but the legislation provided an important foundation for modernizing the role of women in Iraqi society.

In 1968, the Baath Party came to power in Iraq. Like earlier secular modernizers, from Atatürk to Reza Shah Pahlavi, Baath leaders promoted women as a means of achieving their larger objective of rapid industrialization and economic growth. The 1970 Iraqi provisional constitution gave women equal rights under the law, and the government also ratified several international treaties assuring women equal rights.

Raising female education levels became a central component of the government's modernization plans. In 1976, the Baath Party made primary education mandatory for girls. Although upper-class Iraqi girls in urban areas had been attending school for decades, this was a big change for the majority of girls in rural areas. Resistance to girls' education remained strong in conservative communities, particularly in southern Iraq, but the gap between male and female literacy levels steadily narrowed. By the late 1980s, Iraq had one of the highest levels of female literacy in the region.

Increasing women's workforce participation was critical to the Baath Party's efforts to expand the economy. Throughout the 1970s, the Iraqi government encouraged women to work by providing generous maternity benefits, subsidized day care, and transportation. By the end of the decade, nearly half the country's teachers were women. Women also made up a sizable proportion of white-collar professionals, including doctors, dentists, civil servants, construction managers, oil industry supervisors, and accountants. In professional terms, Iraqi women were far ahead of their Arab sisters.

During the Iran-Iraq War in the 1980s, women continued to make gains in the workforce as they filled jobs left empty by men conscripted into the army. But Saddam's invasion of Kuwait in 1990 marked the beginning of a long series of reversals for Iraqi women. The 1990s were a harsh decade, as sanctions and intense political repression took a heavy toll on most Iraqis. Sanctions gripped the country in an economic vise and women felt the brunt of the crisis. They were routinely pushed out of the workforce in favor of men.

Girls' education suffered acutely. Faced with limited resources, parents chose to keep their girls at home. The UN estimates that while female literacy had reached 75 percent by the late 1980s, it declined to less than 25 percent by 2000.[2] In one generation, Iraq went from having one of the region's highest levels of female education to one of the lowest. As a result, by 2003 it was all too common for mothers to be more educated than their daughters. Iraq suffered from one of the biggest gender gaps in literacy of any country in the world, with female literacy rates as much as 30 points lower than male literacy rates.

Women were also hurt in the 1990s by Saddam's decision to turn away from secular policies and embrace religious and tribal traditions as a means of shoring up political support. The last years of Saddam Hussein's rule saw a noticeable rise in religiosity as Iraqis sought solace in the mosque and hewed closer to tribal and religious support systems. In the wake of his Kuwait invasion debacle, Saddam passed a series of laws to curry favor with clerics and tribal leaders. These included easing restrictions on polygamy, curtailing women's ability to travel, enforcing gender segregation in schools, and reducing punishments for "honor" killings.

After the U.S. invasion of Iraq in the spring of 2003, women's groups proliferated in Baghdad. Many were run by well-educated, vocal, secular Iraqi women who had spent years in exile in the West and had now returned to help rebuild their country. Their command of English and ability to write grant requests gave them instant recognition in the Western press and access to nongovernmental and U.S. government funding.

Not surprisingly, many prominent Iraqi women activists are Kurdish. During the 1990s, under protection of the U.S. and British no-fly zone, the Kurds carved out a relatively independent and largely secular

economic and political system. Kurdish women held high-level positions in Kurdish government and business and emerged as natural advocates for women's rights in post-Saddam Iraq. Few of these women's
organizations, however, had much of a grassroots presence, especially in
the conservative Shia south.

These secular women's groups quickly mobilized against Resolution
137. Within weeks, activists representing eighty women's organizations
staged a demonstration in Baghdad's al-Firdaws Square, where the previous spring Iraqis had symbolically toppled Saddam Hussein's imposing statue. They held rallies, press conferences, and high-level meetings
with the American authorities, warning darkly that Resolution 137
would return Iraqi women to the Middle Ages. Women also marched in
the streets of Sulaymaniya and Kirkuk in the north, demanding an overturn of the decree. But none of these demonstrations was large and they
failed to ignite enthusiasm among mainstream Iraqis, who by now were
struggling for survival amid the chaos and violence.

Several of the women activists used their influence to lobby Paul
Bremer, the head of the Coalition Provisional Authority (CPA) and the
United States' chief administrator in Iraq at the time. The CPA wanted
to appear sensitive to women's issues and had supported a number of
programs for women around the country. At the same time, it was
deeply cautious about antagonizing powerful Shia leaders like al-
Hakim, the influential leader of the Supreme Islamic Iraqi Council and
sponsor of Resolution 137.

Pressure from secular Iraqi women's groups did not convince Bremer to veto the resolution, but he did neglect to ratify it for several
months. During that time, secular activists relentlessly lobbied against
Resolution 137. They gathered signatures on petitions and one by one
convinced members of the Governing Council to oppose it. Their
efforts paid off. By March, the Governing Council, no longer under
the thumb of al-Hakim, agreed to cancel the resolution. Around the
same time, the State Department announced a high-profile, $10 mil-
lion initiative to promote the role of women in Iraqi politics. It was a
belated realization that the unbridled religious influences Washington
had unleashed in Iraq would have negative repercussions for women.

In retrospect, these achievements would be the high-water mark for secular women's groups in Iraq. Within a few months, the United States would dissolve the CPA and transfer power back to the Iraqis, leaving the women's groups to navigate the minefield of religious politics—and a conservative Shia majority—largely on their own.

A Modern-Day Zainab

The two-car convoy carrying Salama al-Khafaji sped north toward Baghdad, kicking up a cloud of dust that clung to the leaves of the ancient eucalyptus trees along the side of the road. The rays of the late afternoon sun, still searing hot, glinted off the sluggish, muddy water of the Euphrates River in the distance.

It was the end of May 2004. Salama al-Khafaji, a prominent Shia politician, was returning from Najaf. For weeks, she had been shuttling back and forth between Najaf and Baghdad as she attempted to negotiate a cease-fire with the renegade leader Muqtada al-Sadr. Over the past several months, fighting had escalated between al-Sadr's Mahdi Army and U.S. forces. Al-Khafaji was trying to use persuasion to dial down the violence.

A dentist in her mid-fifties, Salama al-Khafaji was relatively new to politics, but she had taken to it with gusto. Only seven months earlier, she had been catapulted to prominence when she was selected as one of only three women for the Interim Governing Council. Her predecessor, also a woman (and a former Baathist official), had been assassinated in an ambush on her car as she made her way to work. Officials in the powerful Islamic Dawa Party, who knew of Salama from her work teaching Islamic studies to women, nominated her as a replacement.

As darkness began to fall, Salama al-Khafaji's convoy began the most treacherous part of its journey through the militant Sunni area south of Baghdad where Shias were routinely shot, kidnapped, tortured, and murdered. Her drivers instinctively narrowed the distance between their cars and sped up. Her convoy had made the trip numerous times in recent weeks and was known in these parts.

A red Opel sedan passed them heading in the opposite direction. The men in the car swiveled their heads to check out al-Khafaji's group. They recognized her and pulled a quick U-turn to give chase.

As they came up behind her car, they leaned out of their windows and let loose with a fusillade of gunfire from their AK-47s.

Salama al-Khafaji ducked in the backseat. Her driver swerved and floored the accelerator. The spray of bullets narrowly missed her car. As they sped off, she looked through the back window to see the red Opel pushing her other car off the road behind them, shattering its windows with gunshots. She screamed at her driver to stop. Salama's seventeen-year-old son Ahmad was in the other car. But it was too late. The next day, she heard that Ahmad's bullet-ridden body had been found in the canal alongside the road.

Salama al-Khafaji took the news stoically. She tried to find solace by remembering the fortitude of Zainab, the heroine of Karbala. As word spread about the murder of her son, her currency soared. Now known as the mother of a martyr, she was lauded in Shia circles for making the ultimate sacrifice for her country. Her supporters even began to refer to her as Zainab. In a survey the following month, respondents rated al-Khafaji as the most popular female politician in Iraq, and the eleventh-most-popular politician overall.[3]

Secular groups, however, viewed Salama al-Khafaji with hostility. Not only does she wear her religiosity on her sleeve (she always wears the long, black, all-encompassing *abaya*), but in one of her first actions on the ICG, she voted in favor of Resolution 137. Women's groups accused her of simply toeing the line of the conservative Islamic Dawa Party, which had nominated her to the council, against the interests of women. Salama defended her position by arguing that Islamic rules would actually provide better protection to women in divorce and custody proceedings than would secular law.

It is hard to imagine that Salama al-Khafaji actually believed this to be true. Sharia law can be and is widely interpreted, including in the sensitive areas of divorce and custody, but mainstream interpretations usually give fathers sole custody of the children in the case of divorce, starting at the age of seven for boys and around nine, or the age of puberty, for girls. Grand Ayatollah al-Sistani, who on many matters is known as a moderate, advises on his own website that fathers should gain sole custody of the children at the age of two. There is little room to argue that sharia would favor women over Iraq's existing civil law.

It is also not fair, however, to depict Salama al-Khafaji as a mere puppet of the Shia political machine. Within months of landing her position on the IGC, she was challenging the leaders of the Islamic Dawa Party and the Supreme Islamic Iraqi Council on several high-profile issues, including their stance toward Muqtada al-Sadr (they wanted to crush the upstart renegade, rather than negotiate with him).

Clearly, Salama was trying to walk a narrow line. She wanted to be relevant within the newly empowered Shia religious parties, which meant accepting an Islamic framework. Yet she also saw herself as an advocate for women. "I have Islamic ideas on justice, but I am moderate," she insisted. "I have optimism. I can speak with people who are liberal and with those who are from the Islamic party."[4] Conservative and devout, but also determined to establish an active role in society for women, Salama became something of a trailblazer for Islamic feminists in Iraq.

Salama al-Khafaji was used to charting new ground for traditional women in Iraq. From an early age, her father, a self-taught carpenter, had pushed her to seek education and to pursue a career. "He encouraged me to be a doctor or a dentist and he always said, 'You should have been a man.'"[5] She wanted to be an engineer, but was not accepted into the engineering school. Instead, she attended the College of Dentistry and completed a master's degree in dentistry in 1989. Despite the fact that she was an openly pious Shia woman, making her suspect in the eyes of Saddam's Baathist regime, she earned a teaching position at the University of Baghdad. She also opened her own private practice. She remembers those days proudly.

"In Iraq, they say that you have to have a man extract teeth. But I always did my own extractions. So I was famous at the college because they knew that in my practice, I did the extractions myself. My hand is bigger than other women's—and this is from doing my own extractions. Religious women like to have other women do extractions for them."[6]

As she was building her practice, she also began to explore Islamic law and philosophy. She started attending an underground school for Shia women at the home of Sheikh Fatih Kashif al-Ghita. The sheikh came from a long line of religious scholars from Najaf. His great-grandfather was the senior *marja* (Shia authority) in Najaf in the 1930s, a position now held by Grand Ayatollah al-Sistani.

The al-Ghita family is notable not only for its Islamic scholarship, but also for its decidedly progressive stance on women's religious training. For more than a century, women in the family have become distinguished scholars in their own right, although officially they are excluded from Najaf's seminaries.

In his clandestine academy for women, al-Ghita accepted only students who already had at least a college degree. He would then make them take a broad course of study—including philosophy, logic, rhetoric, and jurisprudence—the same curriculum followed by men in the seminaries.[7] Salama al-Khafaji became his star pupil.

Anticipating his eventual arrest, Sheikh al-Ghita taught his students from behind a screen. That way, he could not see their faces and would not be able to reveal their identities if interrogated. In 1998, Saddam's henchmen came for him, and he ended up in the notorious Abu Ghraib prison. After being tortured, the sheikh was sentenced to death for the subversive activity of teaching Shia theology.

Salama al-Khafaji worked with the sheikh's mother, Amal al-Ghita, a determined woman with a Ph.D. in pharmacology, to scrape together enough money to bribe officials on the sheikh's behalf. Their efforts succeeded when his sentence was commuted to life in prison. Amal al-Ghita, well-trained in Islamic scholarship herself, took over the women's classes, getting teaching ideas and reading lists from her son during her prison visits. Sheikh al-Ghita was let out of prison at the end of 2002, on the eve of the U.S. invasion when Saddam Hussein released many political prisoners.

Salama al-Khafaji started to become active in politics soon after the demise of the regime. "I did not plan on entering politics, but after the American invasion I realized that the voice of the majority of Iraqi women—who are religious and not returning exiles—was not being heard," claimed Salama. "I wanted that voice to be heard."[8]

She joined her dentists' union and in June 2003 was elected to its executive committee. It was from that perch that she was tapped by the Islamic Dawa Party to fill the seat on the IGC left empty after her predecessor's assassination.

Before accepting the position, Salama sought guidance from the senior Islamic leaders in the holy city of Najaf, including Ayatollah al-Sistani. She asked the clerics if it was appropriate for her, as a woman, to work in politics, and specifically, to work with the Americans. They told her that not only was it appropriate, but that it was her duty. "They all said, 'This is very important. There have to be some Iraqi people to work with the Americans,'" she recalled.[9]

Salama al-Khafaji's reputation on the IGC was immediately burnished by the fact that she was the only person on the council elected by her peers and not appointed by the Americans.[10] She chose her spiritual guide, Sheikh al-Ghita, as her deputy. Her obvious piety and religious credentials, along with the fact that she was not a returning exile but someone who had toughed it out during the Saddam years, gave her instant credibility within the Shia community. Yet she also espoused relatively progressive ideas about democracy. Even though she voted for Resolution 137, she often spoke on the record about the need for a secular system in Iraq—that a separation of religion and politics was right and necessary.

Her perspectives on democracy and human rights and her outspoken advocacy for an active public role for women made it hard to pigeonhole Salama al-Khafaji simply as a religious conservative. She was one of the rare Iraqi politicians attempting to bridge some of the deep chasms that increasingly divided society. She paid a deep personal price for her efforts. In the wake of the assassination of her son, her husband demanded that she leave politics. When she refused, he divorced her.

Seeking Safety in Numbers

Early in Iraq's new political process, a variety of women's groups began lobbying for a quota—it was not hard for them to anticipate that they would be shut out of Iraqi politics as religious parties solidified their control. Like their politically active sisters in Afghanistan, they wanted a guarantee of at least 25 percent of the seats in parliament for women. They pointed to the fact that Iraqi women had had the right to vote and run for office since 1980. Within two decades, women had come to occupy 20 percent of the seats in Iraq's parliament versus the average for women in the region of less than 4 percent at that time. They had also held several cabinet positions under the Baathists.

Although Salama al-Khafaji disappointed secular women with her vote for Resolution 137, she was an early and ardent supporter of a quota for women in government. Salama well understood the conservative forces she was working with and the need for women to have a voice. She and Sheikh al-Ghita went further than many women's groups, arguing that women should have at least 40 percent of the seats in parliament.

Some U.S. policy makers were sympathetic to Iraqi women's concerns, since it was obvious that the political process was becoming increasingly dominated by conservative Shia groups. Yet the CPA was unwilling to publicly back a quota for women. Again, it was reluctant to challenge the religious powerbrokers on women's issues. Iraqi women, both secular leaders like Maysoon al-Damluji and openly religious women like Salama al-Khafaji, would not take no for an answer on quotas. Their persistence ensured that women would get at least 25 percent of the seats in parliament. In the January 2005 elections for a transitional national assembly, whose main task would be to draft a new constitution, political parties were required to have slates on which every third person was a woman.

In the run-up to these elections, U.S. officials made attempts to encourage women's political participation, particularly secular women. They held leadership training sessions for female candidates to enhance their public speaking and media skills. They funded a series of women's centers to build an advocacy network for women. They also promoted voter education to build public support for the idea of women as candidates. However, of the more than $130 million the U.S. government spent on the January 2005 elections, less than 5 percent was directed specifically toward women.[11]

U.S. efforts were hardly sufficient to counter the trends working against women. Rising levels of violence were becoming a clear deterrent to women's public participation. While both men and women risked assassination and kidnapping amid the growing lawlessness, women had to brave the additional challenge of extreme fundamentalism. Sunni and Shia zealots, although locked in a bloody sectarian battle themselves, indulged in similar acts of violence against women to impose rigid orthodoxy on their communities.

In cities across Iraq, even in the more fashionable districts of

Baghdad, religious conservatives terrorized unveiled women by throwing acid at their faces—a method of attack used with disturbing frequency in Afghanistan and Pakistan as well. In other instances, women had their heads forcibly shaved or were pelted with stones for daring to appear uncovered. In villages terrorized by al-Qaeda in the Sunni Triangle and along the Shia-controlled streets of Basra in the south, extremists assassinated women for wearing makeup or appearing without a headscarf. To leave no doubt about their intentions, the militants would strip the bodies, dress them in scandalous clothing, and dump them in the gutter. Sometimes, the bodies were decapitated and the message "collaborator" was pinned to their chests.

Female politicians and activists became assassination targets. Within weeks of becoming a member of the IGC, gunmen tried to kill Salama al-Khafaji. She barely escaped. In the spring of 2004, assassins also targeted the minister of public works, Nasreen Barwari, a Harvard-trained Kurdish woman who was the only female cabinet member in the interim government. She narrowly escaped but the attack killed three of her bodyguards. In March 2004, Fern Holland, a human-rights activist and lawyer from Oklahoma who helped draft parts of the interim constitution concerning women, was killed along with two co-workers in the town of Hilla, south of Baghdad. It was open warfare on women.

As the January 2005 elections neared, escalating violence called into question whether a fair election could take place. With insurgents promising to attack polling centers, concern ran high that the legitimacy of the elections would be undermined by a low turnout, particularly by Sunni groups who threatened a boycott. U.S. officials, however, remained determined to push forward. They viewed the elections as a crucial milestone for transferring power to an Iraqi democracy. Many Iraqis also remained determined to vote, particularly the Shia, who saw elections as the way, finally, to realize the power of their numbers.

Just weeks before the elections, the United States sponsored a training session for Iraqi female candidates. The session was held in neighboring Amman, Jordan, since security was so fraught inside Iraq. A group of well-intentioned but apparently under-informed U.S. congresswomen traveled from Washington, D.C., to provide sisterly solidarity and technical campaigning advice to the Iraqis. They brought with them samples of bumper stickers and campaign buttons to show the Iraqi women how to build name recognition among voters. They had prepared motivational talks about the importance of getting one's messages out to voters on radio and on television. But after hearing horrifying stories from so many of the Iraqi women—about assassination attempts, kidnappings, death threats to family members—the American congresswomen quietly slipped their campaign props back into their bags.

Fears of assassination led most parties to refrain from even releasing the names of their candidates. Ballots included only numbers and symbols to indicate parties, leaving voters to choose among broad slates. This approach helped the well-organized Shia religious parties, especially those that combined to form the United Iraqi Alliance (UIA). Propelled forward with endorsement from spiritual leader Ayatollah al-Sistani, the UIA got the most votes in the election, securing 140 out of 275 seats in Iraq's National Assembly.[12]

By most accounts, turnout among women was surprisingly strong— about as strong as among men. Ayatollah al-Sistani's encouragement no doubt helped. He issued a fatwa saying that women should be allowed to vote even if their husbands objected. He urged women to follow the example of Zainab and go forth to vote. Across Baghdad and in the southern cities of Najaf and Basra, photos of the aging cleric were plastered on buildings and storefronts, along with his exhortations. "Truly, women who go forth to the polling centers on Election Day are like Zainab who went forth to Karbala."[13]

When the dust cleared on the election, some Western commentators pointed to the high level of female participation, and the fact that women comprised 31 percent of the seats in the new parliament, as evidence that a grand social and cultural transformation was under way in Iraq. With so many women in parliament, they reasoned, Iraq's new government would likely take a progressive stance on women's rights in drafting the new constitution and limiting the role of religion.

This line of reasoning, however, neglected to factor in that half of the women elected came into parliament on the conservative Shia slate of the UIA. Like Salama al-Khafaji, they would be careful about challenging the party line. As Abdulaziz al-Hakim and other leaders of the

UIA made clear, that party line very much included religion. Indeed, they announced that inserting sharia in the constitution was for them a nonnegotiable demand.

Kurds and secular Iraqis were equally adamant about keeping religion out of the constitution. Speaking to a reporter soon after the January 2005 election, Kurdish leader Jalal Talabani, just before he became the new president of Iraq, insisted, "We will never accept any religious government in Iraq. Never. This is a red line for us. We will never live inside an Islamic Iraq." Secular women's groups also joined the fray, warning that the UIA's intent to impose sharia would take women backward. The role of sharia quickly became one of the most contentious issues facing the constitutional drafting committee.

"You Cannot Ignore Our History!"

Sundus Abbas Hasan sat in the audience, her heart pounding as she became increasingly agitated. She was listening to an Iraqi member of parliament drone on about his support for Iraqi women, how he encouraged them to become teachers and healthcare professionals. However, he continued emphatically, they should stay out of politics. "In Iraq," he concluded, "women and politics simply do not work together. It is against our Islamic traditions for women to be leaders."

It was June 2005. For nearly two days Sundus, the founder of the Women's Leadership Institute in Iraq, had been participating in a conference about women's rights and the Iraqi constitution (the drafting process was in full swing). The meeting was sponsored by Women for Women International, an American-based women's rights organization founded by Zainab Salbi, an Iraqi exile, to help women in war-torn countries regain self-sufficiency. The conference, held at a Dead Sea resort in Jordan because of security concerns within Iraq, brought together Iraqi women activists, members of parliament, and the constitutional drafting committee. International legal and constitutional experts, including those with expertise in sharia, also attended. Zainah Anwar, one of the founders of Sisters in Islam, was there. So, too, was a representative from Women Living Under Muslim Laws. They brought with them their considerable experiences of trying to find balance between religion and constitutional freedoms in their own Islamic countries. They well understood how religion in the new Iraqi constitution could be used to limit women's rights.

Sundus could no longer contain her frustration with the speaker. "Sir," she said politely, her soft voice quavering slightly in the microphone, "you are not correct. Women have been deeply involved in Iraqi politics since the 1940s. Women filled Saddam's jails. I don't know where you have been all these years, but I have been in Iraq. I can tell you that Iraqi women have sacrificed. You cannot ignore our history."[14]

There was silence in the room for several seconds. Then a few women started to clap, quickly joined by others. "You know," Sundus remembers, thinking back on that experience, "just getting listened to is an important step. The men refuse to listen to me because I do not wear a hijab." Her long dark hair, tinted with auburn, falls unapologetically on her shoulders.

Sacrifice is something that Sundus knows about all too well. During the years of horrendous violence after the U.S. invasion of Iraq, she lost two siblings. Her sister was killed in an explosion in 2004, leaving behind two teenage sons. Then, in 2007, her brother was killed in another attack. He left behind an infant son, whom Sundus has been raising. Her own mother, overcome by stress, died a few months later.

Sundus Abbas Hasan has lived her whole life in Baghdad. She went to university and got a master's degree in political science. But since she refused to become a member of the Baath Party, her job options were limited. She avoided politics and worked anonymously in a research institute. After the U.S. invasion, her hopes for a better life soared. "I assumed there would be no problems for women. I assumed people returning to the country from overseas would be progressives, they would be democrats," she says wistfully.

"I vividly remember a conversation I had with a member of Iraq's transitional government," she recalls. "When I asked him why there were only three women in the interim government, he told me that they simply couldn't find any qualified women to serve. I knew that was ludicrous. But it gave me the inspiration to start my organization to help develop women's leadership." With financial backing from donors overseas, Sundus founded the Women's Leadership Institute in 2004 to train women in communications, negotiations, and political decision making. She would make sure that Iraq's leaders knew where to find qualified women.

Almost immediately, Sundus and her new organization focused on the drafting of the Iraqi constitution. Like progressive women's groups across Iraq, they were uneasy with the conservative composition of the drafting committee. Based on election results, about half of the committee members came from the Shia United Iraqi Alliance. Of the eight women on the committee, five represented the UIA. The majority of women were there to represent conservative Shia interests, not to advocate on behalf of women.

Sundus came away from the Dead Sea meeting in June with reams of materials, supplied by Women Living Under Muslim Law and Sisters in Islam, about the relationship between customary and religious law, and constitutional law, in various countries. She and other women activists did their best to lobby the constitutional committee for a separation of mosque and state, for exact language to minimize future battles over religious interpretation, and to ensure that religion remained a source of guidance but not a source of discrimination or inequality.

They were fighting an uphill battle. Conservative Shia leaders demanded that Islam be *the* source of legislation for the country and threatened to scuttle talks if Islam did not get a central place in the constitution. The original deadline for negotiations came and went, and still no agreement was reached. The constitutional debate spilled over into an extension period. As the arguments dragged on, then U.S. Ambassador Zalmay Khalilzad intervened to avoid a stalemate. To gain concessions in other areas, he supported provisions that strengthened Islam's influence. Ultimately, the Kurds acquiesced too, both because they had other priorities to defend and because they recognized that conservative Shia leaders were not going to capitulate.

The final version of the constitution designates Islam as the official religion of the state and says that no law can be passed that contradicts its "undisputed" rulings. Yet, in a small but important compromise sought by the more secular Kurds and women's groups, it cites Islam as a basic source of legislation, not the only source as religious leaders demanded. Still, secular democracy as promoted by the Americans never stood a chance given the determination of the newly empowered Shia leaders to promote Islam in the new state. "All of this," Sundus concludes, "was to give authority to religious men. It is not what our country needs."

Women's groups continue to worry about Article 41 of the constitution, the section dealing with personal status law. As foreshadowed by the earlier battle over Resolution 137, Article 41 of the constitution deems Iraqis "free in their personal status according to their religions, sects, beliefs, or choices," but leaves it up to subsequent legislation to define what this means. Some claim that the provision is meant to give Iraqis freedom of choice—allowing Shia to live under Shia law and Sunnis under Sunni law.

Allowing such freedom could lead to a confusing but relatively benign system under which Iraqis choose among different codes and court systems—Sunni or Shia—depending on their background. This is not unprecedented in the region, where in countries like Lebanon and Pakistan, multiple court systems coexist. Sundus, however, views Article 41 as a sectarian disaster. "The reality of Iraqi families is that we are mixed. My family is Shia. Yet both my sisters married Sunnis. How will mixed families deal with the different courts? This law will only divide us."

Secular women also view Article 41 as a harbinger of Iranian-style theocracy—the first step in stripping women of their rights within the family. Given the deep connections between Iraq's Shia leaders and Iran, Iraqi women have good reason to be concerned. Polls do show that a majority of Iraqis want a religious state, and many look to Iran as a model. But even among devout Shia, the model is not necessarily the theocratic extreme of Iran in 1980. The more likely starting point when it comes to women and family laws will be the fluid and deeply contested legal environment of Iran today, where women's rights within Islam are a central topic of debate, not only among the general public but among religious leaders themselves.

Since the Iraqi constitution was adopted, women activists have tried to revisit Article 41 as part of the constitutional review process, but so far their efforts have been stymied. Negotiations to reopen the constitution have focused, and foundered, on the critical frontline political

264 / Paradise Beneath Her Feet

issues of oil wealth redistribution, de-Baathification, and the disposition of Kirkuk. Women's rights have taken a backseat to these deliberations.

For several years, the space for women to protest and argue for their rights seemed to be closing as conservative Shia politicians tightened their grip on power. Women speaking out publicly against Article 41 risked being labeled anti-Shia or even sympathetic to Saddam. Western powers were cautious about interfering. "It's hard for us to lobby strongly and say this is wrong, this is right," said a Western diplomat, succumbing to cultural relativism. "If you put it across too strongly, it comes across as you're not sensitive to their religion or their history."[15]

Several developments, however, hold promise that the space for women activists is opening up again in Iraq. First and foremost, improvements in security are hugely to women's benefit. Civil society in general and women's groups in particular simply cannot organize and be effective in the face of unrestrained violence and terror. Women's groups flourished in the immediate months after the U.S. invasion, but as security deteriorated, they were forced to scale back their activities. Many moved their offices to neighboring countries like Jordan, where they were much less effective, or simply closed up shop. Now, with significant improvements in security, they are once again rebuilding and mobilizing.

Sundus Abbas Hasan is a walking example of how women's groups are benefiting from increased stability. In previous years, her life was regularly threatened. She could barely visit her offices in Basra, a stronghold of Shia militias for several years. Since she refuses to wear a hijab, she was particularly vulnerable to fundamentalist vigilante groups in the south who target non-veiled women. Now, she feels safer traveling there, and increasingly sees other women stripping off their hijabs too. "I am not against hijab," she explains, "but it is critical that we as a country can respect people's choices. If I believed that the problems of my country could be solved if I wore a leaf from a tree, then I would wear it."

The country's evolving political landscape also holds signs of hope for women. Provincial elections in early 2009 indicated a swing of the pendulum back to more of a middle ground, as voters chose secular and nationalist parties over religious parties. While some political power brokers remain committed to the establishment of a Shia Islamic state in Iraq, there are signs of mounting public resistance to a theocratic fait accompli.

Increasingly, that resistance is coming from conservative, *abaya*-clad women themselves. Sundus's organization, the Women's Leadership Institute, works with aspiring female politicians. Many of them are affiliated with the conservative religious parties. In just a few brief years, she has seen these women evolve from silent acquiescence into vocal leaders.

Sundus tells me about Leila, a widow from Basra who was a candidate for the provincial elections held in January 2009. Although she was very active in her work, Leila was also painfully shy and traditional. She hid herself behind her full black *abaya* in public. In the training sessions, Leila asked not to be called on and insisted that she could never speak to the media. Sundus slowly coaxed her out of her shell. She got her to do some mock media training, only for internal use. They started by recording just twenty seconds of tape and playing it back. Then one minute. Then five minutes. Soon, Leila became an expert. "Just before the elections, I saw Leila on one of the evening news shows. She was discussing her platform, making her campaign pitches like a seasoned professional. Of course, she got elected," says Sundus, beaming like a proud parent. "When those women with *abayas* have a bit of opportunity, they can do a lot of things."

In many ways, the quota for women in parliament has provided that "bit of opportunity." The challenge now is for Iraqi female parliamentarians to translate numbers into influence. So far, it has been rough going: The women members have been regularly insulted by their male colleagues and relegated to working on "women's issues." A low point came in the fall of 2008 when the powerful speaker of parliament announced that women make poor leaders because they are constantly worried that their husbands will take a second wife. Incensed, all seventy-four women in parliament boycotted the session the next day, bringing the government to a standstill. The speaker was forced to publicly apologize.[16]

The silver lining of this incident for women was that it showed them they can make change happen when they come together. They are beginning to realize the power of numbers. They are also becoming more skilled as legislators. Women are taking advantage of the training sessions offered to them by Western advisers; they are becoming more active on committees where the actual work of parliament is done; they get high marks for knowing the details of legislation, and for putting aside sectarian differences more quickly than men.[17]

If Iraq's fragile democracy can survive, women—thanks to the quota—will play a significant role in determining the political evolution of the country. One of the most important issues they will continue to face is the role of religion in their lives. Traditional women across Iraq have joined the country's religious awakening. They are taking introductory religious classes. They are attending the mosque. They are setting up special schools to study Islamic jurisprudence in an attempt to go beyond the basics. They see Islam as their key to reentering the public sphere that has been largely closed to them. Like Islamic feminists in other countries around the world, they are learning how to harness the power of religion for their own reform agendas.

Women's groups are strategically working with religious leaders to build support for their causes. Women for Women International, for example, secured a fatwa from Ayatollah al-Sistani saying that it was appropriate for women to work and study outside the home. With this in hand, the resistance they had encountered from traditional women who were reluctant to participate in their income-generation programs melted away. Sundus and her organization also rely on various sheikhs to speak on behalf of women. One in particular, Sheikh Iyad Jamal al-Din, who is also a member of parliament, frequently speaks out on behalf of women's rights. Known as the "secular sheikh" because he believes in the separation of religion and politics, Sheikh al-Din is also a strong advocate for women's rights within Islam.

Another potentially strong ally in Iraqi women's struggle to realize their rights could be the country's judiciary, which has responsibility for interpreting the country's constitution. There are some positive signs that a decent, independent judiciary is emerging in Iraq. Already, Iraq's Supreme Court has upheld various freedoms delineated in the constitution against the wishes of powerful politicians. Over the long term, the composition of Iraq's high court, whether it is packed with clerics as in Iran or with judges trained in civil law along with sharia, will be all-important in determining the religiosity of the laws. The legislation defining the selection of court members will be a crucial area for women politicians in Iraq to engage.

Iraq's future remains uncertain. Will the violence return and shatter the country? Will a strong man reemerge, taking charge of the disparate pieces of the country through brute force? Or will the political process continue to evolve into a truly democratic system, a first for the Arab world? Against long odds, Iraq is slowly putting in place the building blocks of democracy—a free press, an independent judiciary, an active civil society, open and fair elections. Women like Sundus Abbas Hasan are very much part of that process, picking up the pieces and getting on with the job of rebuilding their country.

The challenges for women in Iraq are great: large gaps in education, fragile security, frayed social networks. The devastation of the country's infrastructure in the wake of the bungled U.S. invasion falls heavily on women: lack of adequate electricity and clean drinking water, lack of a reliable police force, the rise of female-headed households due to detained or killed husbands and fathers. Over the long run, navigating the resurgence of conservative Islam may be the biggest challenge for Iraqi women. They will need to learn quickly from the experiences of Muslim women around the world—from Morocco to Iran to Malaysia—who have had to fight for gains for women's rights within an Islamic framework.

Over time, free elections will force Iraq's religious parties to compete for votes, including the votes of women who comprise a majority of the population. At some point, defending religious tradition will not be sufficient to carry the day. The religious parties will have to show that they can govern effectively, that they can deliver. While Iraqi citizens are understandably focused on security and economic issues, second-order issues like legal rights will become more important as the country stabilizes, especially for women. Iraq's courts could become important testing grounds for reconciling sharia with the modern world, especially on thorny questions of gender equality.

In this fluid context, where Islam is an essential part of the cultural fabric and plays a central role in the constitution, women activists will need to utilize a variety of strategies, including Islamic feminism, to push for legal, social, economic, and political gains. Among Iraq's newly empowered Shia majority, there are many strong-willed modern-day Zainabs who, with a bit of opportunity, can and will do many things.

CHAPTER 8

CONCLUSION
Unveiling the Future

Islam calls for equality, justice, compassion, and dignity between all people. Family laws and practices must therefore fulfill this call by promoting these principles and responding to the lived realities of Muslim women and men today.

—Musawah Framework for Action, February 2009

Harnessing Courage

In February 2009, several hundred women and scores of men gathered in Kuala Lumpur to launch a global movement. They came from nearly fifty countries around the world, from sub-Saharan Africa and the Middle East, from South Asia and North America. The participants represented broadly different expertise and experiences—lawyers, judges, scholars, journalists, activists, bloggers, politicians, performers, religious leaders. Many of the women you have read about in this book were there—some meeting each other for the first time, others old friends and longtime collaborators.

The movement, called Musawah ("equality" in Arabic), has set for itself an audacious goal: achieving equality within the Muslim family. Musawah declares this goal important not only because so many Muslim family laws are out of touch with the reality of modern life, but because they are not defensible on Islamic grounds. The movement is taking the fight for equality straight to the heart of the matter—to the texts.

To open the meeting, the organizers showed a powerful video (you can watch it online at www.musawah.org). It starts with a map of the Middle East and the words "7th Century A.D.: Islam Arrives in Arabia. The Most Progressive Feminist Laws of the Age Are Introduced . . . in the Quran." As the map adds green to show the spread of Islam across the region, those progressive feminist laws flash up on the screen:

"Killing of Girl Babies Prohibited."
"I am equal before the eyes of God."
"I have the right to own property."
"I have the right to inherit property."
"I can sign my own contracts."
"I can choose my own husband."
"I can't be forced to marry against my will."
"I can write a marriage contract and impose conditions on my
    husband-to-be."
"I have the right to divorce my husband."
"I am entitled to dignity and respect."
"I am entitled to an education."
"I have the right to think for myself."
"I have the right to lead my people to the right path."

Watching the video, I could only ponder how so many Muslim communities have today strayed from these progressive principles, while at the same time feel inspired by the efforts of these determined women and men to bring their faith back to its original values.

"Today, everything is an 'insult to Islam,'" complains Zainah Anwar, the longtime head of Sisters in Islam and one of the prime movers behind Musawah. "But I ask you, are equality and justice insults to Islam? No, I don't think so. My God and my Islam recognize me as a human being of equal worth and dignity—nothing less." Zainah and I are sharing a few quiet moments at the conclusion of the conference— after all the speeches, the breakout sessions, the working groups, the media events, the journalist briefings have ended and the last partici- pants are packing up and heading home. She looks exhausted but exhil- arated from the whole experience.

"I didn't expect such a response," she continues. "But clearly, there is some major resonance here. Muslim women around the world want to be feminists and they want to enjoy their faith. We had people here from all over the world—scholars from all backgrounds, activists working at the grassroots, policy makers from Islamic governments and the UN system. We are building a collective, global force. We are harnessing courage."

Musawah's launch was three years in the making, although in many respects the movement had been percolating for decades. The idea originated at a 2006 Sisters in Islam meeting on family law that brought together Muslim activists from Turkey and Morocco (two Muslim-majority countries that had just successfully reformed their family laws) with activists from Southeast Asia, Iran, Pakistan, the United States, and the United Kingdom to share strategies and tactics. By the end of that meeting, the participants recognized that there was a need, and an opportunity, to create an international network. Some women's groups have been working for years on family law reform and have much to share with respect to scholarship, strategy, and best practices. An international network would help reform movements around the world reach that critical tipping point. Musawah was born.

As I walked the hallways of the Musawah conference, I saw the anticipated networking breaking out all over the place. In one room, a group of women representing ten different sub-Saharan African countries was meeting to establish their own Musawah caucus. As they sat around the table in their bold-colored traditional dresses, they looked like a menagerie of graceful tropical birds, but they were all business in discussing how they would support each other in pushing back the challenge posed by the rise of sharia in their African societies. In another room, a Saudi activist was sharing her strategies with several Iranians for using new media to organize. Down the corridor, the Moroccan women were meeting with the Afghan women on family law strategies. Islamic feminism was on the move.

Musawah's explicit goal is to promote a holistic approach toward change and reform—one that combines both secular and religious frameworks. Since so much injustice toward women is done in the name of Islam, the group reasons, then explaining why change is necessary and equality is possible within Islam is critical. Some of those who participated in the conference are well-known secularists who in the past have expressed deep reservations about the strategy of appealing to religion. Their touchstone is international human rights; they have long avoided the quicksand of religious discourse at all costs. Their support now for Musawah reflects a grudging acceptance of what some Islamic feminists have been warning about for years: It is dangerous to cede the space of religious authority to conservative voices. Musawah acknowledges that political Islam and identity politics are powerful forces that must be addressed. It acknowledges that the demonizing of women's groups requires new tools for dealing with religious authority; most important, it insists that equality and change are possible within Islam.

Zainah Anwar likes to ask, why is it that you do not need a degree in economics to talk about the economy, but unless you have advanced degrees from al-Azhar in Cairo, you cannot talk about Islam? At the heart of Islamic feminism is Anwar's contention that Muslim women "will no longer be shut up by some verse in the Quran." Across the Muslim world, women are engaging with the texts in an unprecedented fashion—through Quranic study groups, radio shows, Islamic satellite television, through the Internet, and through formal study. In some countries like Iran, the process is more advanced, whereas in others, like Afghanistan, it is just beginning.

Women's rising literacy across Muslim countries, and ultimately their rising religious literacy, is shifting the terms of debate. No longer can women's groups, advocating for more rights, be so easily dismissed as "anti-Islam." Increasingly, women know the texts well enough to challenge them.

The ongoing scholarly process of contextualizing, of recapturing the original meaning of the texts, and of reevaluating the hadith, all of which are so central to Islamic feminism, has the potential to be as transformative in this century as the Christian Reformation was in the sixteenth century. The growing ability of Muslim women to read the Quran for themselves is commensurate with the sea change that occurred when average Christians began to read the Bible directly.

In many ways, the Internet is to Islamic feminism what the printing press was to Martin Luther's reformation. Websites like Women Living Under Muslim Law and Musawah collect and archive relevant information and materials. Musawah, for example, has catalogued various Muslim family laws to show how these supposedly divine laws differ. Musawah's bottom line: Since there are clearly differences among these Islamic laws, they simply cannot be divine and therefore are eligible for reform. Advocacy groups use email to instantaneously bombard policy makers. Activists expose brutality and injustice with simple video footage captured on a cell phone and uploaded to YouTube. For example, the flogging of the seventeen-year-old girl in Swat by the Taliban, captured on a bystander's cell phone, made headline news around the world and helped energize the Pakistani response to the Taliban threat.

Some critics dismiss Islamic feminism as a fringe movement—they say it is too small, too weak, too marginal to move mainstream opinion. For all their good intentions, these women will never be able to overturn 1,400 years of oppressive Islamic law. When I play that critique back to Anwar, she throws her head back and laughs. "We are not going to overturn fourteen hundred years of tradition overnight! We are just at the beginning. These changes take time, but time is on our side."

The tipping point will be reached for women's rights at different times in different countries. In Africa and parts of Asia, many of the restrictions imposed on women in the name of Islam in fact run counter to long-held traditions. They were introduced relatively recently, as a more austere Wahhabi form of Islam spread over the past several decades through Saudi-funded mosques. As women and supportive men find their voices, they are pushing back on these restrictive interpretations of Islam. The clamor for more sharia in society might have already peaked in places like Nigeria and Indonesia.

Change is happening. The success of the women's movement in Morocco in 2004 in reforming the *mudawana*, the family laws, within a framework that satisfied most of the country's Islamists was in many ways a watershed. It showed Muslim women what was possible and energized Muslim women's movements around the world. The growth and persistence of the One Million Signatures Campaign in Iran, and the launch of the transnational Musawah movement, are both direct outcomes.

Progress for women is occurring, although at uneven rates. In Iran, women have recaptured much of the ground they lost with the Islamic Revolution, although it has taken thirty years and much struggle, and some laws remain grossly unequal. In Pakistan, women are working across class lines to promote social change and awareness of rights—constitutional rights, human rights, and Islamic rights. Even disadvantaged rural women, like Muktar Mai, are becoming more aware of their rights and finding the courage to resist the harsh tribal practices they are subjected to in the name of Islam. In Afghanistan, women hold onto the constitutional gains they have achieved while working to improve women's access to basic health and education. In Saudi Arabia, women are plowing ahead academically, graduating from universities in record numbers. They are making gains in the workforce even though they are not allowed to drive and the judicial system remains stacked against them. In neighboring Iraq, women are staking their claim to the political process despite the country's Islamic revival and their distinct disadvantages in educational levels.

Although the headlines from these countries are usually so grim—the religious police beating up another woman in Saudi Arabia for the crime of being seen in public with a man not related to her, the Taliban burning down another girls' school in Afghanistan—the oppressive laws and the violence perpetrated against women in the name of Islam could very well be a last gasp of patriarchy.

Frequently I am asked by interested and concerned people around the world, "What can we do to help?" My first response is that help begins with understanding. Too often, I hear people despair that the unequal treatment of women across the broader Middle East will never change because "that's their culture." But sweeping statements like this fail to appreciate that culture is not immutable. In every country, even your own, at any time, culture is contested. As fast as the Taliban burn down girls' schools in Afghanistan, for example, a dedicated group of parents and teachers rebuild. They are willing to risk their lives to change their own culture. The women in this book are also all struggling—each in her own way—to change culture. We should at least acknowledge and encourage their determination, since a failure to do so leads straight into the trap of cultural relativism.

While moral support is nice, women activists around the world, especially in Muslim-majority countries where they are embattled, also need financial assistance and technical expertise. While it is true that women's groups are vulnerable to the risk of backlash against their international partnerships, this concern is often exaggerated. Women's groups are for the most part *already* accused by their opponents of following a foreign agenda. Moreover, they understand the risks and trade-offs of working with international organizations. They understand their own local conditions sufficiently to determine whether the benefits of international support—by way of technical expertise, financial support, media exposure, and public recognition—help more than hurt. (Musdah Mulia, for example, chose to accept the Woman of Courage Award from the U.S. State Department, calculating that it would enhance her prestige more than detract from her local reputation.) Concerns about backlash can be minimized by keeping international support demand-driven. (The Bush administration's support for democracy promotion in Iran clearly violated this simple principle.)

Likewise, it is critical that international support be channeled through local groups. Dr. Sakena Yacoobi's Afghan Institute of Learning is effective because it understands local conditions and recognizes how to work with the culture, rather than against it. Grassroots initiatives like the National Solidarity Program are also models to follow. They build local ownership and buy-in for the changes at hand.

When the international community does have a direct role in shaping the political situation in a country, as in Afghanistan and Iraq, it should support the demands of local women to improve their rights. Implementing electoral quotas for women in those countries' constitutions enabled a political shortcut of at least a generation. Other leverage points include media access and training for women, education, access to income, and property rights.

It is also important to keep in mind that cultural change happens slowly. We are witnessing just the beginning of what will undoubtedly be a long process of change—in many cases intergenerational change. The process will be uneven, and the outcomes from place to place will no doubt differ. I suspect that over the long term, Islamic feminism, like other reform movements that preceded it, will end up unapologetically secular. Only then will never-ending debates over religious interpretation be removed from politics.

In the meantime, Islamic feminism is an important emotional and intellectual stepping-stone—and tactic—to reconcile religion with the demands of the modern world. Shirin Ebadi, the Iranian Nobel Peace Prize winner, summed it up well: "In an ideal world, I would choose not to be vulnerable to the caprice of interpretation, because the ambiguity of theological debates spirals back to the seventh century . . . If I am forced to ferret through musty books of Islamic jurisprudence and rely on sources that stress the egalitarian ethics of Islam, then so be it. Is it harder this way? Of course it is. But is there an alternative battlefield? Desperate wishing aside, I cannot see one."[1]

At the end of the Musawah conference, a Buddhist monk—a woman, familiar with dealing with issues of patriarchy in her own culture and religion—shared the parable of the baby elephant with the group. Taken from its mother in the wild, the baby elephant was chained to a stake in the ground on the outskirts of the village. It tried and tried to get free, straining at its chains. But it was just not strong enough. Many years later, when the baby elephant had grown into a mighty animal, it remained there tethered to the stake, not realizing that one simple tug would now set it free.

The women I have written about in this book, and the many millions more who are bravely striving for change in their conservative societies across the Middle East, are part of a growing movement. It is only a matter of time until the day comes when they test their chains and break free.

ACKNOWLEDGMENTS

This book is the result of nearly a decade of writing about both the Middle East and the role of women in development. During that time, I traveled the region, interviewed hundreds of experts, visited with numerous non-governmental organizations, examined many different projects in the field, and met with countless government officials and local leaders. All of these experiences provided insight, context, and color. I am grateful to the many people who shared their time and their thoughts with me. In particular, I am most grateful to the women featured in this book who shared the personal stories of their lives. They have throughout this process been my inspiration.

The Council on Foreign Relations has been a wonderful environment in which to undertake this project. My special thanks go to Council President Richard Haass and Director of Studies James Lindsay for their steady support, guidance, and encouragement, and fine editing of the manuscript. In addition, I am grateful for the support of the entire Studies department, including Janine Hill and Amy Baker, and the other incredibly capable people who keep the Council functioning so smoothly, including Irina Faskianos, Lisa Shields, Nancy Bodurtha, Suzanne Helm, Camille Massey, Betsy Gude, Patricia Dorff, Kay King, Jan Hughes, and Jean-Michel Oriel.

The Council would not be such a wonderful place to work without the camaraderie and intellectual stimulation of my colleagues. My thanks to Elizabeth Economy, Laurie Garrett, Steven Cook, Walter Russell Mead, Shannon O'Neil, Max Boot, Adam Segal, Amity Shlaes, and Julia Sweig. I owe special thanks to Mohamad Bazzi, Dan Senor, and Vali Nasr, who provided comments on parts of the manuscript, and also to James Hoge and Gideon Rose, who published two earlier articles of mine in *Foreign Affairs* that helped develop many of the ideas in this book. I am especially grateful to Council President Emeritus Leslie Gelb, who hired me and set me on the path of women and development. Thanks for being such a wonderful mentor, sounding board, and source of encouragement.

Over the years, I have been assisted by a number of terrific research associates and interns who helped with this book at different stages, including Sameen Gauhar, Sierra Burnett, Mehlaqa Samdani, Cambria Hamburg, Atika Khawaja, Andrew Lim, and Ethan Pack. My thanks to all of them. I am enormously indebted to Negar Razavi, a dedicated, thorough, and insightful colleague who tirelessly researched, fact-checked, analyzed, organized, edited, challenged, translated, and improved the book until the end. Finally, John Chen did a wonderful last read through and saved me from several errors.

The Women and Foreign Policy Advisory Council at the Council on Foreign Relations has been a tremendous source of support for me throughout this project. Special thanks to Jewelle Bickford, Marlene Hess, Ann Kaplan, Hutham Olayan, Marnie Pillsbury, Diana Taylor, and Anita Wien. I owe my deepest gratitude to Linda Gottlieb, who encouraged me to write this book in the first place and pushed me all along the way to make the book better. She read the first draft with great attention to detail and provided such helpful comments that I am eternally grateful.

My thanks also go the Ford Foundation and the United States Institute of Peace. Each organization provided funding for my research and travel over the years which facilitated this book.

I am very grateful to the many experts who assisted me throughout this process, providing contacts, answering questions, reading sections of the manuscript, and helping in innumerable ways. My thanks to Haleh Esfandiari, Rina Amiri, Asma Nassery, Clark Lombardi, Barnett Rubin, Ann Elizabeth Mayer, Fatemeh Hagigatchou, Robin Wright, Zainab Salbi, Kavita Ramdas, Geeta Rao Gupta, Zainah Anwar, Amina Wadud, Ziba Mir-Hosseini, Isabel Sadurni, Scott Guggenheim, Nathan Brown, Carol Yost, and Christina Asquith. My special thanks to Masuda Sultan, who so graciously introduced me to people in Afghanistan and provided a safe refuge in Kabul.

At Random House, Kate Medina was a thoughtful, patient, and encouraging editor. She and her wonderful team, especially Frankie Jones and Millicent Bennett, helped steer this book through multiple drafts and significant revisions. Their insightful comments and persistence brought this book to fruition. Charlotte Sheedy, my agent, ably introduced me to and steered me through the New York publishing world. I am thankful for her steady hand, unerring guidance, and enthusiasm.

My most heartfelt thanks go to my family, who have suffered through my endless late nights, long weekends, and travels to faraway places. I thank my parents, who allowed me to explore the world as a teenager and encouraged me to believe that anything is possible. I thank my children for being understanding when work takes me away from home. A special thanks to my son Cullen for traveling with me to Afghanistan and Pakistan. Finally, I can never thank enough my husband Struan, who makes the journey so much fun.

GLOSSARY

Abaya: the head and body covering worn by Muslim women, particularly in the Arab states of the Persian Gulf. *Abayas* are traditionally black and cover everything except the face and hands.

Afghani: the currency used in Afghanistan today.

Alim: a Muslim scholar or individual well-versed in Islamic legal and religious studies. The plural is *ulama.*

Allahu Akbar: "God is great" in Arabic. The phrase is repeated by Muslims in different situations (from showing approval, to times of stress).

Ayatollah: a high-ranking religious authority in Shia Islam. A cleric must study for many years and first achieve the rank of *mujtahid* and then *marja-i taqlid* (see below for definitions) before he can reach the rank of ayatollah, after which he becomes a leading source of imitation on all religious matters for his followers. The highest-ranking ayatollahs are now called "grand ayatollahs," of which there are about a dozen in the world today.

Basij: supposedly a volunteer paramilitary militia in Iran. (Many in fact say the Basijis are paid for their service.) The Basij consists mainly of young religious men who are devoted to the supreme leader. Many young Basijis fought in the Iran-Iraq War. Today, they are often used as additional state security and are known to forcefully disperse, beat, and intimidate Iranian protesters and dissidents.

Burqa: the all-encompassing covering worn by women in Afghanistan, parts of Pakistan, and elsewhere. It is normally blue and covers everything from head to toe, including the face. There is only a small mesh opening near the eyes to allow women some vision.

Chador: the long covering worn in Iran, which covers the head and body. Traditionally, devout Iranian women wore a white or light-colored chador over their headscarf—many still wear these inside their homes. However, since the Islamic Revolution, many devout women have opted to wear the black chador to show their piety and their loyalty to the Islamic Republic.

Dari: an Afghan dialect of Persian, which in modern-day Iran is called Farsi. Dari along with Pashto are the two official languages of Afghanistan.

Deobandi: an Islamic revivalist movement, which began in India as a form of Muslim resistance to British colonialism. In recent years, the movement has spread to other countries and regions. Deobandi thought is characterized by a blend of literal adherence to the Islamic texts and elements of Sufi practices. Many of the extremist groups in South Asia are inspired in part by the teachings of the Deobandi movement.

Dupatta: a scarf worn by South Asian women, which is either worn over the shoulder or used to cover one's head. They are often worn with a *shalwar kameez* (see definition below).

Fatwa: a decision or opinion made by an Islamic scholar, usually to clarify a question about Islamic jurisprudence.

Fiqh: Islamic jurisprudence or the science of understanding Islamic law using legal reasoning and knowledge of the texts.

Haar: a Hindi/Urdu word for a garland of flowers.

Hadith: a narration of the sayings of the Prophet Muhammad—what actions he approved of, his explanations of things, etc. The hadith help clarify some of the ambiguities in the Quran.

Hafiz (also spelled "Hafidh"): an individual who has memorized the entire Quran.

Hajj: the Muslim pilgrimage to Mecca. It is one of the five mandatory pillars of Islam. All Muslims who are capable of performing the Hajj are expected to do so. Because Muslims follow a lunar calendar, the date of the Hajj changes every year.

Hajji: a title given to those who have performed the Hajj.

Halal: actions that are permissible in Islam, usually used in the context of foods that a Muslim is allowed to eat.

Haram: actions that are forbidden by Islam, ranging from adultery to the consumption of pork or alcohol.

Hazara: a word that literally means "one thousand" in Persian and refers to the predominantly Shia, Persian-speaking ethnic group that lives in Afghanistan, parts of northern Pakistan, and Iran. The Hazara are largely believed to be descendants of the Mongols, given their shared physical characteristics. Throughout history, the Hazara have been brutally targeted by the Pashtun majority in Afghanistan, especially under the Taliban.

Hijab: the covering of a woman's head and body with an article of clothing. Some Muslims believe that hijab is required by Islamic law to preserve a woman's privacy, modesty, and morality. However, this view is debated among Muslims. The types of hijab worn by women differ depending on the country. The term "headscarf" is also used generally to describe hijab.

Ijaza: literally means "permission" in Arabic, and refers to the official permission given to a student of Islamic studies by a center of Islamic teaching, allowing the student to become a religious scholar in his or her own right.

Ikhwan: an Arabic term for "brotherhood," often used in reference to the Islamist political party, the Muslim Brotherhood. It was also the name given to the fighters that helped Abdul Aziz Ibn Saud conquer the Arabian Peninsula from 1902 to 1932 to create the modern state of Saudi Arabia.

Imam: a Muslim religious leader who acts as a teacher and leader of prayer in the mosque. For Shia, the title of "imam" refers to the infallible leaders of the com-

munity (depending on the school, there are twelve imams or seven), who succeeded from Ali, the son-in-law of the Prophet.

Ijtihad: literally means self-exertion and refers to a process of applying independent
reasoning to interpret Islamic texts. Depending on the school of Islamic jurisprudence, there are varying degrees to which *ijtihad* can be used. During the time of
the Prophet, the use of *ijtihad* was encouraged. However, the "gates of *ijtihad*" are
said to have been closed in Sunni Islam in the twelfth century, whereas for Shias
it has always been allowed. Sunni scholars have debated whether the "gates of
ijtihad" were really ever closed.

Isnad: a list of individuals who have transmitted the sayings of the Prophet Muhammad (usually the Companions of the Prophet); the reliability of *isnad* determines
the validity of the given hadith.

Jihad: a "striving" or "struggle" for God to improve oneself and society. It is a complicated word with various meanings and connotations. Muslims frame jihad in
different ways; some view it mainly as violent struggle against those who harm
Muslims, while others view it more as an internal struggle to become closer to
God.

Jirga: a Pashto word for a gathering or assembly of tribal leaders in Afghanistan and
Pakistan to settle disputes and make decisions. The *jirga* is expected to make such
decisions by consensus.

Kafir: an "unbeliever" or "infidel" (i.e., a non-Muslim or a Muslim who has committed apostasy). It is often used in a derogatory manner.

Karo Kari: literally means "black male and black female." In Pakistan, it is a term
used to describe individuals who have committed adultery. Once a person is
labeled as such, local tradition allows their family members to punish the accused
person without fear of retribution. This often means physically attacking the person, which at times can lead to murder.

Khulwa: means "seclusion" in Arabic. In Islamic law, it is used to describe when an
unrelated man and woman are alone without proper supervision. According to
strict interpretations of Islam, *khulwa* is a sin and therefore punishable.

Kila: the large, walled compounds built by the landed gentry in parts of Afghanistan
and South Asia. It is sometimes translated as a castle or fort.

Kyai: a Javanese word used to refer to Muslim religious clerics.

Loya Jirga: the "grand assembly" that has historically been called by Pashto leaders
in Afghanistan and Pakistan to discuss issues of national and broad tribal concern.
In the context of modern-day Afghanistan, a *loya jirga* was convened in 2002,
bringing together representatives from all major political and tribal factions in the
country to form a new government. Another *loya jirga* was held in 2003 to
approve the country's new constitution.

Madrasa: literally, a "school" in Arabic. It is used in this general way in both Arabic-
speaking countries and in Iran. However, in other contexts, it refers specifically to
religious schools. In these schools, students learn the religious texts, the history of
the religion, and other skills they need to become religious scholars.

Maghneh: a sleevelike headscarf worn by women in Iran. Since the *maghneh* does not slip or fall easily like other headscarves, it is worn by Iranian women when they work and by girls when they attend school.

Mahram: a person who, according to Islamic law, can act as a male guardian for a woman. He can be a male relative that she is forbidden to marry, as well as her husband and his immediate family. Generally it is agreed that a woman does not need to veil in front of her *mahram.*

Marja-i Taqlid (or simply *marja*): a title reserved for high-ranking religious jurists in Shia Islam. Shia believers follow the rulings and opinions of a *marja* of their own choosing. The highest-ranking *marja* take on the title "ayatollah."

Maulana (Arabic spelling): an honorific title given to learned Sunni scholars and leaders, particularly in South and Central Asia.

Maulvi (Persian spelling): a title similar to *maulana* given to local Sunni Islamic clerics in South and Central Asia.

Murshidat: female religious clergy, trained to provide spiritual guidance. There are now *murshidat* being trained in both Egypt and Morocco.

Mudawana: the name given to the family code of law in Morocco. This family code was revised in February 2004 by the parliament, granting women more rights and power.

Mufti: an Islamic judge or jurist who studies Islamic jurisprudence, and is called upon to issue fatwas on various issues. In some Sunni countries, the highest-ranked mufti or grand mufti is seen as the most important religious authority.

Muftia: a female mufti.

Mujahideen: Muslims who engage in jihad to defend Islam and fellow Muslims. The term is generally used today to refer to those Afghans who fought against the Soviets in the 1980s.

Mujtahid: an Islamic scholar or jurist qualified to independently interpret Islamic law. Usually these individuals have dedicated their lives to studying the texts, and are given the title with the approval of other *mujtahids* of similar or higher rank.

Mujtahideh: female *mujtahids*, of which there have only been a handful in history.

Mullah: a title given to Islamic clergy, particularly in Iran, Turkey, Central Asia, and South Asia. The title is generally given to lower-ranking mosque leaders who have not yet attained the rank of *mujtahid* or ayatollah.

Mushaira: a formal poetry reading in Pakistan and parts of Afghanistan.

Muta: a temporary marriage in Islam. It is allowed according to Shia Islam, but forbidden in Sunni Islam. Some Arab scholars have defined *muta* as a "marriage of pleasure." Unlike a permanent marriage, *muta* is set for a finite period that is agreed upon by both the man and woman. The man is required to pay the woman a dower, and provide for any children that are produced from the marriage.

Mutawa: the religious morality police in Saudi Arabia.

Niqab: the veil that some very conservative women wear across their face, exposing only their eyes. Its use is considered controversial in many parts of the Muslim world.

Pashto: the Indo-European language spoken by the Pashtun people in Afghanistan and parts of western Pakistan.

Pashtun: the dominant ethnic group in Afghanistan and the largest minority in

Pakistan. The Pashtuns have historically been a tribal people. Many aspects of their political leadership, codes of conduct, and relations with one another are based on tribal affiliations and hierarchy—even today.

Panchayat: a local council historically used in Nepal, Pakistan, and India to govern at the village level. In India today, they are constitutionally integrated into the formal government structure, where they play an important role in promoting and managing local development in rural communities across India.

Pasdaran: the Iranian Revolutionary Guard. They are an elite military/security force created in 1979 by Ayatollah Khomeini to serve as loyal forces of the supreme leader who would protect the Islamic system of Iran. The Pasdaran are separate from the regular Iranian armed forces. They also control the Basij (see definition above).

Pesantren: Islamic boarding schools in Indonesia, where traditional Islamic studies, Arabic, and some nonreligious classes are taught. Many of these schools are free or have a low tuition.

Purdah: the practice of secluding women from men. It is sometimes used to mean covering the body instead of physical seclusion. While for the most part, *purdah* is practiced in Muslim countries, it was also a custom in India for some upper-caste Hindu women.

Qazf: giving false testimony. According to Islamic law, the punishment for committing *qazf* is lashings.

Qibla: the direction of Mecca, which Muslims are required to face when they pray.

Rejal: literally means "men" in Arabic. It is a contested word in the context of the Iranian constitution, which states that the president of Iran must be a Muslim and a *rejal.* Since in Arabic, *rejal* is a masculine term, many have interpreted this to mean that the president must be male. However, since the Persian language does not have feminine or masculine, reformers have argued that the term *rejal* simply means "statesman" and because it is gender neutral, it can apply to both men and women.

Salaam Alaikum: literally means "peace be upon you" in Arabic, and is used as a greeting by Muslims and Middle Easterners. One usually replies by saying "*Wa Alaikum Salaam*" (and on you be peace).

Salafism: a branch of Sunni Islam that lies outside the four main schools (or *madhhabs*). Its adherents look back to the period of early Islam to seek guidance from the Prophet and his Companions. Salafis often take a literalist approach to texts, and therefore live an austere life. Wahhabism is closely related to Salafism, and many use the terms interchangeably even though there are Salafis who are not Wahhabis.

Sarpanch: the leader of a *panchayat* or local council in India (see above).

Sayyid: a title given to those who claim to be direct descendants of the Prophet Muhammad.

Shalwar Kameez: the traditional tunic and pants worn by both men and women in the Indian subcontinent and Afghanistan.

Sharia: Islamic law. Nearly all Muslims agree that the two main sources of Islamic law are the Quran and the Sunnah (see definition below). After this, a series of other legal sources are used depending on the school of jurisprudence. Sharia governs many aspects of Muslims' lives, including politics, economics, business, sexuality, and social issues.

Sheikh: an honorific title given to Sunni clergy.

Shia Islam (also referred to as "Shiism"): the second-largest sect of Islam after Sunnism. Shias comprise roughly 15 percent of the world's Muslims. They differ from Sunnis in that they believe that Ali, the son-in-law of the Prophet, and his descendants (the imams) should have succeeded the Prophet Muhammad, rather than Muhammad's friend and follower, Abu Bakr and the other Caliphs. The "partisans" (or Shiat) of Ali went on to form a separate sect of Islam. Shias are concentrated in Iran, Iraq, Lebanon, Central Asia, and South Asia.

Shura: means "consultation" in Arabic. It was a common pre-Islamic decision-making system in the Arabian Peninsula that is spoken of highly in the Quran. Many Muslims believe that all major decisions for the Muslim community should be made through this system of consultation. Today, many Muslim countries call their national and local parliaments *shuras.*

Sunnah: literally means the "way" or "example"; describes the way the Prophet Muhammad lived his life. It includes the various hadith (see definition above) and also descriptions of what the Prophet did during his life.

Sunni Islam (also referred to as "Sunnism"): the largest sect of Islam, comprising nearly 85 percent of the world's Muslims. The word *Sunni* comes from Sunnah (see definition above). Sunni Muslims believe that Muhammad intended his successor to be chosen by consensus, not by hereditary relationship.

Taliban: the plural of *talib*—the Arabic word for student. It refers specifically to the Pashtun extremist Islamist movement in Afghanistan and parts of Pakistan. The Taliban ruled Afghanistan with an iron fist during the 1990s and now continue to wage a war of resistance in both Afghanistan and western Pakistan.

Thobe: the traditional long robe worn by men typically in the Gulf Arab states. It is usually white.

Ulama: the community of religious scholars. It is the plural of *alim.*

Umma: the "community of believers" in Islam; in other words, all Muslims.

Vaize: appointed female preachers in Turkey who have been trained by the state to become spiritual advisers and teachers for the faithful.

Vilayat-i-Faqih (also spelled Velayat-e-Faqih): "guardianship of the Islamic jurists." It is a theory in Shia Islam that Islamic clerics or jurists must rule over the political affairs of state. Ayatollah Ruhollah Khomeini introduced the idea to modern-day Iran during the Islamic Revolution. It is now the basis of the political system in Iran, where a "supreme leader" and high-ranking jurists have the final say in matters of the state—even above the rule of the people. It is a controversial idea and many prominent Shia clerics, both inside and outside Iran, have opposed it.

Vali-i-faqih: supreme leader or jurist. In the system of Vilayat-i-Faqih, this is the highest-ranking religious authority. Ayatollah Khomeini was the first Vali-i-Faqih in the Islamic Republic of Iran. Ayatollah Khamenei is the second.

Wahhabism: an Islamic movement started by Muhammad ibn Abdul Wahhab in the Arabian Peninsula in the eighteenth century. Adherents of Wahhabism take a literalist approach to the religious texts, and try to purge the religion of all non-Muslim customs that have infiltrated the religion over the years. It is often characterized as being more austere than other interpretations of Islam. In Saudi Arabia, it is the official interpretation imposed by the state.

Wakil: a representative or lawyer. It is often used to describe a woman's legal male guardian, such as her husband or father.

Zina: means "fornication" or sex outside the confines of marriage. According to strict interpretations of Islamic law, *zina* is punishable by death.

NOTES

Introduction

1. Khaled Abou El Fadl, *The Great Theft: Wrestling Islam from the Extremists* (New York: HarperCollins Publishers, 2005), p. 6.
2. Ronald F. Inglehart, Miguel Basanez, Alejandro Moreno, eds., *Human Beliefs and Values: A Cross-cultural Sourcebook Based on the 1999–2002 Values Surveys* (Mexico: Siglo XXI Editores, 2004). The World Values Survey (WVS) is a survey of beliefs and values that covers seventy countries representing more than 80 percent of the world's population.
3. Pippa Norris and Ronald Inglehart, "The True Clash of Civilizations," *Foreign Policy*, March/April 2003.
4. Whether or not the "gates of *ijtihad*" were ever really closed is a controversial question among scholars. While the process fell out of favor among some schools of Islamic law, it remained an active process in others. Shia jurists, for example, always continued to practice *ijtihad*.

1. Why Women Matter: *The Payoff from Women's Rights*

1. Geoffrey Loane, interview with the author, Washington, D.C., April 30, 2007.
2. Andrew Natsios, speech delivered at the Global Philanthropy Forum Fifth Annual Conference, Washington, D.C., April 3, 2006.
3. "Women Broadcasters Told to Wear Hijab or Face Death," *The Times Online*, June 5, 2007.
4. I first heard this saying from Christine Grumm, president of the Women's Funding Network, in 2005.
5. Muhammad Yunus, on-the-record meeting at the Council on Foreign Relations, New York, November 16, 2006. (Transcript by Federal News Service, Inc., 2006.)
6. Muhammad Yunus, *Banker to the Poor: Micro-Lending and the Battle Against World Poverty* (New York: Perseus Books Group, 1999), p. 73.
7. "The State of Texas 1967 Marital Property Act," *Handbook of Texas Online*. Available at http://www.tshaonline.org/handbook/online/articles/WW/jsw2.html.
8. Elizabeth King and Andrew Mason, *Engendering Development*, World Bank (Oxford University Press, 2001), pp. 159–60.
9. A similar "controlled experiment" took place in South Africa in the immediate

aftermath of apartheid when there was a rapid expansion in the "Old Age Pension" program. In an effort to close the large gap in benefits received by whites and blacks, the government significantly increased pension payments to blacks. At the time, nearly a third of black children under the age of five lived with a pension recipient. A decade later, economists could clearly chart that girls living with a grandmother who received the increased benefit had experienced markedly better nutrition, as evidenced by their greater weight and height. Girls living with a grandfather experienced no such height-weight improvements. (See Esther Duflo, "Grandmothers and Granddaughters: Old Age Pension and Intra-Household Allocation in South Africa," *World Bank Economic Review* 17 [1], 2003, pp. 13–14.)

10. Mexico's welfare revolution has also been deeply influenced by research demonstrating that women invest in the family more than men. In an effort to break the grip of poor nutrition, bad health, and inadequate education across rural communities, Mexico's government in 1997 launched an innovative social welfare program called Progresa, which means "progress." (The program is now called Oportunidades.) The program distributes cash payments directly to women, and in return, the women ensure that their children attend school and have regular medical checkups. In a particular effort to close the gender gap in secondary education, the program provides scholarships that are up to 15 percent higher for girls to attend school than for boys. Mothers also receive education on basic healthcare and good nutrition, which they pass on to their families through better sanitary conditions and eating habits. More than 4 million families representing nearly a quarter of Mexico's population now receive payments through Oportunidades, and the results have been impressive. During its first decade, school enrollment rates, especially for girls, increased significantly; malnutrition declined and height-weight measures for children improved substantially; and overall poverty rates among Oportunidades participants declined. Moreover, women in the program report that they enjoy higher status in their families and in their communities, and feel more confident that they are able to help their children succeed. (See Carla Salman-Martinez, "Empowering Poor Women in Mexico: A Strategy to Reduce Rural Poverty," GAAP, April 2004.) Oportunidades' focus on women is now being used as a development model for the entire region, even in the United States. In 2007, Mayor Bloomberg launched an innovative antipoverty program in New York City called Opportunity NYC. It is modeled after Mexico's initiative.

11. Roshaneh Zafar, interview with the author, New York, NY, April 17, 2008.

12. Amanda Howe, "Development Dialogue Turns into 'Miracle' for Pakistani Women," *Global Envision*, January 5, 2005.

13. Ibid.

14. Lawrence Summers, "Investing in All the People: Educating Women in Developing Countries," *Economic Development Institute of the World Bank Seminar Paper No. 45*, 1992, p. 7.

15. T. Paul Schultz, "Why Governments Should Invest More to Educate Girls," *World Development* 30 (2), February 2002, p. 29.

16. Lisa C. Smith and Lawrence Haddad, "Overcoming Child Malnutrition in Developing Countries: Past Achievements and Future Choices," International Food Policy Research Institute (IFPRI), February 24, 2000.

17. Heidi Fritschel and Uday Mohan, "The Fruits of Girls' Education," in *The Unfinished*

Agenda: Perspectives on Overcoming Hunger, Poverty and Environmental Degradation, Per Pinstrup-Andersen and Rajul Pandy-Lorch, eds. (Washington, D.C.: IFPRI, 2001), p. 218.

18. King and Mason, *Engendering Development*, p. 83.

19. Ibid., pp. 82–83.

20. Census India (2001). Available at http://censusindia.gov.in/.

21. Azmat Ghani and Christopher Ngassam, "Economic Analysis and Policy Implications of Fertility in Middle East and North African Countries," *Journal of Economics and Economic Education Research*, January 2006, p. 98.

22. Agnes R. Quisumbing, "Gender Differences in Agricultural Productivity: A Survey of Empirical Data," *IFPRI Food Consumption and Nutrition Division Discussion Paper*, July 1995.

23. Agnes R. Quisumbing, "Improving Women's Agricultural Productivity as Farmers and Workers," *Education and Social Policy Discussion Paper No. 37*, The World Bank, July 1994, p. 25.

24. Ibid., p. 35.

25. Food and Agriculture Organization of United Nations (FAO), Gender and Food Security Statistics. Available at http://www.fao.org/gender/stats/ran.htm.

26. Ibid.

27. In sub-Saharan Africa, women now comprise more than three-quarters of young people ages fifteen to twenty-four infected with HIV. Girls' fewer years of education; their early age of marriage, often to significantly older men; their lack of information about sexual and reproductive health; their lack of property, inheritance rights, and control over income; and especially their lack of control on sexual matters all combine to make them particularly vulnerable to HIV infection.

28. Jan Vandemoortele and Enrique Delamonica, "The 'Education Vaccine' Against HIV," *UNICEF*, November 2000, p. 6.

29. A single percentage point increase in the number of girls completing secondary school raises a developing country's overall annual per capita income growth by almost a third of a percent. David Dollar and Roberta Gatti, "Gender Inequality, Income and Growth: Are Good Times Good for Women?" *Working Paper Series No. 1*, World Bank Policy Research Report on Gender and Development, 1999, p. 20.

30. King and Mason, *Engendering Development*, p. 11.

31. "National Campaign on Dalit Human Rights." Available at www.ncdhr.org.in.

32. Mary Anne Weaver, "Gandhi's Daughters: India's Poorest Embark on an Epic Social Experiment," *The New Yorker*, January 10, 2000, p. 50.

33. Esther Duflo, "Gender Equality in Development," *BREAD Policy Paper No. 001*, 2005, p. 20.

34. King and Mason, *Engendering Development*, p. 95.

35. M. Steven Fish, "Islam and Authoritarianism," *World Politics 55.1*, October 2002, pp. 4–37.

36. M. Steven Fish, "Repressing Women, Repressing Democracy," *Los Angeles Times*, October 12, 2003.

37. Since the 1980s, the number of girls born in China has declined markedly compared with male births. As of the 2000 census, almost 117 boys are born for every 100 girls, although in some rural regions, the ratio is as skewed as 135 boys to every 100 girls. (See

John Gittings, "Growing Sex Imbalance Shocks China," *The Guardian*, May 13, 2002.) India faces a similar problem, with parents desperate for boy babies to avoid the burdens of dowry associated with the birth of a girl. Abortion clinics lure customers with advertisements warning, "Pay 500 rupees now rather than 50,000 rupees later," contrasting the cost of an abortion today with a dowry in the future. (See Uma Girish, "For India's Daughters, a Dark Birth Day," *The Christian Science Monitor*, February 9, 2005.)

38. Nicholas Eberstadt, "Power and Population in Asia," *Policy Review*, February/March 2004.

39. Valerie M. Hudson and Andrea M. den Boer, *Bare Branches: Security Implications of Asia's Surplus Male Population* (Cambridge, Mass.: MIT Press, 2005), pp. 187–228.

40. Roughly 30 percent of Muslims live in South Asia, 15 percent in Indonesia, the largest Muslim-majority country in the world, and the rest are spread across Central Asia, sub-Saharan Africa, the non-Arab Middle East, Europe, and North America.

41. *Arab Human Development Report: Creating Opportunities for Future Generations*, United Nations Development Program, 2002, p. vii.

42. *Arab Human Development Report 2005: Toward the Rise of Women in the Arab World*, United Nations Development Program, 2005, p. iii.

2. Gender Jihad: *The Rise of Islamic Feminism*

1. The grand mufti in Saudi Arabia wrote in the *Asharq Al-Awsat* newspaper, "A woman is not permitted to lead a man in prayers. If a woman has reached a level where she desires to lead men and women in prayers, it should be known that her purpose and the purpose of her followers in doing this is not to bring good, rather it is to wage war against Allah and His Messenger."

2. Hesham Hassaballa, "Is she an apostate?" beliefnet.com. Available at http://www.beliefnet.com/Faiths/Islam/2005/04/Is-She-An-Apostate.aspx.

3. Thomas Bartlett, "The Quiet Heretic," *The Chronicle of Higher Education*, August 12, 2005.

4. Amina Wadud, *Inside the Gender Jihad: Women's Reform in Islam* (Oxford, England: Oneworld Publications, 2006).

5. "Memoir" here is a loose term. Mernissi herself admits that several of the characters in this book are actually composite figures of people she knows. (See Fatima Mernissi, *Dreams of Trespass: Tales of a Harem Girlhood* [Reading, Mass.: Perseus Books, 1994].)

6. Mernissi, 1994, p. 9.

7. There are disputes about the timing of the writing of the Quran. It is commonly believed that during the Prophet's lifetime, verses of the Quran were written down in various forms, but they remained scattered. They were not compiled into the collection that we now know as the Quran until after Muhammad's death.

8. Fatima Mernissi, *The Veil and the Male Elite: A Feminist Interpretation of Women's Rights in Islam* (New York: Basic Books, 1991), p. 61.

9. Mernissi, 1991, pp. vii–viii.

10. George Farquhar Graham, *The Life and Work of Syed Ahmed Khan* (London: William Blackwood and Sons, 1985), p. 113.

11. Sayyid Ahmad Khan, "The Rights of Women," in Mansoor Moaddel and Kamran Talattof, eds., *Modernist and Fundamentalist Debates in Islam: A Reader* (New York: Palgrave Macmillan, 2002), p. 159.

12. Ibid., p. 160.

13. Ibid., p. 161.

14. Sir Syed believed that given the current low level of education among Muslim men, women's education was "premature." (See Gail Minault, "Sayyid Mumtaz Ali and 'Huquq Un-Niswan': An Advocate of Women's Rights in Islam in the Late Nineteenth Century," *Modern Asian Studies* 24, 1990, p. 156.)

15. Mansoor Moaddel, "Conditions for Ideological Production: The Origins of Islamic Modernism in India, Egypt, and Iran," *Theory and Society* 30 (5), October 2001, p. 685.

16. Minault, p. 153.

17. Ibid., pp. 155–56.

18. Ibid., pp. 161–62.

19. Although al-Afghani was harshly critical of Sir Syed's political notions, and in particular his obsequiousness to his British colonial masters, they shared a common belief that modern science and technology were critical to eliminating their societies' economic and cultural "backwardness." (See Aziz Ahmad, "Afghani's Indian Contacts," *Journal of the American Oriental Society*, 1969, p. 480.) In spite of his scathing criticisms, many of al-Afghani's arguments regarding modern science, philosophy, and Islam were quite similar to those made by Sir Syed and his followers. As Nikki Keddie argues, the two men's ideas were "almost identical." (See Nikki Keddie, "Religion and Irreligion in Early Iranian Nationalism," *Comparative Studies in Society and History* 4 (3), 1962, p. 280.)

20. Caryle Murphy, *Passion for Islam: Shaping the Modern Middle East: The Egyptian Experience* (New York: Scribner, 2002), p. 46.

21. Some contemporary scholars take issue with depictions of Qasim Amin as a "feminist." Leila Ahmed, for example, points out that Amin's most virulent contempt was directed at Egyptian women whom (based on his very little firsthand experience) he depicted as lazy, materialistic, lacking in basic hygiene, and morally lax. (See Leila Ahmed, *Women and Gender in Islam* [New Haven: Yale University Press, 1993], pp. 157–62).

22. Lee Smith, "Veil of Tears: Whatever Happened to Arab Feminism?" *Slate*, February 19, 2004. Available at http://www.slate.com/id/2095767/.

23. Mansoor Moaddel, "Religion and Women: Islamic Modernism versus Fundamentalism," *Journal for the Scientific Study of Religion*, 37 (1), March 1998, p. 121; Juan Cole, "Feminism, Class, and Islam in Turn-of-the-Century Egypt," *International Journal of Middle East Studies*, 13 (4), November 1981, pp. 394–97.

24. In 1899, only about 10 percent of Egyptian women wore the veil, and a minuscule one-tenth of 1 percent of women were secluded in their homes, all of them in the upper classes. (See Juan Cole, "Feminism, Class, and Islam," 1981, p. 393.)

25. Ahmed, 1993, pp. 155–57.

26. The most notable of these was the journalist Malak Hifni Nasif, who was among the first Egyptian women to contribute regularly to the mainstream press. She objected to unveiling, though not on religious grounds—she believed that veiling was not a religious requirement and those who veiled were no more modest than those who did not. However, she felt that women were accustomed to veiling and should not be rushed to unveil. (See Ahmed 1993, pp. 180–81; Beth Baron, *The Women's Awakening in Egypt: Culture, Society and the Press* [New Haven: Yale University Press, 1994], p. 113.)

27. Michael Hirsh, "Bernard Lewis Revisited," *Washington Monthly* 36 (11), November 2004, p. 13.

28. Murphy, *Passion for Islam*, 2002, p. 50. (See also Richard P. Mitchell, *The Society of Muslim Brothers* [London: Oxford University Press, 1969], on which Murphy bases much of her discussion about al-Banna and the Muslim Brotherhood.)

29. In the run-up to Egypt's 2005 elections, the Mubarak government imprisoned hundreds of Muslim Brotherhood leaders and harassed its peaceful demonstrators. Despite being banned from political activity, the Brotherhood ran candidates as independents and still managed to win 20 percent of parliamentary seats, a record for the party.

30. Raheel Raza, "Calling for Islamic Reformation," *The Toronto Star*, November 23, 2002.

31. El Fadl says that the Quran itself does not mandate that only men can lead prayer, and that the Sunnah is indecisive on the issue. "The Prophet on more than one occasion allowed a woman to lead her household in prayer—although the household included men—when the woman was clearly the most learned in the faith." (See "Fatwa by Dr. Abou El Fadl: On Women Leading Prayer," *Scholar of the House*. Available at http://www.scholarofthehouse.org/onwolepr.html.)

32. Khaled Abou El Fadl, *Speaking in God's Name: Islamic Law, Authority, and Women* (Oxford, England: Oneworld, 2001).

33. Born and raised in Sudan, An-Na'im is a disciple of Mahmoud Muhammad Taha, a prominent Sudanese religious and political intellectual who fought for democracy and human rights and was hanged for apostasy in 1985.

34. Abdullahi An-Na'im. *Towards an Islamic Reformation: Civil Liberties, Human Rights and International Law* (Syracuse, N.Y.: Syracuse University Press, 1990), p. 63.

35. Tariq Ramadan, "Tariq Ramadan on Islamic Feminism and Women's Leadership," Conference on Muslim Youth and Women in the West: Source of Concern or Source of Hope?, Salzburg Global Seminar, May 16, 2007. Available at http://www.youtube.com/watch?v=Do--YdH-888.

36. Tariq Ramadan, *In the Footsteps of the Prophet: Lessons from the Life of Mohammed* (New York: Oxford University Press, 2007), p. 35.

37. Zainah Anwar, interview with the author, Kuala Lumpur, February 2009.

38. Zainah Anwar, interview with the author, Washington, D.C., October 14, 2005.

39. Ibid.

40. Anwar, interview with the author, 2009.

41. "World People's Blog: Zainah Anwar—Malaysia," November 29, 2006. Available at http://word.world-citizenship.org/wp-archive/919.

42. Jane Perlez, "Malaysia's Big Sister Shakes Up Islam Rule," *International Herald Tribune*, February 16, 2006.

43. Anwar, 2005, interview with the author.

44. "World People's Blog: Zainah Anwar—Malaysia," November 29, 2006. Available at http://word.world-citizenship.org/wp-archive/919.

45. Jemma Parsons, "Modelling Syariah in Aceh," *Inside Indonesia*. January–March 2008. Available at http://www.insideindonesia.org/content/view/1044/47/.

46. Hera Diani, "Indonesia: Gender Expert Musdah Speaks with Reason," *The Jakarta Post*, October 3, 2004.

47. Ibid.

48. Alpha Amirrachaman, "Siti Musdah Mulia Stands Up for Her Convictions," *The Jakarta Post*, March 23, 2007.

49. The NU operated as a political party from 1952 to 1984, challenging Indonesia's authoritarian regime. From 1984 to 1998, the organization withdrew from formal politics and renewed its focus on its social agenda. With the return to democratic politics after the fall of President Suharto in 1998, the NU launched a new political party, the National Awakening Party, known by its local acronym PKB.

50. Christopher Candland and Siti Nurjanah, "Women's Empowerment Through Islamic Organizations: The Role of Indonesia's 'Nahdatul Ulama' in Transforming the Government's Birth Control Program into a Family Welfare Program," Case study prepared for the World Faiths Development Dialogue Workshop in New Delhi, India, February 9–11, 2004.

51. Craig Charney and James Castle, "A Democratic Indonesian Tiger?" *The Washington Post*, August 1, 2007.

52. Candland and Nurjanah, p. 12.

53. Julie Chow, "Pacific Currents: Contract Marriages Assailed as Sanctioned Prostitution," *The Seattle Post Intelligencer*, April 11, 2005. Available at http://www.seattlepi.com/national/219556_pac11.html.

54. Emory Law professor Abdullahi Ahmed An-Na'im is one of the Wahid Institute's patrons.

55. Tracy Clark-Flory, "Sex and the Married Muslim," *Salon*, June 6, 2007. Available at www.salon.com/mwt/feature/2007/06/06/kotb/index.html.

56. See http://www.hebakotb.net/.

57. Reham El-Adawi, "Save Your Marriage Now!" *al Ahram Weekly*, October 7–13, 2004.

58. Clark-Flory, 2007.

59. I. M. A. Hassanin, R. Saleh, A. A. Bedaiwy, R. S. Peterson, M. A. Bedaiwy, "Prevalence of Female Genital Cutting in Upper Egypt: 6 Years After Enforcement of Prohibition Law," *Reproductive Biomedicine Online*, Vol. 16, Supplement 1, 2008, p. 27.

60. Al-Qaeda reciprocated by demanding that al-Qaradawi be excommunicated for his "moderate" views.

61. Anthony Shadid, "Maverick Cleric Is a Hit on TV," *The Washington Post*, February 14, 2003.

62. Scholar Margot Badran goes so far as to call Qaradawi a "liberal scholar" when it comes to women's rights. (See her interview with Mohammed Noushad, "Islamic Feminism Means Justice for Women," *The Milli Gazette*, January 16–31, 2004. Available at http://www.milligazette.com/Archives/2004/16–31Jan04-Print-Edition/1631200425.htm.)

63. Lindsay Wise, "Muslim TV preacher reaches out to youth," *The San Francisco Chronicle*, February 26, 2006. Available at http://sfgate.com/cgi-bin/article.cgi?f=/c/a/2006/02/26/MNGEEHDP4Q1.DTL.

64. Samantha Shapiro, "Ministering to the Upwardly Mobile Muslim," *The New York Times Magazine*, April 30, 2006.

65. Robert Worth, "Generation Faithful: Preaching Moderate Islam and Becoming a TV Star," *The New York Times*, January 2, 2009.

66. The religious restructuring also included the establishment of religious education institutions, dedicated religious bodies in mosques, and a fatwa center that would

prevent "confusion and dissension." In effect, the government is asserting greater control over religious authority in an effort to tamp down extremist ideology. (See Mohammed Massad, "Morocco's Female Religious Counselors," *The Daily News Egypt*, September 19, 2007.)

67. Sally Williams, "Mourchidat—Morocco's Female Muslim Clerics," *The Telegraph*, April 30, 2008.

68. "Everywoman—International Women's Day Part 1," al-Jazeera Television, March 8, 2007.

69. Ibid.

70. Ibid.

71. Yigal Schleifer, "In Turkey, Muslim Women Gain Expanded Religious Authority," *The Christian Science Monitor*, April 27, 2005. Available at http://www.csmonitor .com/2005/0427/p04s01-woeu.html?s=widep.

72. Yigal Schleifer, "Turkish Scholars Aim to Modernize Islam's Hadith," *The Christian Science Monitor*, March 11, 2008.

73. Ian Traynor, "Turkey Strives for Twenty-first Century Form of Islam," *The Guardian*, February 27, 2008.

74. "Egypt: First Women Preachers Named," Women Living Under Muslim Law, October 11, 2006. Available at http://www.wluml.org/english/newsfulltxt.shtml?cmd percent5B157 percent5D=x-157-546959.

75. Sharon Otterman, "Fatwas and Feminism: Women, Religious Authority, and Islamic TV," *Transnational Broadcasting Studies* 16, 2006. Available at http://www.tbsjournal .com/Otterman.html.

76. "Road to Ijtehad Is Arduous," *Iran Daily*, October 9, 2006. Available at http://www .iran-daily.com/1385/2681/html/panorama.htm#s179451.

77. Carla Power, "A Secret History," *The New York Times Magazine*, February 25, 2007.

3. Revolutionary Sisters: Iran

1. Some of the women activists I have interviewed over the years have been in and out of prison in Iran. They remain anonymous to protect their identities.

2. Another activist who shall remain anonymous to protect her identity.

3. Shirin Ebadi, *Iran Awakening* (New York: Random House, 2006), p. 51.

4. Monique Girgis, "Women in Pre-Revolutionary, Revolutionary and Post-Revolutionary Iran," *Iranian Chamber Society*, 1996. Available at http://www .iranchamber.com/society/articles/women_prepost_revolutionary_iran1.php.

5. Female literacy under the Shah climbed steadily from close to zero in 1941 when he came to power, to almost 30 percent in 1978 (versus 50 percent for men). Daughters of the more secular urban middle classes comprised nearly 40 percent of university students at the time of the revolution.

6. UNFPA, "Country in Focus: Iran." Available at http://www.unfpa.org/countryfocus/ iran/.

7. *The Iran Crisis—America Held Hostage*, ABC News, November 1979.

8. Mark Bowden, "Among the Hostage-Takers," *The Atlantic Monthly*, December 2004.

9. "The Inside Story of the 1979 U.S. Embassy Capture," Press TV. Available at http://it.truveo.com/Massoumeh-Ebtekar-on-Hostage-Crisis/id/1246638543.

10. Monir Amadi Qomi, interview with the author, Tehran, Iran, May 2007.

11. Rochelle Termin, "Foul Ball: Muslim Women Banned from Sports Participation," *Women Living Under Muslim Law*, April 18, 2008.

12. Although both bills were ratified by parliament in 1998, they went so far beyond what people were willing to tolerate that they were never actually implemented. (See Ziba Mir-Hosseini, "The Rise and Fall of Fa'ezeh Hashemi: Women in Iranian Elections," *Middle East Report No. 218* [Spring 2001], p. 9.)

13. Shirin Ebadi, p. 118.

14. "Shutting Down Zanan," *The New York Times*, February 7, 2008.

15. Nazila Fathi, "Ayatollah, Reviewing Islamic Law, Tugs at Ties Constricting Iran's Women," *The New York Times*, July 29, 2001.

16. Manal Lutfi, "The Women's Mufti: An Interview with Ayatollah Saanei," *Asharq Al-Awsat*, June 4, 2007.

17. Ibid.

18. Ibid.

19. "Ayatollah Mousavi Bojnourdi: "Observing *Hijab* Out of Intimidation and Pressure Is Ineffective," *Payvand*, January 10, 2001. Available at http://www.netnative.com/news /01/jan/1060.html.

20. Manal Lutfi, "Inside Iran: Hujjat al Islam Mohsen Kadivar," *Asharq Al-Awsat*, August 4, 2007.

21. Hugh Sykes, "Iranian Women Battle the System," *BBC News Tehran*, September 5, 2008.

22. In a closely watched Friday prayer, Ali Akbar Rafsanjani continued to energize the reform movement by reminding his fellow clerics and the Revolutionary Guard that the ideal of the revolution was an Islamic Republic. He warned: "If [Iran] loses its Islamic aspect, we will go astray. If it loses its Republican aspect, the Islamic Republic will not be realized." Ali Akbar Hashemi Rafsanjani, as transcribed by U.S. Government Open Source Center, reproduced by Juan Cole on his Informed Comment website. Available at http://www.juancole.com/2009/07/rafsanjanis-friday-prayers-sermon.html.

4. Under the Crescent Moon: Pakistan

1. Benazir Bhutto, *Reconciliation: Islam, Democracy and the West* (New York: Harper-Collins, 2008), p. 17.

2. Bhutto, 2008, pp. 39–40.

3. The only other countries in the world with such a large gender gap in literacy rates are Yemen (70 percent male literacy versus only 30 percent female literacy), Afghanistan (43 percent male versus 13 percent female literacy), and Mozambique (63 percent male literacy versus 33 percent female literacy). (See World Bank "Gender Stats," http://go.worldbank.org/YMPEGXASH0.)

4. Pakistan's Taliban movement shares a tribal Pashtun relationship with Afghanistan's Taliban, but it is a separate, indigenous group with different leadership.

5. Nigar Ahmad, interview with the author, Lahore, Pakistan, March 3, 2008.

6. Haqqani, p. 135.

7. Khawar Mumtaz and Farida Shaheed, *Women of Pakistan: Two Steps Forward, One Step Back?* (London: Zed Books, Ltd., 1987), p. 9.

8. Of course, women to some extent had been mobilized in Pakistan long before Zia. During the 1930s and 1940s, the women's wing of the Muslim League—comprised mostly of wives, daughters, and sisters of prominent Muslim League men—proved crucial in getting Muslim women out of their homes for the first time to advocate for an independent Pakistan. In the wake of Pakistan's independence in 1947, however, the male leadership of the Muslim League was more than happy to see women retreat to their homes. The Muslim League had little interest in baiting the religious and feudal establishments over women's rights. Their priority was consolidating the legitimacy of the new and fragile state.

9. Mumtaz and Shaheed, 1987, p. 131.

10. Dr. Riffat Hassan, interview with the author, Lahore, Pakistan, March 1, 2008.

11. Haqqani, p. 207.

12. Afshan Jafar, "Strategies of Activism: The Campaign to Increase Women's Political Participation in Pakistan," p. 12. Available at http://www.allacademic.com//meta/p_mla_apa_research_citation/2/4/1/9/8/pages241988/p241988–1.php.

13. Socorro Reyes, "Quotas in Pakistan: A Case Study," International Institute for Democracy and Electoral Assistance (IDEA), September 2002.

14. Amnesty International, "Pakistan: Violence Against Women in the Name of Honour." Available at http://www.amnesty.org/en/library/asset/ASA33/017/1999/en/dom-ASA330171999en.html.

15. Pamela Constable, "In Pakistan, Women Pay the Price of Honor," *The Washington Post*, May 8, 2000.

16. Riffat Hassan, "Open Letter to General Pervez Musharraf," February 25, 2000. Available at http://ecumene.org/INRFVVP/musharraf.htm.

17. Mukhtar Mai, *In the Name of Honor*, pp. 9–10.

18. Carla Power, "A One-Woman War on Justice," *Glamour Magazine*, 2006.

19. Power, 2006.

20. Glenn Kessler and Dafna Linzer, "Musharraf: No Challenge from Bush on Reversal: Pakistani President Still Leading Army," *The Washington Post*, September 13, 2005.

21. A poll conducted by WorldPublicOpinion.org found that 70 percent of Pakistanis supported the government's fight against the Taliban in the Swat Valley. (See "Pakistanis Turn on Taliban but Resent US Poll Shows," Reuters, July 1, 2009.)

22. Sonya Fatah, "The Geography of GEO," *Himal Southasian*, September 2005.

23. GEO TV did, however, solicit the input of women's rights activists for the shows.

24. Sohail Akbar Warraich, interview with the author, Kuala Lumpur, Malaysia, March 3, 2008.

25. After the 2002 elections, many of the women in parliament were fully veiled members of the Islamic coalition and the fiercest critics of liberal women's groups in the country. One critic described these women as nothing but "shock troops" who are used by their male party leaders to attack progressive women.

26. Bhutto, 2008, p. 225.

27. When the general election was held in February 2008, the MMA won less than 2 percent of the vote and only a handful of seats in parliament. Jamaat-i-Islami had called for a boycott of the vote on the grounds that with Musharraf's martial law in place it would not be fair. However, the MMA was likely to lose significant ground in the elections, and the boycott was a face-saving way to explain its electoral debacle.

5. Redirecting Jihad: Afghanistan

1. The manual was produced collaboratively by WLP and its partner organizations, Association Democratique des Femmes du Maroc (ADFM in Morocco), Baobab for Women's Human Rights in Nigeria, and the Women's Affairs Technical Committee (WATC) in Palestine. Zainah Anwar from Sisters in Islam was an adviser to the project. (See *Leading to Choices: A Leadership Training Handbook for Women*, Women's Learning Partnership for Rights, Development and Peace, p. i.)

2. Barnett Rubin, *The Fragmentation of Afghanistan: State Formation and Collapse in the International System, Second Edition* (New Haven: Yale University Press, 2002), pp. 70–72.

3. In an effort to introduce a more representative government, King Zahir Shah implemented a new constitution in 1964, one which was debated and revised by a relatively independent *loya jirga*. The constitution provided for elected upper and lower houses of parliament and prohibited members of the royal family from running for parliament or serving as ministers. Notably, two women were included on the Constitutional Advisory Committee. (See Barnett Rubin, p. 73.)

4. Peter Marsden, *The Taliban: War and Religion in Afghanistan* (New York: Zed Books Ltd., 2002), p. 22.

5. "We Want to Live as Humans: Repression of Women and Girls in Western Afghanistan," *Human Rights Watch*, December 2002. Available at http://www.hrw.org/en/node/78609.

6. "Gunmen Kill Director of Women's Affairs in Southern Afghanistan," The Associated Press, September 25, 2006.

7. In a 2007 poll, 74 percent of all women said they support women in government, but only 46 percent of men agreed. (see ABC News/BBC/ARD, "Where Things Stand," *Charney Research*, December 3, 2007.) In a 2009 poll, 60 percent of women in the conservative south of the country supported women holding public office, but only 36 percent of men favored it. (See ABC News/BBC/ARD, "Where Things Stand," February 9, 2009.)

8. Rina Amiri, interview with the author, UN Assistance Mission Afghanistan, Kabul, February 23, 2004.

9. In some districts, particularly in the south and eastern part of the country, women's political participation was very low. In Uruzgan and Zabul provinces, for example, women made up just 9 percent and 10 percent of voters, respectively. (See Amnesty International, "Women Failed by Progress in Afghanistan," October 28, 2004.)

10. Safia Siddiqi, interview with the author, Kabul, Afghanistan, February 28, 2008.

11. Elisabeth Eide, "Safia Siddiqi: Tailor, Jurist, Politician, Poet," Norwegian PEN Centre, July 27, 2005.

12. Three women had run for the deputy chair position, but their male colleagues had not elected them to serve. The women delegates complained that the men were shutting them out of the *loya jirga* leadership. The conference chair, Sibghatullah Mujaddedi, then created a third deputy chair position and selected Safia Siddiqi to fill it.

13. Tom Coghlan, "Women Defy Odds in Afghanistan," *The Daily Telegraph*, November 15, 2005.

14. International Crisis Group, "Afghanistan's New Legislature: Making Democracy Work," *Asia Report*, No. 116, May 15, 2006, p. 6.

15. Declan Walsh, "Afghanistan Convenes New Era," *San Francisco Chronicle*, December 19, 2005.

16. "Women Gain Ground in Afghan Polls," *The Daily Star*, November 23, 2005.

17. Scott Baldauf, "Afghan Parliament Debates Chaperones for Women," *The Christian Science Monitor*, February 15, 2006.

18. Shukria Barakzai, interview with the author, Kabul, Afghanistan, February 27, 2008.

19. Heidi Vogt and Rahim Faiez, "Afghanistan Rewrites Marital 'Rape' Law," *The Toronto Star*, July 10, 2009.

20. Sayed Sawayz, interview with the author, Kabul, Afghanistan, February 26, 2008.

21. Rasna Warah, "Afghan Women's Struggle Behind the Veil," UN-HABITAT. Available at http://ww2.unhabitat.org/mediacentre/documents/feature13.pdf.

22. The grants are calculated at the equivalent of $200 per family, up to $60,000 per community. A village needs a minimum of twenty families to qualify for a grant. (Susanne Holste, interview by phone with author, December 13, 2007.)

23. Clare Lockhart, interview with the author, New York, December 3, 2007.

24. Sawayz, 2008.

25. Data on the exact number of Afghan villages are unreliable. Estimates range from 25,000 to 45,000.

26. Isobel Coleman, "Beyond the Burqa: The Future of Afghan Women's Rights," *Georgetown Journal of International Affairs*, Summer/Fall 2004, p. 63.

27. Sawayz, 2008.

28. Greg Warner, "The Schools the Taliban Won't Torch," *Washington Monthly*, December 2007.

29. "Frequently Asked Questions about the NSP," National Solidarity Program, Afghanistan. Available at http://www.nspafghanistan.org/faqs.shtm#Q6.

30. Holste, 2007.

31. Warner, 2007.

32. Scott Guggenheim, interview with the author, New York, June 30, 2009.

33. Isobel Coleman and Swanee Hunt, "Afghanistan Should Make Way for Its Female Leaders," *The Christian Science Monitor*, April 24, 2006.

34. Scott Baldauf, "The West Pushes to Reform Traditionalist Afghan Courts," *Christian Science Monitor*, February 21, 2006.

35. Ibid.

36. Alissa Rubin, "Afghan Women's Quiet Revolution Hangs by a Thread," *Los Angeles Times*, January 21, 2007.

37. The mullah is referring to "Naqis-ul-Aql," a commonly cited hadith that describes women as being emotional and deficient of reason.

38. Nilofar Sakhi, interview with the author, Kabul, Afghanistan, March 1, 2008.

6. Channeling Khadijah: Saudi Arabia

1. Although Wahhabism and Salafism are often used interchangeably in the West, they have different histories and therefore different connotations. Both are concerned today with strict, literalist interpretations of sharia. However, some Salafis view Wahhabism as a derogatory term, because of its fanatical association. While all Wahhabis are Salafi in their orientation, not all Salafis are Wahhabis.

2. A bitter point of contention within the Muslim world is Saudi Arabia's transformation

of Mecca. Over the past several decades, the Saudis have razed any sites that might be construed as shrines in an effort to discourage idolatry. Numerous historical buildings have been demolished, both to satisfy Wahhabi interests and to make way for high-rise developments. This same narrow interpretation of Islam is what the Taliban in Afghanistan used to destroy the giant statues of Buddha in Bamiyan. (See Elizabeth Farnsworth, "Inside the Kingdom Part III," *PBS Newshour*, February 19, 2002. Also see Rachel Huff, "Dissident Watch: Sami Angawi," *Middle East Quarterly*, Winter 2006.)

3. Madawi al-Rasheed, *A History of Saudi Arabia* (Cambridge, England: Cambridge University Press, 2002), p. 17.
4. Khaled Abou El Fadl, *The Great Theft: Wrestling Islam from the Extremists* (New York: HarperCollins, 2005), p. 56.
5. Rachel Bronson, *Thicker Than Oil: America's Uneasy Partnership with Saudi Arabia* (Oxford, England: Oxford University Press, 2006), p. 28.
6. Faiza Saleh Ambah, "Saudi Women Recall a Day of Driving," *The Christian Science Monitor*, December 7, 2005.
7. Dr. Haifa Jamal al-Lail, interview with the author, Jeddah, Saudi Arabia, February 23, 2006.
8. Al-Rasheed, *A History of Saudi Arabia*, p. 121.
9. Ibid., p. 124.
10. Dr. Haifa, interview with the author, Jeddah, Saudi Arabia, February 16, 2008.
11. Dr. Saleha Mahmood Abedin, interview with the author, Jeddah, Saudi Arabia, February 17, 2005.
12. "Saudi Police 'Stopped' Fire Rescue," *BBC News*, March 15, 2002.
13. "Saudi Arabia: Religious Police Role in School Fire Criticized," *Human Rights Watch*, March 15, 2002. Available at http://hrw.org/english/docs/2002/03/15/saudia3801_txt.htm.
14. Christopher Dickey and Rod Nordland, "The Fire That Won't Die Out: A Tragedy at a Girls' School in Mecca Gives Saudi Rulers an Opening to Break Down Ancient Barriers, But Will They?" *Newsweek*, July 22, 2002.
15. It was a struggle for Faisal too. In 1975, he was shot dead by his nephew who, it is commonly thought, was avenging the death of a brother killed by Saudi police a decade earlier while fighting to stop the introduction of television to the kingdom. (See Rachel Bronson, pp. 136–37.)
16. Eleanor Doumato, "Women and the Stability of Saudi Arabia," *Middle East Report*, No. 171, July–August 1991, p. 36.
17. "Shobokshi Article Provokes Vibrant Debate," *Arab News*, July 16, 2003.
18. Sabria Jawhar, interview with the author, Jeddah, Saudi Arabia, February 17, 2005.
19. Between 2003 and 2009, the crown prince/king convened eight "National Dialogues" covering a range of issues from reducing extremism in Saudi society to the concerns of youth, the kingdom's job crisis, and health.
20. Omar al-Midwahi, "Remarks on Women's Rights Cause Uproar," *Asharq Al-Awsat*, June 15, 2004.
21. Hussein Shobokshi, interview with the author, Jeddah, Saudi Arabia, February 2005.
22. Sabria Jawhar, interview with the author, Newcastle, Great Britain, May 15, 2008.
23. "Transcript: Saudi King Abdullah Talks to Barbara Walters," *ABC News*, October 14, 2005.

24. Rachel Bronson, *Thicker Than Oil*, p. 210.

25. Eleanor Doumato, p. 34.

26. Sabria Jawhar, interview with the author (by email), May 17, 2008.

27. Madawi al-Hassoon, interview with the author, Jeddah, Saudi Arabia, February 18, 2006.

28. Jawhar, interview with the author, Jeddah, Saudi Arabia, 2005.

29. Samir al-Saadi and Maha Akeel, "Madawi: First Woman to Run for JCCI Post," *Arab News*, September 18, 2005.

30. Samar Fatany, "Challenges Remain in Path to Women's Progress," *Arab News*, January 2007.

31. Sonia Verma, "Saudi Arabia Stands by Its Arrest of an American Woman in Starbucks," *Fox News*, February 19, 2008.

32. "The Jeddah Economic Forum Studies the Economic Reforms in a Number of Countries," *Ain al-Yaqeen*, January 24, 2003.

33. "Saudi King Breaks Ground for New Co-Ed University," *International Herald Tribune*, October 21, 2007.

34. In 2006, MIT was granted 121 patents versus 92 patents that year for all Arab countries.

35. Sheikh Obeikan, interview with the author, Riyadh, Saudi Arabia, February 15, 2005.

36. Hussein Shobokshi, interview with the author.

37. Zaki Yamani, interview with the author, Jeddah, Saudi Arabia, February 18, 2005.

7. Daughters of Zainab: Iraq

1. At the time, the party was known as the Supreme Council for the Islamic Revolution in Iraq (SCIRI). It changed its name in May 2007 to the Supreme Islamic Iraqi Council. Abdulaziz al-Hakim died of lung cancer in August 2009.

2. "Background on Women's Status in Iraq Prior to the Fall of the Saddam Hussein Government," *Human Rights Watch*, November 2003.

3. Mohamad Bazzi, "Female Iraqi Poised to Take Power," *Newsday*, January 24, 2005.

4. Alissa J. Rubin, "A Painful Road to Leadership," *Los Angeles Times*, November 2, 2005.

5. Rubin, 2005.

6. Bazzi, 2005.

7. Bazzi, 2005.

8. Bazzi, 2005.

9. Rubin, 2005.

10. Bazzi, 2005.

11. "Rebuilding Iraq: U.S. Assistance for the January 2005 Elections," *GAO Report Number 05–932R*, September 7, 2005.

12. As suspected, many Sunni Arabs boycotted the elections, depressing their representation in parliament. They ended up with roughly 2 percent of the seats in parliament although they represent about a third of the population. Shia and Kurds had high turnouts, resulting in their parties being overrepresented in parliament.

13. Ahmed H. al-Rahim, "The Sistani Factor," *Journal of Democracy* 16.3, 2005, pp. 50–53.

14. Sundus Abbas Hasan, interview with the author, Kuala Lumpur, Malaysia, February 17, 2009.

15. Tina Susman, "Iraqis Divided by Treatment of Women in the Constitution," *Los Angeles Times*, October 9, 2007.

16. Jim Michaels, "Iraq's Female Lawmakers Make Strides," *USA Today*, October 26, 2008.
17. Ibid.

8. Conclusion: *Unveiling the Future*

1. Shirin Ebadi, *Iran Awakening* (New York: Random House, 2006), p. 122.

INDEX

Ibn Saud, King Abdul Aziz, 206–207, 209
Ibn Saud, Muhammad, 206
Ibrahim, Hafez, 3
ID cards, 230
ijtihad, xxiii–xxiv, 30, 47, 84, 93, 100, 113, 147, 150
Ikhwan(Saudi Arabia), 206–207
illiteracy, 9, 17, 36, 37, 130, 133, 140, 143, 162, 182
income, xxvii, 6, 10, 21, 186
India, 11, 19, 20, 27–28, 41–45, 50, 127, 132, 142
  British rule, 42
  caste system, 23
  Islamic feminism in, 41–45
  panchayat revolution, 22–25
Indonesia, 50, 53, 59–64, 78, 99–100, 188, 272
  Islamic feminism in, 59–64
  tsunami, 60
  villages, 188–89, 191–92
infant mortality, 7, 202
inflation, 207
inheritance, 43, 44, 112, 248
Institute for Women's Studies and Research (IWSR), 85–86, 91–94, 96
insurance, 14–15
Interim Governing Council (IGC), 248, 251, 252, 255, 256
International Congress on Islamic Feminism, 33
International Food Policy Research Institute, 20
International Rescue Committee (IRC), 169, 170
International Women's Day, 226
Internet, 29, 114, 211, 217, 226, 232, 240, 244, 270, 271–72
Iqbal, Muhammad, 147
Iqbal International Institute, 149–50
Iran, xxviii, 22, 50, 58, 75, 78, 81–125, 131, 168, 177, 216, 224, 263, 270, 272–73, 274
  Ahmadinejad government, 83, 86, 94, 95, 100, 103, 111, 114, 117, 123, 124–25
  anti-Americanism, 94, 95
  democratization, 124–25, 274
  dress code, 86, 88, 94, 95, 102, 107, 111, 112, 113, 115, 118, 121, 125
  female education, 85, 88–89, 119–21
  female religious leaders, 75

film, 125
Iran-Iraq War, 84, 89, 91, 106, 250
Islamic feminism, 81–125
  Khatami government, 99, 109–111, 113, 114
  Khomeini regime, 82, 86–89, 90–92, 95, 105, 115, 116
  laws, 86, 87–88, 90–94, 111–12, 117
  politics and government, 82–84, 86–101, 104–111, 114, 124
  reform movement, 83, 84, 109–111, 114
  Revolution, xiii, xxi, 52, 86–89, 95–96, 106, 116, 216, 273
  Revolutionary Guards, 96, 110
  Saanei as women's mufti, 111–14
  women's journals, 105–111
  women's sports, 101–104
Iraq, xxviii, 7, 22, 27, 50, 78, 206, 224, 237, 241–67, 273
  Baathist regime, 244, 245, 249, 254, 256, 261
  constitution, 247, 248, 260–64
  dress code, 246, 253, 258, 264, 265
  economy, 249
  education, 249, 250
  extremism, 245, 257–58
  Gulf War (1991), 217, 224, 225, 250
  Iran-Iraq War, 84, 89, 91, 106, 250
  Islamic feminism in, 241–67
  judiciary, 266, 267
  laws, 245–52, 253, 260, 266, 267
  modernization, 249
  politics and government, 244, 247–67
  post-Saddam, 246–48, 251–67
  Resolution 137, 248, 251, 253, 256, 257, 263
  sectarian tensions, 243–63
  U.S. invasion of, xxi, 68, 248, 250, 252, 261, 264, 267
  violence, 244–45, 253, 257–59, 261
Iraq War, xxi, 68, 248, 250, 252, 261, 264, 267
Islam, xii, xvi, xviii, xix, xxiii, 7, 14, 26, 49–53, 245, 266–67, 275
  attitudes toward women, 28, 29–30, 34, 43, 54, 112, 145–46
  authority, 38–39
  extremism, 7–8, 26–27, 50–52, 64, 71–73, 126–31, 142, 170–76, 206–207, 216–18, 237
  female preachers, 71–78

About the Author

ISOBEL COLEMAN is a senior fellow for U.S. foreign policy at the Council on Foreign Relations, where she also directs the council's Women and Foreign Policy program. Her writing has appeared in publications such as *Foreign Affairs*, *Foreign Policy*, the *Financial Times*, the *International Herald Tribune*, *USA Today*, and *The Christian Science Monitor*. She is a frequent speaker at academic, business, and policy conferences and a guest commentator on networks including CNN, the BBC, Al Jazeera, and NPR. She lives in the New York area with her husband and children.

ABOUT THE TYPE

The text of this book was set in Janson, a typeface designed in about 1690 by Nicholas Kis, a Hungarian living in Amsterdam, and for many years mistakenly attributed to the Dutch printer Anton Janson. In 1919 the matrices became the property of the Stempel Foundry in Frankfurt. It is an old-style book face of excellent clarity and sharpness. Janson serifs are concave and splayed; the contrast between thick and thin strokes is marked.